LEGAL PLURALISM AND DEVELOPMENT

Previous efforts at legal development have focused almost exclusively on state legal systems, many of which have shown little improvement over time. Recently, organizations engaged in legal development activities have begun to pay greater attention to the implications of local, informal, indigenous, religious, and village courts or tribunals, which often are more efficacious than state legal institutions, especially in rural communities. Legal pluralism is the term applied to these situations because these institutions exist alongside official state legal systems, usually in a complex or uncertain relationship.

Although academics, especially legal anthropologists and sociologists, have discussed legal pluralism for decades, their work has not been consulted in the development context. Similarly, academics have failed to benefit from the insights of development practitioners.

This book brings together, in a single volume, contributions from academics and practitioners to explore the implications of legal pluralism for legal development. All of the practitioners have extensive experience in development projects; the academics come from a variety of backgrounds, and most have written extensively on legal pluralism and on development.

Brian Z. Tamanaha is the William Gardiner Hammond Professor of Law at the Washington University School of Law. He is the author of six books, most recently *Beyond the Formalist-Realist Divide* (2009) and *Law as a Means to an End* (2006). He is the recipient of the inaugural Dennis Leslie Mahoney Prize in Legal Theory (2006) and the Herbert Jacob Book Prize (2002). Tamanaha has delivered a number of high-profile lectures in the United States and abroad. Prior to becoming an academic, he worked for two years as Assistant Attorney General in Yap State, Federated States of Micronesia.

Caroline Sage is a Senior Social Development Specialist at the World Bank. She previously headed the World Bank Justice for the Poor program, which focuses on legal empowerment and mainstreaming justice and conflict management concerns into broader governance and development efforts. She has written numerous articles and edited books on law and development and continues to lead an in-depth research effort focusing on these issues as part of the Justice for the Poor program.

Michael Woolcock is Lead Social Development Specialist in the Development Research Group at the World Bank and one of the founders of the World Bank's Justice for the Poor program. He also teaches part-time at Harvard University's Kennedy School of Government. He has published extensively on the social dimensions of economic development, most recently *Contesting Development* (2011) and *History, Historians and Development Policy* (2011). From 2006 to 2009 he was the founding Research Director of the Brooks World Poverty Institute at the University of Manchester.

Legal Pluralism and Development

SCHOLARS AND PRACTITIONERS IN DIALOGUE

Edited by

BRIAN Z. TAMANAHA
Washington University School of Law

CAROLINE SAGE
The World Bank

MICHAEL WOOLCOCK
The World Bank

CAMBRIDGE
UNIVERSITY PRESS

University Printing House, Cambridge CB2 8BS, United Kingdom

One Liberty Plaza, 20th Floor, New York, NY 10006, USA

477 Williamstown Road, Port Melbourne, VIC 3207, Australia

314-321, 3rd Floor, Plot 3, Splendor Forum, Jasola District Centre, New Delhi - 110025, India

79 Anson Road, #06-04/06, Singapore 079906

Cambridge University Press is part of the University of Cambridge.

It furthers the University's mission by disseminating knowledge in the pursuit of education, learning and research at the highest international levels of excellence.

www.cambridge.org
Information on this title: www.cambridge.org/9781107019409

© Cambridge University Press 2012

This publication is in copyright. Subject to statutory exception and to the provisions of relevant collective licensing agreements, no reproduction of any part may take place without the written permission of Cambridge University Press.

First published 2012
First paperback edition 2013

A catalogue record for this publication is available from the British Library

Library of Congress Cataloging in Publication data
Legal pluralism and development : scholars and practitioners in dialogue / [edited by] Brian Z. Tamanaha, Caroline Sage, Michael Woolcock.
    p.   cm.
Includes bibliographical references and index.
ISBN 978-1-107-01940-9 (Hardback)
1. Legal polycentricity – Economic aspects. 2. Law and economic development. I. Tamanaha, Brian Z. II. Sage, Caroline Mary. III. Woolcock, Michael J. V., 1964–
K236.L44   2012
340´.115–dc23   2011044845

ISBN 978-1-107-01940-9 Hardback
ISBN 978-1-107-69090-5 Paperback

Cambridge University Press has no responsibility for the persistence or accuracy of URLs for external or third-party internet websites referred to in this publication, and does not guarantee that any content on such websites is, or will remain, accurate or appropriate.

Contents

Contributors	*page* vii
Preface	xv
Acknowledgments	xix

Introduction: Legal Pluralism and Development Policy – Scholars and Practitioners in Dialogue 1
Caroline Sage and Michael Woolcock

PART I. ORIGINS AND CONTOURS

1 Historical Perspectives on Legal Pluralism 21
Lauren Benton

2 The Rule of Law and Legal Pluralism in Development 34
Brian Z. Tamanaha

3 Bendable Rules: The Development Implications of Human Rights Pluralism 50
David Kinley

4 Legal Pluralism and Legal Culture: Mapping the Terrain 66
Sally Engle Merry

5 Toward Equity in Development When the Law Is Not the Law: Reflections on Legal Pluralism in Practice 83
Daniel Adler and Sokbunthoeun So

PART II. THEORETICAL FOUNDATIONS AND CONCEPTUAL DEBATES

6   Sustainable Diversity in Law   95
    H. Patrick Glenn

7   Legal Pluralism 101   112
    William Twining

8   The Development "Problem" of Legal Pluralism:
    An Analysis and Steps toward Solutions   129
    Gordon R. Woodman

9   Institutional Hybrids and the Rule of Law as a Regulatory
    Project   145
    Kanishka Jayasuriya

10 Some Implications of the Application of Legal Pluralism to
    Development Practice   162
    Doug J. Porter

PART III. FROM THEORY TO PRACTICE

11 Legal Pluralism and International Development Agencies:
    State Building or Legal Reform   177
    Julio Faundez

12 Access to Property and Citizenship: Marginalization in a
    Context of Legal Pluralism   197
    Christian Lund

13 The Publicity "Defect" of Customary Law   215
    Varun Gauri

14 Unearthing Pluralism: Mining, Multilaterals, and the State   228
    Meg Taylor and Nicholas Menzies

15 The Problem with Problematizing Legal Pluralism: Lessons
    from the Field   237
    Deborah H. Isser

Index   249

Contributors

SCHOLARS

Lauren Benton is Professor of History and Affiliate Professor of Law at New York University. She is the author of numerous books and articles on law, global history, and economic development, including *A Search for Sovereignty: Law and Geography in European Empires, 1400–1900* (2010); *Law and Colonial Cultures: Legal Regimes in World History, 1400–1900* (2002), which was awarded the J. Willard Hurst Prize and the World History Association Book Prize; *Invisible Factories: The Informal Economy and Industrial Development in Spain* (1990); and a volume edited with Alejandro Portes and Manuel Castells, *The Informal Sector: Studies in Advanced and Less Developed Countries* (1989). Benton received her PhD in Anthropology and History from Johns Hopkins University and her AB from Harvard University. She is currently serving as Dean for Humanities at NYU.

Julio Faundez holds an LLB degree from Universidad Católica de Chile, and LLM and SJD degrees from Harvard University. He is Professor of Law and is currently the Head of Warwick Law School. He has written extensively on law and democratization in Chile and Latin America (*Marxism and Democracy in Chile*, Yale, 1989; and *Democratization, Development, and Legality: Chile 1831–1973*, Palgrave, 2007). He also publishes widely in the area of legal reform and governance (*Good Government and Law*, Macmillan, 1997; and *On the State of Democracy*, Routledge, 2007). He is co-editor in chief of the *Hague Journal on the Rule of Law* (Cambridge University Press) and editor of Routledge's book series Law, Development and Globalization.

Varun Gauri is a Senior Economist in the Development Research Group of the World Bank. His research focuses on politics and governance in the social sectors and aims to combine quantitative and qualitative methods in economics and social science research. He is leading research projects on the impact of legal strategies to claim economic and social rights and on the impact of international laws and norms on development outcomes. He has published papers on a wide variety of topics, including social rights and economics, public interest litigation, the effect of local-level dispute resolution on economic outcomes, the political economy of government responses to HIV/AIDS, the strategic choices of development non-governmental organizations (NGOs), the use of vouchers for basic education, and immunization in developing countries. He is the author of *School Choice in Chile: Two Decades of Educational Reform* (University of Pittsburgh Press, 1998) and the editor (with Daniel Brinks) of *Courting Social Justice: Judicial Enforcement of Social and Economic Rights in the Developing World* (Cambridge University Press, 2008). Since joining the World Bank in 1996, he has served on and led a variety of operational tasks in the World Bank, including operational evaluations, investments in privately owned hospitals in Latin America, a social sector adjustment loan and several health care projects in Brazil, and a study of the decentralization of health care in Nigeria. He was also a core team member of the 2007 *World Development Report*.

H. Patrick Glenn is the Peter M. Laing Professor of Law at McGill University, where he teaches principally in the fields of comparative law, private international law, and civil procedure. A member of the International Academy of Comparative Law and a Fellow of the Royal Society of Canada, he has also been a Bora Laskin National Fellow in Human Rights Research and a Killam Research Fellow. In 2006 he received the Prix Leon-Gérin from the government of Quebec for his contribution to the social sciences. He has published *Legal Traditions of the World* (4th ed., Oxford University Press, 2010) and *On Common Laws* (Oxford University Press, 2005).

Kanishka Jayasuriya is currently Professor of International Politics, University of Adelaide. Prior to this, he was Principal Senior Research Fellow at the Asia Research Centre (ARC), Murdoch University. He has written extensively on the rule of law, legal institutions, and regulatory reform, particularly in relation to the Asia Pacific. Some of his books include *Towards Illiberal Democracy in Pacific Asia* (Macmillan, 1995); *Law, Power and Capitalism in Asia* (Routledge, 1999); *Reconstituting the Global Liberal Order* (Routledge, 2005); and *Statecraft, Welfare and the Politics of Inclusion* (Palgrave/Macmillan, 2006).

David Kinley holds the Chair in Human Rights Law at the University of Sydney. He has previously held positions at Cambridge University, the Australian National University, the University of New South Wales, Washington College of Law, and American University; most recently he was the founding Director of the Castan

Centre for Human Rights Law at Monash University (2000-2005). He was a Senior Fulbright Scholar in 2004, based in Washington, DC, and Herbert Smith Visiting Fellow at the Faculty of Law, University of Cambridge, during the first half of 2008. He is author or editor of eight books and more than sixty articles, book chapters, reports, and papers. He has also worked for fifteen years as a consultant and adviser on international and domestic human rights law in Vietnam, Indonesia, South Africa, Thailand, Iraq, Nepal, Laos, China, and Myanmar/Burma, and for a number of organizations, including the United Nations High Commissioner for Human Rights, the World Bank, the Ford Foundation, AusAID, and the Asia Pacific Forum of National Human Rights Institutions, as well as a number of transnational corporations and NGOs. He also previously worked for three years with the Australian Law Reform Commission and for two years with the Australian Human Rights Commission. His latest books include *Civilising Globalisation: Human Rights and the Global Economy* (Cambridge University Press, 2009), *Corporations and Human Rights* (Ashgate, 2009), and *The World Trade Organisation and Human Rights: Interdisciplinary Perspectives* (Edward Elgar, 2009) Another edited collection titled *Principled Engagement: Promoting Human Rights in Pariah States* was published by UNU Publications in 2010.

Christian Lund has worked on land and politics issues in West Africa for twenty years. He is the author of *Local Politics and the Dynamics of Property in Africa* (2008) and *Law, Power and Politics in Niger* (1998). He is the editor or co-editor of *Politics of Possession* (2009), *Twilight Institutions: Public Authority and Local Politics in Africa* (2007), *Securing Land Rights in Africa* (2003), and *Negotiating Property in Africa* (2002). He is Director of the Graduate School in International Development Studies at Roskilde University.

Sally Engle Merry is Professor of Anthropology and Director of the Law and Society Program at New York University. Her work explores the role of law in urban life in the United States in the colonizing process and in contemporary transnationalism. Her recent books are *Colonizing Hawai'i: The Cultural Power of Law* (Princeton University Press, 2000), which received the 2001 J. Willard Hurst Prize from the Law and Society Association; *Human Rights and Gender Violence: Translating International Law into Local Justice* (University of Chicago Press, 2006); *The Practice of Human Rights: Tracking Law between the Local and the Global* (co-edited with Mark Goodale, Cambridge University Press, 2007); and *Gender Violence: A Cultural Perspective* (Blackwell, 2008). She has authored or edited four other books: *Law and Empire in the Pacific: Hawai'i and Fiji* (co-edited with Donald Brenneis, School of American Research Press, 2004); *The Possibility of Popular Justice: A Case Study of American Community Mediation* (co-edited with Neal Milner, University of Michigan Press, 1993); *Getting Justice and Getting Even: Legal Consciousness among Working-Class Americans* (University of Chicago Press, 1990); and *Urban*

Danger: Life in a Neighborhood of Strangers (Temple University Press, 1981). She has recently published articles on women's human rights, violence against women, and the process of localizing human rights. She is past president of the Law and Society Association and the Association for Political and Legal Anthropology and president-elect of the American Ethnological Society. In 2007 she received the Kalven Prize of the Law and Society Association, an award that recognizes a significant body of scholarship in the field. She is the winner of the 2010 J. I. Staley Prize of the School for Advanced Research for her book *Human Rights and Gender Violence*.

Brian Z. Tamanaha is William Gardiner Hammond Professor of Law at Washington University School of Law. He is the author of six books and several dozen articles covering various topics in legal theory, including the rule of law, law and development, law and society, and legal pluralism. Prior to becoming an academic, he worked for two years as Assistant Attorney General in Yap State, Federated States of Micronesia.

William Twining is Quain Professor of Jurisprudence Emeritus, University College London, and a regular Visiting Professor at the University of Miami School of Law. For the first seven years of his career, he taught law in Khartoum and Dar-es-Salaam, and he has kept in touch with the region ever since. His recent works include *General Jurisprudence: Understanding Law from a Global Perspective* (2009), *Human Rights: Southern Voices* (2009), and the 2009 Bernstein Lecture at Duke University on "Normative and Legal Pluralism" (in press).

Gordon R. Woodman is Emeritus Professor of Comparative Law at Birmingham Law School, University of Birmingham, United Kingdom. He spent the first fifteen years of his career working on law faculties in universities in Ghana and Nigeria and has been at Birmingham Law School since 1976. He studies and writes about law in Africa, customary laws generally in the modern world, and related issues in legal theory concerning the nature of customary law and the theory of legal pluralism. He has spent periods of research in Papua New Guinea, the United States, Barbados, Tanzania, and Malaysia. He has been a consultant for governments, aid agencies, nongovernmental organizations, and the World Bank, as well as an expert witness in court proceedings that involve issues of African law. He has been Editor-in-Chief of the *Journal of Legal Pluralism and Unofficial Law* since 1994. He has edited and contributed to a number of books in these fields, including *People's Law and State Law* (Foris, 1985, edited with Antony Allot), *Indigenous Law and the State* (Foris, 1988, edited with Bradford W. Morse), *Between Kinship and the State: Social Security and Law in Developing Countries* (Foris, 1988, edited with Franz von Benda-Beckmann and others), *African Law and Legal Theory* (Dartmouth, 1995, edited with A. O. Obilade), *Local Land Law and Globalization* (LIT Verlag, 2004, edited with Ulrike Wanitzek and Harald Sippel), *Law and Religion in Multicultural Societies*

(DJØF, 2008, edited with Rubya Mehdi and others), and numerous published papers.

PRACTITIONERS

Daniel Adler is a Governance Specialist with the World Bank in Cambodia. He works on a mixture of Cambodian and regional issues with a focus on land and natural resources management. Relevant publications include *Justice without the Rule of Law? The Challenge of Rights-Based Industrial Relations in Contemporary Cambodia* (with Michael Woolcock) and *Interim Institutions and the Development Process: Opening Spaces for Reform In Cambodia and Indonesia* (with Caroline Sage and Michael Woolcock).

Deborah H. Isser is Senior Counsel, Legal and Judicial Reform, for the World Bank and the former Senior Program Officer in the Rule of Law Center for Innovation at the United States Institute of Peace. At USIP, she directed projects on the role of non-state justice systems in post-conflict societies and on addressing property claims in the wake of conflict. Most recently, her work has involved research and policy facilitation on the role of customary justice in Liberia and Southern Sudan and assistance on the development of mechanisms to address land and property claims of the displaced in Iraq. She is the editor of a forthcoming volume, *Customary Justice in Post-Conflict Societies*, and co-author of "Looking for Justice: Liberian Experiences with and Perceptions of Local Justice Options." Previously, she was a senior policy adviser in the Office of the High Representative in Bosnia and Herzegovina, where she focused on economic reform and efforts to address serious crime and corruption. From 2000 to 2001, she was a special adviser for the U.S. Mission to the UN. She received the Department of State's Distinguished Honor Award for her work on UN peacekeeping reform in the context of the Brahimi Report. She was also a member of the team responsible for settling U.S. arrears to the UN. Isser received a JD from Harvard Law School, an MALD from the Fletcher School of Law and Diplomacy, and an AB from Columbia University. She has taught courses on rule of law at Georgetown and George Washington Law School.

Nicholas Menzies is a Justice Reform Specialist in the Justice Reform Practice Group of the World Bank's Legal Vice Presidency with a BA/LLB from the University of Sydney and an MPP from the Hertie School of Governance, Berlin. He has worked at the intersections of plural legal systems as a land and natural resources lawyer for indigenous communities in Australia, on legal empowerment and access to justice issues in Cambodia, and in providing policy advice to the Papua New Guinean cabinet across a range of matters – from participatory budgeting and micro-enterprise development to gender-based violence. Nicholas has also worked in progressive political advocacy, building social movements for political, cultural, and environmental action. At the World Bank, Nicholas works on mainstreaming justice into development programming in East Asia, the Pacific, and West Africa.

Doug J. Porter is Economics and Governance Coordinator for the World Bank's work in Timor-Leste and the Pacific Islands. Doug holds a PhD from the Australian National University, and his work in conflict-affected countries includes long-term assignments in Kenya, Uganda, Malawi and Zambia, Cambodia and Vietnam, Pakistan, and southern Philippines. During 2007 and 2008, Doug was based in Timor-Leste, working on public finance management and is currently leading a study of the Solomon Islands' long-term growth prospects. He is a contributor to the 2011 *World Development Report: Conflict, Security and Development* and is preparing case studies on Timor-Leste, conflict in Melanesia, and public finance management in conflicted settings. His research interests include the political economy of institutional change, with a special interest in decentralization, state-society relations, and justice reforms. Doug is the author of several books and articles, including *Development beyond Neoliberalism? Poverty Reduction, Governance, Political Economy* (Routledge, 2006) and is currently working on a study of post-conflict transition in Cambodia titled *Winning the Peace: New Institutions, Neo-Patrimonialism and Post-Conflict in Cambodia* (Michigan University Press, 2010).

Caroline Sage is a Justice Reform Specialist in the Legal Vice Presidency of the World Bank. She currently heads up the Justice for the Poor program, which focuses on legal empowerment and mainstreaming justice and conflict management concerns into broader governance and development efforts. The program is currently operating in nine countries across Africa and the East Asia and Pacific region. Caroline's research interests include regulatory and justice-focused reforms in fragile and conflict-affected environments, with a particular focus on legal pluralism, customary institutions, state-society relations, and the role of law in processes of social change. She has written numerous articles and has edited books on law and development and continues to lead an in-depth research effort focusing on these issues as part of the Justice for the Poor program. Caroline holds undergraduate degrees in history and film and graduate degrees in law and anthropology.

Sokbunthoeun So is a Governance Analyst (Consultant) at the World Bank Country Office in Cambodia. He is also an Advisor on Democratic Governance and the Public Sector Reform Program at the Cambodia Development Resource Institute. His recent research focuses on the issue of access to land, land tenure security, land registration, democratic governance, and decentralization and deconcentration Reform in Cambodia. Dr. So was a Fulbright Fellow between 2002 and 2004.

Meg Taylor, a national of Papua New Guinea, received her LLB from Melbourne University, Australia, and her LLM from Harvard University. She practiced law in Papua New Guinea and serves as a member of the Law Reform Commission. She was Ambassador of Papua New Guinea to the United States, Mexico, and Canada in Washington, DC, from 1989 to 1994. She is co-founder of Conservation Melanesia and has served on the boards of the World Wildlife Fund–United States and the

World Resources Institute. She was a member of the World Commission on Forests and Sustainable Development. In addition, she has served as a board member of a number of companies in Papua New Guinea in the natural resources, financial, and agricultural sectors.

Michael Woolcock is Lead Social Development Specialist in the Development Research Group at the World Bank and one of the founders of the World Bank's Justice for the Poor program. He also teaches part-time at Harvard University's Kennedy School of Government. He has published extensively on the social dimensions of economic development, most recently *Contesting Development* (2011) and *History, Historians and Development Policy* (2011). From 2006 to 2009 he was the founding Research Director of the Brooks World Poverty Institute at the University of Manchester.

Preface

CAROLINE SAGE AND MICHAEL WOOLCOCK

This volume emerged from a desire to enhance the quality and frequency of dialogue between scholars and practitioners of legal pluralism. Too often, it seemed to our group within the World Bank legal department that scholars of legal pluralism were operating at a level several steps removed from the concrete challenges faced by practitioners in the field, whereas practitioners, for their part, too often encountered or reported on vexing instances of legal pluralism in particular contexts but failed to connect their work to, or engage substantively with, the broader literature on this issue. The reasons for this divide are in part a product of familiar differences pertaining to each group's respective training, professional identity, and career incentives and an abiding sense that the others' knowledge is only of tangential relevance to their immediate concerns. Even so, it's hard to argue that this separation generates optimal outcomes for either party or for newcomers to the field of legal pluralism seeking to discern how theory, research, and policy inform (or might inform) one another.

The first motive behind this volume, then, was a pragmatic one: namely, a conviction that both scholarship and practice are enhanced by regular, open, constructive interaction. The second and related motive was our conviction that scholars and practitioners could have a distinctively fruitful exchange, one transcending the diversity of views that one expects to encounter in more traditional professional gatherings. In our experience, "diversity" in such settings is still largely diversity of a particular kind (e.g., people coming at an issue from a range of well-known theoretical perspectives), with the corresponding debates largely centered on finer points of disagreement. These "family fights," so to speak, may be no less heated, but they are the debates one expects and to which one is trained to respond; they take place within a familiar intellectual space, with the rules and roles of participants, for the most part, well rehearsed and well understood. Although much can be gained from such debates, of course, there is a danger that they will unfold along well-worn tracks and that a flurry of activity surrounding individual trees will deflect attention from more pressing issues facing the forest. Alternatively, precisely because the interests and incentives of senior academics and frontline practitioners so often diverge, the nature and extent of the similarities and differences between them may be less clear ex ante, creating the potential for some initial sense of unease about the appropriate tone and terms of debate. Conscious of these potential strengths and weaknesses, we sought the involvement of individuals whose work (whether scholarly or applied) and temperament (capacity for frank but collegial exchange) we knew, wagering that a well-managed gathering among a relatively small number of such people over two days would yield insights that a more orthodox professional gathering would not. We hope that the contributions gathered here affirm that the wager paid handsome dividends, though their capacity to stimulate further such exchanges elsewhere would be the highest form of vindication.

The third motive was somewhat more focused and strategic: for World Bank staff engaged in these issues, especially those contributing to a global field-based research and development program known internally as Justice for the Poor, it was to ensure that their work program was sufficiently grounded not only in the prevailing literature but also in the immediate frame of reference of its leading academic contributors. Most of the World Bank's analytical staff are economists, and they enjoy almost daily input from a veritable parade of Nobel laureates and other high-profile members of their profession, in the process ensuring that the World Bank's work programs in economics are imbued with a correspondingly refined content and legitimacy and supported by close professional coalitions borne of ongoing face-to-face interactions across the scholar-practitioner divide. It was our sense that this model was entirely desirable and feasible for fields other than economics and that, specifically, the resources and "convening power" of the World Bank could be harnessed to bring together various bank staff working on legal pluralism and some of the leading scholars of this field. As we discuss in the Introduction, engaging constructively with legal pluralism is an inherently problematic issue for development agencies of all kinds, so – for both ethical and pragmatic reasons – it is vital that the leading scholarly minds inform and refine this work.

BRIAN Z. TAMANAHA

As an academic who has been critical of World Bank development activities, I was wary when first approached by members of the Justice for the Poor program to help them organize a gathering between scholars and practitioners to explore the topic of legal pluralism. Within academic circles, the World Bank is viewed with suspicion for its perceived economic policies and formulaic approaches to legal development. This exchange was an ideal opportunity for academics to learn about views within the bank, as well as a chance to communicate our views to people in the bank.

It has indeed proved to be a fruitful interaction. Academics and practitioners, in their appreciation of the implications of legal pluralism, share a great deal more in common than might appear at first glance. The main difference is that scholars have the luxury of thinking about the situation from a distance, whereas practitioners have projects to carry out within constraints that limit what can be accomplished. These contrasting perspectives are evident in the essays: the academic pieces are more general, abstract, and conceptual, whereas the practitioner pieces are grounded in concrete situations and tasks. The pieces are not directly responsive to one another, because we thought that would be too artificially restricting for both sides. But our two-day gathering at the World Bank generated a genuine dialogue on a set of shared themes that influenced the final contributions. Readers of this collection, we hope, will benefit from reading essays from both perspectives within the covers of a single book.

Acknowledgments

We wish to thank those staff at the World Bank not immediately affiliated with the Justice for the Poor program who gave up valuable time to give us their insights and feedback on this project. Many thanks to John Berger, our editor at Cambridge University Press, and to two anonymous reviewers, both of whom provided helpful feedback on the draft manuscript. We are particularly grateful to Nimalka King, Teresa Marchiori, and Susanne Skoruppa for their excellent work completing the numerous logistical tasks associated with the workshop and subsequent editorial activities as the various written contributions were prepared for publication. We thank Patricia M. Carley for her editing assistance. More broadly, we thank the Government of Australia's Agency for International Development (AusAID) for its major contribution to the analytical (and other) work of the World Bank's Justice for the Poor program, which made this particular project possible.

Brian Z. Tamanaha
Caroline Sage
Michael Woolcock

Introduction

Legal Pluralism and Development Policy

Scholars and Practitioners in Dialogue

Caroline Sage and Michael Woolcock

For the vast majority of people in today's low-income or conflict-affected countries, everyday life entails negotiating between the claims of multiple rules systems and regulating institutions of varying authority, legitimacy, coherence, and capacity, any of which can, depending on the issue, exert their influence or be appealed to in the quest for justice or conflict management. In many of these countries, everyday transactions, such as marriage, inheritance, and land exchange, may fall under different (or multiple) legal orders and jurisdictions, ranging from the legal or administrative institutions of the state (sometimes at multiple levels) to religious authorities and traditional, cultural, or community-based systems, each of which may interpret and thus adjudicate a given issue in very different ways.[1] Legal pluralism – the coexistence of multiple legal systems within a given community or sociopolitical space (Merry 1988; Benda-Beckmann 2002) – is a normal state of affairs in all societies, but it presents distinctive challenges and opportunities in low-income or conflict-affected countries.

Development theorists and practitioners have tended to either blindly ignore the ubiquitous phenomena of legal pluralism or regard it as a constraint on development, a defective condition that must be overcome in the name of modernizing, state building, and enhancing "the rule of law." Efforts were often made to codify and transform what were seen as informal and idiosyncratic local systems into something more "legible" and uniform within the umbrella of the state (Escobar 1995; Scott 1998). Another prevailing assumption was that the transformation of such rules systems was largely a technical exercise, one optimally achieved by the adoption of legal systems deemed to be effective elsewhere. Programmatic efforts to build state

---

[1] Legal pluralism also often characterizes issues over which there is larger-scale contestation, such as who controls national budgets, security forces, and natural resources. Our focus in this volume is predominantly on local-level manifestations, even as we acknowledge the importance of national and international instances of legal pluralism (see Berman 2006; Michaels 2009).

legal systems in these countries via this approach, however, have often fared poorly (Haggard, MacIntyre, and Tiede 2008). Despite the deployment of vast resources over several decades, many state legal systems remain weak or dysfunctional, while non-state systems continue to operate. That such "schemes to improve the human condition have [so often] failed" (Scott 1998) is testimony to the resilience, importance, and complexity of prevailing rules systems (Carothers 2006; Scott 2009) and the inherent flaw in the idea that the ways in which people structure, regulate, and understand their lives can be rapidly transformed via external technical fixes.

Although the development community has tended to regard legal pluralism as a "problem," people living under such circumstances, especially the poor and marginalized themselves, do not necessarily share this view. If the state legal system under which one lives is perceived as captured, corrupt, inefficient, or hostile, or if engaging with it requires traveling great distances, waiting in long lines, completing complex forms, enduring humiliating treatment, and paying prohibitively expensive fees, only to receive an unsatisfactory outcome (or no outcome at all), it may be beneficial to have other options available. People in these situations often understand the norms and processes of the local religious, traditional, or customary justice system and are eminently familiar with the key decision makers presiding over them, whereas the state legal system may remain obscure, remote, expensive, slow, and unaccountable. When disputes arise, an overwhelming majority of these people eschew the state legal system and instead seek redress in a range of non-state institutions, which to them are accessible (geographically, administratively, and financially), efficient, and socially legitimate.

As such, the key tension of legal pluralism is its potential to be both a problem and an opportunity. The fact that development organizations have tended to perceive legal pluralism in low-income countries as a problem can be understood from a number of perspectives. Primarily, it stems from a series of widely held underlying assumptions: that law must be uniform, comprehensive, and monopolized by the state; that the rule of law consists of a single model or form to which all constituent legal systems must conform; and that political and economic development depend on conforming to this model (because of the greater "predictability," "efficiency," and "justice" such conformity will allegedly provide). Related, but perhaps less intentional, explanations stem from the near monopoly of the discipline of economics in setting development agendas and approaches (Rao and Woolcock 2007) or the institutional imperatives of large bureaucracies to make complex social realities legible, actionable, and measurable – preferably in three bullet points or a simple diagram.

Despite this history, in recent years development organizations have begun to reexamine some of the underlying assumptions about legal pluralisms and to explore the opportunities that might exist in contexts where legal pluralism is a pervasive reality. This undertaking, however, is fraught with its own concerns and unknowns. An uncritical embrace of legal pluralism, for example, might exacerbate the already seemingly impossible task of building the state legal system and might worsen legal uncertainty. Moreover, the norms and procedures of many customary or traditional justice systems raise real concerns about gender equity, human rights, due process, and capture by the traditional elite; many of these systems have been seriously distorted by oppressive colonial histories or more recent forms of state or non-state violence. Importantly, it is difficult to adequately gain the knowledge base necessary to engage with context-specific idiosyncratic systems that do not fit into a clearly understood model (McGovern 2011); without such knowledge, how can one design technical solutions? How can these tensions be acknowledged and addressed in constructive ways? What role, if any, can external agencies play in facilitating a domestic policy dialogue that ensures that these tensions are addressed in ways that are perceived to be fair, legitimate, and effective, especially by those groups whose voices and interests are otherwise marginalized? Under what conditions can the "lessons" of any such experiences from different times and places be applied elsewhere?

The contributors to this volume comprise leading scholars of legal pluralism and experienced development practitioners, brought together here to engage in a critical dialogue on the key analytical and applied issues. The purpose of this volume is to enhance the analytical rigor underpinning the development community's engagement with legal pluralism, not so much because the particular interactions presented here yield "the answers" (they do not), but because they demonstrate to scholars and practitioners of legal pluralism the mutual benefit of engaging in sustained dialogue, a process we believe is underused but potentially of mutual benefit. The various contributions to this volume were initially presented at a workshop hosted by (and held at) the World Bank and have benefited greatly from the lively debate that ensued. It is crucial to point out up front that the aim was not to craft a "unifying" theory of legal pluralism and development or to identify "best practice" policy solutions to inherently complex problems. We hope instead that these contributions demonstrate that enhancing rigor and relevance at the nexus of legal pluralism and development policy is instead an emergent phenomenon, arising from an ongoing commitment to understanding and nurturing the political spaces wherein diverse (and often opaque) rules systems – their forms, jurisdictions, sources of legitimacy, modes of dispute resolution, and enforcement mechanisms – can be recognized, and the tensions between them constructively addressed. We hope that the tone and content of this volume, which includes contributions from people representing an array of disciplines, regional expertise, theoretical perspectives, and professional standpoints, embodies this principle.

The challenges and opportunities of legal pluralism can be addressed more constructively through open debate, we contend, but they have been a stumbling block for (large) development agencies over many decades, suggesting that a more structural concern must be addressed if more constructive engagements between different normative orders and legal systems are to be brokered (Toomey 2010). Even with the best of intentions, the imperatives of development agencies constrain them to conceive of legal pluralism as a particular *kind* of development problem – that is, a variant on more familiar development problems. Unfortunately, seeking solutions through orthodox approaches is often itself a central part of the problem.

WHY IS ENGAGING WITH LEGAL PLURALISM SO DIFFICULT FOR DEVELOPMENT AGENCIES?

In high-income countries, rule of law systems have emerged over time in ways that provide, for the most part, a coherent, overarching set of enforceable procedures ("meta-rules"[2]) for regulating a vast array of socioeconomic interactions and political relationships – from the most personal of family ties to the management of natural resources to the structuring of state institutions – as well as determining which issues fall under whose jurisdiction (North, Wallis, and Weingast 2009; Fukuyama 2011). Such systems have emerged conjointly with the modern state as the ordering principles structuring government and the ways in which such governments govern. So understood, a rule of law system is not an immutable or fixed end state, but a perpetual work in progress, an ongoing effort to constructively accommodate numerous (sometimes contending) normative orders while adapting in legitimate ways to new social realities. As such, "the law" itself is not a stand-alone "sector" operating at a high level of abstraction or autonomy, but rather a constituent element infusing all aspects of everyday life, from buying train tickets and car insurance to determining the rights and obligations of citizenship. All "policies" are expressed in, and made actionable by, law, and all laws, by extension, are a subset of broader rules systems governing society (Sage and Woolcock 2008).

The political dynamics underpinning the historical emergence of different rule of law systems remain a subject of ongoing scholarly inquiry (Tamanaha 2005, 2008; Glenn 2010),[3] with little consensus on what such knowledge implies for development policy. Even so, "building the rule of law" now enjoys the broadest possible endorsement across the North/South, left/right, and disciplinary divides and has been hailed by World Bank president Robert Zoellick as the highest-priority development policy issue. For its part, however, the international development community has a mostly unhappy record of engagement with legal development over many decades, a record borne, as we contended previously, of strong – but too often flawed – underlying assumptions about the nature of "the law," its institutional embodiment, and the mechanisms by which legal reform can be brought about, especially at the local level.

---

[2] Meta-rules, as articulated in Barron, Smith, and Woolcock (2004), are higher-order rules that provide a basis for mediating between (and, where necessary, reconciling) lower-order rules. At the level of individual decision making, see also Sunstein and Ullmann-Margalit (1999) on the related idea of "second-order decisions."

[3] See also the influential writing of Amartya Sen (2009) on this subject.

In too many instances, development actors have presumed that a rule of law system is an institutional form that can and should be transplanted into contexts in which it is otherwise absent – that is, where the "problem" of legal pluralism prevails. Building the rule of law is thus a project that "develops" contexts that are either "pre-legal" or suffused with legal pluralism. The underlying assumption, consistent with reforms sought in other sectors in development (such as education and public financial management), is that the "functionality" of a legal system is a direct product of its "form" – that is, what it "does" stems from what it "looks like" (Pritchett, Andrews, and Woolcock 2010).[4] Ipso facto, enhancing the effectiveness of a given legal system is often construed in development policy circles as being largely a matter of replicating the practices understood within, or that can most plausibly appeal to, the frames of reference of external professionals: adopting particular legal codes, passing legislation, signing resolutions, building courthouses, and holding training ("capacity building") seminars.[5] But there is no single or universal rule of law system, and even putatively similar systems can generate a strikingly diverse range of outcomes in particular settings. Every legal tradition, though it may share broadly similar philosophical and historical roots with those of others, is unique in its constitutive elements and particular application, in how it is connected to the particular culture, polity, and economy in which it is embedded.

Despite decades of trying and the expenditure of billions of dollars, the "law and development" effort – which overtly sought to transplant Western commercial and criminal codes into developing countries – is now widely agreed (even by its original protagonists) to have been a great disappointment. But the organizational imperatives to continue its practices live on;[6] the same kinds of legal development programs are tried time and again. The instincts of development professionals – underpinned and reinforced by their career incentives, especially in large organizations – are to regard the rule of law problem as a variant on other familiar technical problems (such as engineering), one that has a knowable solution that can be readily discerned and implemented by "experts." They are inclined to think that efforts to date have so often failed largely for want of adequate resources, domestic "capacity,"

---

[4] Critics of "institutional isomorphism" (DiMaggio and Powell 1983) and organizational "monocropping" (Evans 2004) have provided compelling explanations of why these phenomena are so prevalent: metrics of success in such instances are inherently problematic, so credibility is inferred on the basis of having adopted a "best practice"; when uncertainty is high (as in civil war or post-conflict settings), the imperatives to justify one's actions in this way are even stronger.

[5] Recent legal reform initiatives in the Solomon Islands aptly reflect this. Millions of dollars have been spent in regional centers to construct state-of-the-art courthouses and jails to address the "tensions" (civil war) from the early 2000s; the buildings use locally sourced materials and conform to indigenous architectural styles. They certainly look like modern judicial institutions, but, unfortunately, they are yet to function as one; a year after its opening, the jail has only a handful of inmates, and the courthouse has been used twice. Meanwhile, little dent has been made in the hundreds of backlogged cases stemming from the everyday disputes that affect most Solomon Islanders most of the time.

[6] For a review of some of the most recent initiatives, see Trubek and Santos (2006).

"political will," or donor "coordination" (Pritchett and Woolcock 2004). Even in the most propitious of circumstances, however, engaging in legal reform and seeking to respond effectively to the challenges and opportunities of pervasive legal pluralism is a qualitatively different challenge from building roads, immunizing children, and fertilizing crops (important and difficult as these tasks are), because legal systems, and rules systems more broadly, are social inventions. Like languages (which are also a form of rules system), social inventions draw their salience and strength from the acquiescence of those using them, becoming meaningful, actionable, and legitimate through idiosyncratic political and cultural processes. Reforming or enhancing social inventions (such as legal systems) is a different kind of policy problem, and as such these require different kinds of solutions, informed by correspondingly different kinds of analytical and assessment frameworks from those that tend to dominate most (large) development agencies.

Institutional imperatives to regard legal and judicial reform as merely a variant of other development problems are compounded by the bureaucratic nature of development agencies (like the World Bank), which demands that such reforms and systems to implement and manage them, be made legible, broadly understandable, and actionable. For fiduciary and quality control mechanisms to work at scale in such an organization, project documents need to be written and assessable by non-specialists, providing results indicators that can be easily measured; the privileging of templates, bullet points, matrices, or the simple triangle to deftly link together fundamental aspects of social life leaves little space for the inherent complexities that characterize a given context. To get approval to support a particular initiative or policy reform, staff must present a coherent, persuasive story about how certain actions will lead to expected change in a given context in a given time frame (usually three to five years);[7] these imperatives encourage staff to present knowledge that is either not known or perhaps even not knowable as clearly legible within the existing apparatus of institutional categories, discourse, and frameworks. Such representations tend to say more about the context within which they are written than the social realities they purport to represent. Personal career incentives of course come into play as well, with staff rewarded for delivering "successful projects" and providing policy responses that demonstrably "work." Even more highly prized are those projects and policies that meet predetermined targets such as the Millennium Development Goals, and with a minimum of political controversy. There are few

---

[7] Such short time frames are themselves deeply problematic. As the World Bank itself observes in its World Development Report 2011 on conflict and security (World Bank 2011), achieving a one-standard-deviation improvement in its "rule of law" indicator took forty-one years, on average, among the twenty *fastest*-reforming developing countries. For those not "reforming" at all, or even regressing, the time frame is essentially infinite (or at least unknown). Sustaining political support and justifying financing for development initiatives whose impact – even when implemented by the best people, with adequate financial backing and administrative cooperation – may not be apparent for multiple decades is a serious challenge for our contemporary international aid architecture.

incentives, however, to document the real activities and complexities of everyday development practice: the constant negotiations, exchange of ideas, and building of networks, partnerships, and understanding across all spectrums of a given society, the development community, and within the development agency itself, as well as the political maneuvering required to get any initiative off the ground. It is in these spaces that development practitioners come in contact with legal pluralism in all its forms, but it is these stories – and this understanding of what all these exchanges are actually about and why they so often stall – that are rarely told.

The fact that the analytical and empirical work in large development organizations (such as the World Bank) tends to be dominated by economists also complicates the task of responding effectively to legal pluralism. Paradoxically, for all its apparent sophistication and rigor, economics can provide (or justify) the "simple" answers that large bureaucracies require.[8] Although there is a vibrant sub-field on "law and economics" (see Cooter and Ulen 2007), for example, its prevailing assumption is that the content and effectiveness of the law is best understood via the tools of neoclassical economics. Ontologically, this gives rise to a view of "the law" (and companion concepts, such as "property rights" and "contracts") that largely assumes similarity across different contexts; such assumptions, in turn, justify certain preferred epistemological entry points for empirical research, strongly favoring comparative econometric analysis over the more context-specific (idiosyncratic) findings of anthropology, sociology, and history (Woolcock, Szreter, and Rao 2011).[9] Such economic methods based on quantitative data collection and analysis – generally gleaned from individual people or events – tend to overlook or undervalue the inherently relational and inherently contested nature of socioeconomic life. This is particularly problematic for the analysis of legal orders that are fundamentally about establishing rules that define and govern relationships and allow for peaceful contestation; in turn, institutional transformation implies a shift in relationships and

---

[8] In principle, one might imagine that "small" development agencies (e.g., specialist nongovernment organizations), many of them inspired by rights-based or political concerns rather than economics, may be inherently better placed to respond to the specific legal issues of poor communities. This may be so in certain instances, but small is not always beautiful, especially when considerable leverage (symbolic and/or substantive) is required to move and sustain a legal reform agenda in a more inclusive direction or at scale.

[9] Commenting on recent work by economists studying the causes of civil war, McGovern (2011, 353) astutely observes that the "extensive and intensive qualitative research required to obtain context-specific knowledge is neither a luxury nor... a kind of methodological altruism to be extended by the softhearted." It is, in purely positivist terms, the epistemological due diligence work required before one can talk meaningfully about other people's intentions, motivations, or desires. The risk in foregoing it is not simply that one might miss some of the local color of individual "cases." It is one of misrecognition. Analysis based on such misrecognition may mistake symptoms for causes or view two formally similar situations as comparable despite their different etiologies. To extend the medical metaphor one step further, misdiagnosis is unfortunate, but a flawed prescription based on such misrecognition can be deadly.

the rules and norms that govern them, all of which is likely to be deeply contentious (Barron, Diprose, and Woolcock 2011).

Even if different theoretical and methodological approaches are largely complementary, too often the "disciplinary monopoly" (Rao and Woolcock 2007) at large agencies manifests itself in a very narrow rendering of what counts as a question and (most important) what counts as an answer. This is deeply problematic for development policy, especially, as indicated, in the field of legal and judicial reform, because it largely precludes, from the outset, the very possibility of engaging with questions of legal pluralism on its own terms. However, the absence of different disciplinary perspectives in shaping approaches to development should not be seen as the fault of economists alone. Among the social sciences, the discipline of economics has been by the far the most adept at translating research and analysis into policy solutions and practical action (thereby bridging the divide between theory, research, and practice), whereas other disciplines, such as anthropology, with its uncomfortable relationship to colonial histories, has until recently actively steered clear of development policy and practice. As a consequence, other disciplinary perspectives that have come to the table in more recent years find it difficult to do so on their own terms without being sidelined or steamrollered. It is undeniable that the ability to work effectively in the World Bank (and other large development agencies) is helped greatly by an ability to understand and communicate with economists. At the same time, establishing partnerships and collaborative relationships with leading social scientists in academia or research institutions was one of the primary motivations behind the workshops and meetings that led to this publication.

None of this is to say that alternative approaches cannot be pursued, even in an institution like the World Bank.[10] However, doing so brings with it an added complexity: on the one hand, rule systems and justice institutions provide frameworks and spaces for contestation and innovation, while on the other hand, these systems and institutions themselves emerge from these same processes. How it is that broadly coherent and legitimate "rule of law" systems emerge in any given country context is only clear with the benefit of hindsight; they are not (or are very rarely) the product of anyone's grand design, and they inherently entail conflict because their articulation and consolidation over time necessarily benefit some while (actually or potentially) being costly to others (North et al. 2009). For this reason, mechanisms for addressing conflict need to be incorporated into the design of interventions seeking to facilitate the emergence of "rule of law" systems.

If development agencies and the disciplines that dominate their analytical frameworks struggle in general to engage adequately with legal pluralism, responding more constructively to the challenges and opportunities that legal pluralism presents

---

[10] A key theme of the World Bank's Justice for the Poor program, for example, is that "building the rule of law" fundamentally requires local organizational innovation and that processes of reform at the local level must be undertaken on the basis of a detailed understanding of the context in which they will occur (see Sage, Menzies, and Woolcock 2010).

requires a clear articulation of exactly why it is a development issue. It is to this that we now turn.

LEGAL PLURALISM AS A DEVELOPMENT ISSUE

Legal pluralism characterizes those situations in which there are multiple legal and normative orders governing everyday life (Merry 1988). The phenomenon of legal pluralism per se is not unique to developing counties – social norms and multilayered legal systems are ubiquitous in developed countries, as when states in a federation have different laws pertaining to criminal penalties, or the United States seeks to accommodate the particular rules governing Native American communities – but it is experienced most intensely in such contexts because (a) there is often no credible overarching system for mediating between these different orders; (b) such orders may be deeply embedded in broader political and cosmological systems, which themselves may be incommensurate; and (c) there may be so many qualitatively different and contending orders in a given context, yet (d) each of these elements, individually or collectively, may be fluid, relatively weak, and/or overwhelmed by the wider array of social challenges they now confront. Let us address each of these aspects in turn.

Legal pluralism becomes a development issue when

(a) There Are Weak or Absent "Meta-Rules." In many respects, the development of a rule of law system entails forging a set of enforceable agreements about how to manage the contending claims of subordinate legal and normative orders. International law is perhaps the highest embodiment of such agreements – for example, when it helps individual countries sort out their differences on trade. But agreements can also emerge at lower units of analysis in developing countries in settings of high legal pluralism, thereby constituting an organic set of "meta-rules" (Barron et al. 2004) for mediating everyday disputes between contending orders. To the extent that external agents can facilitate the emergence of such "meta-rules" (e.g., through carefully designed development projects or supporting paralegal intermediaries), they can be said to be building "interim institutions" (Alder, Sage, and Woolcock 2009) that attempt to engage constructively with competing legal-normative orders in ways that allow for nonviolent contestation around points of difference without predetermining the final end state.

(b) Different Normative Orders Are Embedded in (Incongruent) Political and Cosmological Systems. As Gauri (2009) stresses, a defining characteristic of many non-state legal systems is their conjoined status with political structures and the encompassing-meaning systems by which people make sense of what happens to them.[11] Although this can also be said for state legal systems – that they reflect and

---

[11] On the importance of intersubjective meaning for development policy, especially in "fragile" states, see Gauri, Woolcock, and Desai (2011).

serve to reinforce prevailing political structures and value systems – such systems also ensure some level of "separation of power" by making clear distinctions between the core functions of state to enact, to implement, and to adjudicate the law. In non-state systems, this separation of functions and powers may not exist. In such systems, political power vested in ruling elites also tends to confer discretionary power to determine the rules, whereas both the rules and the rulers themselves may embody (and/or draw their legitimacy from) cosmologies that are deeply constituent of people's identities, beliefs, aspirations, and values. In some contexts, this may lead to outcomes that upset liberal sensibilities and thus become (deeply) problematic for development practitioners to engage with. Upholding the integrity of a community's system may be seen as a higher priority than discerning what is "just" for a given individual, as when a community facing a rape charge asserts the primacy of restoring group "harmony" and family "honor" over prosecuting the individual perpetrator. Moreover, if a feature of rule of law systems is the formal separation between politics, law, and religion, in many developing country settings (and indeed for certain groups within developed countries, such as Aborigines in Australia), these "powers" remain fused, their separation unthinkable. As Polanyi (1944) long ago argued, in the course of the development process, transactions of all kinds that were once deeply embedded in familial and cosmological relations became increasingly separated, giving rise to widespread conflict as identities and power relations were reconfigured. In many respects, these processes continue to play themselves out in developing countries today; as such, legal pluralism is less a "problem" (to be "fixed" by "experts") than a pervasive empirical reality whose political salience is only enhanced by deeper processes of social change.

(c) *The Volume and Diversity of Contending Orders Is Large.* Legal pluralism in developing countries can differ in degree from counterpart situations in developed countries because of the sheer volume and diversity of (often contending) legal-normative orders. In any given social realm – but particularly one characterized by high ethnic diversity – different religions, different forms of "customary" law, different layers of state law (national, regional, and local), and indeed the administrative requirements of different development projects together constitute the prevailing "rules of the game" that those seeking justice must navigate. Much of this legal pluralism will be "unobservable" in a statistical sense and thus difficult to detect (let alone understand) via the dominant modes of enquiry (e.g., large-scale household surveys) typically used to plan, to implement, and to assess orthodox development projects and policies.[12] Moreover, standard "development" activities, such as the provision of roads, schools, telecommunications, and public transport, only serve

---

[12] This is not to say, of course, that local justice issues cannot (or should not) be assessed using household surveys (and the statistical analysis to which such data give rise); it is just a far more vexing issue than collecting information on (say) standard demographic categories, which itself is hard enough. Indeed, see Himelein, Menzies, and Woolcock (2010) for a "second best" attempt to construct an instrument (based on various isolated initial efforts) for assessing local justice issues via household surveys.

to increase the likelihood that these diverse orders will come into contact with one another (and thereby generate conflict). Even the most carefully designed projects themselves constitute a complex array of new rules and procedures, likely adding additional layers (and potential confusion and conflict) to an already diverse situation (Barron, Diprose, and Woolcock 2011). Consequently, development projects can *intensify* rather than mitigate legal pluralism and its potential discontents.

(d) Fluid and Weak Non-State Justice Systems Become Overwhelmed. A defining characteristic of many systems described as customary or traditional is that their precepts are expressed in oral form, their application and limits determined by a village elder. This gives such systems considerable fluidity, a virtue of which can be their capacity to adapt to new circumstances and to evade control by the state.[13] A corresponding vice, however, is that the same fluidity can give rise to rulings that can be used to consolidate the interests, resources, and status of elites at the direct expense of more marginalized groups.[14] In many contexts, local systems that may previously have incorporated a range of checks on the abuse of power have been distorted beyond recognition through deliberate co-option by the colonial or independent state, or through serious social upheavals such as civil strike or conflict. In such situations of legal pluralism, the various constituent legal-normative orders may be individually weak – courts may be underresourced and with long backlogs, the police may be corrupt, religious leaders may be inadequately trained, and village elites may focus exclusively on their own concerns – leaving the poor little option but to "forum shop" between orders in the quest for justice. Even if the various legal-normative orders are sufficiently stable, legitimate, and robust, they may be simply overwhelmed by the volume and complexity of the challenges now confronting them, challenges they were not designed to handle, such as large-scale inflows of migrants or negotiations with outside investors who require very particular notions of "property rights." In a world of mass transit, cellular telephones, television, and the Internet, even the most isolated communities are becoming aware of alternatives, of opportunities to interact with others who do not share their language, religion, culture, or rules system. Thus, globalization challenges and intensifies all forms of legal pluralism.

In the face of these contending pressures, the response from the international community to date has at best a very mixed record. Responding to this challenge in an operationally relevant way requires an alternative theory of change and diverse forms of empirical evidence. A key starting point is the recognition that legal pluralism

---

[13] As Scott (1985) famously put it, such strategies were often one of the "weapons of the weak," a way of retaining some semblance of advantage in contests with vastly more powerful entities, such as states and firms.

[14] Rule of law systems also ideally respond to the need for change but do so through agreed-upon and broadly legitimate procedures; see point (a) above. A corresponding concern of rule of law systems is that when they are introduced quickly and via external decree, they can consolidate and legitimize (at least in the minds of elites) an otherwise highly inequitable situation (Mattei and Nader 2008).

is an empirical fact in most contexts and becomes a policy "problem" largely to the extent that its constituent legal-normative orders inadequately cohere with one another, or indeed with the dominant development norms. Whether and how to bring about this coherence is less a technical issue awaiting the insight of a team of legal experts than a political process that can be managed in more or less equitable ways. In this sense, development is largely a process of facilitating "good struggles" (Alder et al. 2009), in and through which the content and legitimacy of legal reform takes place.

ENHANCING THE DIALOGUE BETWEEN LEGAL PLURALISM SCHOLARSHIP AND PRACTICE

Forging a stronger dialogue between scholars and practitioners of legal pluralism provides one possible avenue for responding in constructive ways to some of the issues and dilemmas identified in this Introduction. Whereas a great deal of intellectual thought has been given to this topic from a range of perspectives and disciplines, this has yet to really find its way to informing what development practitioners actually do. To this end, this volume presents the work of a dozen leading scholars of legal pluralism, drawn from the disciplines of anthropology, history, law, political science, and sociology, who have, in their own way, addressed the nexus between legal pluralism and development. The chapters by these scholars have, in turn, been commented on by legal development practitioners – people with extensive experience working with governments and civil society organizations to bring about positive change in legal settings in particular countries. This gives the volume a very distinctive and, we hope, innovative and instructive tone: it draws on the leading scholarship but interprets it through the pragmatic lens of those who must do something constructive with it in actual countries under real constraints.

The book is divided into three thematic sections.

1. *Origins and Key Ideas.* What does legal pluralism mean to different scholars and practitioners, and how has its relationship to development been understood? What do we know – historically, politically, and philosophically – about how legal systems, and more specifically "rule of law" systems, have evolved?

The opening five chapters provide a broad introduction to legal pluralism and its various manifestations in development debates. Following this introductory chapter, Lauren Benton provides, in Chapter 1, a historian's perspective, arguing that contemporary challenges associated with legal pluralism can be fruitfully understood as instance in the early twenty-first century of much longer-standing situations, especially those associated with the behavior of early modern empires, where various forms of law were deployed both by the imperial order and by subjects seeking to resist or accommodate that order. Brian Z. Tamanaha, in Chapter 2, extends these arguments into contemporary development policy debates surrounding legal pluralism and the rule of law, arguing that, although both terms remain deeply contested, more fruitful interaction between them requires a deeper appreciation of their constituent characteristics and the societal context within which any attempt at "reform" takes place.

In Chapter 3, David Kinley provides an overview of an area of particular contention in legal pluralism, namely, human rights, arguing that concerns about their alleged rigidity are misplaced and that they must always (as they have in the past) be understood and adjudicated in their appropriate political context. In Chapter 4, Sally Engle Merry draws on a case study of a women's court in Gujurat, India, to explore the significance of the concepts of legal consciousness, legal culture, and legal mobilization for developing an applied (and more comprehensive) theory of legal pluralism. These opening contributions are followed in Chapter 5 by some reflections on legal pluralism in Cambodia by Daniel Adler and Sokbunthoeun So; they argue that political economy considerations must be central to understanding the quest for justice faced by marginalized groups, especially in contexts characterized by entrenched power differentials and deep patrimonial ties connecting firms, the executive, and judiciary. In such circumstances, merely strengthening the formal legal system serves only to further entrench the interests and power of well-connected elites.

2. *Theory and Concepts.* As rule of law systems have emerged and evolved, how have citizen groups influenced the timing and content of decisions or concessions by the state to extend the rule of law, especially to the poor, and to require (at least in principle) the state itself to be subject to its precepts?

The next four chapters explore the idea of legal pluralism in greater theoretical detail. In Chapter 6, H. Patrick Glenn takes up the challenge of providing some foundations for an alternative formulation of legal pluralism that helps to account for past policy disappointments – which he argues have focused excessively on adopting Western models – while also outlining a more hopeful path forward that adopts a perspective concerned with sustainable diversity in law. Chapter 7, by William Twining, provides an overview of some of the key concepts associated with legal pluralism and explores some of their jurisprudential implications, and Gordon R. Woodman, in Chapter 8, provides his own analysis of why legal pluralism has proved to be such a persistent "problem" for development policy, contending that the primary culprit has been an exclusive focus on the state as the object of reform and failure to appreciate that heightened complexity and uncertainty is likely to accompany attempts at reform. In Chapter 9, Kanishka Jayasuriya examines the fascinating topic of institutional hybrids, arguing that the logic of development assistance conspires to seek a "technology of jurisprudence" by which to resolve the challenges of legal pluralism it encounters in novel institutional environments. These contributions are followed in Chapter 10 by some reflections by Doug J. Porter on the applications and implications of different conceptions of legal pluralism for development practice, especially as it pertains to decentralization and the regulation of service delivery in post-conflict settings.

3. *Applications and Practice.* Legal pluralism can be simultaneously part of the problem and part of the solution for poor people seeking justice. Under what conditions does it become one or the other? How can external agents facilitate processes of change that minimize the "problems" while retaining some of the valued features of the "opportunities"?

The final grouping of chapters focuses on the specific challenges and opportunities that legal pluralism presents to development policy, development strategies, and development agencies. In Chapter 11, Julio Faundez considers the implications of whether international development agencies construe legal pluralism as part of a state building or a legal reform agenda. This distinction matters, he argues, because engaging with non-state justice systems presents qualitatively different challenges to development agencies than the more familiar tasks of enhancing the capacities of states, the former being inherently less amenable to uniform responses. Christian Lund explores similar dilemmas at a more micro level in Chapter 12, where he considers the particular ways in which legal pluralism complicates understandings of such seemingly clear and conventional concepts as "property" and "citizenship." In Chapter 13, Varun Gauri engages with the difficult topic of the limits of customary law, arguing that they often suffer from a "publicity deficit" that in turn shields both local and international systems from critique and from orthodox mechanisms of accountability. The volume concludes with two contributions by practitioners: in Chapter 14, Meg Taylor and Nicholas Menzies look at the salience of legal pluralism in the (often deeply contentious) debates surrounding natural resource extraction, with a particular focus on Papua New Guinea; and in the final Chapter 15, Deborah H. Isser draws on her extensive field experience in Liberia, Southern Sudan, and Mozambique to argue that justice reform in general and legal pluralism in particular need to be addressed not as abstractions, but as concrete, context-specific challenges faced by everyday people, for which the most effective response is likely to be one that takes seriously the task of understanding particular manifestations of legal pluralism on its own terms.

CONCLUDING REMARKS

In the early decades of the twenty-first century, the development community finds itself confronted with an array of serious challenges pertaining to the reform of institutional mechanisms for mediating relations between peoples, firms, states, and international actors, and doing so in ways that are broadly perceived to be legitimate, equitable, and effective. Most obviously in the Middle East but also in contexts as diverse as the European Union, fast-growing China, democratic India, urban Brazil, and rural Africa, wholesale institutional transformation is a defining feature of our age, and its effects are often experienced most consequentially by those least able to respond effectively, namely, the poor and marginalized. These are surely challenges for legal professionals, but they are also complex political, economic, and social challenges, and as such their resolution must draw on the larger storehouse of knowledge – empirical, theoretical, and experiential – available for this purpose.

The overt attempt to reform legal and judicial institutions is a particular kind of development problem; it is one that history and social consensus now demands that we (everyone, whether professional or everyday citizen) confront, but it is also one with which our prevailing aid architecture, with its corresponding structures and imperatives, struggles mightily. Responding more constructively to this challenge requires in the first instance appropriate humility; our record to date is hardly flattering. In the second instance, it requires identifying more precisely what kind of challenge it is and then harnessing the best and most appropriate forms of evidence to inform the debates that necessarily surround it so that reform – if and when it is deemed to be required – takes place in ways that are ultimately owned, implemented by, and accountable to domestic actors and that serve the interests and aspirations of that society's most vulnerable. The efficacy and trajectory of this reform is likely to be clear only in hindsight, and the dynamics surrounding it will ultimately be forged in the messy crucible of domestic politics. Even so, and in its own very circumscribed way, we hope that more frequent and fruitful dialogue between scholars and practitioners of legal pluralism can be part of that process.

REFERENCES

Adler, Daniel, Caroline Sage, and Michael Woolcock. 2009. "Interim Institutions and the Development Process: Opening Spaces for Reform in Cambodia and Indonesia." BWPI Working Paper 86, Brooks World Poverty Institute, University of Manchester.

Barron, Patrick, Claire Q. Smith, and Michael Woolcock. 2004. "Understanding Local Level Conflict in Developing Countries: Theory, Evidence and Implications from Indonesia." Social Development Papers, Conflict Prevention and Reconstruction Paper 19, World Bank, Washington, DC.

Barron, Patrick, Rachael Diprose, and Michael Woolcock. 2011. *Contesting Development: Participatory Projects and Local Conflict Dynamics in Indonesia*. New Haven, CT: Yale University Press.

Benda-Beckmann, Franz von. 2002. "Who's Afraid of Legal Pluralism?" *Journal of Legal Pluralism* 47: 37–82.

Berman, Paul Schiff. 2006. "Global Legal Pluralism." *Southern California Law Review* 80: 1155–238.

Carothers, Thomas, ed. 2006. *Promoting the Rule of Law Abroad: In Search of Knowledge*. Washington, DC: Carnegie Endowment for International Peace.

Cooter, Robert, and Thomas Ulen. 2007. *Law and Economics*. 5th ed. Reading, MA: Addison-Wesley.

DiMaggio, Paul, and Walter W. Powell. 1983. "The Iron Cage Revisited: Institutional Isomorphism and Collective Rationality in Organizational Fields." *American Sociological Review* 48 (2): 147–60.

Escobar, Arturo. 1995. *Encountering Development: The Making and Unmaking of the Third World*. Princeton, NJ: Princeton University Press.

Evans, Peter. 2004. "Development as Institutional Change: The Pitfalls of Monocropping and the Potentials of Deliberation." *Studies in Comparative International Development* 38 (4): 30–52.

Fukuyama, Francis. 2011. *The Origins of Political Order: From Prehuman Times to the French Revolution*. New York: Farrar, Straus and Giroux.

Gauri, Varun. 2009. "How Do Local Level Legal Institutions Promote Development? An Exploratory Essay." Justice and Development Working Paper Series 6/2009, World Bank, Washington, DC.

Gauri, Varun, Michael Woolcock, and Deval Desai. 2011. "Intersubjective Meaning and Collective Action in 'Fragile' Societies: Theory, Evidence and Policy Implications." Policy Research Working Paper 5707, World Bank, Washington, DC.

Glenn, H. Patrick. 2010. *Legal Traditions of the World*. 4th ed. New York: Oxford University Press.

Haggard, Stephan, Andrew MacIntyre, and Lydia Tiede. 2008. "The Rule of Law and Economic Development." *Annual Review of Political Science* 11 (June): 205–34.

Himelein, Kristin, Nicholas Menzies, and Michael Woolcock. 2010. "Surveying Justice: A Practical Guide to Household Surveys." Justice and Development Working Paper 11/2010, World Bank, Washington, DC.

Mattei, Ugo, and Laura Nader. 2008. *Plunder: When the Rule of Law Is Illegal*. New York: Blackwell Publishing.

McGovern, Mike. 2011. "Popular Development Economics: An Anthropologist among the Mandarins." *Perspectives on Politics* 9 (2): 345–55.

Merry, Sally Engle. 1988. "Legal Pluralism." *Law & Society Review* 22 (5): 869–96.

Michaels, Ralf. 2009. "Global Legal Pluralism." *Annual Review of Law and Social Science* 5: 243–62.

North, Douglass C., John Joseph Wallis, and Barry R. Weingast. 2009. *Violence and Social Orders: A Conceptual Framework for Interpreting Recorded Human History*. New York: Cambridge University Press.

Polanyi, Karl. 1944. *The Great Transformation*. Boston, MA: Beacon Press.

Pritchett, Lant, Matt Andrews, and Michael Woolcock. 2010. "Capability Traps? The Mechanisms of Persistent Implementation Failure." Working Paper 234, Center for Global Development, Washington, DC.

Pritchett, Lant, and Michael Woolcock. 2004. "Solutions When *the* Solution Is the Problem: Arraying the Disarray in Development." *World Development* 32 (2): 191–212.

Rao, Vijayendra, and Michael Woolcock. 2007. "The Disciplinary Monopoly in Development Research at the World Bank." *Global Governance* 13 (4): 479–84.

Sage, Caroline, Nicholas Menzies, and Michael Woolcock. 2010. "Taking the Rules of the Game Seriously: Mainstreaming Justice in Development." In *Legal Empowerment: Practitioners' Perspectives*, ed. Stephen Golub, 19–37. Rome: International Development Law Organization.

Sage, Caroline, and Michael Woolcock. 2008. "Breaking Legal Inequality Traps: New Approaches to Local Level Judicial Reform in Low Income Countries." In *Inclusive States: Social Policy and Structural Inequalities*, ed. Anis Dani and Arjan de Han, 369–93. Washington, DC: World Bank.

Scott, James C. 1985. *Weapons of the Weak: Everyday Forms of Peasant Resistance*. New Haven, CT: Yale University Press.
———. 1998. *Seeing Like a State: How Certain Schemes to Improve the Human Condition Have Failed*. New Haven, CT: Yale University Press.
———. 2009. *The Art of Not Being Governed: An Anarchist History of Upland Southeast Asia*. New Haven, CT: Yale University Press.
Sen, Amartya. 2009. *The Idea of Justice*. London: Allen Lane.
Sunstein, Cass, and Edna Ullmann-Margalit. 1999. "Second-Order Decisions." *Ethics* 110 (1): 5–31.
Tamanaha, Brian. 2005. *On the Rule of Law: History, Politics, Theory*. New York: Cambridge University Press.
———. 2008. "Understanding Legal Pluralism: Past to Present, Local to Global." *Sydney Law Review* 30 (3): 375–411.
Toomey, Leigh T. 2010. "A Delicate Balance: Building Complementary Customary and State Legal Systems." *Law and Development Review* 3 (1): article 6.
Trubek, David, and Alvaro Santos, eds. 2006. *The New Law and Economic Development: A Critical Appraisal*. New York: Cambridge University Press.
Woolcock, Michael, Simon Szreter, and Vijayendra Rao. 2011. "How and Why Does History Matter for Development Policy?" *Journal of Development Studies* 47 (1): 70–96.
World Bank. 2011. *World Development Report 2011: Conflict and Security*. Washington, DC: World Bank.

PART I

Origins and Contours

1

Historical Perspectives on Legal Pluralism

Lauren Benton

INTRODUCTION

Historical research represents our richest vein of information about the workings of legal pluralism. Before the long nineteenth century, all legal orders featured jurisdictional tensions without strong claims of legal hegemony by states. In a world in which multicentric legal orders were the norm, jurisdictional complexity created continuities across diverse regions and polities. Merchant diasporas, religious communities, and maritime traders used their knowledge of the workings of plural legal orders to position themselves strategically in new settings. Jurisdictional conflicts shaped the institutional context of expanding long-distance trade, urbanization, and the rise of global capitalism.

What can we learn from the history of legal pluralism in considering its relation to economic development? Legal history provides an analytic guide to grasping the complexities of current legal patterns and behavior, with particularly helpful insights emerging from the study of empires. Empires necessarily involved layered constructions of sovereignty while also producing patterns of legal pluralism that corresponded to – with varying degrees of precision – categories of cultural difference. Imperial officials gave sustained thought to familiar problems, such as the relation of law and governance, the effects of legal pluralism on the production and control of revenue, and the regulation of distant and hidden economic activities (Benton 2002; Burbank and Cooper 2010).

The comparative study of legal pluralism in empires reveals repeating patterns across substantively very different legal orders. One pattern is a tendency for subjects situated everywhere within an empire to adopt both rhetoric and strategies referencing the law of the imperial center. In early modern empires, such behavior often took the form of declarations and legal maneuvering designed to demonstrate subjects' loyalty to sovereigns. Such strategies cut across jurisdictional divides and flourished in situations of supposed marginality. This behavior represents an example of a pervasive practice I refer to as "legal posturing" (Benton 2010a, chap. 1).

A second relevant finding, confirmed by historical studies of plural legal orders in empires, consists of the observation that legal actors – again, at all levels – tended to show a preference over time for adjudication in forums that seemed to provide a greater possibility of enforcement of rulings. In many imperial settings, this preference aided in the integration of conquered populations; the same trend sometimes quickened the pace of the relative decline of the legal practices of cultural minorities. It is important to note that the merging of legal cultures often occurred despite imperial policies intended to preserve subordinate communities' jurisdictions.

By keeping in view the jurisdictional jockeying of imperial legal orders, we gain new perspective on the role of legal pluralism at major turning points in the development of international law. In particular, it becomes possible to understand nineteenth-century prohibition regimes as forming through jurisdictional restructuring within and across global empires – a view that contrasts with traditional narratives of the rise of international law. Similarly, understanding the pervasiveness and persistence of strategies of appealing to imperial legal authority allows us to appreciate the effects on legal behavior of robust claims to the dominance of state law over subordinate jurisdictions in later centuries.

This chapter considers the relevance of all of these findings for an understanding of the relation of legal pluralism and development. I do not evaluate how legal pluralism intersected with economic growth in the past. Instead, I suggest that historical analysis points toward the usefulness of several counterintuitive strategies for promoting judicial reform in plural legal orders. Highlighting the search for predictability of legal outcomes and engagement with jurisdictional politics, historical analysis allows us to understand how legal actors perceive the stakes of institutional change and to examine the ripple effects of policy interventions. Efforts to widen the scope of action, including broadening economic choices, for particular groups requires calibrating the power of legal authority held by a variety of non-state and state actors. The historical study of legal pluralism moves us away from a focus on the architecture of plural legal orders or the normative content of distinctive spheres of law and encourages sustained comparative analysis of shifting jurisdictional boundaries and other contingent legal structures.

JURISDICTIONAL POLITICS

Early modern societies were plural legal societies. Empire-states and smaller polities alike tended to recognize the legal authority of multiple religious and cultural communities.

States and sovereigns often reserved for themselves jurisdiction over crimes defined as challenges to sovereign authority, and they sometimes insisted on review of capital criminal charges or other major cases. But it was possible to live very near the heart of sovereign power without coming into contact with the sovereign's courts, even when commercial disputes, criminal prosecutions, or family matters arose requiring recourse to the law.

Such plural legal orders took a variety of forms. In the Ottoman Empire, non-Muslim religious communities regulated their own affairs, whereas their members in most cases could elect to bring legal actions in qadi courts as well as in their own community forums. In West Africa, polities hosted merchant diaspora communities that maintained separate quarters in towns and were permitted oversight over their own members, except with regard to capital crimes. Atlantic European empires shared a pattern of tensions between secular and canon law that modeled a jurisdictional order in which legal authorities claimed purview over different classes of acts and actors (Benton 2000).

The prominent role of merchant diasporas in long-distance trade in the early modern world depended on the replication of a loose jurisdictional order across substantively different legal systems. Armenians across the Ottoman Empire and Central Asia remained under the authority of Armenian community leaders for the resolution of many kinds of disputes (Curtin 1984). The Portuguese in West Africa inserted themselves as traders in host polities with the understanding that they would take up the status – familiar both to them and to their hosts – of subordinate but semi-independent guest communities. Even captive Africans were able to act on expectations of being part of a plural legal order; in creating communities of runaway slaves, or maroons, in the New World, they negotiated subordinate jurisdictions and agreed to assign major cases to colonial authorities (Benton 2002, chap. 2).

These multijurisdictional orders were never static. Conflicts continually shifted jurisdictional boundaries. And in particular conjunctures, legal actors perceived the stakes of defining those boundaries as very high and imagined them as connected clearly to the protection of group interests. Jurisdictional politics forged odd alliances and produced occasional flash points. In expanding empires, conquered subjects sometimes sought to maintain preexisting legal forums, but, just as often, they maneuvered to be defined as political insiders without a separate legal status. Conquerors disagreed about the degree to which they should recognize the legal equality of subject peoples. European empires grappled with such questions as whether or when to admit the testimony of non-Christians and whether to assert jurisdiction over violent acts committed by non-Europeans against members of their own communities. Jurists explicitly addressed such questions, but they did not do so in a vacuum; subordinate and conquered subjects engaged in jurisdictional jockeying that influenced the actions of imperial officials, whose reports and letters posed the questions taken up by scholars (Benton 2002, 2010a; Ford 2009).

Several phenomena associated with legal politics in early modern multijurisdictional orders are relevant to understanding the relation of development to legal pluralism in later centuries. Two patterns in particular deserve comment. The first is the speed with which various groups adapted to new legal systems and learned to use new law to their advantage. The second is the migration of cases and litigants to particular forums, especially courts perceived to offer reliable enforcement of judgments.

A striking example of rapid adaptation to imposed law is that of American Indians and their response to Spanish rule. Within a generation after the conquest of Tenochtitlan, Spaniards had begun to shape a formally different legal status for Indians in conquered areas. Though considered Spanish subjects, Indians were awarded a status analogous to that of *miserables*, a category of subjects whose actions in Spain fell under the protection of the church and the jurisdiction of ecclesiastic courts (the category included widows, orphans, and the poor). In Spanish America, a new post of *protector de Indios* (protector of the Indians) was created, and special courts were erected for considering Indian litigation. The litigious Spaniards were perhaps less surprised than their historians have been to find that Indians across Spanish America soon became active litigants in the Spanish system. In the sixteenth century, some suits were brought against Spaniards by Indians, but most of the litigation in the Indian General Court in New Spain involved Indian groups suing other Indian groups over access or rights to resources like land and water. Indian forums, which the Spanish had not acted to dismantle, faded in influence and importance, so that a recognizably distinct "Aztec law," for example, soon disappeared, and Indian legal culture emerged as a hybrid of past practices and new strategies crafted in response to Spanish institutions (Kagan 1981; Borah 1983; Cutter 1995; Kellogg 1995; Owensby 2008).

This active participation in the colonial legal order by Indians continued through the colonial period. Historians have traced in some detail the legal engagement of Andes Indians in the late eighteenth century. At a time when Indians in the Andes were engaged in revolts against imperial officials – mainly in response to increasing tax burdens under the Bourbon reforms – we find records of dogged persistence in pursuing legal avenues of redress. Even while promoting violent attacks against local officials, Indian groups sent representatives on long treks to present their cases to *audiencias* (colonial high courts), appealing to imperial authorities directly and emphasizing Indians' status as loyal – and specially protected – imperial subjects. Such strategies showed Indians' sophisticated understandings of jurisdictional tensions and related legal politics (e.g., Serulnikov 2003).

Examples from half a world away confirm the pattern of quick adjustment to new legal conditions. Soon after the British East India Company acquired administrative oversight in three populous regions by assuming the Mughal imperial title of *dewani* in 1765, the company designed a new plural legal order in which the application of English law was restricted to cases involving British subjects and company officials, and Hindu or Muslim law continued to be applied in other cases. Accustomed to sophisticated legal tactics in the plural legal order of the Mughal Empire, Indian litigants did not passively observe these jurisdictional divides but actively exploited them, selectively bringing cases to forums controlled by company officials. Both the fluidity of the plural legal order and the growing volume of litigation in colonial courts remained features of the legal system through the nineteenth century and contributed to the gradual Anglicization of Indian law (Galanter 1989; Benton 2002; Travers 2007). We observe a similar pattern among some Jewish communities under Ottoman rule. Courts presided over by Jewish community leaders did not disappear and continued to be officially tolerated (and sometimes cultivated), but Jews routinely brought particular kinds of disputes, especially those over property, to Ottoman courts (Cohen 1984; Inalcik 1989; Barkey 2010).

In short, we find a broad pattern of rapid adjustment to, and pervasive participation in, newly constructed legal systems. Within a very short period in environments of rapid legal change, it is no longer possible to speak of cultural clashes in the law. Precisely because they already operated in multicentric jurisdictional orders, both colonizers and colonized peoples understood that the new plural legal orders represented flexible frameworks and that those structures were shaped by legal strategies such as forum shopping, appeals, and defensive litigation. Further, even as they adopted sophisticated tactics to take advantage of jurisdictional complexity, legal actors sought access to those legal forums they thought could provide the greatest chance of enforcement for legal rulings. They often began and pursued legal actions in local or alternative forums, but they also raced to the top, that is, to forums under the close control of imperial officials. Indians appeared routinely in Spanish courts; Jews pursued commercial disputes in Ottoman courts; Hindus brought cases directly to the Supreme Court in India; and French West African subjects, often seeking to define themselves as French imperial citizens, bypassed local forums in favor of appeals to officials in France.

I return later to a discussion of the relevance of such patterns to an understanding of legal pluralism and development in the twenty-first century. I first want to examine one other striking aspect of legal behavior in the early modern world. As hallmarks of the age, the expansion of long-distance trade and the creation of global empires generated an unusual array of opportunities for legal improvisation.

LEGAL POSTURING

The records compiled in early modern empires are filled with accounts of subjects very far from home performing ad hoc legal rituals. They often did so while making only vague references to legal sources, precedents, or instructions. Only a minority possessed formal legal training; most agents relied instead on understandings of the law assembled from memories of encounters with the law at home or from law stories recounted by others. This deference to imagined legal procedures was consistent with an insistent referencing of law in the construction of colonial political communities and in new developments in commerce and production.

Again, we can find examples from early and late centuries and from distant parts of the world. European agents operating on behalf of a wide variety of sovereign sponsors made ad hoc arrangements to stake claims to imperial territories, referencing Roman law doctrines in flexible and vague ways (Benton and Straumann 2010). In the late eighteenth century and into the first decades of the nineteenth century, British colonial governors and garrison commanders in disparate parts of the empire declared martial law in moments defined imprecisely as emergencies, then devised ad hoc procedures and represented them as conforming to an amorphous body of military law (Hussain 2003; Kostal 2008; Benton 2010a, chap. 4). A great deal of writing from and about empires, including many chronicles we have labeled travel literature, represented forms of legal writing: briefs prepared in relation to ongoing cases, salvos to deflect litigation or prosecution, and documents intended to provide legal support for imperial claims or bids for patronage (Benton 2010a, chap. 1).

Significantly, sojourners and settlers rarely positioned themselves outside the imperial legal order. Although their actions sometimes shaped new jurisdictions or challenged existing jurisdictional claims, even self-proclaimed rogues and rebels tended consistently to reference, usually in vague ways, known or imagined doctrines, procedures, and precedents. Perhaps the most striking example of such legal posturing is found in the strategies of pirates. Only a tiny percentage of pirates flew the black flag or considered themselves as operating permanently outside the law. Many more of them constructed careful legal stories and amassed paper trails to protect themselves from prosecution. Even in the midst of open raiding, pirates carried multiple flags and passes in order to be able to represent themselves as connected to one or another legitimate sponsor, depending on the circumstance and the nature of legal jeopardy they encountered. Other people called these mariners pirates or smugglers; they defined themselves as privateers and traders (Benton 2006; Karras 2009).

Though sometimes prompted or encouraged by the weakness of imperial oversight, this type of legal posturing contributed to forces of institutional consolidation. Legal posturing focused attention on the ties between subjects and sovereigns. It also pointed to questions we might think of as constitutional, that is, focused on issues pertaining to the proper relation of delegated legal authorities – expedition commanders, ship captains, garrison commanders, colonial governors, and others – to imperial legal authority. The most important "rules" invoked in these processes were "rules about rule," or changing propositions about how to compose and fix the relation of multiple authorities within a plural legal order.

PLURALISM AND GLOBAL ORDER

States' claims to legal hegemony developed in an ad hoc and incomplete way, gathering force particularly over the long nineteenth century. This global historical trend altered the configuration of legal pluralism even as state-centered legal orders remained jurisdictionally complex. In some cases, including many colonial settings, the result was paradoxically to reanimate projects of recognizing the legal authority of "traditional" communities. For example, Britain championed the legitimacy of alternative dispute resolution in African colonies, an approach that carried little of the tension associated with African-led legal forums in earlier periods precisely because it represented "traditional" forums as explicitly subordinate to, and ultimately subject to intervention by, the courts of the colonial state (Chanock 1985; Mamdani 1996; Roberts 2005).

The right of intervention was a power that British colonial officials in particular spilled a great deal of ink attempting to define. In India, colonial officials sought to enumerate precisely the conditions under which Britain's recognition of local jurisdiction might be set aside. In the second half of the nineteenth century, particular attention was focused on the Indian princely states, which formally retained legal authority within their borders while existing clearly within a field of power that British officials interpreted as including the right to suspend the normal operation of the law. Some officials articulated this prerogative as the power to decide when law stopped and politics began. Others looked to the law for a rationale for intervention, arguing, for example – much like imperial sovereigns of centuries before – that because the ties between sovereigns and subjects transcended jurisdictional boundaries, the sovereign could reach anywhere to punish transgressions against the imperial power. This arrangement constituted a kind of legal pluralism, but one in which imperial authority hovered as a more immediate, and potentially menacing, presence (Benton 2008).

The shift contributed to and was informed by another salient trend: the rise to prominence of a distinction between civilized states as parts of the international legal order and uncivilized states as polities queuing for entrance into that order (Gong 1984). The history of this doctrine has been clearly documented by historians of international law, but its relevance for understanding legal pluralism has not been much appreciated. The emerging doctrine of civilization encouraged observers to begin to associate legal pluralism with earlier states of economic and social development. If we define legal pluralism as jurisdictional complexity and combine this perspective with an understanding of the active creation of new subordinate jurisdictions within colonial societies of the long nineteenth century, then this distinction is exposed as a myth. But the view carried forward powerfully as attached to a new vision of territorial sovereignty as the defining characteristic of nation-states, and of nation-states (rather than empires) as the constitutive polities of positive international law. In this regard, legal pluralism took on associations it did not have in the early modern world: it came to signify the incomplete political, territorial, and legal control of colonies and of new states formed from the dissolution of empires (Anghie 2007; Benton 2010a).

Much like plural legal orders within polities, the international system is a plural legal order composed of unequally powerful polities. In the long nineteenth century, the project of identifying international norms was spearheaded by Britain, which acted – to the extent that it was able – as an enforcer of practices it favored, in particular seeking to prohibit certain practices globally, such as slave trading, piracy, and other forms of non-state violence (Thomson 1994). But constructing a prohibition regime was not the same as simply exercising hegemony. As with continuities across regions and polities of the early modern world, it required the replication of similar jurisdictional configurations across the global order.

The example of the prohibition regime of the abolition of the slave trade is especially illuminating in this regard. Britain banned the trade in 1807, and a period of attempting to control the trade through unilateral action was followed in 1815 by a shift to a strategy of forming bilateral treaties to draw other states into the prohibition regime. Although some historians have described this shift as one involving the birth of positivist international law, a closer examination of abolition debates and legal cases involving the interception of slave ships reveals a more complex story. In addition to promoting treaties to control the trade, abolitionists understood that effective implementation would be impossible without a tightening of imperial criminal jurisdiction so that traders faced not just the threat of commercial penalties by British-led "international" courts, but also the danger of criminal penalties imposed under the laws of various jurisdictions within British and other imperial polities. Reproducing the claim of an expansive imperial criminal jurisdiction became central to abolition in law (Benton 2010b).

The example could be expanded to include other global prohibition regimes to show that shifts in the international legal regime depended as much on the replication of similar structures in polities' legal orders as on the substance of interstate agreements. Like the historical studies of law in empires, this history instructs us, in assessing the legal environment for economic development, to look for moments of synchronic movement in legal structures across separate polities. Promoting new international norms in part depends on incremental changes within formally disconnected but similarly structured plural legal orders.

DEVELOPMENT AND LEGAL PLURALISM

As robust models of state sovereignty entered political and legal discourse, legal pluralism was reimagined as the outcome of processes generating new spheres of unregulated labor and commerce in the heart of advanced industrial economies. Much of the literature on the informal economy has focused on its costs and benefits and on the implications for growth. Analyses of unregulated spheres of economic activity as elements of plural legal orders have tended to preserve a distinction between advanced and developing countries by advocating the acceleration of a progressive process, presumed to be stronger in advanced countries, of bringing informal economic activities into the realm of state regulation. This objective can supposedly be achieved, as de Soto and others have argued, by lowering the barriers to participation in state legal practices and institutions (De Soto 2002, 2003; cf. Portes, Castells, and Benton 1989). This approach represents one example of the treatment of legal pluralism as a special "problem" for, and obstacle to, development (Tamanaha, Woodman, this volume).

We would again do well to draw from historical studies of legal pluralism of empires in evaluating this perspective. As we have seen, even in places with little legal infrastructure far from centers of power, imperial agents played up their connections to distant sovereigns and enacted legal procedures as they remembered them. It would be at odds with this history to expect that social actors in settings where the state clearly claims legal hegemony would not actively reference state law, however inaccurately or opportunistically. Further, and by analogy, we would expect to find contemporary legal actors making such references to state law both explicitly and implicitly. Even if they express preferences for non-state legal forums and processes, legal actors continue to depend in various ways on their knowledge, however imperfect, of the legal procedures, penalties, and principles operating in state legal forums.

Patterns of participation in unregulated activities by employers and workers do, in fact, suggest that their actions reflect understandings of state law and not a straightforward preference for alternative law or lawlessness. We know, for example, that in unregulated piecework or sweatshop labor, both employers and workers show acute awareness of the terms and conditions of employment in the state-regulated sector. Paradoxically, it appears that the assumption of the centrality of state authority can even make off-the-books labor more appealing (Benton 1994). Participants do not give up their recourse to state law, in other words; they suspend that recourse under certain conditions, sometimes by choice but often through necessity or coercion. Their relation to state law is altered, not absent.

This point brings us to the broader question of how legal pluralism relates to the project of promoting the rule of law as a framework for development. In his classic analysis of the construction of the rule of law in late eighteenth-century England, E. P. Thompson sought to move away from a view of law as a tool wielded by elites to narrowly support their power and interests (Thompson 1975). He argued that the legitimacy of the rule of law in England derived from the strategic perception of the plebeian class that the law could occasionally produce just outcomes. This mere possibility of justice pervaded commoners' legal strategies and prevented them from rejecting state law, even as they struggled to preserve alternative, communal social practices.

The limitations of Thompson's approach stemmed not from his affirmation of the rule of law as a "universal good" despite its reinforcement of inequalities. The analysis suffered instead from a failure to push far enough the notion that people engaged the law strategically, drawing on shared fragments of understanding about legal processes and principles. Subsequent studies have reminded us that rule of law is produced through the politics of legal pluralism, rather than the other way around (for example, Burbank [2004] on Russian peasants at court). A productive approach to legal pluralism and development might ask under what conditions the mere possibility of just outcomes in state law translates into pervasive recognition of the legitimacy of legal institutions. It also would begin with an investigation of legal strategies and the circulation of knowledge about the law rather than with attempts to characterize the contents and constraints of normative orders. Thompson's plebeians, after all, did not recognize the rule of law because it fit within a particular normative order, nor did they imagine themselves as occupying a fully separate normative order that was oppositional to state law. Even in defying the law, they acted in ways that supported its legitimacy without intending to do so. In the process, they constructed new associations with law and arrived at new interpretations of norms.

This critique brings us to the view that because jurisdictions may share some normative content and rules, and because legal authorities recognize porous borders between jurisdictions, it makes sense to understand legal pluralism as a multijurisdictional field rather than as a structure comprising multiple entities such as normative orders (Woodman, this volume), systems of rules (Tamanaha, this volume), or spheres of law (Merry, this volume). An emphasis on jurisdictional politics leads us to privilege analysis of patterned conflicts as objects of study rather than seek to render the architecture or characterize the content of realms within a plural legal order. It is this perspective that allows us to see that reforms designed to lift the underground economy into the regulated sector as a legally focused development policy might, like integrationist imperial policies, have the unintended consequence of producing greater jurisdictional complexity. The barriers between non-state and state legal processes do not submit to easy surgery partly because the barriers are illusory – that is, state law is always present – and partly because new forms of unregulated activity emerge in response to institutional change.

CONCLUSION

Is there any way, given the fluidity of legal politics, to draw lessons from the historical study of legal pluralism in crafting interventions designed to promote development? A brief disclaimer must be offered first. Some political scientists promise to draw from the analysis of past and present predictions for the future. Few historians would make the same claim. Some historical patterns repeat themselves, but the smallest changes in context can create enormous differences in outcome. And whereas contemporary polities have characteristics in common with the multilayered, fluid jurisdictional orders of polities in the past, they exist in a world in which territorial sovereignty, national economic policy, and (sometimes) democratic institutions are claimed by nation-states within the context of an interstate legal regime.

Still, some possible lessons have emerged. First, we note that even when recourse to particular forums undermines social cohesion and cultural continuity, legal actors tend to seek out, over the long term, legal authorities that they perceive offer the best chance at enforcing judgments. A clustering of cases in colonial state courts for this reason was responsible for strengthening central and secular jurisdiction in relation to local or religious forums in many historical settings. We might conclude from this finding that the attraction of predictability of enforcement would produce only a preference for "high" state law. But it would be just as reasonable to imagine that improving the consistency of legal outcomes *anywhere* within the legal order might affect practices across many jurisdictions. That is, there is nothing intrinsically preferable to litigants about state forums; their preference is for reliability of outcomes and enforcement. In seeking ways to make justice more widely available, we might adopt interventions that are merely possible over reforms that are institutionally ambitious but also more elusive. Conversely, we might unapologetically identify especially active litigation forums as places where small reforms can reach large audiences.

A second tentative conclusion derives from the finding that state law casts a shadow over what appear to be "non-state" legal processes. Even before the emergence of strong claims to state legal hegemony, legal actors cultivated flexible strategies that allowed them to assert independence while also posturing in ways that reaffirmed their ties to sovereign authority. Historical studies show us that people act on the basis of stories they have heard or experiences they have had with law, and they do so even in situations or places of seeming lawlessness. Taken together, these findings point toward the importance of the circulation of information about law, especially state law, and they caution us against accepting characterizations of behavior as lawless or distant from state controls. The policy implications of such conclusions may be varied, but one possible conclusion is the value of efforts to enhance the quality and reach of information about selected state legal processes. Groups regarded as legally marginal might benefit from referencing state law, even if they do so in non-state forums.

A third, intriguing historical finding is that in global reform movements, assistance to people in positions of social weakness has been advanced effectively through reforms designed to scale back the legal prerogatives attached to some jurisdictions. This pattern is true even with regard to programs of global change associated with the promotion of universal principles, such as the abolition of the slave trade. This finding may translate into a recommendation for less emphasis on championing the legal rights of the poor and more on regulating the prerogatives of people and institutions with authority over them. Efforts to eradicate child labor, for example, may depend as much or more on restricting the legal authority of heads of households as on promoting the rights of child laborers. In general, if history guides us at all, progressive institutional change may be thought of as requiring some consolidation of political and legal authority in ways that reorder existing semiautonomous jurisdictions, even while generating new jurisdictional tensions. Historical studies of global institutional change also suggest that such change depends on synchronous, widely repeated shifts in structures of legal pluralism. Reforms replicated across numerous, distant local settings might prove as influential as attempts to shift international opinion with regard to particular reform measures.

To some degree, to be sure, a deep historical analysis introduces an element of skepticism about public or cross-national policies designed to alter institutional contexts. At the margins, we see room for supposing that interventions designed specifically to enhance the incentives for deference to some forums over others, to circulate information about some practices of state law, to contain the scope of particular jurisdictions, and to replicate institutional innovations can help to create conditions conducive to justice and economic development. Legal politics will always drive the outcomes of such reforms as conflicts continue to shape new jurisdictional tensions.

REFERENCES

Anghie, Antony. 2007. *Imperialism, Sovereignty, and the Making of International Law.* Cambridge: Cambridge University Press.
Barkey, Karen. 2010. "Ottoman Imperial Management of Diversity: The Costs and Benefits of Legal Pluralism." Paper presented at the symposium "New Perspectives on Legal Pluralism," Newberry Library, Chicago, April 23.
Benton, Lauren. 1994. "Beyond Legal Pluralism: Towards a New Approach to Law in the Informal Sector." *Social and Legal Studies* 3 (2): 223–42.
———. 2000. "The Legal Regime of the South Atlantic World: Jurisdictional Complexity as Institutional Order." *Journal of World History* 11 (1): 27–56.
———. 2002. *Law and Colonial Cultures: Legal Regimes in World History, 1400–1900.* Cambridge: Cambridge University Press.
———. 2006. "Constitutions and Empires." *Law & Social Inquiry* 31 (1): 177–98.
———. 2008. "From International Law to Imperial Constitutions: The Problem of Quasi-Sovereignty, 1870–1900." *Law and History Review* 26: 595–620.
———. 2010a. *A Search for Sovereignty: Law and Geography in European Empires, 1400–1900.* New York: Cambridge University Press.
———. 2010b. "Slave Trading Is Not a Piratical Offense: Abolition and Legal Pluralism in the British Empire." Paper presented at the symposium "New Perspectives in Legal Pluralism," Newberry Library, Chicago, April 16.
Benton, Lauren, and Benjamin Straumann. 2010. "Acquiring Empire by Law: From Roman Doctrine to Early Modern European Practice." *Law and History Review* 28 (1): 1–38.
Borah, Woodrow. 1983. *Justice by Insurance: The General Indian Court of Colonial Mexico and the Legal Aides of the Half-Real.* Berkeley: University of California Press.
Burbank, Jane. 2004. *Russian Peasants Go to Court: Legal Culture in the Countryside, 1905–1917.* Bloomington: Indiana University Press.
Burbank, Jane, and Fred Cooper. 2010. *Empires in World History.* Princeton, NJ: Princeton University Press.
Chanock, Martin. 1985. *Law, Custom, and Social Order: The Colonial Experience in Malawi and Zambia.* Cambridge: Cambridge University Press.
Cohen, Ammon. 1984. *Jewish Life under Islam: Jerusalem in the Sixteenth Century.* Cambridge, MA: Harvard University Press.
Curtin, Philip. 1984. *Cross-Cultural Trade in World History.* Cambridge: Cambridge University Press.
Cutter, Charles. 1995. *The Legal Culture of Northern New Spain, 1700–1810.* Albuquerque: University of New Mexico Press.

De Soto, Hernando. 2002. *The Other Path: The Economic Answer to Terrorism*. New York: Basic Books.
———. 2003. *The Mystery of Capital*. New York: Basic Books.
Ford, Lisa. 2009. *Settler Sovereignty: Jurisdiction and Indigenous People in America and Australia, 1788–1836*. Cambridge, MA: Harvard University Press.
Galanter, Marc. 1989. *Law and Society in Modern India*. Delhi: Oxford University Press.
Gong, Gerrit. 1984. *The Standard of "Civilization" in International Society*. New York: Oxford University Press.
Hussain, Nasser. 2003. *The Jurisprudence of Emergency: Colonialism and the Rule of Law*. Ann Arbor: University of Michigan Press.
Inalcik, Halil. 1989. *The Ottoman Empire: The Classical Age 1300–1600*. New Rochelle, NY: Orpheus Publishing. First published 1973 by Weidenfeld & Nicolson.
Kagan, Richard. 1981. *Lawsuits and Litigants in Castile, 1500–1700*. Chapel Hill: University of North Carolina Press.
Karras, Alan. 2009. *Smuggling: Contraband and Corruption in World History*. Lanham, MD: Rowman & Littlefield.
Kellogg, Susan. 1995. *Law and the Transformation of Aztec Culture, 1500–1700*. Norman: University of Oklahoma Press.
Kostal, Rande W. 2008. *A Jurisprudence of Power: Victorian Empire and the Rule of Law*. Oxford: Oxford University Press.
Mamdani, Mahmoud. 1996. *Citizen and Subject*. Princeton, NJ: Princeton University Press.
Owensby, Brian. 2008. *Empire's Law and Indian Justice in Colonial Mexico*. Stanford, CA: Stanford University Press.
Portes, Alejandro, Manuel Castells, and Lauren Benton, eds. 1989. *The Informal Economy: Studies in Advanced and Less Developed Countries*. Baltimore: Johns Hopkins University Press.
Roberts, Richard. 2005. *Litigants and Households: African Disputes and Colonial Courts in the French Soudan, 1895–1912*. Portsmouth, NH: Heinemann.
Serulnikov, Sergio. 2003. *Subverting Colonial Authority: Challenges to Spanish Rule in Eighteenth-Century Southern Andes*. Durham, NC: Duke University Press.
Thompson, Edward P. 1975. *Whigs and Hunters: The Origin of the Black Act*. New York: Pantheon Books.
Thomson, Janice E. 1994. *Mercenaries, Pirates, and Sovereigns: State-Building and Extraterritorial Violence in Early Modern Europe*. Princeton, NJ: Princeton University Press.
Travers, Robert. 2007. *Ideology and Empire in Eighteenth-Century India: The British in Bengal*. New York: Cambridge University Press.

2

The Rule of Law and Legal Pluralism in Development

Brian Z. Tamanaha

After decades of disappointing progress in building the rule of law in societies that suffer from poorly functioning legal systems, the development community has turned its attention to legal pluralism. Legal pluralism is a prominent feature in many development contexts, with both negative and positive implications for the rule of law. The negative questions revolve around whether or to what extent the presence of multiple coexisting legal forms hampers or detracts from efforts to build the rule of law. The positive questions revolve around whether alternative legal forms in situations of legal pluralism might satisfy rule of law functions that failing state legal systems are unable to provide. This chapter explores these questions.

Two limitations of this exploration – the first involving application and the second involving theory – must be acknowledged at the outset. Rule of law development projects take place around the world in extraordinarily varied situations, each of which is unique. Observations about the interaction between the rule of law and legal pluralism, therefore, can be offered only as broad generalizations. Whether these generalizations apply – and what their concrete implications are – depends on the circumstances at hand. What is relevant to isolated islands in the Pacific, for example, may have no application to rural areas in Africa or to jungles or favelas in Latin America. Nothing in this essay applies everywhere, and for some contexts the themes taken up here will have little bearing. This chapter sets out a framework for thinking about matters, not a formula with concrete application.

A theoretical limitation arises because theorists sharply disagree about the meaning and implications of the rule of law *as well as* about the meaning and implications of legal pluralism (Tamanaha 2004, 2008). One highly contested notion is hard enough to manage, but working with two such notions in tandem threatens to defeat the exploration before it begins. To avoid getting bogged down in irresolvable theoretical disputes, I posit a basic working formulation of each. The *rule of law* means that government officials and citizens are bound by and generally abide by the law. *Legal pluralism* refers to a context in which multiple legal forms coexist. These are minimalist formulations of vastly complicated ideas. Although legitimate objections can be raised against each, and other formulations could have been offered in their place, they represent sound understandings of these notions, and their pared-to-the-bone quality makes it possible to examine the interaction between them.

STATE LEGAL SYSTEMS IN DEVELOPMENT

To begin, a set of broad generalizations will be offered about the relative power and functional capacity of state legal systems in development contexts. In societies with well-established legal systems, the state legal system is highly differentiated (legislatures, police, prosecutors, judges), with amply funded and solidified legal institutions, well-trained and disciplined legal officials, a well-educated legal profession, and a substantial body of legal knowledge that developed gradually over time in connection with internal social-political-economic dynamics. Government officials and the public identify with and feel some obligation to abide by the state legal system. Failures in the legal system and lawbreaking among officials and citizenry are normal conditions at the margins, but by and large the system operates effectively because of the combination of broad voluntary compliance backed up by the threat of coercive sanctions imposed on violators.

Rule of law development projects are undertaken in societies that lack these basic characteristics (Tamanaha 2011). They have fewer differentiated and entrenched state legal institutions; fewer financial, material, and human resources; defectively trained and disciplined legal officials; a poorly established legal profession; and an inadequately developed body of legal knowledge (with a greater proportion of transplanted legal norms derived from external sources). The presence and power of the state legal system may be weak or may have a limited reach (e.g., hardly any presence in distant or inaccessible rural areas, ineffective in the slums of megacities). The populace may be wary of the state legal system. Law may be perceived as alien or inscrutable; it is sometimes written in a language different from the vernacular of groups within society. Or it may be seen as corrupt or incompetent or inefficient or prohibitively expensive. Or it may be seen as a tool of the elite. Or it may be dominated by a particular ethnic or religious subgroup in society. Or it may be stained by a history of oppressive authoritarian rule or by the use of the law by political or economic elites as a means of economic predation. When a combination of these conditions holds, a substantial proportion of the populace will not identify with state law – they will not see it as *their* law, serving *their* needs.

What makes rule of law development so difficult is that a failing state legal system cannot be fixed by focusing on legal institutions in isolation. Take judicial reform – a favorite of law and development projects. Training judges accomplishes little by itself. A sizable group of trained legal practitioners is needed to handle cases and to help develop legal practices and shared legal knowledge. Competent clerks and transcribers with adequate office space and equipment are necessary to process cases and record proceedings. Judicial compensation must be set at a level sufficient to attract qualified individuals and to lessen the temptation to corruption. Judges must resist the influence of prejudices, class or group loyalties, the calls of friendship or extended networks of relations, or other inappropriate factors. Judges must not be subject to intimidation from warlords, drug lords, organized crime, terrorists, or other dangerous elements, including other government officials. The public generally must comply with judicial rulings, and judicial orders must be backed by effective sanctions when voluntary compliance is not forthcoming. Political leaders, military leaders, the economic elite, the police, and government officials must abide by judicial rulings, including rulings that go against their interests or frustrate their desires. As this list illustrates, functioning legal systems require a host of secondary supportive conditions, involving a confluence of social, economic, cultural, and political factors.

When the background conditions that support legal systems are woefully inadequate, as is the case in many development contexts, the legal system will be dysfunctional, reform efforts will be stymied, and the populace will avoid or despise the legal system. As one development practitioner in Africa noted, more "than 80 to 90 percent of day-to-day disputes in Africa are said to be resolved through nonstate systems such as traditional authorities" (Piron 2006, 291). The UK Department for International Development estimates that "in many developing countries traditional or customary legal systems account for 80% of total cases" (Golub 2006, 118). This might well be an understatement.

If a state legal system is stuck in a dysfunctional state, viewed negatively by the populace, with reform efforts persistently failing, it is sensible to explore alternatives that might satisfy legal functions. But the development community has been slow in coming to this realization. Two recent reports of the United Nations secretary-general emphasizing the importance of "United Nations support for the rule of law" focus almost exclusively on efforts to build state legal institutions, listing "court administration, legal drafting, judicial accountability, . . . prison management, reparations, prosecutions, international and mixed tribunals, legal training, land and property rights, international humanitarian, human rights and refugee law, constitutional law, institution-building, public administration reform and so on" (United Nations 2006, 7). Only passing mention was given to "the presence of traditional and customary systems" (United Nations 2004, 12).

THE RULE OF LAW BRIEFLY

Before turning to legal pluralism, several implications of the stipulated definition of the rule of law – government officials and citizens are bound by and abide by the law – must be drawn out. At a minimum, it assumes that legal rules exist and that government officials and citizens know what the rules require in connection with their actions (the rules must be declared in advance and made public). Otherwise, it is impossible to be bound by and abide by the law. The rule of law operates at two levels: it imposes legal limitations on and coordinates the behavior of government officials, and it imposes legal limitations on and coordinates the behavior of citizens (Tamanaha 2009).

Government officials are subject to two distinct types of legal limitations. The first limitation is that government officials *must abide by valid laws in force* at the time of any given governmental action. Officials must remain within established legal bounds when exercising the power attached to their public positions. If they wish to do something that is legally prohibited or not authorized by current law, the law must be changed to remove the prohibition or grant the authorization before the actions can be taken. Citizens benefit because they are apprised in advance – by consulting the relevant legal rules – of the range of actions they can engage in without fear of government interference or reprisal. (For convenience, I label limits on officials the "vertical" effect because it relates to the relationship between government and citizens.) The second limitation *imposes restrictions on the law itself*, controlling the lawmaking power of state officials. This limitation sets a higher hurdle than the first because it imposes legal restrictions that cannot be altered through ordinary legal processes. Versions of such limits include the constitution of a given country, binding international law, human rights provisions, and religious or natural law proscriptions. State lawmakers are prohibited (at least in theory) from enacting laws that contravene these legal constraints.

Legal limitations on citizens (including corporations) establish rules that govern social intercourse. (I label this the "horizontal" effect because it relates to the relationship between citizens.) This includes property rights, contracts, injuries or harms inflicted on one another (tort law), familial obligations, and crimes against persons or property. Legal rules help to coordinate social behavior and maintain social order. These rules secure the person and property of citizens from interference by others and facilitate and effectuate transactions. Disputes that arise between citizens are resolved in accordance with these rules.

A frequent misunderstanding must be preempted here. To say that state law helps to establish rules for social intercourse and maintain social order emphatically does not mean that it is the main source of social order or that the entire realm of social behavior is or should be governed by state law. That is neither possible nor desirable. Multiple normative orders exist within every society, including customs, morality, religious norms, social etiquette, workplace norms, business norms, and more. The presence, scope, and penetration of state law vary by subject matter and location. Certain matters, like banking or corporate law, are thickly governed by state law. Certain societies are more permeated by state legal regulations than others. But state law can be marginal or even nonexistent in many social arenas. To conform to the rule of law requires that whatever state law addresses should be generally adhered to, but it does not entail that law covers everything. The scope of coverage of state law varies widely among societies, and nothing in the rule of law necessitates that state law covers the same things everywhere.

It must also be kept in mind that nothing in the rule of law itself – at least not in the bare terms set out here, known in legal theory as the "thin" or "formal" version of the rule of law (Tamanaha 2004) – entails that the legal rules must be good or just in content or application. The law can be bad, unfair, or harsh yet still be consistent with the rule of law (think of former racial segregation laws in the United States). An oppressive legal order can satisfy the rule of law as long as the rules exist in advance and government officials and citizens abide by the rules.

A final clarification relates specifically to legal pluralism. The notion of the rule of law is typically applied to state law, and sometimes to international law. The standard analysis reflects this state law thrust. However, the pared-down definition I adopt in this essay – government officials and citizens are bound by and abide by the law – does not specify any particular type of "law." This generic quality allows it to be applied more broadly to other forms of law, as I demonstrate in the course of this chapter.

LEGAL PLURALISM INVOLVING CUSTOM, TRADITION, AND RELIGION

A common form of legal pluralism involves the presence of norms and institutions identified with custom, tradition, or religion, or with informal or village tribunals, operating alongside state legal institutions. Colonization in the eighteenth and nineteenth centuries was a major source of these types of legal pluralism (Benton 2001). Transplanted legal regimes imposed by colonizers on subject lands mainly addressed the affairs of colonial government (taxes, maintaining colonial rule), economic matters (protecting commercial interests), and relations among expatriate settlers or mixed cases between settlers and indigenous people (Mommsen and de Moor 1992). Initially, colonizing powers often used indigenous leaders and institutions for indirect rule and otherwise largely left them alone. Over time, as colonial rule was extended, state legal systems selectively incorporated customary or religious laws (subject to repugnancy clauses) and recognized or created customary or village tribunals to handle local matters (family law, customary and religious norms, minor disputes). Colonization thus produced legal pluralism, grafting or erecting a variegated mix of legal systems: transplanted state legal systems focused on matters of government and commerce alongside modified indigenous laws and institutions, with mutual interpenetration and hybrid combinations of both (Tamanaha 2008). The legacy of these historical arrangements continues today, decades after the end of colonization. Legal arrangements like this also exist in places where colonization was not a factor, when indigenous rulers developed state legal institutions but did not (could not or saw no need to) extend the reach of state power into the hinterlands or over distinct ethnic or religious groups within the territory that maintained a degree of autonomy from central government.

A multitude of such arrangements exist, no two exactly alike. Customary, village, traditional, religious, or informal courts or councils, or leaders or elders, handle social disputes and other problems, applying their own norms in their own ways. Some are officially recognized by and incorporated within the state legal system, enjoying symbolic and financial support from the state, whereas others operate independently of the state. Some are decades-old standing institutions that take on the trappings of state courts, whereas others are occasional informal bodies that meet only when the need arises. Some make decisions oriented toward the application of rules, whereas others strive to reach a consensual resolution that satisfies all of the parties involved and repairs the breach in the community. Although they frequently are called "customary," "traditional," or "religious" courts or tribunals, these are contemporary institutions that deal with everyday problems.

A few preliminary propositions are offered about these tribunals with the caveat that what is stated may not hold in a given context. In contrast to most state legal institutions in development contexts, these institutions are *of* the community, closer in derivation and proximity, and hence more accessible to members of the community. Its norms and processes, its modes of decision making, are understood by members of the community. The proceedings are less costly, more timely, and often do not require the intermediation of legal professionals. The decision makers are known to or recognized by the community. Remedies or sanctions issued by decision makers rely on the acquiescence of the parties and on community support, which usually necessitates that the result be perceived by the community as acceptable (either owning to the appropriateness of the outcome, belief in fairness of the proceedings, or deference to the status of the decision makers).

These local tribunals must not be overly idealized. The norms they enforce may be objectionable, their processes may be skewed, and decision makers may have warped motivations or be self-interested or corrupt. They may fail to meet due process standards like neutrality, opportunity to be heard, and equal application of the rules without regard to the identity or status of the parties. The fact that they are *of* the community does not necessarily mean they are *for* the entire community, nor is it always the case that everyone in the community respects them. Furthermore, certain customary or religious norms, especially those imposing harsh punishments or unequal treatment of women or enforcing caste systems, may chafe against human rights and women's rights. But they usually enjoy at least one major advantage over state legal systems: they work in ways that people understand and can generally anticipate. This awareness provides the participants with a greater sense of control over their fate, and it makes the decision makers more accountable because what they are doing can be evaluated against shared community standards and expectations.

Now let us apply the definition of the rule of law to these legal forms.

When members of the community understand and identify with these local tribunals, when they are more accessible, when the orientations and norms of the decision makers are familiar, it is more likely that people in the community will feel an allegiance to them. When this holds, basic rule of law functions can be filled by these legal forms irrespective of whether they are officially recognized as part of the state legal system. The core "horizontal" (person-to-person) functions of the rule of law – to help coordinate behavior and resolve disputes between members of a community – are achieved by these local norms and institutions. The high percentage of people in development contexts who currently take their disputes to non-state legal institutions for resolution is evidence of their usefulness.

These institutions, however, might not be adequate substitutes for state law on all horizontal matters. Crossover situations – when a dispute involves members of different communities or religious groups, or between a person attached to traditional ways and a person who rejects those ways – are problematic. For example, when a dispute arises between a commercial enterprise and a local merchant or member of the community, the commercial enterprise may have structured the transaction relying on state legal norms that are incompatible with customary or religious norms. To have a traditional or informal tribunal resolve these types of disputes may be contrary to the prior expectations of at least one of the parties, making it difficult to produce a consensus decision and perhaps generating uncertainty for future transactions.

With respect to vertical (government-to-person) functions, these institutions cannot replace an essential benefit provided by the rule of law: erecting legal restraints on government officials (which also is poorly achieved by state legal systems in many development contexts). Customary and religious legal institutions cannot do this because usually they do not address or enforce state legal norms, and their coercive power is limited. Notwithstanding this crucial incapacity, non-state legal norms and institutions can sometimes erect vertical legal constraints on government officials in other ways. A few postcolonial legal regimes accord superior status to customary law in a way that trumps state legal provisions, or they reserve for traditional or religious authorities certain geographical regions or subject matters beyond the reach of government officials. Religious and traditional authorities, in turn, are themselves subject to religious and customary legal restrictions, which is a type of vertical restraint.

Although the foregoing discussion focuses on the contrast between state law and customary or informal or religious norms and institutions, pluralistic situations manifest all sorts of interaction. Customary institutions and religious institutions may be in conflict with one another. This occurs in Afghanistan, where battles wage between tribal elders in the name of traditional institutions against the Taliban bringing strict Islamic norms. When different groups live side by side in tension, the contest can be between two customary systems or two religious systems, over which norms and institutions will prevail within the community or over mixed interaction between members of different communities. Another variation can be found in urban favelas or slums, where unofficial norms established and enforced by the community, or by criminal gangs, de facto govern property transactions and maintain social order more effectively than the state legal system (Santos 1977). The potential combinations that can arise in legal pluralism are limitless.

It also must be emphasized that, although the analysis thus far highlights clashes between coexisting legal systems, the relationship between coexisting systems can be complementary and mutually reinforcing. State legal systems that incorporate or recognize customary or religious regimes benefit by providing locals with a forum that serves their needs, whereas the state maintains some control by setting the terms of incorporation and (sometimes) by paying local authorities; customary or religious tribunals and leaders, on their part, benefit by securing state funding and by enjoying the boost of status and authority (and sometimes coercive backing) that follows from state recognition.

LEGAL PLURALISM INVOLVING CAPITALISM AND LIBERAL RIGHTS

Colonization brought on the first wave of legal pluralism. A second wave is occurring today, consisting of two distinct strains. Legal norms and institutions attached to global capitalism (the first strain) and to liberal democratic norms (the second strain) are now being exported to societies around the world with different social, cultural, economic, and political underpinnings and legal systems. Several notable parallels are evident in the first and second waves of legal pluralism. During colonization as well as today, much of the impetus for and models applied in legal transplantation came from outside, and the process on the receiving end was less than consensual. Economic motives were the prime movers of colonization (then) as well as in the spread of global capitalism (now). Missionaries brought Christianity to the natives then; today, Western development organizations and nongovernmental organizations (NGOs) proselytize about capitalism, democracy, human rights, and women's rights. In both waves, those exporting law assumed that their version was *the* right or best model, using templates taken from home to build legal regimes elsewhere. As occurred with colonization, the result today is a hodgepodge of coexisting, potentially clashing social and legal norms and institutions. Each strain of the modern wave is be taken up sequentially below.

The spread of global capitalism, a historical process set in motion several centuries ago, must not be conflated with the efforts to promote economic development made by the modern development community. The former involves an epic transformation around the globe in the organization of economic activities – albeit with many impoverished areas excluded; the latter involves the ideas and activities of (mostly) Western-funded development organizations. The spread of capitalism is an undeniable fact, manifested in the rise of the Asian tigers, the collapse of communism, and the recent growth of China, India, and Brazil (see Frieden 2007), whereas programs to promote economic development, which concentrate on regions left behind, are widely considered a failure (Easterly 2006). The spread of global capitalism owes relatively little to the activities of the development community.

The bulk of the funding for law and development activities is provided by institutions like the World Bank, whose primary mission is to advance economic development. Law is touted as a *means* to advance the economic development *end* (Tamanaha 2011). The standard package includes laws on incorporation, securities, antitrust, banking, intellectual property, commercial transactions, protections for foreign investors, and property rights and contract enforcement. This was the law component of the "Washington Consensus" plank of market-friendly reforms actively pushed around the world in the 1980s and 1990s.

A conventional set of assumptions about the role law plays in economic development is taken as articles of faith among many in the development community. The protection of property secures the fruits of one's labor, which encourages people to devote greater efforts to productive activities. The enforcement of contract enables people to engage in transactions with assurances that they will be carried through, expanding the range of contracting parties to include strangers at a distance over time, increasing the number of transactions. Society benefits from property and contract laws because encouraging productive activities and economic transactions increases aggregate social wealth (Dam 2006). A prominent voice from the South, Peruvian economist Hernando de Soto, highlighted the special economic significance of property rights (De Soto 2000). A great deal of land in development contexts is not officially titled, especially where registering title is a lengthy and costly process. In the absence of legal recognition, he argued, property cannot be used as collateral to secure loans; people are less inclined to improve the property (fearing they will lose it), and the market for real property is artificially constrained. As a result, much of the potential wealth and capital in developing societies is locked up unproductively.

Many law and development projects conducted in the name of economic development have increased legal pluralism. This pluralism (the coexistence of multiple legal forms) almost invariably follows whenever legal regimes are transplanted from elsewhere. Titling projects, which rank high on the development agenda, are a prime example. Property in many societies is conceived of and controlled in a variety of ways that do not match freehold ownership by individuals. In such societies, family and clan members possess various capacities to use land – to cross it, graze their animals on it, collect its fruits, till it – and others must be consulted about uses of the land. The process of titling extinguishes much of this, because use and access rights are not recognized by standard legal titles and banks do not favor encumbered collateral. When property is titled in situations like this, individuals are confronted with conflicting rule systems – state law granting freehold ownership versus communal use and possession rights – that confer different advantages and disadvantages.

Traditional leaders, for instance, can officially register and sell or borrow against property, dispossessing members of the community and altering access to and the distribution of land in ways that were not possible under customary systems. The dispossessed can no longer live off the land and will be forced to find other ways to feed and house their families. Women stand to be adversely affected because ownerships rights in many cultures, if reduced to a single titular "owner," often favor men (Manji 2006). The broader social structure can also be disrupted because social relations in many local communities revolve around the land.

Although titling projects have been promoted to bring clarity to property ownership, the immediate consequence of these projects may be the opposite because of legal pluralism (Easterly 2006, 95–97). Two coexisting bodies of law, state and customary, clash in a manner that unsettles both, allowing competing claimants to point to different legal sources in support of their conflicting positions. (An increase in pluralism does not always result: granting official legal title to squatters in urban slums to acknowledge their de facto possession-based ownership might reduce legal pluralism and enhance certainty.) State law may assert that official title is superior, but people within the community can effectively place a cloud over ownership by resisting state-issued titles.

The foregoing example is negative, but legal pluralism might also hold positive implications for the rule of law and economic development. Commercial enterprises that prefer to avoid state legal systems – because of corruption, ineptitude, delay, or bias – can resort to (or create) alternatives, like independent commercial arbitration or a tribunal instituted by the merchants themselves that operate apart from the official legal system. Encouraging alternative legal institutions that compete with state law increases legal pluralism, but for the positive purpose of satisfying rule of law functions – resolving disputes – that go unmet by failing state legal systems.

The second strain of the contemporary wave of legal pluralism goes beyond economic development. In the past decade, development efforts have placed a growing emphasis on democracy, human rights, women's rights, labor rights, environmental protection, and access to justice for the poor. These initiatives are often bundled with rule of law promotion.

Unlike the economic development strain, these efforts often take direct aim at the culture and order of a society. The spread of capitalism visits sweeping changes on cultures and societies: drawing people from the country to the city, bringing women into the workplace, imposing work discipline, controlling the daily rhythm, providing money to families and communities from external sources, offering a broader range of goods for consumers, increasing exposure to mass media, and much more. The disturbances of cultures and societies that result, however, are mostly side effects rather than intended consequences of global capitalism.

By contrast, human rights and women's rights initiatives directly target the culture, society, and polity when challenging harsh or discriminatory treatment of low caste, the poor, children, women, or social outcasts (homosexuals, criminals, and so forth).

The transformative consequences of global capitalism on local culture and society might well be more thoroughgoing, but the indirect versus direct nature of the consequences matters greatly in how they are received. People who eagerly seek the economic fruits of capitalism are less wont to protest its adverse cultural side effects, whereas human rights and women's rights initiatives are viewed as frontal assaults on their way of life – which they rise to defend – offering little in return in the eyes of those who oppose the changes (although beneficiaries, like women, may embrace them).

Legal pluralism produced in connection with this broader development strain is dynamic and multisided. NGOs press human rights or women's rights (with women's rights now often couched as human rights) as universally applicable and superior to customary and religious traditions (Quraishi 2011). In defense of the challenged norms or practices (for example, relating to divorce rights, domestic violence, and inheritance of property), traditional leaders cite customary or religious norms and institutions. State legal systems may be caught in the middle when they officially recognize human rights or women's rights while they also recognize the validity of customary and religious law. In these contexts, several legal regimes are in play – international law, state law, customary law, and religious law – the parties invoking whichever system aligns with their preferred goals.

These broader development initiatives are not always or inevitably set against culture and society – it depends on the situation, the objectives, and strategic alignments that arise among parties. Environmental NGOs that seek to limit mining or deforestation by multinational corporations, for example, can find allies in traditional leaders who wish to preserve their lands and way of life or to secure a bigger share of the economic benefits of the activities. In these situations, international law advocated by the NGOs and customary law advocated by local leaders will join and be pitted against corporate actors supported by government officials who cite the authority of state law–issued mining or forestry licenses.

The cumulative consequence of the first and second waves is to enhance legal pluralism across several dimensions: by increasing the raw number of legal regimes, by increasing the layering and nesting of legal regimes, by placing more legal regimes side by side within a single community, by multiplying the ways in which these coexisting regimes interact and interrelate, and by creating hybrid blends that join qualities of more than one regime.

THE UNIQUE QUALITIES OF LEGAL PLURALISM IN DEVELOPMENT

The academic literature on legal pluralism is filled with reminders that legal pluralism exists in *all* societies, Western and non-Western, North and South, developed and developing. That is doubtless correct – but it is like observing that the sun shines everywhere, from the Arctic Circle to the Arabian Peninsula. What is significant here lies not in the similarities between Western and non-Western contexts about legal pluralism but in the essential differences.

In Western societies, the primary locus of law was gradually established within the state over the course of the fifteenth through the nineteenth centuries, when the state system coalesced in Europe (see Van Creveld 1999). Prior to this, the Medieval period was marked by a rich plurality of coexisting legal systems, including local customary law, Germanic customary law, feudal law, law of merchants, law of separate guilds, canon law of the Catholic Church, and Roman law (see Tamanaha 2008, 377–81). The consolidation of the state system involved several key developments: establishing the supremacy of monarchs within territorial boundaries; creating the public/private distinction around the separation between public office and the person who occupies it, between public resources and private resources (previously the monarch's resources came mainly from personal holdings, and officials were members of the king's personal staff), and between public functions and private activities; and building a government bureaucracy that included royal courts and tax collectors. The unification of law within the state was a central aspect of these developments. In the course of this consolidation, other preexisting forms of law, like customary law and canon law, lost their independent "legal" status. They either were absorbed into the state legal system – as occurred with the law merchant and family law aspects of canon law – or were shunted to the private side of the public/private divide, where they lived on as private rule systems, but shorn of their previous full-fledged legal status. Through a slow and lengthy process, legal systems in the West thus arrived at their centralized monopoly position.

Development settings today differ in several crucial respects: multiple legal forms with legal status continue to exist alongside state law (law has not been consolidated in the state); state legal institutions and legal traditions are younger and less entrenched; the public/private divide is poorly established; and many legal institutions and norms did not evolve over time in connection with society but have been transplanted from external sources (colonization, global capitalism, liberal democratic rights).

Legal pluralism will remain a reality in development contexts for the foreseeable future (although in some locations, interrelations with state law may become better articulated with the passage of time). This currently entrenched state, reinforced by path dependence, is deepened by the contrast between the sociocultural normative ordering of developing societies and the normative underpinnings of state legal systems. This normative contrast was set in place during colonization and is fed today by the continuous external assault on these societies by global capitalism and liberal norms. This clash can be erased only if cultures and societies around the world converge to better match the normative underpinnings of law brought in from the outside. Western societies have never had to grapple with this sharp normative contrast because capitalism, liberalism, and their legal systems collectively developed in sync with their own cultures and societies. Therein lay the pivotal difference.

This leads to an alternative way to perceive the current situation in development contexts. Rule of law projects, which focus almost exclusively on building state legal systems, are implicitly informed by an unstated assumption that the trajectory in developing nations matches that of Western countries – that law will be (must be) consolidated within the state. But this is a problematic assumption for at least two reasons. A different path has brought these societies to their contemporary plural legal arrangements, which are now entrenched. And the state system in Western countries is now undergoing change, devolving away some of its former monopoly powers, giving up limited aspects of its sovereignty to transnational bodies or greater autonomy to subterritories, and delegating some of its legal functions to private actors (private security, privately run prisons, private arbitration, and so forth) (Tamanaha 2008). The entrenchment of pluralism makes unification in the state more difficult, whereas the ongoing devolution of legal functions to private actors suggests that state consolidation of legal authority might not be necessary or desirable.

Rather than an unfinished stage of legal development, legal pluralism is more aptly viewed as a reality in its own right – a functional arrangement that reflects and manages the normative inconsistencies between the society and the state legal system. It may be prudent, in this light, for state legal systems in development contexts to eschew the standard claim to possess a monopoly over law, exercising instead a narrower scope of authority focused mainly on the affairs of a functioning government and the modern economy, and dealing with high crimes. The bulk of ordinary social intercourse can perhaps be better dealt with through local tribunals that are continuous with the surrounding normative ordering. In many locations, rural and urban, this de facto division already exists.

Two barriers stand in the way of embracing this perception of legal pluralism. First, the strongly held assumption that the state must hold a monopoly over law paints these as defective legal systems rather than intelligent accommodations to existing circumstances. Second, many local tribunals fail the Western tests of legitimacy. They are usually dominated by males; they might not conform to norms of due process and procedural fairness; they might not strictly apply the rules (compromising to achieve consensus or peace); they might visit harsh punishments or apply inequitable rules; they might resort to ordeals, magic, or other unorthodox modes; and so forth. These societies have their own norms, institutions, and ways of doing things that do not always conform to Western institutions and norms. Nonetheless, these tribunals are accessible and understandable to the people, and they can provide fora to resolve disputes and help maintain social order.

Legal pluralism can comport with and serve rule of law functions even when they do not meet what the West considers to be standard legal requirements. It is an alternative constellation of law within society that has arisen out of these circumstances and can operate in ways that meet the needs of the community. This is the positive takeaway of this exploration.

INSTRUMENTALISM AND UNCERTAINTY

Legal pluralism also has worrisome implications, however. The main negative implication for the rule of law is the increase in legal uncertainty that it potentially creates. All legal systems suffer from uncertainty and excessive instrumentalism (Tamanaha 2006). In situations of legal pluralism, however, these problems are magnified. The presence of coexisting legal systems fuels strategic resort to law to advance particular agendas, several examples of which are offered in the course of this chapter. Legal disputes usually center on which party has the better case under the law; disputes in contexts of legal pluralism present an additional layer of questions about which law controls when two or more contrasting legal regimes point toward different outcomes. This puts at issue the respective authority and power of the competing legal systems themselves. Uncertainty is increased – ex ante as well as after a dispute arises – for everyone in situations of legal pluralism because of the ever-present latent potential for a clash of legal regimes. This uncertainty, moreover, can encourage legal disputes because an apparently solid legal position is vulnerable to being unsettled by a challenge grounded on a competing legal regime. Conflict of law rules that exist on paper or officially prescribed legal hierarchies that purport to resolve clashes between coexisting legal regimes might not dampen this uncertainty. The bottom line in these clashes is not the authority a given legal regime claims to possess but, in the end, which result can be made to stick. Social and political power may matter more in the resolution of these disputes than law.

Legal pluralism, to draw out the crucial point, provides fertile terrain for intensifying legal disputes, with competing legal systems strategically used by the parties as weapons in the fight. This scenario leads to the virtual antithesis of the rule of law.

DEVELOPMENT ACTIVITIES AND LEGAL PLURALISM

Development projects must be sensitive to and anticipate the implications of legal pluralism, which can be good or bad, depending on one's objectives and the circumstances at hand. The success of these projects may by stymied or facilitated by the presence of other legal forms. When contemplating legal pluralism, an eye should be cast in two directions: on the legal institutions themselves and on strategic actors in a given social arena. (Development organizations must remember that they too count as such strategic actors.) Each legal form present should be evaluated for its operational capability; the amount of financial, martial, or political resources it can enlist; which way its norms point; and its relative standing, power, and relations vis-à-vis other coexisting legal forms and other relevant actors (especially economic, political, and military elites). *Power* includes the ability to impose sanctions – ranging from social disapprobation to coercive force – as well as to rally public opinion. The people who staff legal institutions and who have a stake in them and benefit from them must also be considered – including their personal interests and ideological commitments. It is essential to anticipate who stands to gain or to lose by a particular course of action, contemplating not only the immediate parties but also the coexisting legal institutions themselves and the people who are vested in them.

Another point, which relates to the previous one, is that there must be a significant local constituency that supports the achievement of the goals pursued by development projects. They must see those goals as desirable, beneficial, legitimate, and/or just. This need not be a majority of people. If it is to have a chance of succeeding, it must reflect the views or have the support of a measurable number of people. Ideally, some of those people should occupy leadership positions or carry influence within that society. This counsel is perhaps obvious, but it still must be emphasized. Development initiatives ultimately depend on the hard work and commitment of people from and within the society to realize those goals. This is especially difficult if it involves change or goes against conventional practices and norms. Only if people believe in the goals and see a path by which they can be achieved will the necessary effort be made.

Finally, it must be kept in mind that legal development activities are often active *sources* of legal pluralism. Legal pluralism is sharpened when a clash arises between cultural and legal norms. That is what occurs when development organizations promote titling projects or advance human rights or women's rights agendas that run contrary to entrenched cultural or religious norms. The design and evaluation of these projects should consider not only their objectives and the likelihood of their attainment, but additionally whether the project itself will exacerbate legal pluralism in a manner that worsens legal uncertainty and generates divisive battles within law that accomplish little. Social change can be brought about in a variety of ways, including education and exposure to new ideas. When law is used as a coercive mechanism to force change on recalcitrant people, it may prompt a backlash that includes not just lawbreaking behavior and avoidance of legal officials, but also resentment toward the law that undermines the long-term efficacy of the law itself.

REFERENCES

Benton, Lauren. 2001. *Law and Colonial Cultures: Legal Regimes in World History, 1400–1900*. New York: Cambridge University Press.
Dam, Kenneth W. 2006. *The Law Growth Nexus: The Rule of Law and Economic Development*. Washington, DC: Brookings Institution Press.
De Soto, Hernando. 2000. *The Mystery of Capital: Why Capitalism Triumphs in the West and Fails Everywhere Else*. New York: Basic Books.
Easterly, William. 2006. *The White Man's Burden: Why the West's Efforts to Aid the Rest Have Done So Much Ill and So Little Good*. New York: Penguin.
Frieden, Jeffry A. 2007. *Global Capitalism: Its Fall and Rise in the Twentieth Century*. New York: W. W. Norton & Company.

Golub, Stephen. 2006. "A House without a Foundation." In *Promoting the Rule of Law Abroad: In Search of Knowledge*, ed. Thomas Carothers. Washington, DC: Carnegie Endowment for International Peace.

Manji, Ambreena. 2006. *The Politics of Land Reform in Africa: From Communal Tenure to Free Markets*. London: Zed Books.

Mommsen, Wolfgang, and Jaap de Moor, eds. 1992. *European Expansion and Law: The Encounter of European and Indigenous Law in 19th- and 20th-Century Africa and Asia*. Oxford: Berg Publishers.

Piron, Laure-Helene. 2006. "Time to Learn, Time to Act in Africa." In *Promoting the Rule of Law Abroad: In Search of Knowledge*, ed. Thomas Carothers. Washington, DC: Carnegie Endowment for International Peace.

Quraishi, Asifa. 2011. "What If Sharia Weren't the Enemy? Rethinking International Woman's Rights Advocacy on Islamic Law." *Columbia Journal of Gender and Law* 20 (5).

Santos, Boaventura de Sousa. 1977. "Law of the Oppressed: The Construction and Reproduction of Legality in Pasargada." *Law & Society Review* 12 (1): 5–126.

Tamanaha, Brian Z. 2004. *On the Rule of Law: History, Politics, Theory*. Cambridge: Cambridge University Press.

———. 2006. *Law as a Means to an End: Threat to the Rule of Law*. New York: Cambridge University Press.

———. 2008. "Understanding Legal Pluralism: Past to Present, Local to Global." *Sydney Law Review* 30 (3): 375–411.

———. 2009. "A Concise Guide to the Rule of Law." In *Relocating the Rule of Law*, ed. Gianluigi Palombella and Neil Walker. Oxford: Hart Publishing.

———. 2011. "The Primacy of Society and the Failures of Law and Development." *Cornell International Law Journal* 44 (2): 209–47.

United Nations. 2004. "The Rule of Law and Transitional Justice in Conflict and Post-Conflict Societies." Report of the Secretary General, United Nations Security Council, United Nations, New York.

———. 2006. "Uniting Our Strengths: Enhancing United Nations Support for the Rule of Law." Report of the Secretary General, United Nations General Assembly Security Council, United Nations, New York.

Van Creveld, Martin. 1999. *The Rise and Decline of the State*. Cambridge: Cambridge University Press.

3

Bendable Rules

The Development Implications of Human Rights Pluralism

David Kinley

ENDS AND MEANS

Within the context of development, human rights have an uncertain place (Sano 2000). The problem is not at the highest levels of generality, where the goals of human rights and development readily intertwine. Here we can happily agree that both seek the alleviation of poverty, the betterment of the lives of the marginalized, and the promotion of self-respect and fulfillment built on basic levels of economic capacity, social acceptance, and (at a stretch) political voice. It is in terms of perspective, and to a lesser extent practice, that we encounter problems. Human rights stated in law and with attendant legal obligations, imperatives, instructions, and institutionalized dispute settlement regimes give the impression of rigidity and immediacy. By contrast, development perspectives emphasize the need for flexibility in the face of nuanced and often highly elastic problems. However, to the extent that modern human rights are enshrined in law (international and/or domestic), they do secure some purchase within development thinking and practice. This is largely through the now well-established mediums in development work of programs promoting the rule of law, gender equity, justice, and law reform, as well as governance and general institutional capacity initiatives. It is a foothold borne of surrogacy. The protection and promotion of human rights seldom constitute the explicitly stated objects of a development project; rather, human rights are seen, at most, as a supplementary resource informing the project's principal ends and their protection (hopefully) as one of its desirable by-products.

I'd like to thank the organizers of and participants in the World Bank's Legal Pluralism and Development Policy workshop, on which the book is based, for their constructive comments and criticisms of this chapter, especially Daniel Adler, its official commentator. I am also very grateful to Christine Ernst for her research assistance and editorial acumen in the finalization of the piece.

PURPOSE

The purpose of this chapter is to examine human rights in their legal clothing through the lens of how they both reflect and limit the ideas of legal pluralism. In so doing it will, necessarily and importantly, recognize human rights in their other guises – philosophical, economic, social, and political – to reconcile what the law of human rights says it does, and what it does in practice.

In seeking to adopt a global perspective, the chapter focuses on international human rights law (IHRL). Generally, IHRLs purport to provide three things:

(i) they enunciate broad statements of rights (mostly of individuals) and responsibilities (mostly of states);
(ii) they stipulate the circumstances in which those rights can legitimately be limited and responsibilities curtailed or suspended. That is, exceptionally, in times of public emergency, but more regularly, when other rights might be infringed; in the interests of public order,[1] health,[2] or national security;[3] and to protect public morals;[4]
(iii) and, in order to help both right holders and duty bearers to understand the extent of their respective jurisdictions, they appeal to the desirable goals of global/regional/community peace and security, borne of securing basic standards of liberty, justice, fairness, and equality.[5]

THE INHERENT ELASTICITY OF HUMAN RIGHTS

Certainly, notions of legal pluralism played little or no formal part in the formulation of these basal features of IHRL. Rather, the qualifications or "elbow room" represented by the limitation clauses in (ii) is the consequence of political pragmatism. It is an answer, in other words, to the question of how to frame international human rights instruments that exerted normative force on the behavior of states, while at the same time recognizing their competence to mitigate, curtail, or suspend rights "where necessary." This faintly Faustian pact is as familiar to international lawyers as it is to diplomats and politicians.

Since their inception, however, these limitation clauses have been used as a vehicle for protecting pluralistic sensibilities. Thus, although the Universal Declaration

---

[1] See, for example, International Covenant on Civil and Political Rights (ICCPR), arts. 12(3), 14(1), 18(3), 19(3), 21, and 22(2); International Covenant on Economic, Social and Cultural Rights (ICESCR), art. 8(1).
[2] See, for example, ICCPR, arts. 12(3), 18(3), 19(3), 21, and 22(2).
[3] See, for example, ICCPR, arts. 12(3), 13, 14(1), 19(3), 21, and 22(2); ICESCR, art. 8(1).
[4] See, for example, ICCPR, arts. 12(3), 14(1), 18(3), 19(3), 21, and 22(2).
[5] For example, the preamble to the Universal Declaration of Human Rights (UDHR) describes recognition of human rights as the "foundation of freedom, justice and peace in the world." Similarly, the preamble to the European Convention on Human Rights provides that fundamental freedoms are the "foundation of justice and peace in the world."

of Human Rights (UDHR) is widely understood as reflecting a set of common basic norms, it is accepted, equally, that the differing cultures and contexts from which they are drawn necessitate some differences in the manner and form of their implementation. As Mary Ann Glendon notes of the UDHR:

> One of the most common and unfortunate misunderstandings today involves the notion that the Declaration was meant to impose a single model of right conduct rather than provide a common standard that can be brought to life in different cultures in a legitimate variety of ways.

Glendon (2001, xviii–xix) adds that such standards as contained in the UDHR "can serve as a basis for discussion across ideological and cultural divides."[6]

As such, an alternative understanding of the role played by the permissible limitations on rights stipulated in IHRL is to view them not just as the consequences of compromise, but also as doors through which differences can be channeled and managed – in other words, not to see them necessarily as "limiting," but potentially as a means of engagement and inclusion by which states can interpret and apply rights in ways that reflect their inescapably varied histories, cultural mores, political circumstances, and legal traditions.

If we are to consider these provisions as instruments of dialogue and debate, there can be no denying their success in terms of the attention they receive. By far, the greatest proportion of human rights jurisprudence *and* human rights policy occurs within the space provided by these limitations. Even a cursory glance at the methods and outputs of the various international human rights institutions advertises this fact. But it is on closer examination that one realizes how endemic the issue is.

It is evident, for instance, in the "subsidiarity principle" widely employed in IHRL, which avoids prescribing a precise format for the domestic implementation of international obligations. Instead, as formulated in the International Covenant on Civil and Political Rights (ICCPR), it requires states to take "the necessary steps, in accordance with its constitutional processes... to adopt such laws or other measures as may be necessary to give effect to the rights recognized in the present Covenant."[7] The scope of subsidiarity encompasses the notion of *Drittwirkung*, which connotes the horizontal application in domestic law of guarantees expressed in international law. What this means in practice is that by the use, for example, of such terms as "to ensure to all persons subject to their jurisdiction the free and full exercise of th[e] rights and freedoms [herein],"[8] human rights treaties compel signatory

---

[6] P. C. Chang, the Chinese delegate to, and vice chair of, the United Nations Commission on Human Rights responsible for drafting the UDHR, was clearly of this view. Eleanor Roosevelt, the chair of the commission, noted in her memoirs that, from the very outset, she saw Chang as a "pluralist" with regard to what versions of "ultimate reality" should be reflected in the declaration, a position that she certainly did not disapprove of, as quoted in Glendon (2001, 47).

[7] ICCPR, art. 2(2).

[8] American Convention on Human Rights, art. 1(1).

states to ensure not only that the state agencies do not violate individuals' rights (a vertical relationship) but also that they put in place means to ensure that private or non-state actors do not do so either (a horizontal relationship).[9] Forged in the crucible of Germanic jurisprudence, this principle has been adopted and adapted by the European Court of Human Rights (ECtHR)[10] and is now commonly recognized and applied in human rights jurisprudence worldwide. The application of the principle illustrates the capacity of human rights law to accommodate concepts beyond those expressly articulated in human rights instruments.

An acceptance of pluralistic approaches also underpins the drawing of jurisdictional boundaries, whereby individual complaints of human rights abuse typically will not be entertained by international tribunals until complainants "have exhausted all available domestic remedies" (in the words of the *First Optional Protocol to the ICCPR*).[11] For those cases that do reach the international tribunals, some degree of allowance is made for differences between states in the application of IHRL that reflects certain moral and ethical beliefs, or political, social, and economic circumstances. The most sophisticated and widespread deployment of such legal leeway has been by the ECtHR through its use of "margin of appreciation" as a principle of legal interpretation of the nature and extent of states' obligations under the European Convention on Human Rights (ECHR).[12] The principle is, in effect, a device for extending to states a limited scope of discretion. Importantly, it is not considered dispensatory, but rather necessary and indeed even desirable, in order to encapsulate the breadth of *legitimate* differences of opinion as mediated through the legal organs of state. In other words, it both embraces legal pluralism and uses it as a sanitizing filter. As Onder Bakircioğlu explains:

> The role of discretion is indispensable not only for bridging the gap between the law and changing realities of dynamic social organisms, but also for answering the particular questions of a given case in the absence of overall enacted or case law. In other words, judges are entitled to exercise discretion to make fair decisions in a specific case, without being locked into a formula that might not be applicable to every scenario. (Bakircioğlu 2007, 711)

The alacrity with which international human rights tribunals extend such discretion to states, and especially to their judges, can be looked at from another angle as well: the relative infrequency with which domestic tribunals invoke a particular feature

---

[9] On the concept of *Drittwirkung*, see Engle (2009). The concept is especially well developed in the jurisprudence of the ECtHR and the ACtHR; on the former, see Engle (2009), and on the latter, see Inter-American Court of Human Rights (2003).
[10] See *X and Y v. The Netherlands* [1985] 8 EHRR 235, para. 23, and the line of cases that have followed it: see Krzeminska-Vamvaka (2009, 49–50).
[11] Article 2.
[12] See *Handyside v. UK* [1976] 1 EHRR 737, and the line of cases that have followed it (see Hutchinson 1999).

of IHRL that appears to demand singular objectivity. This is the common IHRL requirement that domestic laws cannot be "arbitrary" with regard to their impact on rights protections. The term *arbitrary* is used throughout the ICCPR both in conjunction with and as an alternative to *unlawful*. The latter sense is especially interesting in the present context. By insisting that rights must not be curtailed in ways that are either unlawful *or* arbitrary,[13] it effectively permits the United Nations (UN) Human Rights Committee to pronounce on the legitimacy (at least in a human rights sense) of a state's laws and even its legal system.[14] It is the very nature of this scope that effectively curtails the Human Rights Committee's invocation of this provision beyond occasionally.

Pluralistic strains are perhaps most evident in the political and diplomatic interactions between states and the international human rights bodies. Such relations are often characterized as engaging rather than didactic, and as suggestive rather than admonitory (Steiner, Alston, and Goodman 2008). There are exceptions – the judgments and sanctions of the ECtHR and the American Court of Human Rights, for example, which are quite different from the nonbinding "views" of the UN human rights treaty bodies[15] – but overall, these interactions are couched in language that promotes assimilation of the human rights cause rather than conversion to it.

We should expect as much, given the conceptual provenance of rights. From the ancient natural rights theorists, such as Aquinas and Aristotle, to the Enlightenment philosophers, such as Hobbes, Kant, Mill, Locke, and Rousseau, to the more positivistic-minded modern thinkers, including Ignatieff, Fredman, Raz, Sandel, and Sen, this political dimension of rights has been not only acknowledged but

---

[13] See, for example, art. 17(1) of the ICCPR, which reads: "No one shall be subjected to arbitrary or unlawful interference with his privacy, family, home or correspondence, nor to unlawful attacks on his honour and reputation."

[14] See, for example, the ICCPR's Human Rights Committee's views in *Toonen v. Australia*, where it held that laws in the state of Tasmania that criminalized homosexuality between consenting adults "arbitrarily interfere[d] with Mr. Toonen's right [to privacy] under article 17, paragraph 1": Human Rights Committee, *Toonen v. Australia* (1994), CCPR/C/50/D/488/1992 [8.6]. Prohibitions on arbitrariness are also evident in the ECtHR's jurisprudence on art. 5 of the ECHR. In *Assanidza v. Georgia*, the ECtHR held that "to detain a person for an indefinite and unforeseeable period, without such detention being based on a specific statutory provision or judicial decision, is incompatible with the principle of legal certainty ... and arbitrary, and runs counter to the fundamental aspects of the rule of law": *Assanidza v. Georgia*, Application No. 71503/01 [2004] EHHR 140 at [175]. Similarly, in *Filiz and Kalkan v. Turkey*, the ECtHR held that in detaining the applicant for eight days without judicial intervention, Turkey breached art. 5 of the ECHR, which aims "to protect the individual against arbitrary interference by the State with his right to liberty": *Filiz and Kalkan v. Turkey*, Application No. 34481/97 [2002] EHRR 509 at [23], [25]–[27].

[15] The ECHR has relatively strong enforcement mechanisms. Under arts. 33 and 34 of the ECHR, an application alleging a breach of the convention can be brought before the ECtHR by any state party, person, nongovernmental organization, or group of individuals. The court's decision is binding, and the execution of the judgment by the parties is monitored by the Committee of Ministers of the Council of Europe: David Harris et al., *Law of the European Convention on Human Rights* (2009), pp. 4–5. By contrast, the UN human rights bodies do not have the same authority; their determinations of individual complaints result in "a view" rather than "a judgment," which is an important distinction.

also embraced as essential to their enunciation, invocation, and implementation. Despite the fact that the narrative of human rights is promoted by many, and believed by many more, to speak in a single voice, it is in reality a voice speaking at least three languages – philosophical, legal, and political.[16] And it is in the language of philosophy, and especially politics, where there lies the greatest room for legal interpretation that is not straightforwardly singular, but rather, often and unavoidably, plural.

That said, the history of the modern conception of human rights has hardly been consistent on this point. The sixty-odd years of the UDHR have been marked, first, by the creation of the rift between the supposed status (juridically and practicably) of civil and political rights (labeled first generation and justiciable) and economic, social, and cultural rights (labeled second generation and nonjusticiable), and, second, by ongoing efforts to repair it. This was a very politico-legal rift borne of misaligned dichotomies of the Cold War (socialism *versus* liberal democracy; social order *versus* individual freedom; and equality *versus* liberty). The response to it at the international level was equally politico-legal. In perhaps the most celebrated of the attempts to bridge the divide, the UN-auspiced *Vienna Declaration and Program of Action* adopted by the World Conference on Human Rights in 1993 stated:

> All human rights are universal, indivisible and interdependent and interrelated. The international community must treat human rights globally in a fair and equal manner, on the same footing, and with the same emphasis. While the significance of national and regional particularities and various historical, cultural and religious backgrounds must be borne in mind, it is the duty of States, regardless of their political, economic and cultural systems, to promote and protect all human rights and fundamental freedoms. (art. 5)

The rift was certainly insidiously destructive to the effort to establish a coherent system of international human rights law, but it was not all groundless. This all-embracing response, therefore, was an overreaction. Logically, it bears the distorting hallmarks of compromise – on the one hand appealing to the singular, unifying characteristics of human rights, while on the other accepting the need to admit multiple influences and perspectives on their promotion and protection. Philosophically, it provides little by way of guidance as to how, in practice, to resolve the needs to prioritize rights promotion and to reconcile differences between rights.

What this high-water mark of universalism has precipitated, albeit unintentionally, is a more sophisticated debate about human rights relativism. There is now a deeper examination of the need for, and the extent to which, differences of legal tradition, culture, politics, and economics can legitimately be taken into account by states when they are fulfilling their obligations under international human rights law.

---

[16] This is how Tony Evans (2004) frames it in his critique of the concept of universal human rights.

Ida Elisabeth Koch's (2009, 3) extensive analysis of the status of socioeconomic rights vis-à-vis civil and political rights as practiced in states today is a good example of this type of approach. Although she uses the Vienna Declaration Article 5 denotation as the entry point for her study, she very quickly concludes that "human rights are *not* in practice treated as 'indivisible, interrelated and interdependent,' and they are certainly not treated either 'on the same footing' or 'with the same emphasis.'"

THE SIGNIFICANCE OF NONLEGAL DIMENSIONS

There are those both inside and outside the human rights community who might view all this apparent equivocation as heresy, or at least as a threat to the integrity of human rights and to the purity of their message. But that is to misunderstand the reality of international human rights law as it is both stated and practiced, as well as the facilitative dimensions of human rights that ought to allow for their wider application. The latter point is especially significant in terms of our concern in this chapter with the development implications of human rights pluralism. The amenability of human rights should be seen as an opportunity for development strategists and practitioners in their engagement in "good struggles" (see Sage, Tamanaha, and Woolcock 2011). It is a chance to see anew the utility of human rights as a tool of rhetoric and as a process that supports development ends rather than being irrelevant to or pitted against them (Kinley 2006).

The "bendability" of human rights rules is not a sign of their weakness or a diminution of their universal aspirations, and still less a triumph of politics (or culture or economics) over law. Rather, it is a feature of the vital role that these other, nonlegal dimensions play in the exposition and deployment of human rights. International human rights law is not absolutist and uncompromising – no matter how zealously some seek to argue the case – nor can it ever be.

In some places, this accommodation is more apparent than in others. Take, for example, the situation in many Pacific Island countries, the constitutions of which typically declare that both culture and human rights must, together, form the foundations of their nation-states (New Zealand Law Commission 2006, 22). Custom, including customary law, still plays a very important part in the social orders of all of these states. As the New Zealand Law Commission (2006, 41) notes, "the vast majority of disputes in many Pacific countries, especially in Melanesia, are resolved by customary means." It is certainly true that such means are not always easily reconciled with human rights laws,[17] but equally, there is a relatively long history under international law of recognizing that custom is itself an expression and exercise of a human right (Scaglion 2003). Such recognition stretches from

---

[17] On the difficulty of reconciling certain customary norms with human rights, see New Zealand Law Commission (2006, 83–146). For a critical perspective of Sharia law and its ability to accommodate human rights objectives, see Chamblee (2004).

the UDHR's guarantee of "the right freely to participate in the cultural life of the community"[18] and the protection of the right of self-determination under Article 1 of both of the covenants (ICCPR and International Covenant on Economic, Social and Cultural Rights) through to the preservation and promotion of indigenous legal and juridical customs under the *ILO Convention 169 on Indigenous and Tribal Peoples (1991)* (Arts. 8 and 9) and the *UN Declaration on the Rights of Indigenous Peoples (2007)*.[19] Within the legal systems of the countries themselves, there is a small but growing number of cases in which courts in particular are being called on to reconcile potentially opposing norms.[20] For example, where customary laws restrict the inheritance of land to men, courts can mitigate their discriminatory effects by ensuring that male heirs meet their obligations to support their female family members.[21]

The most serious roadblock to reconciling customary law (as a particular instance of legal pluralism) and human rights law lies in viewing each as monolithic and unbending. To do so is a serious mistake. Both are evolving, and both impact on each other. To look again at the experience in the Pacific, it is essential "to recognise and value different cultural perspectives of human rights and to accept that Pacific cultures are, like all cultures, complex... [and] change over time as a result of internal and external forces," as Konai Helu Thaman puts it (1998, cited in New Zealand Law Commission 2006, 73). Helu adds, tellingly, in the context of the Pacific, where religion is so strong, "[i]f Christianity can be adopted as a Pacific religion, why not human rights?"[22]

Donovan and Assefa (2003) are driven by the same sense of what is practicable. In their study of homicide and the conflicts between human rights and customary law in Ethiopia, they draw on lessons learned in Latin America in the 1980s. This they characterize as implementing a "strategy of ranking human rights," whereby one focuses "enforcement efforts on the most fundamental rights, such as the right to life, the right against torture and the right not to be enslaved and relegate enforcement of other rights to the backburner" (Donovan and Assefa 2003, 540).[23]

Accepting these practical realities of how legal systems actually work in different communities and cultures pushes us toward the general principle that it is essential to consider international law as a product of, and as being continually shaped by, a sort of "global legal pluralism." This, for Mireille Delmas-Marty (2009, viii), is

---

[18] UDHR, art. 27(1).
[19] See also the rights of minorities to enjoy their own culture under art. 27 of the ICCPR and art, 30 of the Committee on the Rights of the Child (CRC), and the right to participation in cultural activities under art. 5 of the CESCR.
[20] See New Zealand Law Commission (2006, 168–79).
[21] See ibid., 12–13.
[22] See ibid.
[23] Donovan and Assefa draw on the work of A. Hoekema, "Aspects of Legal Pluralism in the Federal Set-up of the Ethiopian State" (unpublished paper on file in the law library of the Ethiopian Civil Service College, 1998).

a circumstance where "law among nations and beyond single nations develops through cross-referencing, through efforts to harmonize, and through the creation of hybrid rules of substance and procedure."

All that said, however, there are limits. There are lines drawn in the sand. We as individuals, communities, and states will and must make a stand on certain interpretations, ultimately deeming them to be acceptable or not. It is undeniable that there are better interpretations, understandings, and applications of international human rights law than others. Certainly, some readings are insincere, hypocritical, or perverse,[24] but even these help to mark out the extremities of unconscionability. So, it is within this arena of contestation that one must find the room for plurality of thought over the establishment and interpretation in law of the minimum standards of human existence that permit individual dignity to be secured and respected in the vast multiplicity of human circumstances. If there ever was a legal construct that could *not* – at least not in any detail – be definitively designed as a "one size fits all" it has to be human rights.

GRAMMATICAL FEATURES OF HUMAN RIGHTS LAW

So, there it is. The proposition that the fine print of human rights law is ill defined – or at least, is in a constant state of definition and redefinition (which amounts to the same thing) – that encourages pluralistic interpretation and debate. The framework within which this occurs is more settled. There are certain "adjectives" and "adverbs" that adhere to the grammar of international human rights law[25] that delineate the boundaries of deliberation and help to guide us in understanding how and in what ways human rights pluralism impacts on development. They stress the importance of the growth and impact of pluralism from below, not as imposed from above. "Pluralism cannot be decreed," as Delmas-Marty rightly asserts, imposed, as it were, by a legal or human rights hegemon (Delmas-Marty 2009, 5). With this in mind, the last part of the paper identifies the placement, manner, and form of these boundaries and tries to explain their relevance to the goals of modern development policy and practice. There are six such "grammatical" features.

1) The first of these is *empowerment*. This is the potential borne by enunciations of human rights to empower individuals both in terms of political rhetoric and legal process. Human rights laws can and do provide voice and leverage

---

[24] In fact, all states are prone to stray into these areas at times, but for the more blatant examples, see the most recent reports of the Democratic People's Republic of Korea to the Human Rights Council (A/HRC/WG.6/6/PRK/1, 27 August 2009), Saudi Arabia to the CEDAW (CEDAW/C/SAU/2, 29 March 2007), Myanmar to the CRC (CRC/C/70/Add.21, 5 November 2003), and the United States to the Committee against Torture in 2005 (CAT/C/48/Add.3, 29 June 2005.

[25] I am here borrowing from and adapting Uprendra Baxi's characterization of human rights as a modern-day "grammar of governance" (Baxi 2002, 8).

to those on the outer edges of societies, including the poor,[26] and they can do so across a range of different societies, cultures, legal systems, political economies, and governance structures. They are used as revolutionary tools in autocracies, accountability measures in democracies, instruments of reform in transitionary political systems, and reconciliatory stabilizers in post-conflict states.[27] To be sure, there are obstacles to empowerment encountered in each of these circumstances (and in some they are obviously much greater than in others), but the potential is always there. It is the assistance that such potential receives from the penumbra of factors and influences that surround the claims and enforcement of human rights that will determine the translation of potential into practice. The promotion of economic wealth and distributive equity; the establishment of robust institutions of governance that are transparent and accountable; and the maintenance of security and social order through means that are fair, open, and proportionate all are factors that bear directly on the need for individuals to invoke their human rights guarantees, as well as their ability to do so effectively. The breadth of development programs typically supported today by multilateral and bilateral aid agencies (at least in the West) reflect this broad-church approach. It is indeed through these vital ancillary dimensions to the story of empowerment through human rights that the development agencies exercise their greatest leverage (OECD 2006).

2) The second is the *universal appeal* of human rights. The emphasis here is on the actuality of their "intuitive appeal"[28] rather than on their contested universality. The openness of the universalizing project – ongoing, dialogic, and ever refining – should be lauded as one of the attractive features of human rights law. It provides the doorway through which to beckon non-lawyers and non–human rights specialists, the wary and hesitant, and even the human rights skeptics. Critical perspectives of human rights should be embraced – countered or amended if necessary or, of course, accepted – but embraced nonetheless. This means engaging with anthropological analyses that underscore divergences and partiality between peoples over the status of, and respect for, human rights and the consequences – positive as well as negative – of such differences for claims of human rights universality.[29] It means debating incisive

---

[26] See, for example, how Darrow and Tomas frame the World Bank's iconic "Voices of the Poor" study in 2000 in human rights terms (Darrow and Tomas 2005, 477–78).

[27] See Golub (2010).

[28] See Gearty (2008). And from this widely shared intuition comes the strongly binding notion of empathy for one's fellow human beings: see Kinley (2007).

[29] Marie Bénédicte Dembour: "As an anthropologist I do not see how one can say that human rights exist on a universal plane, nor do I see that human rights are such a good thing that it would be wonderful if they existed on a universal plane." But despite the fact that "human rights are not an empirical constant in humanity," she is nonetheless interested in examining "whether the world *as you and I know it* may well demand something like a framework of human rights": Dembour (2006, 2–3).

cultural critiques of the Western monopolization of human rights discourse (as argued by Mutua 1996) and heeding calls for "truly inter-civilizational dialogue" (according to Yasuaki 1999) to try to overcome such prejudices. It also means engaging with the various perspectives of human rights that emphasize their porosity to political context (Kennedy 2002), to philosophical framing (that human rights are a "value-oriented co-ordination" tool, in Habermas's terminology, the employment of which coordinates competing interests "based on the ability [of competing groups] to adduce reasons which can convince all parties" [Fredman 2009, 35],[30] and to cultural biases [whereby the goal, as Abdullahi An-Na'im (1990, 339) states, is to "seek ways to support and legitimize the particular human right in terms of values, norms and processes of change belonging to the relevant cultural tradition"]). Human rights are not above, beyond, or separate to any of these pluralizing forces, but constituted by them.

3) The third feature relates to the *programmatic dimensions* of human rights. For more than fifty years, considerable effort at the international level has been made to put some explanatory meat onto the bones of the starkly stated duties of states expressed in IHRL. The intention has been to establish some uniformity in standards or outcomes while leaving open the possibility of differences in method and approach. The ECtHR has produced a sizable jurisprudence on the nuances involved in protecting basic civil and political rights, and various UN human rights treaty bodies (especially the Committee on Economic, Social and Cultural Rights; the Committee on the Elimination of Racial Discrimination; the Committee on the Elimination of Discrimination against Women [CEDAW]; and Committee on the Rights of the Child [CRC]) have provided guidance regarding the parameters within which the progressive realization of economic and social rights can be achieved. With respect to the latter, these efforts to explain and guide have been broader and shallower. As a rule, international tribunals have been barred from addressing complaints in the same way they do civil and political rights (or at least have been reluctant to do so). But even here, some ground has been made up by the involvement of civil society organizations alongside states and international organs in the production of aids like the Limburg Principles and the Maastricht Guidelines, which advance notions like "core minimum standards" of economic and social rights and what practical steps these entail. They have also been instrumental in attempts – incomplete and inchoate as they are – to align socioeconomic rights with development objectives (Uvin 2004; Darrow and Arbour 2009), as represented by the debates over human rights–based approaches to development (Darrow and Tomas 2005), the existence of a right

---

[30] Fredman (2009) draws on J. Habermas, *Between Facts and Norms: Contributions to a Discourse Theory of Law and Democracy* (Cambridge, MA: MIT Press, 1996).

4) The fourth grammatical feature draws out the *process orientation* of human rights. All international human rights regimes have processes through which states may be called to account regarding their compliance with the legal obligations to which they have signed up. In certain respects, this particular feature overlaps with the programmatic features of human rights under the previous point. But the processes I am concerned with here encompass human rights complaints and dispute settlement mechanisms as well as other forums for debate, deliberation, and direction. They also include periodic reporting and review, face-to-face hearings, country visits, technical assistance and advisory services, complaint handling and dispute settlement, sanctions, and enforcement follow-up, which are variously employed across the UN and regional human rights regimes.[31] All of these processes have a degree of regulatory formality, but there are also other informal avenues for dialogue and assistance within and around them. Indeed, it is often at this end of the spectrum of these accountability mechanisms that the greatest accommodation is made for pluralistic interpretations of human rights laws. The apparatus of the African Union (AU) that oversees the Banjul Charter (the African Charter on Human and Peoples' Rights), for example, has been designed to promote dialogue, conciliation, and recommendations rather than admonishment. It is true that an African Court of Human and Peoples' Rights finally (eight years after the adoption of its protocol in 1998) opened for business in 2006, but thus far only twenty-five of the fifty-three states of the AU have ratified the court's protocol, and the court itself has passed judgment in only one case.[32] Contemporaneous efforts to merge this court with the AU's other court (the African Court of Justice) have been greeted with even less enthusiasm, with only twenty-one signatories and (at the time of this writing) only two ratifications of the new court's protocol.[33] The AU's principal human rights organ therefore remains the African Commission on Human and Peoples' Rights, whose modus operandi has always been to settle disputes (between states or between individuals and states) through diplomatic negotiations that accord most closely with traditional African means of dispute settlement. As the commission's body of "jurisprudence" of such dispute settlement has grown, so

---

[31] See, generally, Chapters 9 and 10, which canvass the methods used by the Human Rights Council and Human Rights Committee, respectively, to hold states to account.

[32] *Judgment in the matter of Michelot Yogogombaye v. The Republic of Senegal*, application No. 001/2008 (15 December 2009), at http://www.african-court.org/en/cases/latest-judgments/.

[33] To be titled the African Court of Justice and Human Rights, the protocol to the new Court's Statute has been ratified only by Libya and Mali (as of August 2010), http://www.au.int/?q=treaties/OAU%26AU±treaties.

has its reputation and its wider acceptance among the member-states of the union (Jallow 2007).[34]

5) The fifth feature is the importance of the *international/domestic nexus* to the protection and promotion of IHRL. In terms of providing space and opportunity for the particular to influence the general, there is little to rival this fundamental axiom of international law. As the principal (though not sole) agents on the international stage *and* as the preeminent seats of effective legal implementation and enforcement, states are the conduits through which international law is channeled. In terms of IHRL, this necessitates recognizing the importance of domestic governments, societies, and cultures embracing human rights goals in the face of the relative powerlessness of international human rights regimes to do much about it if states cannot or do not want to play ball. Much of the overall aim of international human rights laws and the operations of its institutional apparatus is therefore focused on nurturing this capacity and will in domestic governments. The programmatic and procedural features discussed under points 3) and 4) are key to this endeavor, providing, respectively, international measures of guidance and accountability that, though directed toward all states equally, are nevertheless open to differential domestic adaptation.

6) The sixth and final factor yields a somewhat skewed dimension on human rights pluralism. It stems from the growing importance of the *international/international nexus*. This is the arena of global law that operates beyond purely *international* intercourse to encompass *supranational* relations. With the plethora of international lawmaking or regulatory organs now in place (estimated to be more than two thousand), each covering a particular area of international interest or concern, inter- or supranational legal specialism has become rife. The International Law Commission's 2006 report on the expansion and diversification of international law as finalized by Martti Koskenniemi (2006, para. 1.9) characterized the consequence of these circumstances as the fragmentation of international law. A peculiar consequence of such differentiation or plurality has been to invigorate the search for connections and common ground and resulted in a sort of "bricolage that attempts . . . to connect legal ensembles," to use Delmas-Marty's artful terminology. To be sure, there is cross-disciplinary competition, and there are conflicts in all this, but there have also been exchanges, especially between judicial/arbitral bodies, based on the sharing, borrowing, and/or insertion of regulatory principles,

---

[34] Though not sharing the same design, the American Commission on Human Rights enjoyed preeminence in human rights dispute settlement in Latin American during the 1970s and 1980s for the same reasons of pursuing negotiated rather than enforced settlements of disputes. Since those times, however, the commission's sister body, the American Court of Human Rights, has grown considerably in stature, and its output increased accordingly.

techniques, approaches, and processes, amounting to what some see as a system of global administrative law (Kingsbury, Krisch, and Stewart 2004). International development law and IHRL are both familiar sites for exchanges with other international law categories, as well as with each other.[35] There is, in other words, a vibrant "circulation of legal ideas through networks of academics, lawyers, and judges [that] entails a mixture of legal cultures" (Maduro 2009, 358).[36]

CONCLUSION

This essay is a brief examination of the choreography of human rights' seemingly impossible dance between the promise of universal prescription and the practice of facilitating difference. On closer inspection, it is their expression in international human rights *law* that reveals the inherent indeterminacy of human rights and their necessary openness to some degree of differential application – in a word, their "bendability." The development of a legal framework through which this process of qualification is mediated and regulated is a lot more sophisticated than is commonly supposed. It is far from perfect, but it is also far from crude opportunism. It is, furthermore, a framework that readily accommodates limited legal (as well as political, cultural, and economic) plurality. Parallel disciplines, such as the law (as well as the politics and economics) of development, can see this as an opportunity to engage with human rights – indeed, even to enlist human rights law to the development cause. Not through the artificiality of overblown claims of "human rights approaches to development" or the doomed efforts to resurrect the idea of a "right to development," but through an adoption of human rights on their own, innately accommodating terms. These can and should properly be read as vehicles sufficiently flexible to bend to the multifarious demands of development, but not so bendable as to dispense with standards that are widely accepted and adhered to. It is not the easiest of tricks to master, but to do so will bolster the means and methods of achieving not just the goals of development, but also those of human rights.

REFERENCES

Alston, Philip. 2005. "Ships Passing in the Night: The Current State of the Human Rights and Development Debate Seen through the Lens of the Millennium Development Goals." *Human Rights Quarterly* 27 (3): 755–829.

---

[35] On international development law intersections with international trade and financial regulation, see Sarkar (2009, 125–49); and on international development law and international human rights law, see Kinley (2009, chap. 3).

[36] Maduro quotes Neil Walker's perspective of this "legal openness to external legal arguments as one of sympathetic consideration": Maduro (2009, 358).

An-Na'im, Abdullahi. 1990. "Problems of Universal Cultural Legitimacy for Human Rights." In *Human Rights in Africa: Cross-Cultural Perspectives*, ed. A. An-Na'im and F. Deng, 331–67. Washington, DC: Brookings Institution Press.

Bakircioğlu, Onder. 2007. "The Application of the Margin of Appreciation Doctrine in Freedom of Expression and Public Morality Cases." *German Law Journal* 8 (7): 711–34.

Baxi, Upendra. 2002. *The Future of Human Rights*. New Delhi: Oxford University Press.

Chamblee, L. Elizabeth. 2004. "Rhetoric or Rights: When Culture and Religion Bar Girls' Right to Education." *Virginia Journal of International Law* 44 (4): 1073–1143.

Darrow, Mac, and Louise Arbour. 2009. "The Pillar of Glass: Human Rights in the Development Operations of the United Nations." *American Journal of International Law* 103 (3): 446–501.

Darrow, Mac, and Amparo Tomas. 2005. "Power, Capture and Conflict: A Call for Human Rights Accountability in Development Cooperation." *Human Rights Quarterly* 27 (2): 471–538.

Delmas-Marty, Mireille. 2009. *Ordering Pluralism*. Oxford: Hart Publishing.

Dembour, Marie B. 2006. *Who Believes in Human Rights?* Cambridge: Cambridge University Press.

Donovan, Dolores, and Getachew Assefa. 2003. "Homicide in Ethiopia: Human Rights, Federalism and Legal Pluralism." *American Journal of Comparative Law* 51 (3): 505–52.

Engle, Eric. 2009. "Third Party Effect of Fundamental Rights (Drittwirkung)." *Hanse Law Review* 5 (2): 165–73.

Evans, Tony. 2004. "Universal Human Rights: 'As Much Round and Round as Ever Onward.'" *International Journal of Human Rights* 7 (4): 155–68.

Fredman, Sandra. 2009. *Human Rights Transformed: Positive Rights and Positive Duties*. Oxford: Oxford University Press.

Gearty, Conor. 2008. "Doing Human Rights: Social Justice in a Post-Socialist Age." Speech delivered at the launch of the Las Casas Centre on Social Justice, Oxford, November 25.

Glendon, Mary Ann. 2001. *A World Made New: Eleanor Roosevelt and the Universal Declaration of Human Rights*. New York: Random House.

Golub, Stephen, ed. 2010. *Legal Empowerment: Practitioners' Perspectives*. Rome: International Development Law Organization.

Hutchinson, Michael. 1999. "The Margin of Appreciation Doctrine in the European Court of Human Rights." *International and Comparative Law Quarterly* 48 (3): 638–50.

Jallow, Hassan. 2007. *The Law of the African (Banjul) Charter on Human and Peoples' Rights*. Bloomington, IN: Trafford Publishing.

Inter-American Court of Human Rights. 2003. *Juridical Condition and Rights of the Undocumented Migrants (Advisory Opinion Requested by the United Mexican States)*, Case No. 18/03.

Kennedy, David. 2002. "The International Human Rights Movement: Part of the Problem?" *Harvard Human Rights Journal* 15: 101–25.

Kingsbury, Benedict, Nico Krisch, and Richard Stewart. 2004. "The Emergence of Global Administrative Law." International Law and Justice Working Paper 2004/1, Global Administrative Law Series, School of Law Institute for International Law and Justice, New York University.

Kinley, David. 2006. "Human Rights and the World Bank: Practice, Politics and Law." In *The World Bank Legal Review: Law, Equity, and Development*, vol. 2, ed. C. M. Sage and M. Woolcock, 353–83. Leiden: Martinus Nijhoff Publishers.

———. 2007. "Human Rights Fundamentalisms." *Sydney Law Review* 29 (4): 545–76.

———. 2009. *Civilising Globalisation*. Cambridge and New York: Cambridge University Press.
Koch, Ida E. 2009. *Human Rights as Indivisible Rights: The Protection of Socioeconomic Demands under the European Convention on Human Rights*. Leiden: Martinus Nijhoff Publishers.
Koskenniemi, Martti. 2006. *Fragmentation of International Law: Difficulties Arising from the Diversification and Expansion of International Law*. Report of the Study Group of the International Law Commission, UN Doc. A/CN.4/L.682, United Nations, New York.
Krzeminska-Vamvaka, Joanna. 2009. "Horizontal Effect of Fundamental Rights and Freedoms: Much Ado about Nothing? German, Polish and EU Theories Compared after *Viking Line*." Jean Monnet Working Paper 11/09, Jean Monnet Center for International and Regional Economic Law and Justice, New York University School of Law.
Maduro, Miguel. 2009. "Courts and Pluralism." In *Ruling the World? Constitutionalism, International Law and Global Governance*, ed. J. Dunoff and J. Trachtman, 356–80. Cambridge and New York: Cambridge University Press.
Mutua, Makau. 1996. "Ideology of Human Rights." *Virginia Journal of International Law* 36 (3): 589–658.
New Zealand Law Commission. 2006. *Converging Currents: Custom and Human Rights in the Pacific*. Wellington: New Zealand Law Commission.
OECD (Organisation for Economic Co-operation and Development). 2006. *The Development Dimension: Integrating Human Rights into Development: Donor Approaches, Experiences and Challenges*. Paris: OECD.
Sage, Caroline, Brian Tamanaha, and Michael Woolcock. 2011. "Legal Pluralism and Development Policy." In *Legal Pluralism and Development: Dialogues for Success*, ed. Caroline Sage, Michael Woolcock, and Brian Tamanaha. New York: Macmillan.
Sano, Hans O. 2000. "Development and Human Rights: The Necessary, but Partial Integration of Human Rights and Development." *Human Rights Quarterly* 22 (3): 734–52.
Sarkar, Rumu. 2009. *International Development Law: Rule of Law, Human Rights and Global Finance*. New York: Oxford University Press.
Scaglion, Richard. 2003. "Legal Pluralism in Pacific Island Societies." In *Globalization and Cultural Change in the Pacific Islands*, ed. V. Lockwood, 86–101. Upper Saddle River, NJ: Prentice Hall.
Steiner, Henry, Philip Alston, and Ryan Goodman. 2008. *International Human Rights in Context: Law, Politics, Morals: Texts and Materials*. 3rd ed. New York: Oxford University Press.
Uvin, Peter. 2004. *Human Rights and Development*. Bloomfield, CT: Kumarian Press.
Yasuaki, Onuma. 1999. "Towards an Intercivilisational Approach to Human Rights." In *The East Asian Challenge for Human Rights*, ed. J. Bauer and D. Bell, 103–23. Cambridge: Cambridge University Press.

4

Legal Pluralism and Legal Culture

Mapping the Terrain

Sally Engle Merry

The concept of legal pluralism has proved enormously fruitful in challenging ideas about the centrality of state law and increasing awareness of the diversity of ways that individuals interact with the law. In exploring access to justice, it is essential to recognize the variety of forms of justice that individuals have available to them, the nature of each regime, the relations among them, and the variations in accessibility of each. However, in assessing the contribution of legal pluralism analysis to questions about access to justice, it is important to define the constituent units of legal pluralism carefully. The concepts of legal culture and legal consciousness are valuable frameworks for describing the distinct legal spheres within a legally plural field. Moreover, the concept of legal mobilization, along with its relationship to legal culture and legal consciousness, provides a dynamic way of understanding how legal pluralism affects access to justice in practice.

Using these concepts, it is possible to ask, in what ways are legal spheres different? How does that difference affect the kinds of justice they deliver? How do these differences shape the extent to which individuals resort to each sphere? How do different patterns of mobilizing distinct legal spheres shape legal culture and legal consciousness? This chapter seeks to clarify some of these issues by unpacking the meanings of legal culture, legal consciousness, and legal mobilization and then showing how disentangling these concepts contributes to our understanding of legal pluralism. It then uses a case study to illustrate these concepts. The case study focuses on the *nari adalat*, a women's court developed in Gujarat in western India. Inspired by the Indian women's movement, human rights ideas, and the long-established village governance and judicial system of the *panchayat*, the *nari adalat* is a new legal forum embedded within other legal institutions. It expands the plurality of legal spheres for everyday life in Gujarat and increases access to justice. This means that it has the potential to provide a new form of legal mobilization and to foster a different legal culture and legal consciousness.

THE CONCEPT OF LEGAL PLURALISM

The concept of legal pluralism, as used within anthropological scholarship, describes the multiple forms law takes within particular communities, regions, or nations. Legally plural situations have different but coexisting conceptions of permissible actions, valid transactions, and ideas and procedures for dealing with conflict in the same social field (Merry 1988; K. Benda-Beckmann 2001; F. Benda-Beckmann 2002, 38). They are typically organized around differing conceptions of justice. A critical concern of work in legal pluralism is the nature of the interactions among legal spheres.

The most obvious forms of legal pluralism are the product of colonialism. During colonialism, the colonial power typically added a new layer of law and justice conceptions over existing ones. On occasion, colonial law recognized earlier systems of law, such as the British colonial incorporation of Hindu, Muslim, and Christian personal law into the administration of the Indian empire. The systems often have incompatible standards and procedures, and it is not unusual for individuals to engage in forum shopping among them (K. Benda-Beckmann 1981, 1984).

Although some of the first work on legal pluralism imagined that relatively separate legal systems coexist, as they did in the dual legal systems common to British colonialism (see Mamdani 1996), Sally Falk Moore's notion of the "semi-autonomous social field" argued that regulatory subgroups existed in industrial societies as well (1973). Rather than seeing plural legal systems as circumscribed and bounded, she argued that they are semiautonomous, operating within other social fields but not entirely governed by them. Building on this conceptualization, legal pluralism research explores both the nature of each legal system and its intersections with others. There are global, regional, national, and local legal systems, such as international law, European Union law, national law, and local regulations, layered on top of informal modes of ordering in families, communities, and workplaces. Forms of normative ordering exist outside state law in all societies, sometimes based in institutions such as universities or corporations as private law (Macaulay 1986) and sometimes governing social life in more informal ways.

To a large extent, the roots of contemporary pluralities of global law are buried in the colonial era. Although there were significant transplants and transnational adoptions of law in the period before 1500, the imperial era from the sixteenth to the twentieth centuries represented an unprecedented expansion of legal systems, primarily from the colonial powers in Europe and North America to Latin America, Asia, and Africa. At the same time, the nature of law itself in metropoles was transformed, incorporating concepts of race and difference into its basic fabric and developing new technologies of governance and rule (Comaroff and Comaroff 1991, 1997; Fitzpatrick 1992; Benton 2001, 2009). The legacy of this historical process is a complex legal pluralism, in which overlapping, porous, and contradictory legal systems coexist with one another. The colonial process created a layered system of legalities of unequal powers and distinct jurisdictions.

Legal borrowing has continued apace in the postcolonial era, as newly emerging democracies such as those in Eastern Europe have borrowed legal codes from elsewhere. There has been extensive adoption of constitutions, commercial codes, and discrete legal systems from one country to another. Finally, there has been an expansion in international law, originally focused largely on the regulation of commerce and relations between states, but increasingly, in the postcolonial era, seeking to regulate the legal relations between citizens and their states, economic relationships, the cultural integrity of indigenous peoples, and the status of vulnerable populations such as racial minorities, women, and children. As the human rights system has expanded in the postwar period, it has reached into new domains of social life. Thus, the contemporary world holds a rich diversity of coexisting, overlapping, contradictory, and complementary systems of law at the local, national, and international levels, a system produced to an important extent by processes of colonialism and postcolonialism. The diverse and sometimes fragmented rules and courts that make up international law have been described as global legal pluralism (Berman 2005a, 2005b).

The result is a layered legal pluralism. The geological metaphor suggests simple contiguity and chronological order, but in practice, each system affects the operation of the other. Change comes through appeals from one system to another or through multiple and overlapping jurisdictions leading to forum shopping and inconsistency. As the systems interact with one another, they redefine one another's concepts and practices, although not equally, because legal spheres typically differ in power and influence. Over time, these interactions change the constituent legal systems. Imposed or introduced systems are also transformed by these interactions as parts of them are mobilized and others resisted. Moreover, introduced systems are rarely adopted in whole cloth but are appropriated piecemeal or in an altered condition. The important question for understanding legal pluralism and access to justice is the relationship among the constituent layers. The current process of globalization and associated efforts to expand rule of law systems has fostered the formation of a new layer of law. This includes global regulation of trade, commerce, and labor rights as well as legal regimes to protect human rights.

Understanding law in contemporary postcolonial societies requires an archeology of law: a historical unpacking of this complexity. Postcolonial states now confront hybrid systems of law, sometimes remnants of dual legal systems designed to provide separate justice to European and "native" peoples. Such systems were thought of as European law and customary law, but customary law systems were typically produced through interactions between European law and local law. These interactions occurred under conditions of unequal power relations and expanding capitalism. Noncolonized peoples sometimes appropriated extensive aspects of European law in order to construct a "civilized" society that could take a place in the European order of sovereign nations instead of in the ranks of the colonies, a strategy pursued by Thailand as well as Hawaii (Merry 2000).

Even in noncolonized states, law is deeply pluralized. Noncolonized states often incorporate indigenous peoples or immigrant communities with separate legal systems. Legacies of internal colonialism leave subordinated populations struggling to retain distinctive sovereignties and legal orders, such as indigenous peoples. Privatization has increased reliance on non-state forms of governance, ranging from internal judicial procedures within organizations to private policing and surveillance systems. The spread of alternative dispute resolution mechanisms to many aspects of legal regulation has diversified the procedures of law along with its outcomes and forms of regulation. All of these non-state forms of law interact with state law, shaping the nature of state law itself.

An increasingly powerful transnational law system provides the legal regulation for transnational business, whereas a burgeoning human rights system located in transnational actors such as the United Nations (UN) and nongovernmental organizations (NGOs) augments and at some points displaces nation-state systems of rights and protections for citizens. Legal transfers and transplants are rapidly Americanizing the law in many parts of the world, particularly in the area of commercial law. The modern development agenda promotes reforms of courts and the expansion of the rule of law in Latin America, Africa, and Asia (Carothers 2006). At the same time, ethno-national movements and indigenous peoples in various parts of the world are clamoring for political sovereignty and autonomous legal orders, relying on human rights law. Postcolonial states strive to quash these demands, seeking legal unification as the basis for nation building. Movements of illegal immigrants and refugees create pockets of alternative legalities among groups denied full citizenship in the states they inhabit. Thus, shifting form of legal regulation and changing relations between legal orders are fundamental to the changes in the shape of legal pluralism accompanying contemporary globalization.

The plurality of legal spheres only increased with the globalization of labor and capital and the concomitant expansion of international forms of regulation and governance in the late twentieth and early twenty-first centuries. The burgeoning transborder movements of people, capital, ideas, and products spawned a proliferation of systems of regulation. Global legal regimes such as human rights, women's rights, and indigenous rights have emerged, along with mechanisms to regulate the circulation of intellectual property, trafficked persons, and illegal migrants. Globalization has produced new regional and global legal orders and fostered new kinds of interactions between these and local and national legal orders.

The emergence of transnational legal regulations has redefined sovereignty and, some argue, fostered the fracturing of the nation-state. It creates legal space to demand autonomous local legalities and self-determination. Native self-determination – the assertion of a separate legal system and identity – is often framed in terms of international law (Biolsi 1995; Jackson 2007; Speed 2008). Yet these claims confront the struggles of postcolonial states to unify their legal systems and crush localisms. Thus, this new pluralism represents a shift from the centrality of the state as the source of legal ordering to a more layered and contested social field. The creation of the modern state involved efforts to capture and control disputing processes, to extinguish local forms, and to develop uniformity, but there was always a tension – some resistance to this capture in the form of legalities that are not within state control. The rise of new, internationally based forms of legal pluralism shifts this balance between state and local law.

Indeed, legal pluralism can be seen as the key concept in a postmodern view of law (Santos 1995, 456). In making this argument, Santos adopts the metaphor of the map to suggest that law is a system of signs that, like maps, represent or distort reality through the mechanisms of scale, projection, and symbolization (1995). Different legal orders, like maps, have different scales, different forms of projection and centering, different systems of symbolization. A theory of unequal but mutually constitutive legal orders leads to new questions: How do these systems interact and reshape one another? To what extent is the dominant system able to control the subordinate? How do subordinate systems subvert or evade the dominant system? Are there ways in which the disputing strategies of subordinate users reshape the dominant system? To what extent do contests among plural legal systems explain historical change? To address these questions, this chapter suggests looking at legal pluralism through the lens of three distinct concepts: legal culture, legal consciousness, and legal mobilization.

LEGAL CULTURE

The constituent units of legal pluralism are distinct legal regimes, typically with separate rules, logics, and practices. There are of course overlaps and similarities as well as differences among them. One way to describe these regimes is as more or less distinct legal cultures. In this sense, each has a shared set of ideas about justice, about how to determine truth, and about how to rectify injustice. These legal regimes are often linked to a particular group or territory.

One way to analyze legal culture, developed by Clifford Geertz in the early 1980s, is to see law not just as a bounded set of norms, rules, and principles but as a frame within which the world is made sense of, "part of a distinctive way of imagining the real" (1983, 184). In his interpretive theory of culture, culture is a system of meaning, incorporating symbols that are shared and public. These symbols and systems of symbols constitute, communicate, and alter structures of meaning in the domain of law as well as other domains of social life (1983, 182). Geertz advocates a hermeneutic approach rather than a functional one, arguing that "meaning, not machinery" is the fundamental problem (1983). The concept of legal culture in this tradition sees law as a set of cultural principles and categories crystallized into legal concepts (see also Rosen 1989, 2006). To compare Islamic, Indic, and customary *adat* law in

Indonesia, for example, he seeks to evoke a culture by picking key terms and using these as avenues to explore systems of thinking and practice. His analysis is based not on behavior but on cultural categories embodied in key terms (Geertz 1983, 183). For example, to analyze how lower courts address day-to-day social problems and conflicts, this approach focuses on how the court renders interpretations of them in terms of a particular "legal sensibility" enshrined in the judicial forum (Geertz 1983). Law is local knowledge, "vernacular characterizations of what happens connected to vernacular imaginings of what can" (Geertz 1983, 215). Work in this tradition explores the fundamental categories of meaning embedded in law and culture. Thus, it provides a way to contrast the distinct cultural spaces that constitute a legally plural social field.

LEGAL CONSCIOUSNESS

Legal consciousness is a term developed to describe the way individuals experience and understand the law and its relevance to their lives. In their study of the way Americans respond to a variety of problems, Patricia Ewick and Susan Silbey argue that legal consciousness refers to a limited set of narratives that ordinary Americans have about the law, which they characterize as "before the law," "with the law," and "against the law" (1998). These represent three distinct schemas, or cognitive maps, through which individuals see themselves in the world. These are ways of understanding how the law works with relationship to the self. Anyone may have more than one schema, deployed at different times depending on the situation.

Legal consciousness is defined through experience. An individual's legal consciousness grows out of the cultural space in which he or she lives but is also inflected by his or her own experience. The person who feels entitled to use the law and has an experience that reinforces his or her view will probably develop a different legal consciousness than the person who is ignored or finds his or her claims belittled. Legal consciousness is, in other words, acquired as part of an individual's cultural repertoire but can change with experience, particularly experiences with the legal system. From a legal pluralism perspective, the multiple legal spheres in any social field will be understood differently depending on a person's experience, identity, and embeddedness in various cultural groups. In other words, an individual will develop and refine his or her legal consciousness with relation to each legal sphere he or she encounters.

For example, the battered women's movement in the United States emphasizes to women who have experienced domestic violence that they have the right not to be hit no matter what they do, and that battering is a crime for which they are entitled to help from the state (Merry 2003). For women whose experience shows that the police and courts support the criminalization of domestic violence, the idea that domestic violence is a crime may well become part of their legal consciousness. However, those who find the police and courts dismissive, the penalties trivial to nonexistent, or the system corrupt are unlikely to adopt a legal consciousness defining domestic violence as a crime. They will retain a skeptical legal consciousness about the role of law for domestic violence cases. They may, of course, have different experiences with different legal spheres, so that they see themselves as entitled to help from one legal sphere but not another. In any legal sphere, positive experiences will reinforce legal consciousness within that sphere, whereas negative ones will diminish that consciousness. Despite significant efforts to teach people that they have rights, including human rights, without positive feedback it tends to disintegrate. Thus, the extent to which an individual adopts a consciousness of legal entitlement in any legal regime depends on its response to his or her requests for help.

Legal consciousness is also based on ideas about who is entitled to make a claim. Claims are based on membership in communities, regions, nations, or the international world. In order to make claims on a state legal system, for example, it is necessary for an individual to conceive of himself or herself as a citizen in a cultural and social as well as a legal sense. James Holston argues that in the growing population of the urban poor in Brazil, there is an increasing consciousness of citizenship and a concomitant rise in political activism and sense of entitlement (2008). Those who assert human rights claims tend to imagine themselves as world citizens as well as members of states and communities. Many forms of local justice are available to those who identify with a community or ethno-national group (see Merry 1993). In sum, legal consciousness is the interpretive framework an individual develops based on his or her socialization into various culturally patterned legal spheres and his or her experiences with them.

LEGAL MOBILIZATION

Another approach to understanding legal pluralism is through an examination of legal mobilization. This concept describes the tendency for various individuals and groups to define their problems as legal ones and take them to some legal regime for help or settlement. Once individuals decide that they have a grievance that demands action, they typically choose among a series of legal or quasi-legal forums (see Nader and Todd 1978; Benda-Beckmann 1981). How people handle a problem depends on how they conceive it in the first place and what kinds of options they think are available to them, as well as the costs and benefits of each. Costs and benefits can be financial, moral, social, or religious, among others.

Research on dispute processes show that not all problems are thought of as legal issues, nor do those who think their problems are legal necessarily take them to the legal system. When and how a problem becomes a legal one is highly contextual. Some research has tracked the trajectory of disputes, exploring when and why a person comes to see an experience as injurious and under what conditions that problem is brought to the attention of the legal system (Mather and Yngvesson 1980/81; Felstiner, Abel, and Sarat 1981; Merry 1990). Some problems are more readily defined as legal than others, and some problems, even when thought of as legal, lead to relatively little mobilization of the formal legal system. Civil rights violations (Bumiller 1992) and street harassment (Nielsen 2006) are both examples of this reluctance to use the law. Some groups refuse to define their problems as legal or to mobilize the legal system. For example, in her study of a Southern Baptist community, Carol Greenhouse found a religiously based reluctance to take problems to the legal system and a preference for prayer (Greenhouse 1989), and Carol Greenhouse, David Engel, and Barbara Yngvesson analyze variations in the way Americans in different communities mobilize the law (1994).

Social movements also mobilize the law, both at the domestic level by calling on civil rights and at the international level by referring to human rights (McCann 1994; Keck and Sikkink 1998; Merry et al. 2010). Social movements may use law directly in litigation strategies or more aspirationally as a source of standards and norms and common ground for building alliances. Even in the absence of litigation, rights concepts such as human rights offer fertile sources of inspiration for activists and contribute to the use of law "from below" (Rodriguez-Garavito 2005; Santos and Rodriguez-Garavito 2005). Social movements that mobilize legal arguments are likely to enhance the legal consciousness of state law, international law, or other legal spheres.

As the discussion of these concepts suggests, understanding legal pluralism requires the analysis of a social field in terms of its constituent legal cultures and the varieties of legal consciousness and practices of legal mobilization among its population. Clearly, these are interconnected phenomena. The choice of forum depends on an individual's legal consciousness, which is itself a product of the social world in which he or she lives. Experience with one or another forum can shift a person's views about his or her legal consciousness and thus the forum to which he or she will appeal next time. A pattern of shifting legal consciousness will gradually redefine local legal cultures. Recourse to human rights forums, for example, if they provide some kind of framework and help to a complainant, can lead to a new legal consciousness of rights and ultimately to a new sense of entitlement. Meanwhile, the creation of new legal regimes offers new opportunities for legal mobilization, leading to a new legal consciousness. Finally, the changes in legal culture, engendered by social movements that mobilize legal regimes, can inspire new practices of legal mobilization.

A CASE STUDY OF LEGAL PLURALISM: THE *NARI ADALAT*

In order to demonstrate the value of addressing these three dimensions of legal pluralism, I examine the operation of a new legal forum, the *nari adalat* or women's court, created in India in the mid-1990s to promote women's human rights, particularly in situations of domestic violence. These courts merged ideas of women's human rights, Indian feminism, women's empowerment and development, and traditional local governance by councils. They were formed by local women leaders paid a stipend by a women's empowerment program to develop community development programs. After some consultation concerning local needs, village women in one part of western India organized women's courts to help with domestic violence, divorce, and dowry returns. Although the ideology and training the women received focused on empowerment and human rights, the women who developed and maintained these courts joined local norms, government authority, and references to human rights to settle everyday problems. The *nari adalats* added a new legal sphere to the already existing system of state law and legal aid services, village *panchayats*, and informal family and community mediation.

The *nari adalat* in Gujarat state was thriving when I visited one of its sessions in 2005 along with Peggy Levitt; N. Rajaram of the Department of Sociology, Maharaja Sayajirao University of Baroda; and Vaishali Zararia, our research assistant. We were working together on a National Science Foundation–funded study of the vernacularization of women's human rights in four parts of the world (Levitt and Merry 2009; Rajaram and Zararia 2009). The research focused on two women's NGOs in each of the following locations: Beijing, China; Baroda, India; Lima, Peru; and New York City. The court met once a week in the village square of a town called Padra – a hot, dry plaza with a large tree in the center that was surrounded by a raised concrete platform. The police station faced the square on one side, the courthouse on another. About fifteen women of middle age, including some gray-haired older women, traveled there each week from surrounding villages and towns. They held a court for women seeking help with problems such as husbands who beat them or who refused to return a portion of their dowry following their divorce.

Although a community court, or *panchayat*, is a familiar feature of village and caste life in rural, small-town India, a *panchayat* consisting only of women is highly unusual. The *nari adalat* was inspired by a women's development program funded by the Dutch government and administered by the Indian government's Department of Education. The program created local women's collectives, or *sanghas*, and asked each to identify problems they wanted to redress. Domestic violence and divorce emerged as core issues. The women created a women's *panchayat* with support from the women's development program and later from a local women's NGO. Its members received several weeks of training in feminism, law, and human rights from national NGOs in Delhi. When we visited the court, it had been operating for almost fifteen years. Most women volunteered; only two or three leaders received a small stipend for their work. Because violence in the home was a major concern to many of the village women, the women's collectives developed a system of women's courts to handle domestic violence, divorce, and other family conflicts.

The system of *nari adalats* emerged in Gujarat in 1995 and in Uttar Pradesh in 1998 (ICRW 2002, 34). These were informal courts intended to handle women's legal problems. A 2001 study reported that in the six years since they had been initiated, the four *adalats* in the Vadodara district had handled about 1,200 cases of marital violence, harassment, divorce, maintenance, property, and child custody and successfully resolved a majority of these. The clients were mostly low caste and tribal women (Krishnamurthy 2002, 3).

We watched one case in which a young woman dressed in a demure green dress with a head scarf complained that her husband beat her. The husband, who had been summoned to appear at the court, retorted that she deserved to be beaten because she was such a poor cook. The women seated in judgment raised their voices as one to challenge this claim, arguing that young women don't deserve to be beaten under any circumstances. Undeterred, the man's father, standing by his son's side, reiterated that the woman deserved what she got. Although the woman's father, who lingered timidly in the background, said nothing in his daughter's defense, the *nari adalat* leaders sternly criticized the husband. A crowd of some twenty-five to thirty men stood on the outskirts of the circle, watching with fascination as the husband was upbraided and told not do this again. Some of the people in the audience were lawyers, dressed in white shirts and black pants, hoping to pick up a case. During this public event, new standards were articulated for how husbands should treat their wives, performed in front of this mixed-gender audience.

The women of the *nari adalat* are informal leaders in the villages surrounding this town, but they are also connected to the state. They record all cases in an official book, require small filing fees, and issue decisions on legal stamp papers. Some also resolve cases on their own in their hometowns for a small fee. The support of local headmen, the use of state legal formalities, access to a government of India jeep through the women's development program, and occasional support by police all help convince male defendants that they must appear and face the accusations of their wives and family members. However, the women "judges" also say they are part of an NGO. Their work is currently supported by an NGO, and its origins were in the work of a women's NGO also connected to the state.

These women say they are using human rights. But when we asked them what human rights mean, they said that they didn't really know and wanted to know what we thought. In their practices of case handling, they told women that they should stand up for themselves, that they did not have to be hit, and that if they divorced their husbands, they could take some of their dowry property with them. Yet their opposition to domestic violence bore little resemblance to the human rights documents that laid the foundation for their intervention. They did not cite articles, sections, or texts from the Committee on the Elimination of Discrimination against Women. Instead, they insisted that women should stand up for themselves and modeled that through their own actions. They translated the language of human rights produced in New York, Geneva, Vienna, and Beijing into a set of ideas that made sense locally. They argued that a woman can oppose the violence of her husband and family, which in many places is a radical idea. Thus, this new legal regime articulated a legal culture concerning women's position in the family and the relevance of the local courts to domestic violence that combined Indian law, Indian feminism, and human rights.

The *nari adalat* is new, but caste *panchayats* as judicial forums are ancient in India (see Galanter 1989), and the village *panchayat* is a widely established government initiative. In 1974, the government of India's Committee on the Status of Women issued a report, *Towards Equality*, that proposed establishing women's *panchayats*, although they had not yet been created at the time. As the focus on women's development shifted from a concern with women's welfare in the 1960s to the productive roles of women within the modernization paradigm in the 1970s and 1980s to a more feminist vision bent on challenging social inequalities and promoting a radical vision of women's empowerment in the mid-1980s, however, the idea of a women's *panchayat* reemerged (Sharma 2008). The Women's Development Program in Rajasthan and the *Mahila Samakya* program, the development program that inspired the *nari adalats*, both developed local women's empowerment groups. These programs drew on leaders of the women's movement in India, who were connected to global feminist movements, to train local leaders.

Nari adalats developed in Gujarat, Uttar Pradesh, and a few other states from a government-initiated program to develop women's collectives in villages. They were also shaped by a long tradition of women's movement activism against violence against women. The parent program, called *Mahila Samakhya* (MS), is a national-level rural women's "empowerment" program started by the Department of Education of the government of India in 1989 with funding from the Dutch government (ICRW 2002). The MS program endeavored to promote gender equality, development, and social change by empowering poor women and providing them with the knowledge and self-confidence to make changes (Poonacha and Pandey 1999, 161; ICRW 2002, 32–65; Sharma 2006). The program introduced human rights ideas to its clientele of poor, illiterate women, many of whom are tribals or Dalits, low-caste people. Domestic violence was a core concern (ICRW 2002, 70).

The philosophy of the MS program is that decision making should rest with local-level collectives. The program depends on a cadre of women activists, or *sahyoginis*, who develop and encourage *sanghas*, or women's collectives, in each village. Each *sahyogini* works with a cluster of ten villages. The MS program straddles the government/NGO divide, claiming whichever identity seems most helpful at the moment (Sharma 2006). It functions in the autonomous fashion of an NGO in some contexts and as a government program in others. Personnel are paid by the government but are not government employees and receive less than government workers (Sharma 2006). The largely female workforce lacks job security, pensions, and health benefits and is poorly paid.

During the first four years of the MS program, participants were trained by Jagori, a feminist resource and training center in Delhi (see Krishnamurthy 2002, 42). Seventeen women were trained as paralegals with a feminist critique of the legal system and alternative definitions of violence against women and divorce (ICRW

2002, 49). When I visited Jagori in 2001, the director said that the program puts a strong emphasis on women's rights but that they were inspired more by national than international law. They sometimes refer to international conventions and treaties, but Indian sources of inspiration are more important. The *nari adalat* articulates and enacts this diverse set of legal principles.

The *nari adalat* consists of a core team of *sahyoginis* and selected *sangha* women, most of whom have poor literacy skills and many of whom are Dalits, people of low caste status (ICRW 2002, 36). The members of the *nari adalat* tour the district, meeting on regular days and times in public places near government offices to dispense legal advice and settle marital disputes (Poonacha and Pandey 1999, 161–78). They are not paid, nor is their transportation covered. They have no legal authority but rely on pressure and shaming. Like the parent MS program, they straddle the government/NGO divide, claiming either identity as it seems helpful (Sharma 2006).

> Krishnamurthy's ethnography describes how *nari adalats* move creatively between community and state to gain recognition in the villages and access to formal institutions (2002, 12, 51). The women meet in government compounds close to police and local government offices, assert their status as part of the official MS program, use state symbols such as files, stamp paper, and seals, call on the police for protection, and cite formal laws to support their decisions as they were trained to do by urban activists. At the same time, they reflect the communities they come from. They use humor and shaming to pressure litigants, adjust their meeting times to the rhythms of village life, and use their knowledge of local practices, customs, and social networks to gather evidence and negotiate agreements. They do not try to end marriages but emphasize the rights of the woman within marriage (ICRW 2002, 51). Their authority is limited, and they seem to be most successful in helping women arrange divorces and escape violent marriages, particularly among poor families. They are less successful with wealthy families and with cases of rape and molestation, which require greater evidentiary effort (2002, 99).

Nevertheless, an International Center for Research on Women (ICRW) study in 1999–2000 indicated that the operation of these courts and the closely related *mahila panch* (Women's Councils) made violence in the home a more open and public offense. ICRW evaluations of these programs indicate that *sangha* and *sahyogini* women and those who experienced the *nari adalats* were more aware of their rights and better able to speak up (2002, 40–41, 54). A counterculture based on resisting violence in terms of the intrinsic rights of women is developing slowly, largely in local terms: "Research documented the innovative ways in which activists use their local knowledge to reshape and reinterpret community idioms, phrases and beliefs to create and persuade the community to adopt new perspectives" (ICRW 2002, 72). As they promote the ideology of human rights, some women say they have learned to stand up for themselves.

LEGAL PLURALISM AND THE *NARI ADALAT*

The *nari adalat* is only one of several alternative approaches that a woman might take to solving everyday problems of violence and divorce. During the 1980s, the women's movement established centers to provide women with legal aid, health care, and counseling and branched out into a wide range of issues such as employment generation and slum improvement work (Kumar 1995, 75–83). In towns near the *nari adalat*, some women took similar problems to an NGO that offered legal aid through a lawyer who volunteered her time. She helped them use the courts or resolve problems through more informal legal means.

Women facing domestic violence can also use the formal legal system, filing a complaint with the police. India's penal code covers domestic violence, defined as cruelty by a husband or his relatives to his wife, in section 498A of the Indian Penal Code (Lawyers' Collective 1992, 36). A legal aid handbook dates the law to 1983 and says it is the "first time the crime of violence specifically against a woman by her husband was recognized in law" (Lawyers' Collective 1992, 36). The term *domestic violence* was unknown until recently, according to an attorney at the Lawyers' Collective, with the term *cruelty* used instead.

Another alternative in domestic disputes involving dowry is special dowry police stations. These special police stations were established in 1989 in Bangalore (Poonacha and Pandey 1999, 76–77) and in 1983 in Delhi (interview, Special Cell 2001). Each of the nine police districts of Delhi has such a cell. In 2001, I visited a dowry police station in Delhi called a Special Cell for Crimes against Women and Children. This station handles about 7,500 cases a year and has eighteen police inspectors working there. It also runs a police helpline available around the clock. The commissioner of police emphasized to me that this is not a police station, but a place that deals with domestic violence and dowry, generally through reconciliation and a settlement. In 2000, 23 percent of cases were reconciled through counseling, including those resolved with the assistance of professional counselors from the Central Social Welfare Board. However, this system tends to define all marital problems, including violence, as derived from dowry disputes.

In 2005, India passed a domestic violence law that focuses on protecting women rather than punishing perpetrators. The law contains provisions for protection orders prohibiting domestic violence as well as entering the home or workplace of the person aggrieved or making any attempt to contact that person or alienating any assets held by both parties, including a woman's *stridhan* (the property a woman brings to the marriage). It protects a woman's right to reside in her home of marriage. It also creates a system of protection for officers to assist the court in carrying out these provisions and provides for imprisonment for those who violate protection orders. Thus, this law offers a series of remedies other than punishment of the perpetrator.

Despite this range of options available through the legal system, many women do not turn to a legal forum at all, but seek help within systems of family and neighborhood. And some simply endure the violence and dispossession in the belief that there is no alternative. This comparison shows that there is a series of alternatives open to battered women, although they differ significantly in cost, accessibility, and effectiveness. The strength of the *nari adalat* is that it is one of the most accessible, requiring only a small filing fee, and it is committed to supporting women. It is one option within a legally plural world.

CONCLUSIONS

The women's court is a new legal regime that offers another legal option for women. Women who previously sought help from the caste or village *panchayat* or the state legal system now have another choice. Not only has the *nari adalat* changed patterns of legal mobilization, but it has also changed the legal culture. Using ideas of empowerment, "standing up for yourself," and human rights, the *nari adalat* articulates and enacts a new understanding of women's roles in marriage and husbands' rights over them. The women's court calls male authority into question and challenges the automatic inheritance of property through male descent groups. As women mobilize this legal regime so that their cases are heard in the public square, a new cultural view of women's roles and of the responsibility of legal institutions is articulated and performed to a large and attentive male audience. Women's rights over part of their dowry at divorce and their rights not to be treated cruelly, although principles already embedded in Indian law, are made explicit by the actions of the *nari adalats*. This adds one more dimension to an already plural legal regime.

As they participate in this forum, it appears that these women develop new ideas about their entitlement to help from the legal system. Insofar as the court is able to enforce its decisions, it helps them develop a new legal consciousness of their rights and their entitlement to legal help. In one case, a woman came to the court complaining about being beaten, and her husband and his father standing behind him shouted back that she had performed her housework poorly and deserved it. In front of the audience of perhaps forty men standing around, the cluster of women who made up the court rose up as one, shouting back that he should not hit her, no matter what she does. Although it is hard to know to what extent this woman developed a new consciousness, it is clear that her experience of violence was being redefined as a violation, and that this was done in a public setting with a large number of male observers. She returned the next week for further assistance from the women's court. As the legal mobilization of such a forum leads to a changed legal consciousness, it will be used more often, especially if it is able to act effectively to help women. Such practices can change broader cultures of gender and violence and perhaps even the legal culture itself.

In sum, theoretically disentangling the concepts of legal culture, legal consciousness, and legal mobilization helps to illuminate how legal pluralism affects access to justice for the poor and marginalized populations that have traditionally been excluded from legal regimes or denied justice when they seek them out. It provides insight into why such populations might not use existing legal institutions and suggests approaches to making them more available and more frequently used. And it shows how new, more accessible options can transform everyday practices and consciousness.

REFERENCES

Benda-Beckmann, Franz von. 2002. "Who's Afraid of Legal Pluralism?" *Journal of Legal Pluralism* 47: 37–82.

Benda-Beckmann, Keebet von. 1981. "Forum Shopping and Shopping Forums: Dispute Processing in a Minangkabau Village in West Sumatra." *Journal of Legal Pluralism* 19: 117–59.

———. 1984. *The Broken Stairways to Consensus: Village Justice and State Courts in Minangkabau*. Dordrecht: Foris Publications.

———. 2001. "Transnational Dimensions of Legal Pluralism." In *Begegnung und Konflikt – eine kulturanthropologische Bestandsaufname*, ed. W. Fikentscher, 33–48. Muenchen: Verlag der Bayerischen Akademie der Wissenschaften, C. H. Beck Verlag.

Benton, Lauren. 2001. *Law and Colonial Cultures: Legal Regimes in World History, 1400–1900*. Cambridge: Cambridge University Press.

———. 2009. *A Search for Sovereignty: Law and Geography in European Empires, 1400–1900*. Cambridge: Cambridge University Press.

Berman, Paul Schiff. 2005a. "Towards a Cosmopolitan Vision of Conflict of Laws: Redefining Governmental Interests in a Global Era." *University of Pennsylvania Law Review* 153 (6): 1819.

———. 2005b. "From International Law to Law and Globalization." *Columbia Journal of Transnational Law* 43 (2): 485–556.

Biolsi, Thomas. 1995. "Bringing the Law Back In: Legal Rights and the Regulation of Indian-White Relations on Rosebud Reservation." *Current Anthropology* 36 (4): 543–71.

Bumiller, Kristin. 1992. *The Civil Rights Society: The Social Construction of Victims*. Baltimore: Johns Hopkins University Press.

Carothers, Thomas. 2006. "The Rule-of-Law Revival." In *Promoting the Rule of Law Abroad: In Search of Knowledge*, ed. Thomas Carothers, 3–15. Washington, DC: Carnegie Endowment for International Peace.

Comaroff, Jean, and John L. Comaroff. 1991. *Of Revelation and Revolution: Christianity, Colonialism, and Consciousness in South Africa*. Vol. I. Chicago: University of Chicago Press.

Comaroff, John L., and Jean Comaroff. 1997. *Of Revelation and Revolution: The Dialectics of Modernity on a South African Frontier*. Vol. II. Chicago: University of Chicago Press.

Ewick, Patricia, and Susan S. Silbey. 1998. *The Common Place of Law: Stories From Everyday Life*. Chicago: University of Chicago Press.

Felstiner, William L. F., Richard L. Abel, and Austin Sarat. 1981. "The Emergence and Transformation of Disputes: Naming, Blaming, Claiming." *Law and Society Review* 15 (3/4): 631–54.

Fitzpatrick, Peter. 1992. *The Mythology of Modern Law*. New York: Routledge.

Galanter, Marc. 1989. *Law and Society in Modern India*. Delhi: Oxford University Press.

Geertz, Clifford. 1983. *Local Knowledge: Further Essays in Interpretive Anthropology*. New York: Basic Books.

Greenhouse, Carol. 1989. *Praying for Justice: Faith, Order, and Community in an American Town*. Ithaca, NY: Cornell University Press.
Greenhouse, Carol, David Engel, and Barbara Yngvesson. 1994. *Law and Community in Three American Towns*. Ithaca, NY: Cornell University Press.
Holston, James. 2008. *Insurgent Citizenship: Disjunctions of Democracy and Modernity in Brazil*. Princeton, NJ: Princeton University Press.
ICRW (International Center for Research on Women). 1999–2002. *Domestic Violence in India*. 5 vols. Washington, DC: ICRW.
ICRW (International Center for Research on Women). 2002. *Women-Initiated Community-Level Responses to Domestic Violence*. Vol. 5 of *Domestic Violence in India*. Washington, DC: ICRW.
Jackson, Jean. 2007. "Rights to Indigenous Culture in Colombia." In *The Practice of Human Rights: Tracking Law between the Global and the Local*, ed. Mark Goodale and Sally Engle Merry. Cambridge: Cambridge University Press.
Keck, Margaret E., and Kathryn Sikkink. 1998. *Activists beyond Borders: Advocacy Networks in International Politics*. Ithaca, NY: Cornell University Press.
Krishnamurthy, Mekhala. 2002. "In the Shadow of the State, in the Shade of a Tree: The Politics of the Possible in Rural Gujarat." Bachelor of Arts thesis, Harvard University. Manuscript on file with the author.
Kumar, Radha. 1995. "From Chipko to Sati: The Contemporary Indian Women's Movement." In *The Challenge of Local Feminisms: Women's Movements in Global Perspective*, ed. Amrita Basu, with the assistance of C. Elizabeth McGrory, 58–87. Boulder, CO: Westview. Repr. Delhi: Kali for Women, 1999.
Lawyers' Collective. 1992. *Legal Aid Handbook: Domestic Violence*. Vol. 1. Delhi: Kali for Women.
Levitt, Peggy, and Sally Engle Merry. 2009. "Vernacularization on the Ground: Local Uses of Global Women's Rights in Peru, China, India and the United States." *Global Networks* 9 (4): 441–61.
Macaulay, Stewart. 1986. "Private Government." In *Law and the Social Sciences*, ed. Leon Lipson and Stanton Wheeler. New York: Russell Sage Foundation.
Mamdani, Mahmood. 1996. *Citizen and Subject: Contemporary Africa and the Legacy of Late Colonialism*. Princeton, NJ: Princeton University Press.
Mather, Lynn, and Barbara Yngvesson. 1980–81. "Language, Audience, and the Transformation of Disputes." *Law and Society Review* 15 (3/4): 775–822.
McCann, Michael. 1994. *Rights at Work: Pay Equity Reform and the Politics of Legal Mobilization* Chicago: University of Chicago Press.
Merry, Sally Engle. 1988. "Legal Pluralism." *Law and Society Review* 22 (5): 869–96.
———. 1990. *Getting Justice and Getting Even: Legal Consciousness among Working-Class Americans*. Chicago: University of Chicago Press.
———. 1993. "Sorting Out Popular Justice." In *The Possibility of Popular Justice: A Case Study of American Community Mediation*, ed. Sally Engle Merry and Neal Milner. Ann Arbor: University of Michigan Press.
———. 2000. *Colonizing Hawai'i: The Cultural Power of Law*. Princeton, NJ: Princeton University Press.
———. 2003. "Rights Talk and the Experience of Law: Implementing Women's Human Rights to Protection from Violence." *Human Rights Quarterly* 25 (2): 343–81.
Merry, Sally Engle, Peggy Levitt, Mihaela Serban Rosen, and Diana H. Yoon. 2010. "Law from Below: Women's Human Rights and Social Movements in New York City." *Law and Society Review* 44 (1): 101–28.

Moore, Sally Falk. 1973. "Law and Social Change: The Semi-Autonomous Social Field as an Appropriate Subject of Study." *Law and Society Review* 7 (4): 719–46.
Nader, Laura, and Harry Todd, eds. 1978. *The Disputing Process: Law in Ten Societies*. New York: Columbia University Press.
Nielsen, Laura Beth. 2006. *License to Harass: Law, Hierarchy, and Offensive Public Speech*. Princeton, NJ: Princeton University Press.
Poonacha, Veena, and Divya Pandey. 1999. "Responses to Domestic Violence in the States of Karnataka and Gujarat." Research Centre for Women's Studies, SNDT Women's University, Mumbai.
Rajaram, N., and Vaishali Zararia. 2009. "Reducing Gender Injustice in a Globalizing World: Challenges in Translating Women's Human Rights in Baroda, India." *Global Networks* 9 (4): 462–84.
Rodriguez-Garavito, Cesar A. 2005. "Nike's Law: The Anti-Sweatshop Movement, Transnational Corporations, and the Struggle over International Labor Rights in the Americas." In *Law and Globalization from Below: Towards a Cosmopolitan Legality*, ed. Boaventura de Sousa Santos and Cesar A. Rodriguez-Garavito, 66–91. Cambridge: Cambridge University Press.
Rosen, Lawrence. 1989. *The Anthropology of Justice: Law as Culture in Islamic Society*. Cambridge: Cambridge University Press.
———. 2006. *Law as Culture*. Princeton, NJ: Princeton University Press.
Santos, Boaventura de Sousa. 1995. *Towards a New Common Sense: Law, Science and Politics in the Paradigmatic Transition*. New York: Routledge.
Santos, Boaventura de Sousa, and Cesar A. Rodriguez-Garavito. 2005. "Law, Politics, and the Subaltern in Counter-Hegemonic Globalization." In *Law and Globalization from Below: Towards a Cosmopolitan Legality*, ed. Boaventura de Sousa Santos and Cesar A. Rodriguez-Garavito, 1–27. Cambridge: Cambridge University Press.
Sharma, Aradhana. 2006. "Cross-Breeding Institutions, Breeding Struggle: Women's 'Empowerment,' Neoliberal Governmentality, and State (Re)Formation in India." *Cultural Anthropology* 21 (1): 60–95.
———. 2008. *Logics of Empowerment: Development, Gender and Governance in Neoliberal India*. Minneapolis: University of Minnesota Press.
Speed, Shannon. 2007. "Exercising Rights and Reconfiguring Resistance in the Zapatista Juntas de Buen Gobierno. In *The Practice of Human Rights: Tracking Human Rights between the Local and the Global*, ed. Mark Goodale and Sally Engle Merry, 163–93. Cambridge: Cambridge University Press.

5

Toward Equity in Development When the Law Is Not the Law

Reflections on Legal Pluralism in Practice

Daniel Adler and Sokbunthoeun So

The relationship between the rule of law and equity is now a recurring theme in contemporary development discourse both internationally (World Bank 2005a) and in Cambodia (World Bank 2007). The reasons for focusing on law in discussions of equity in Cambodia are not difficult to understand. The country aspires to be a liberal democracy, and law features prominently in the way liberal democracies promise to deliver on equity.[1] In such systems, a free public sphere ensures that debate and discussion can take place with equal participation from all citizens (Gabardi 2001, 551). Democratic accountability should ensure that the law is a legitimate expression of the public interest. As Kant put it most succinctly, in a just society "legislative power can only belong to the united will of the people" (Axtmann 1996, 18). Further, liberal ideals associated with the judiciary (independence, guarantees of procedural fairness, judicial review of executive acts, equality before the law, access to justice, and so forth) mean – again, theoretically – that the institutions responsible for the execution and enforcement of the law will work to promote equity in practice. The fact that both state and market actors are embedded in this sort of regulatory and institutional framework makes liberal democracy one possible model for an equitable society.

This model is associated with prosperity, and as such there are good reasons why developing countries might want to work toward it. Cambodia's constitution is unequivocal in its commitment to liberal democracy, and since 1992, the assumption underlying the provision of more than $5 billion in international development assistance has been that the country requires support to make this transition (Chanboreth and Hach 2008). Unfortunately, the question of how to support a country like Cambodia to develop institutions that function in a way that

---

The argument set out in this chapter draws significantly on that elaborated in Adler, Porter, and Woolcock (2008).

[1] Posner (2003) goes so far as to describe the relationship as "inescapable."

reasonably approximates the general models described in previous chapters is inherently difficult to answer.

The post–Cold War confidence in the inevitability of democratic transitions supported a high degree of consensus about how to assist this process. The characteristics of the desired system are defined. Development assistance then provides a technical shortcut; it helps to import regulatory frameworks and corresponding institutional arrangements. Aid serves as a financial incentive to fuel their adoption and implementation. Various kinds of "conditionality" remind governments of their commitment to stay the course. More recently, support is also provided to civil society groups to animate "citizen demand" and/or to undertake various watchdog functions to promote observance of the new rules and norms in practice.[2]

The logic underlying this approach has been persuasive. New policies, laws, and regulations create an "enabling environment" for development (Bhatnagar 1992, 17). Citizens are "empowered to make demands" both political and administrative on government (World Bank 2005b, 2). Officials from the legislature and executive respond positively to new patterns of incentives and sanctions, and this leads to "behavior change among public officials," which in turn leads to "more accountable government" (World Bank 2007, 26). The problem, however, is that "people and institutions alike are embedded in wider social contexts that structure their choices, behaviour, and development" (Bevir 2005, 35). Thus, existing institutions can be highly resilient to changes in policies, individual leaders, or external circumstances and demands (March and Olsen 1989, 1995).

This is not to suggest that law and regulation are unimportant to institutional performance and, in turn, to equitable outcomes. Law is an important part of finding new ways for the state to engage with the task of leveling the "economic and political playing fields" (World Bank 2005a, pt. III). But development actors must in practice deal with the fact that institutions and how they perform reflect not just formal law or policy, but also prevailing social, economic, and political relations. Put another way, formal laws and regulations introduced to promote greater equity can hope to achieve this only if they become "embedded" in these relations. Drawing on examples from Cambodia, this chapter seeks to explore how this process of embedding occurs or fails to occur and how it might be supported.

This chapter addresses these questions through the lens of legal pluralism. Legal pluralism, borrowing an early and often cited description from Griffiths, is a situation in which

> ... law and legal institutions are not all subsumable within one "system" but have their sources in the self-regulatory activities of all the multifarious social fields present, activities which may support, complement, ignore or frustrate one another, so that the "law" which is actually effective on the "ground floor" of society

---

[2] This sketch of current development orthodoxies is adapted from Craig and Porter (2006, 54ff.)

is the result of enormously complex and usually in practice unpredictable patterns of competition, interaction, negotiation, isolationism, and the like. (Griffiths 1986, 39)

From the perspective of legal pluralism, state law is just one source of regulatory norms. As Lund (this volume) suggests, the state has an overarching authority, but its authority is not always the main one and can be contested. To be sure, it can represent a particularly powerful and/or legitimate normative order, but it is not one that can be separated from other orders such as those deriving from customary, religious, project, and/or local law, all of which provide alternative bases for claiming rights (Meinzen-Dick and Pradhan 2002). This state of affairs is at one level mundane, as it is common to most if not all social fields; however, "the relative pluralism of their legal aspect is one dimension in which social fields vary" (Griffiths 1986, 1).

The argument presented in this chapter is that the concept of legal pluralism is useful in understanding how regulation works in countries such as Cambodia, (a) which have, in a relatively short time, been subject to multiple overlays of precolonial, colonial, socialist, and liberal modes of regulation, and (b) where – as a consequence of war, revolution, and rapid internationalization – the state lacks institutions that enjoy the crucial mixture of authority and legitimacy. In such circumstances, it follows that (i) state law will fall short of playing its idealized role as the overarching normative order to which all other orders must yield; (ii) social and administrative behavior will be regulated by multiple competing sets of norms; and (iii) both the regulators and the regulated will engage in "forum shopping," which means that they will seek to engage the normative order that they perceive as most favorable to their cause.

Legal pluralism is also a useful analytical tool because it provides an empirical corrective to a series of assumptions associated with the "long dominant view that law is a unified and uniform system administered by the state" (Tamanaha 2008, 2), which underpins not only "most legal scholarship about the way law works" but also mainstream approaches to law and development (Davies 2005, 92). Problematic consequences of assumptions associated with this view include, for example, a focus on the formal legal system as the primary regulatory framework for governance, the treatment of an absence of law on the books as an absence of law, justice sector reform efforts that stress the process of drafting law and building model institutions for its enforcement (even where these are unlikely to deliver the desired social and economic transformations), and the treatment of actions that do not comply with the law on the books as simply "illegal" (even though it may be more fruitful analytically to think about them as acts consistent with a competing normative order).

In the Cambodian context, we often hear that the country has good law, but problems with implementation. What is meant is that the content of the law reflects international or other idealized standards of what the content of law should be (akin to Sen's [2009] "transcendental institutionalism") but that desired changes in behavior are not taking place. An analysis from the perspective of legal pluralism suggests that it may be more helpful to think of the situation as one in which the law is not in fact the law. People are playing by rules of a game, but it is another game – one backed by power that the law cannot match. Good law – it is argued here – is law that is effective in promoting desired outcomes.

In the sections that follow, this paper elaborates on the previous discussion of the dilemmas of promoting good law in settings characterized by entrenched legal pluralism, drawing on examples from the land sector in Cambodia.

LAND IN CAMBODIA: A CASE OF MULTIPLE COMPETING NORMS

Issues of legal pluralism in Cambodia are well illustrated in relation to land. Despite the fact that few households have formal title, tenure is more secure than is generally assumed. This may appear to be a strange claim in a country where land disputation is such a high-profile issue, but assertions of general tenure insecurity are nevertheless difficult to substantiate. Data from the 2004 Cambodian Socio-Economic Survey, a nationally representative household survey, indicate that only 1.8 percent of plots are reported as having ever been subject to a conflict. Of these disputes, two-thirds would appear to be minor, having been resolved (presumably at the local level) in three months or less. Another relevant statistic from the same data is that although only 49.3 percent of plots are reported as having any official certification of ownership, 77 percent are able to be used as collateral for a loan. These findings are supported by a variety of qualitative and quantitative sources, suggesting that tenure insecurity is concentrated among vulnerable groups, particularly poorer households that occupy lands outside core residential or farming zones, such as those that are or were forests, floodplains, seasonal lakes, marshes, and informal urban settlements – that is, land contested by the state (O'Leary 2005; CAS and World Bank 2006; CAS, World Bank, and GTZ 2006). Through the lens of legal pluralism, it is suggested that one of the key characteristics of these vulnerable areas is that their use is subject to – and occurs in and through – multiple conflicting norms.

Case study research suggests at least three sets of norms at work: (i) *historical social norms*: in particular, the concept of usufruct – namely, the idea that vacant land can be occupied and that the act of farming land gives rise to ongoing usage rights – is deeply embedded (despite civil war and changes in state law); (ii) *neopatrimonial administrative conventions*: a competing set of norms deriving from both previous regulatory regimes and practices that empower government officials at various levels to authorize transactions over lands within their administrative jurisdiction;[3] and (iii) *formal statute*: norms derived from the 2001 Land Law and other regulations

---

[3] The concept that patronage-based structures may be legal in a sociological sense though illegal in a formal sense is not novel (see, for example, Teubner [1991–92] with regard to the mafia and Zhang and Jing [2006] with regard to Guanxi rule in China).

currently in force (CAS et al. 2006). As Sokha et al. (2007) point out, each of these regimes is again subject to its own set of internal contradictions and inconsistencies, creating an added order of plurality.

The Land Law affirms and limits the historical social norms of land tenure in Cambodia. On the one hand, it is affirming in that it allows conversion of possession rights (usufruct) into ownership if such possession occurred under certain conditions prior to the adoption of law in August 2001. On the other hand, it limits by restricting legal possession, most notably of "state public land" and lands that entered into private possession after the promulgation of the law.

Unable to take on its idealized role, that of a meta-norm around which all other norms should harmonize, the Land Law becomes one of a number of norms and practices to which people may turn in their struggles to secure land rights. Competing claims emerge even where none appears to be "legal" in the narrow sense of the word. Where these different sets of norms – social, administrative, and statutory – line up, there is little conflict, and efforts at formalization run smoothly. Where, however, these sets of norms compete, conflict arises, with conflicting parties basing their claims on different normative orders. The problem with the emergence of these sorts of "competing (il)legalities" is that elites are often better able to "forum shop" – that is, select the normative framework most likely to legitimize their claims. Thus, Cambodian villagers may still resort to land clearing, although this has been made illegal by the Land Law. They will, however, remain tenure insecure while powerful elites with better access to the state leverage the normative order of patronage to secure better "rights" to the same pieces of land.

It is in this context – acknowledging the role of state law as a significant, though not exclusive reference point around which contests over land rights occur – that we move to consider the successes and limitations of current regulatory approaches.

CURRENT REGULATORY APPROACHES: SUCCESSES AND LIMITATIONS

The government acknowledges the problems described in the previous section and is attempting to deal with them by strengthening the role of state law in land management. This approach has proved successful in allowing the issuance of land titles on both a systematic and a sporadic basis. Since 2005, more than 1 million titles have been issued.

Sporadic (applicant-initiated) titling, a relatively expensive service attracting high levels of fees (both formal and informal), is unlikely to have a positive equity impact. Initial studies on systematic titling, in which whole communes go through the titling process (and in which fees are substantially lower), indicate that the titling process has a range of benefits, including improving access to credit, reducing disputes, and increasing land value. Although these benefits do not exclude the poor, they have been observed to benefit the high- and middle-income households to a greater extent and thus to have an "inherently regressive element" (Markussen 2007, 25; see also O'Leary 2005; Deutsch 2006).

It has also been suggested that the systematic titling process is unable or fails to recognize the usage rights of particularly vulnerable groups, such as indigenous communities, urban slum dwellers, and marginal settlements (O'Leary 2005; CAS et al. 2006). Thus, Markussen (2007, 9) notes that there are strong incentives for the systematic titling process to work in areas where there are "a large number of small, easy-to-measure plots," typically those characterized by "highly productive rice fields." However, these are precisely the areas in which preexisting tenure systems are best embedded, where the least conflict occurs, and where the interests of the poorer majority are least at risk. Further, as systematic titling progresses, the poor, who often live on or farm marginal areas, have been observed to be excluded from titling because they are deemed to be occupying state land or living in informal settlements (Markussen 2007, 25).

In short, it would appear that the titling process can currently be executed in two situations: first, if it is activated and financed by elites (in the case of sporadic titling), and second, if it represents the formalization of substantially pre-embedded local understandings about land use (in the case of systematic registration), in which case more modest per-plot incentives provided by donors are adequate to finance the process. The persistent strength of preexisting norms is demonstrated by the fact that even post titling, most sales are carried out in the "traditional" fashion by contract endorsed by the village chief and commune head rather than by registration with the cadastral authorities, as required by the 2001 Land Law (CCC 2007).

The situation with regard to state land reflects similar patterns. Despite the restrictions placed on new occupations of state land put in place by the 2001 law, other norms and incentives prevail. On the one hand, ordinary citizens assume the right to clear and occupy vacant lands for residential, agricultural, and speculative purposes, yet on the other hand, government representatives conduct discretionary transactions over what they see as state land (CAS and World Bank 2006). A set of new institutions for state land management established under the Land Law is geared toward the development of transparent bureaucratic processes for the administration of such lands. To date, however, these have been difficult to implement on a broad scale as they struggle to grapple with the competing normative frameworks and systems of incentives that keep state land de facto outside the formal regulatory system. The challenge then goes back to the old Hobbesian problem:

> When most people obey the law, the government can enforce it effectively and (relatively) cheaply against the few individuals who break it. But when obedience breaks down on a large enough scale, no authority is strong enough to police everyone. In such a setting, with enforcement becoming less and less effective,

individuals have an incentive to follow their own interests, regardless of any paper constraints. (Rapaczynski 1996, 88)

CONFLICT AND CONFLICT RESOLUTION

Tensions between multiple rule systems suggest multiple sources of legitimacy; hence, existing systems of power are fractured, dynamic, and susceptible to change. The land disputes that have characterized Cambodia's development over the past fifteen years mark the clashing of these rule systems and the variant ideas of what is fair or just that they produce.

In the absence of formal institutions that are able to deal with major conflict in a way that is perceived as fair, the poor use a variety of advocacy strategies to gain extra leverage in their negotiations with wealthier or more powerful parties. In the most successful cases, the poor act collectively to approach powerful administrative officials, often district and provincial governors, to intervene on their behalf. Appeals to the media, local human rights nongovernmental organizations, and national-level institutions have also proven useful. When formal law is drawn upon in these cases, it is to legitimate multifaceted bargaining strategies rather than with any expectation that the state could be relied on to enforce the law in an equitable fashion.

Such strategies have the potential to shift decisions in favor of the poor in individual cases. There is, however, little in the way of institutional structure for this sort of bargaining. As such, collective action around land issues tends to be local, ephemeral, and targeted at powerful individuals within the administration. Although cases in which collective action has successfully improved the responsiveness of the state to the needs of the poor have been documented (CAS and World Bank 2006, 36), the results of such action are highly contingent. The state may respond violently to collective action, and the bargaining position of the poor is generally inferior to that of the powerful individuals they confront. Alternatively, court proceedings (civil or criminal) may be used against those engaging in collective action (even peacefully).[4] Those with economic and political power not only posture (Benton, this volume) with the formal rules (regardless of the reality of their legal positions), but they also commandeer the power of the state to enforce their claims. For the poor, though, success is about gains at the margins in contexts where contestation offers no direct way for gains to create precedents and procedures that are then "fixed" legally or administratively.

---

[4] In a neopatrimonial system, the law is often applied selectively to bestow legitimacy on administrative transactions of dubious legality and to protect well-connected groups or individuals from prosecution. The point that the "discretionary, and often exactingly severe, use of the law against the political enemy or the vulnerable can be an efficient means of oppression" is captured most succinctly in the quote attributed to Brazil's President Getulio Vargas (1930–45, 1950–54): "For my friends, everything; for my enemies, the law."

CONCLUSION

In examining the situation with regard to land in Cambodia, we see that regulation has been most successful where it attempts largely to formalize, rather than radically transform, existing social norms and power relations. Areas in which the (pro-poor) transformative power of the law is called on have been those where progress has been most challenging. For this reason, the transformation, foreseen in the Land Law, of state land management from the patrimonial to the bureaucratic realm has remained largely unrealized.

When the poor contest actions of the powerful, the discourse is more often political than legal. In this contest, the poor will mobilize to "forum shop" to secure their interests in much the same manner as elites (though with very different resources). As a consequence, political gains seldom find expression in formal regulation, but rather require further iterations of political mobilization, the support of patrons, and extralegal action.

Bringing the lens of legal pluralism to development practice reminds us that "the Law" may not be the law. As such, it is a helpful corrective to any simplistic assumptions we may hold about the progressive force of law in processes of social and political change. Decentering the law in this way also helps us to focus on the structural nature of many "problems of implementation" – those that emerge from the fact of competing norms and the competing sources of authority and power with which they are associated, rather than a lack of awareness or capacity. Recalling the plural nature of the legal contexts within which we engage suggests a pragmatic (though potentially radical) approach to empowerment – one that supports people in navigating (or indeed challenging) the rules as they exist rather than the rules as we might imagine them to be. At the same time, the objective of supporting equity in development requires us to put forward theories of change that are explicit about the ways in which law and its institutions develop. Less encouragingly for the practitioner having exposed the concept of law to a more critical, empirical analysis that requires a focus on the nature of power and authority in a particular context, the lens of legal pluralism often suggests circumspection with regard to our ability to effect desirable change and caution against the potential for well-intentioned action to have negative consequences – not necessarily assets in the institutional environment of big development, with its inherent limitations and, to paraphrase Ferguson (1990, 69), hunger for promising candidates of the sorts of interventions development agencies are capable of delivering.

REFERENCES

Adler, Daniel, Doug Porter, and Michael Woolcock. 2008. "Legal Pluralism and Equity: Some Reflections on Land Reform in Cambodia." Justice for the Poor Briefing Note 2, no. 2, World Bank, Washington, DC.

Axtmann, Roland. 1996. *Liberal Democracy into the 21st Century: Globalization, Integration and the Nation State.* Manchester: Manchester University Press.
Bevir, Mark. 2005. *New Labour: A Critique.* London: Routledge.
Bhatnagar, Bhuvan. 1992. "Participatory Development and the World Bank: Opportunities and Concerns." In *Participatory Development and the World Bank,* ed. B. Bhatnagar and A. Williams, 13–30. Washington, DC: World Bank.
Bratton, Michael, and Nicholas van de Valle. 1997. *Democratic Experiment in Africa: Transition in Comparative Perspective.* New York: Cambridge University Press.
CAS (Center for Advanced Study) and World Bank. 2006. "Justice for the Poor? An Exploratory Study of Collective Grievances over Land and Local Governance in Cambodia." CAS and World Bank, Phnom Penh.
CAS (Center for Advanced Study), World Bank, and GTZ (German Development Cooperation). 2006. "Towards Institutional Justice: A Review of the Work of Cambodia's Cadastral Commission in Relation to Land Dispute Resolution." GTZ and World Bank, Phnom Penh.
CCC (Cooperation Committee for Cambodia). 2007. "Land Titling and Poverty Reduction: A Study of Two *Sangkat* in Prey Nup District, Sihanoukville Municipality." CCC and the NGO Forum on Cambodia, Phnom Penh.
Chanboreth, Ek, and Sok Hach. 2008. "Aid Effectiveness in Cambodia." Wolfensohn Center for Development Working Paper 7, Brookings Institution, Washington, DC.
Craig, David, and Doug Porter. 2006. *Development Beyond Neoliberalism: Governance, Poverty Reduction and Political Economy.* London: Routledge.
Davies, Margaret. 2005. "The Ethos of Pluralism." *Sydney Law Review* 27 (1): 87–112.
Deutsch, Robert. 2006. "Beneficiary Assessment of Land Title Recipients under the Land Management and Administration Project (LMAP)." Report prepared for the Cambodian Ministry of Land Management, Urban Planning and Construction, Phnom Penh. Unpublished.
Ferguson, James. 1990. *The Anti-Politics Machine: "Development," Depoliticization, and Bureaucratic Power in Lesotho.* Minneapolis: University of Minnesota Press.
Gabardi, Wayne. 2001. "Contemporary Models of Democracy." *Polity* 33 (4): 547–68.
Griffiths, John. 1986. "What Is Legal Pluralism?" *Journal of Legal Pluralism* 24 (1): 1–56.
March, James, and Johan Olsen. 1989. *Rediscovering Institutions: The Organizational Basis of Politics.* New York: Free Press.
———. 1995. *Democratic Governance.* New York: Free Press.
Markussen, Thomas. 2007. "Land Titling in Cambodia – findings from a Field Trip." Photocopy, World Bank, Washington, DC. Unpublished.
Meinzen-Dick, Ruth S., and Rajendra Pradhan. 2002. "Legal Pluralism and Dynamic Property Rights." CAPRi Working Paper 22, International Food Policy Research Institute (IFPRI), Washington, DC.
O'Leary, Declan. 2005. "Pilot Independent Review of Systematic Land Titling Field Systems and Procedures." Photocopy. Unpublished.
Posner, Richard A. 2003. *Law, Pragmatism and Democracy.* Cambridge, MA: Harvard University Press.
Rapaczynski, Andrzej. 1996. "The Roles of the State and the Market in Establishing Property Rights." *Journal of Economic Perspectives* 10 (2): 87–103.
Sen, Amartya. 2009. *The Idea of Justice.* Cambridge, MA: Belknap Press.
Sokha, Pel, Pierre Le Meur, Sam Vitou, Lan Laing, Pel Setha, Hay Leakhena, and Im Sothy. 2007. "Land Transactions in Rural Cambodia: A Synthesis of Findings from Research on Appropriation and Derived Rights to Land." Études et Travaux en Ligne 18, Éditions du Gret, Nogent-sur-Marne.

Tamanaha, Brian. 2008. "Understanding Legal Pluralism: Past to Present, Local to Global." *Sydney Law Review* 30 (3): 375–411.

Teubner, Gunther. 1991–92. "The Two Faces of Janus: Rethinking Legal Pluralism." *Cardozo Law Review* 13 (5): 1443–62.

UNHCHR (United Nations High Commissioner for Human Rights). 2007. *Land Concessions for Economic Purposes in Cambodia: A Human Rights Perspective*. Phnom Penh: UNHCHR.

World Bank. 2005a. *World Development Report 2006: Equity and Development*. Washington, DC: World Bank.

———. 2005b. "e-Bharat: Project Information Document." World Bank, Washington, DC, http://siteresources.worldbank.org/INTEDEVELOPMENT/Resources/INDoeBharat0PID1.pdf.

———. 2007. "Sharing Growth: Equity and Development in Cambodia. Equity Report 2007." Report 39809, East Asia and the Pacific Region, World Bank, Washington, DC.

Zhang, Jianwei, and Yijia Jing. 2006. "Legal Pluralism in the Governance of Transitional China." *Chinese Public Affairs Quarterly* 2 (3): 208–33.

PART II

Theoretical Foundations and Conceptual Debates

6

Sustainable Diversity in Law

H. Patrick Glenn

The field of law and development has been a recognizable one for approximately a half-century. Its intellectual origins lie in the spirit of optimism and reconstruction that followed World War II. The field has been through a number of recognizable stages or movements, notably an initial period in the 1970s characterized by an effort to transfer Western legal methods and education to jurisdictions characterized as less developed, and more recently by a "new" law and development movement better informed and more nuanced than previously was the case. In spite of a half-century of experience, however, evaluations of the success of the law and development endeavor appear overwhelmingly negative. The World Bank concept paper for this conference (now largely integrated into the introduction to this volume by Sage and Woolcock) speaks of "a mostly unhappy record of engagement" that is now "widely agreed (even by its original protagonists) to have been a failure," though there would be continuing imperatives.[1] In these circumstances it appears salutary to speak of the need for an "alternative theory," though such a theory, according to the concept paper, would necessarily start from the "empirical fact" of what is designated as "legal pluralism."[2]

This salutary effort to seek an alternative theory may be situated in a larger historical process of reflection of the World Bank on the relations between law, in its many forms, and economic development. In spite of the doubtful results of early law and development efforts, the World Bank accepted the necessity of legal projects in the 1990s, when attention initially was given to the "technical" problems or exercises of perfecting court structures and operations, drafting legislation, dealing with corruption, and further means of implementing the "rule of law" (Maru 2009, 6). Subsequently, there was a shift to recognize the importance of "local forms of

---

[1] World Bank (2009, 5, 7); and see B. Z. Tamanaha, "The Primacy of Society and the Failures of Law and Development," *Cornell International Law Journal* 44 (2): 209–47.
[2] World Bank (2009, 4).

justice," and a "relatively recent" development consisted of attention being given to legal services for the poor (Maru 2009, 6). Some movement is thus visible from initial, nonlegal projects to legal ones and then to legal ones in a broad sense, encompassing many and diverse legal traditions and their relations to one another, all of these within the World Bank's broad mission of poverty reduction. An alternative theory appears entirely compatible with this ongoing process of reflection.

The failure of previous law and development efforts does not appear to be due to a lack of either talent or money. Some of the world's best legal talent has been brought to bear on the problems, and very large sums of money have been spent. The failure appears rather to have been conceptual, as suggested by the need for an alternative theory. Thus, some critical consideration of the underlying concepts that have driven law and development projects appears necessary. Subsequent attention is to be given to an alternative theory, that of sustainable diversity in law.

I. THE CONCEPTS DEPLOYED IN LAW AND DEVELOPMENT

The concepts underlying previous law and development efforts appear to be four in number: (i) the concept of development itself; (ii) the concept of custom or customary law; (iii) the concept of the rule of law; and, most recently (though for at least two or three decades), (iv) the concept of legal pluralism.

A. Development

Etymological sources tell us that the contemporary sense of the word *development* (originally, "to remove from the confines of an envelope") is a product of the Enlightenment. It is strikingly Western in its affirmative sense of *making* as opposed to *becoming* bigger or more elaborate. Its Western origins are even more evident when the application of the word to social conditions is considered, because the dichotomy between "developed" and "developing" countries originated only in the mid-twentieth century, replacing in some measure that between "civilized" and "uncivilized" nations or peoples.[3] The process of development has thus been described as "from tradition to modern states,"[4] the state being the archetypal form of Western social organization, although modernity has been seen elsewhere in the

---

[3] For rejection of "uncivilized" nations from the purview of international law, Y. Onuma, "When Was the Law of International Society Born? An Inquiry of the History of International Law from an Intercivilizational Perspective," *Journal of the History of International Law* 2 (2000): 1–66.

[4] Barron, Smith, and Woolcock (2004), referring also at 15 to a "truly modern state"; though for the notion of modernity originating in the twelfth century, following the Cluniac reforms of civil and religious authority, H. Berman, *Law and Revolution* (Cambridge, MA: Harvard University Press, 1983), 112. For criticism of efforts of imposition of state structures, J. C. Scott, *Seeing Like a State: How Certain Schemes to Improve the Human Condition Have Failed* (New Haven, CT: Yale University Press, 1999).

world as "ultimately only a part of the larger traditional framework of European civilization – the part pretending to be independent of its historical roots" (Kim 1993–94, 19).

"Developing" countries are thus seen as progressing toward an eventual end point, with both the progression and the end point as Western in origin and in design. It is Western-modeled law and development, and because the great part of the population of the world is not Western in either origin or belief, it has recently been concluded that "[d]evelopment is conflict."[5] To the extent that local elites become dependent on an international order ("extroverted"), they further distance themselves from the governed, weaken the reactive capacity of the political system, and promote a shift toward authoritarianism (Badie 2000, 156, citing Algeria in 1988, Congo in 1991). Conflict is not limited, however, to that which may exist between a local, indigenous form of life and a model Western one (the contrast between "society," on the one hand, and state-citizen relations, on the other); there also is local conflict that preexists the arrival of Western forms of development and may be exacerbated by the arrival of Western funding, technology, and armament. Discussion of development thus often overlooks the conflict it provokes or exacerbates. There is no development if people are killing one another, for whatever reason.

Therefore, there are justifiable proposals for abandonment of the language and concept of development.[6] In addition to the conflict it provokes and exacerbates, it has led to the entirely unjustifiable dichotomy between developing and developed countries,[7] because there is no country in the world that can be said to be developed, either in the sense of being beyond growth or in the sense of having eliminated human want and need. All countries are therefore developing ones, and the language of development thus washes out in terms of meaningful consequences. This would not mean an end, however, to what can rightfully be described as foreign aid or what the French call *la coopération*, and countries could still be described in terms of having high or low consumption. This might usefully shift attention to other questions, notably that of sustainability. In French-language debates, there is now also discussion of *décroissance*, though there appears to be no exact equivalent in the English language. It is being said, however, that Western social sciences are now "postdevelopmental" (Badie 2000, 1).

---

[5] C. Sage, N. Menzies, and M. Woolcock, "Taking the Rules of the Game Seriously: Mainstreaming Justice in Development – the World Bank's Justice for the Poor Program," in *Legal Empowerment: Practitioners' Perspectives*, ed. S. Golub (Rome: International Development Law Organization, 2009), 31; and for the notion of "ethnocide" in the context of nation-states, R. Stavenhagen, *Ethnic Conflicts and the Nation-State* (London: Macmillan, 1996), 9.

[6] O. de Rivero, *Le Mythe du développement* (Paris: Editions de l'Atelier, 2003) (need to abandon broad Western model, develop autonomous criteria for, e.g., water, food, and energy).

[7] No definition is available for either, and qualification as a developing country is largely a question of self-identification for the purpose of qualification for aid. The World Trade Organization (WTO) allows challenge by other countries, however, to self-identification; see WTO, "Who Are the Developing Countries in the WTO?," http://www.wto.org/english/tratop_e/devel_e/d1who_e.htm.

B. *Customary Law*

Unwritten forms of law encountered in foreign aid efforts are invariably described as "customary" law, taking up the expression that has become commonplace in Western languages since the rise of written law in Europe over the course of the last thousand years. The process of transformation of unwritten law into what is known as "custom" was a long and difficult process, inextricably linked to the emergence of state law (Glenn 1997). The process eventually gave rise to a definition of custom that reduced it to repetitive *practice*, even under a present sense of obligation.[8] Custom thus became what certain people *do*, in an observable manner, and law was thus reduced to observable fact, stripped of normative force. The requirement of a sense of obligation on the part of participants is also mere fact, because what is required is its existence and not any justifiable reason for the sense of obligation.

Custom in its Western sense thus becomes not the normative teaching of a past that continues to live and persuade, but present, observable reaction to whatever may be remembered of it. Locke even converted it to de facto habits.[9] The definition is dissented from by some anthropologists and philosophers[10] but has become so firmly anchored in Western legal thinking, for local, Western reasons, that it is almost impossible to overcome. Transposed to non-Western jurisdictions, it is inevitably seen as a rejection of the normative force of that which has been adhered to, for many millennia, as sacred teaching. If development *is* conflict, development anchored in a dichotomy between law and custom, or even law and customary law, is certain to exacerbate the conflict.[11]

C. *The Rule of Law*

The notion of the rule of law dates at least from Dicey's adoption of it, arguing notably for submission of executive authority to review by superior courts of general jurisdiction (Dicey 1902, 183, 189, 191, 322). It has subsequently expanded in content and would now include submission of disputes to preestablished rules, transparency

---

[8] See, for customary international law, *The Restatement (Third) of the Foreign Relations Law of the United States*, s. 102 ("a general and consistent practice of states followed by them from a sense of legal obligation").

[9] J. Locke, *An Essay Concerning Human Understanding*, 29th ed. (London: Thomas Tegg, 1841), 274 (2.33.6) ("Custom settles habits of thinking in the understanding... which, once set a-going, continue in the same steps they have been used to, which, by often treading, are worn into a smooth path...").

[10] C. Geertz, *Local Knowledge* (New York: Basic, 1983), 208 ("The mischief done by the word 'custom' in anthropology, where it reduced thought to habit is perhaps only exceeded by that which it has done in legal history, where it reduced thought to practice.") O. Correas, "La Toría General del Derecho Frente al Derecho Indígena," *Critica Juridica* 14 (1994): 21 (favoring "unwritten law").

[11] Customary law is usually admitted to be law if it is so declared by a written source of law, whether legislative or judicial, applying the test of repetitive practice under a sense of obligation and derives its force from its adoption by the written source. Notions of "religious law" appear less objectionable, however.

in the legislative and adjudicative processes, impartial and independent adjudication, a right to legal counsel, and even human rights in general. It is thus often taken by "Western political and legal thinkers" as "an absolute given with universal applicability" (de Jong and Stoter 2009, 313). Yet because it is unquestionably rooted in Western legal traditions as both an expression and an institutional form, it necessarily implies adoption of fundamental features of those traditions.[12] There are (at least) four ensuing problems.

The first problem is that, although there is widespread agreement on the necessity of the rule of law, there is no agreement on its essential characteristics.[13] It exists nowhere in abstract form, such that its advocacy dissolves into advocacy of one or another of its national exemplifications. This will be seen as partisan and ultimately unjustifiable in other places, because all of the present exemplifications of the rule of law derive their legitimacy from precise historical contexts and circumstances. Judges are tenured in England but elected in many U.S. states. They are subject to extensive disciplinary measures in European continental jurisdictions but very little disciplinary control in common law jurisdictions. In some jurisdictions, they are civilly liable; in others, immune. Review of the administration may be vested in courts of general jurisdiction or special courts attached to the administration itself. Legal professions are divided or fused. The list of major and substantial differences among Western jurisdictions, all proclaiming their adherence to the rule of law, is endless. It is difficult to implement something when no one knows what it ultimately is.

The second problem is that the rule of law today gives every indication of failing in the Western jurisdictions from which it originated. This is perhaps most evident in common law, adversarial jurisdictions, but there are equally important problems in civilian countries. In the common law countries, litigation has become largely impossible for many ordinary people on financial grounds. Litigation rates in many

---

[12] R. W. Gordon, "The Role of Lawyers in Producing the Rule of Law: Some Critical Reflections," *Theoretical Inquiries in Law* 11 (2010): 444, Article 15, www.bepress.com/til/default/vol11/iss1/art15 (rule of law "surprisingly underspecified. But plainly it is a transplant of a simplified and idealized model of Western, and especially Anglo-American, judicial systems."). For a recent effort of quantitative assessment of rule of law by country, see the World Justice Project, "The Rule of Law Index: Measuring Adherence to the Rule of Law around the World" (2009), World Bank, www.worldjusticeproject.org. The list of criteria includes government and officials accountable under the law; laws "clear, publicized, stable and fair" that "protect fundamental rights"; accessible, fair, and efficient process by which laws enacted, administered, and enforced; access to justice provided by competent, independent, and ethical adjudicators, attorneys, or representatives, judicial officers with adequate resources and reflecting population they serve.

[13] See B. Tamanaha, *On the Rule of Law: History, Politics, Theory* (New York: Cambridge University Press, 2004), 3, citing notably O. Taiwo, "The Rule of Law: The New Leviathan?," *Canadian Journal of Law and Jurisprudence* 12 (1999): 152 ("There are almost as many conceptions of the rule of law as there are people defending it."); F. Neate, ed., *The Rule of Law* (London: LexisNexis, 2009), with "perspectives" (p. vii) on the subject from many parts of the world and contrasting, at p. 262, the "pragmatic" approach of Singapore with the "academic" Russian position.

Western jurisdictions, most notably the United Kingdom, have plummeted.[14] The trial, the hallmark of common law dispute resolution, is said to be "vanishing" in the United States.[15] There is a widespread phenomenon of parties representing themselves (pro se representation) in spite of the real necessity of legal counsel in adversarial proceedings. In civilian jurisdictions, even the large numbers of resident judges, using investigative forms of procedure, are unable to overcome the vast backlog of cases, with ensuing delays in the administration of justice (Perrot 2008, 12). In both common law and civil law jurisdictions, there is now widespread resort to arbitration by sophisticated players who choose to avoid state-centered rule of law institutions, leading to claims of an autonomous international arbitral order (Gaillard 2008). Why either of these common law or civil law implementations of the rule of law should be exported to non-Western jurisdictions is not evident. They both appear radically unsuitable for any program of justice for the poor.[16]

The third problem recently has been highlighted by Amartya Sen in his book *The Idea of Justice* (Sen 2009). It is that of the disconnect of any rule of law project from the actual results of its implementation. This disconnect flows, according to Sen, from a philosophy of justice fixated on an underlying idea of "transcendental institutionalism" or "getting the institutions right," as opposed to relative comparisons of justice and injustice. Justice-enhancing changes or reforms, however, demand comparative assessments, not simply immaculate identification of "*the* just society" or just institutions (Sen 2009, 5, 6, 401). This fixation on institutions, as opposed to material or substantive justice, places into sharper relief the contrast between idealized institutions and their actual reception in jurisdictions outside those of their origin. There is always some measure of disjunction; it is exacerbated if the underlying philosophy discounts the importance of actual results, either explicitly or implicitly. The problem may be exacerbated by the practice of funding agencies of evaluating projects by success in moving money "out the door," measuring outputs and not outcomes (Sarfaty 2009, 669).

The fourth problem has already been discussed in relation to the concepts of development and customary law. Like them, the concept of the rule of law is

---

[14] For the United Kingdom, *The Economist*, October 26, 2002, 34 (60 percent decline in commercial cases from 1996 to 2001), and for sharper declines thereafter, L. West, "Woolf: Ten Years On," *Commonwealth Lawyer* 18 (2009): 37.

[15] M. Galanter, "The Vanishing Trial: An Examination of Trials and Related Matters in Federal and State Courts," *Journal of Empirical Legal Studies* 1, no. 3 (2004): 459. For criticism of the role of lawyers in the process, see Gordon, "The Role of Lawyers in Producing the Rule of Law," 448 (lawyers' interests may support aspects of "variously defined" rule of law projects but "just as often subvert or impede"); 450 (lawyers profit from "delay and complexity"); 465 (far too much expected of judges and lawyers in rule of law projects).

[16] For remarkably mild criticism of access to justice in Western jurisdictions, see the World Justice Project, "The Rule of Law Index," 18 ("The greatest weakness in Western Europe and North America appears to be related to the accessibility of the civil justice system.... These are areas that require attention from both policy makers and civil society to ensure that all people, including marginalized groups, are able to benefit from the civil justice system.").

unquestionably Western in origin and in content.[17] Like them, it inspires resentment and provokes conflict. De Jong and Stoter (2009, 318) thus have recently written that "[t]he very assumptions underlying the rule of law are currently based on individualistic and egalitarian Western values. When these are automatically taken as a starting point for international law-making, mismatches, dissatisfaction and conflict are bound to arise." The conflict is exacerbated when, as is often the case, those in control of the apparatus of the state exploit it for personal gain, becoming the *WaBenzi* (people of the Mercedes Benz) in the eyes of the local population. Imposing a corrupt version of the rule of law is never intended but is often an inevitable result of rule of law endeavors. Local lawyers can be very much part of the problem and not part of the solution. Levels of resentment may vary from jurisdiction to jurisdiction, but the greater the ideal role of displaced indigenous law, the greater the resentment is likely to be. This is perhaps most evident in Islamic jurisdictions, where rule of law endeavors imply the elimination of traditional sources of Islamic law, the "defining characteristic" of Muslim societies.[18]

D. *Legal Pluralism*

The language of "legal pluralism" became current in the late twentieth century as a means of capturing the phenomenon of law beyond the state, a phenomenon that had largely disappeared during the period of state construction in Europe, North America, and many colonies. The language thus fulfilled a useful function in calling attention to the existence of many different legal orders that had been ignored by Western legal theory. The greater part of the legal pluralism literature, however, is empirically driven, providing either "thick" descriptions of particular informal legal orderings or second-order descriptive theories, such as those distinguishing between weak or state legal pluralism, on the one hand, and strong or new legal pluralism, on the other.[19] There is a clear normative dimension to this empirical work, because it is corrosive of state authority in some measure, but the content of the work has been

---

[17] See Gordon, "The Role of Lawyers in Producing the Rule of Law"; and for criticism of rule of law effort as imposition of the "American judicial model" as a means of global governance, N. Rajkovic, "Global Law and Governmentality: Reconceptualizing the 'Rule of Law' as Rule 'through' Law," *European Journal of International Relations* (forthcoming).

[18] W. Hallaq, "'Muslim Rage' and Islamic Law," *Hastings Law Journal* 54 (2003): 1714–15 ("modern- isation" and "decimation" of Islamic law as main cause of Islamic alienation); and see J. Holbrook, "Legal Hybridity in the Philippines: Lessons in Legal Pluralism from Mindanao and the Sulu Archipelago," http://ssrn.com/abstract=1486169 at 19 for tendency of colonial and early government in the Philippines "to marginalize and devalue Muslim normative obligations that led to four hundred years of armed conflict"; and 45 for "non-accommodating approaches. . . . as incendiary agents for additional conflict."

[19] J. Griffiths, "What Is Legal Pluralism?," *Journal of Legal Pluralism* 24 (1986): 5; G. R. Woodman, "Legal Pluralism and the Search for Justice," *Journal of African Law* 40 (1996): 157–58, and again in this volume; E. Melissaris, *Ubiquitous Law* (Farnham, UK: Ashgate, 2009), 27 (the latter rejecting the distinction).

directed to demonstrating, in Griffiths's language, that legal pluralism is "the fact," whereas legal centralism would be myth, ideal, or illusion.[20] Legal pluralism thus has been primarily concerned with demonstrating "the state of affairs"[21] of adherence to multiple legal orders, as opposed to developing legal concepts or instruments that facilitate the relations between different legal orders or traditions, though there have been exceptions.[22]

Criticism of legal pluralism work thus is centered on its empirical or descriptive dimensions. Benda-Beckmann concludes that a review of the field illustrates how "little conceptual progress as been made,"[23] whereas Melissaris views legal pluralism theories as "reducing themselves to either a legal theory that views law from well within a legal system or just a sociological, external recording of legal phenomena..."[24] Others have been more robust. Koskenniemi finds that legal pluralism "ceases to pose demands on the world" (Koskenniemi 2005, 16), and Michaels states that it exhibits a "propensity toward essentialized and homogenized concepts of culture and law" as well as even a "romantic preference" for plurality and locality (Michaels 2009, 244).

Should legal pluralism be seen as a problem or a solution? As a solution, it appears too normatively weak to respond to the highly normative (Western) insistence on development and the rule of law. It appears impossible, however, to conclude that it is a problem, because a problem generally is thought to be that which is amenable to solution or elimination. Legal pluralism appears to be rather the state of play, or the underlying default position of all laws, that is present as much in high-consumption jurisdictions (both historically and presently) as in low-consumption jurisdictions.[25] State law is unavoidable in the present configuration of the world. Non-state law has never been eliminated and can never be eliminated; lawyers have always worked with multiple laws and will continue to do so. The essential is in how this is done. It is unlikely, moreover, that it can be successfully done by concentrating either on understanding context or pursuing a justice orientation or by drawing

---

[20] Griffiths, "What Is Legal Pluralism?," 4, also at 2 for a definition of legal pluralism "suitable for a descriptive theory of law"; and see B. Tamanaha, "Understanding Legal Pluralism: Past to Present, Local to Global," *Sydney Law Review* 30 (2008): 396 that "Griffiths was right that legal pluralism is a fact...."

[21] Griffiths, "What Is Legal Pluralism?," 2.

[22] See, e.g., S. E. Merry, "Legal Pluralism," *Law and Society Review* 22 (1988): 879 ("The existence of legal pluralism itself is of less interest than the dynamics of change and transformation"; and see Woodman (2008, 35, and text below accompanying note 30).

[23] F. von Benda-Beckmann, "Comment on Merry," *Law and Society Review* 22 (1988): 897.

[24] Melissaris, *Ubiquitous Law*, 29.

[25] In high-consumption jurisdictions, this is most evident in the persistence of claims of aboriginal peoples, or in constitutional guarantees of the free exercise of religion, which have led state courts to recognition or even application of religious laws, and also in highly developed forms of Western commerce. See, for example, for state adoption of trade customs and usages in unwritten form, J.-P. Beraudo, "Faut-il avoir peur du contrat san loi," in *Mélanges Paul Largarde* (Paris: Dalloz, 2005), 96–98.

sharp distinctions between citizens and the state, on the one hand, and society, on the other. Such binary distinctions may be seen as part of the problem, even where intended to provoke, to the extent that they reinforce tendencies to separate and divide without providing any instruments of conciliation. Yet it is measures of conciliation that are required, given the inevitability of living among many laws.

Diversity of laws is thus inevitable and should be seen as sustainable.

II. SUSTAINABLE DIVERSITY IN LAW

The case for sustainable diversity in law is part of a larger project of coexistence of peoples or *convivencia* that the United Nations (UN) Human Development Programme has designated as "one of the central challenges of our time" (UNDP 2004, 1). The extent of the problem may be seen in the listing by CrisisWatch of some seventy-five crisis jurisdictions representing approximately 40 percent of the states of the world.[26] These crisis jurisdictions are indicators of the failure of the idea of the "nation-state" on the ground, though also of its continuing lethal attraction to various groups perceived as "minorities" within existing state structures.

The prevalence of violence within so-called nation-states, and across their borders, appears to be having some effect on discussions of economic development. Barron et al. (2004, 1) have concluded that "development actors," including the World Bank, bilateral donors, and nongovernmental organizations, have "in recent years increasingly come to see conflict reduction and post-conflict reconstruction as part of their mandate." Concentrating on the "rebuilding" of "war-torn states," del Castillo (2008, chap. 4) concludes that transition to peace represents a "development plus" challenge, though by this she means that objectives of peace should prevail at all times over those of economic development. There should be, moreover, a new form of measurement of the success of efforts of conciliation. In the African context, Huyse and Salter (2008, 3) observe a move away from a de facto dichotomy (impunity *or* trials) to "multiple conceptions of justice and reconciliation," citing a report of the UN secretary-general on transition justice (United Nations 2004, 12) that states that "due regard must be given to indigenous and informal traditions for administering justice or settling disputes." Faundez (in this volume) speaks of non-state justice as an "indispensable component" of development work, whereas Mabiala (2009, 81) insists on "preventive" justice in the transformation and prevention of disputes.

Violence is endemic within states for many reasons, including greed, the struggle for resources, long-standing enmities, and other easily identified factors. Underlying

---

[26] *CrisisWatch*, no. 79, March 1, 2010, www.crisisgroup.org/library/documents/crisiswatch/cw_2010/cw79.pdf. Though there are indications of an overall decline in war in the world since the end of colonialism, violent conflicts *within* states now make up more than 95 percent of armed conflicts. Human Security Centre, *Human Security Report 2005: War and Peace in the 21st Century* (New York: Oxford University Press, 2005), 8.

these immediate factors, however, are deeply rooted beliefs in differing normative orders or legal traditions, which often may be seen not simply as a means of dispute resolution but as entire ways of life. Each of these legal traditions represents one or more fundamental truths to their adherents, and such fundamental truths often give rise to intractable resistance to deviation or change and ensuing violence. Unwritten laws are often based on animist forms of religion and devotion to a cosmic order; Islamic law is an entire way of life, extending to prayer and personal hygiene, based on sacred sources. Each of these normative orders contains truths recognizable by the others. Animist or chthonic beliefs contain a truth of the need for environmental protection, which is increasingly recognized by nonanimist people. Islamic law in its financial dimensions refuses highly leveraged forms of speculative investment, and this is increasingly seen as wisdom in Western jurisdictions. Civil and common law traditions, in spite of possible differences in their effects on economic development, are seen as traditions of liberty and empowerment, notably through the concept of subjective or human rights, and the concept of rights is recognized everywhere Western laws are known. The search for reduction of violence among adherents to these traditions can therefore be formulated more positively in terms of the necessary preservation of their different truths. It is through guaranteeing preservation of these truths that violence can be avoided. Violence can thus be avoided, and truths preserved, if each of the legal traditions is accorded mutual respect and recognition. Given such a point of departure, individual and particular decisions can then be taken without prejudice to ongoing harmonious relations of peoples and their legal traditions. There is, however, a great need for the development of more precise techniques of sustainable diversity in law.

A. *Techniques of Sustainable Diversity in Law*

How should one think about states and the diversity of laws within them? The language most frequently used is that of minorities and the accommodation of difference, which assumes the perspective of the national territorial state and the unity of its laws. This is not the perspective, however, of those who resist the law of the state on the grounds of alternative legal orders. From such a different legal perspective, it is not a question of accommodating *difference* in the form of an alternative legal order and given a presumptive unity, but of accommodating any form of unity, including that of the state. Sustaining the diversity of laws therefore means abandoning the presumption that law is defined in terms of state law or, put differently, requiring that the law of the state be normatively justified in local circumstances, just as alternative legal orders must be justified in local circumstances. This is as it should be, because state legal orders cannot be taken as positive social facts when they clearly are not. They require normative justification most clearly in jurisdictions with high levels of legal diversity, though there now would be a "burgeoning" group of so-called normative positivists even within Western jurisdictions

(Coleman 2007, 600). Such normative justification will result in the accommodation of those legal unities that meet acceptable thresholds of social acceptance and legitimacy. The legal unities may be found in the positive law of a territorial state, the religious law of a transnational legal order, or the unwritten law of a tribe divided by a national boundary. Some combination of them may be required. These are the diverse laws whose recognition represents the "state of affairs" in most jurisdictions of the world, though largely without theoretical justification. They represent legal unities because they are deeply rooted as laws and have maintained their normative attraction in spite of the close presence of alternatives. They are ineradicable, which is the most important reason for their recognition.

The concept paper for this conference echoes earlier writing in calling for "meta-rules" as a means of accommodating diverse legal unities. The need for "meta-rules" is also spoken of, however, in less formal terms of "forging a set of enforceable agreements about how to manage the contending claims of subordinate legal and normative orders" (World Bank 2009, 2.3). In a similar manner, a paper by Barron et al. (2004, 34) speaks of the need for "meta-rules," though also of "endeavouring to establish mediating institutions." Both of these papers point out the importance of the second-order activity of conciliating different legal orders, though the language of both would allow a differentiation between "meta-rules," on the one hand, and either "agreements" or "mediating institutions," on the other, as a means of conciliation. The distinction, given historical knowledge of choice-of-law processes, appears to be an important one.

The best-known "meta-rules" in the world are those of modern private international law, by virtue of which different legal problems are assigned to particular national laws according to the domicile of the parties, the place where a person acts, and so forth. These types of meta-rules are highly unsuitable for the process of conciliation of laws within states. They assume distinct territorial laws, whereas within most states it is also possible to choose nonterritorial (religious or unwritten) laws. They also conflictualize legal relations (the "conflict of laws") in assuming underlying conflict and the constant need for win/lose decisions. There is, moreover, little by way of "enforceable agreements" between states, and the notion of conflict of conflict of laws rules is well known.

The so-called U.S. revolution in the conflict of laws may provide a more promising means of conciliating laws within a state. U.S. law now generally rejects formal meta-rules of choice of law in favor of a *process* of interpretation of local laws in order to determine their application in space. Decisions are highly casuistic, with no individual case being of system-wide consequence. The science or subject of private international law or the conflict of laws thus declines in visibility (though not necessarily in importance). This deconflictualization of the subject has much to recommend it in the context of violence-prone jurisdictions. Winners and losers become much harder to identify, and major efforts of research are required to have even some idea of what might be occurring in the forest of individual decisions.

A further historical model of the conciliation of diverse laws, this time within a single territory, has been that of "personal laws" or *conflits interpersonnels*. This is still a widely used model in India, Israel, Lebanon, Singapore, South Africa, and elsewhere. There is a considerable literature on the subject (Aoun 2009). State adoption of meta-rules that formally authorize personal laws are often, moreover, a reflection of religious laws that define their application in personal or religious terms and not state or territorial terms.[27] There is much to commend such rules if they can be agreed on. Beyond the cases of meta-rules that formally authorize personal laws, there is also a less widely recognized phenomenon by which non-state law is applied over a potentially large range of subjects and for particular peoples: in the case of religious laws by virtue of constitutional guarantees of religious liberty, and in the case of unwritten laws in decisions involving judicial recognition of aboriginal rights and aboriginal title. These may be seen as informal personal laws and may apply even in matters of crime.[28] The formal application of personal laws has been limited to specific areas of law, usually those of family law and successions, and has been the result of state edict, which may or may not have resulted from "agreement" by the parties concerned. It may or may not be accompanied by separate court structures. There is reluctance on the part of state officers to accept such a formal deviation from the application of state laws. It has, however, been irresistible in many jurisdictions because of the political significance of "minority" populations within the states concerned and has proven to be compatible with state structures.

Without suggesting a binary choice, some form of continuum can thus been seen between formal systems of meta-rules, at one end of the continuum, and less visible processes or methods of interpretation and (casuistic) decision making at the other end. The latter processes or methods are facilitated in some measure by conceiving of the legal orders in question not as autonomous and conflicting systems but as bodies of normative information or simply as legal traditions (Glenn 2005, 894–97). In the language of the concept paper,[29] there will be less insistence on the "integrity of ... systems" if there is no concept of systemic integrity, as opposed to the simple integrity of particular rules or principles.

The sustainable diversity of law that is being discussed here presents obvious similarities, with proposals for the development of "mediating institutions" and "interim institutions" that have been made in World Bank literature, also described as a more "process-oriented approach" (Adler, Sage, and Woolcock 2009, 2, 4,

---

[27] For persistence of Islamic jurisdictions in applying Islamic law to Islamic people, K. Zaher, *Conflits de civilisations et droit international privé* (Paris: L'Harmattan, 2009), 284ff. ("Les justifications du principe de la personnalité des lois").

[28] For submission by state officials of even criminal cases, including those of murder, to informal institutions (jurga, shira) in Afghanistan, USAID, *"Afghanistan Rule of Law Project"* (Washington, DC: USAID, 2005), 10, 11, http://pdf.usaid.gov/pdf_docs/PNADF590.pdf.

[29] World Bank (2009, 3), speaking generally of "political and cosmological systems" in spite of the nonsystemic character of most legal traditions of the world.

16–17). As with these proposals, there would be no given "end point" of the process of bringing about the sustainable diversity of laws. The notion of sustainable diversity, however, is not one that sees the process as "interim" in the sense of provisional or temporary as opposed to mediating. Sustainable diversity implies the absence of a given end point other than sustainable diversity itself. It is as good as it gets.[30]

There are obvious criticisms, however, that can be made of the concept of sustainable diversity of laws. These may inspire further justification.

B. *Critiques and Justification of Sustainable Diversity in Law*

The idea of sustainability diversity in law is incompatible with almost all contemporary legal theory, which assumes (i) an underlying problem of conflict and a need for uniformity and the rule of law as means of conflict resolution; (ii) equality in the enforcement of law and human rights; and (iii) the rule of law as an instrument of economic development. All of these concepts or positions have been developed, however, in the course of development of Western national legal systems, which now require normative justification in the face of alternatives that may be more deeply rooted. Each of them must be addressed.

The concept paper for this conference states that "standard 'development' activities... only serve to increase the likelihood that... diverse orders will come into contact with one another (and thereby generate conflict)" (World Bank 2009, 1, 3). It is clear enough that people conflict; it is much less clear, however, that the contact between legal orders must generate conflict. Conciliation of laws may well provide a major means of conciliation of peoples. The major treatise on the conflict of laws in the United Kingdom has stated flatly that "laws may differ but they do not conflict,"[31] yet in spite of this professional view the relations of national laws remain defined largely in terms of the "conflict of laws." If law is not thought of in terms of incompatible and conflicting systems, however, there is less potential for conflict. There was little confusion and no perceived conflict in English legal history until the emergence of the nation-state from the seventeenth century. Multiple laws coexisted in nonconflictual relationships, even within the same territory.[32] Much of

---

[30] For such a conclusion even in the context of European law, with "overlapping" and incompletely harmonized lawmaking processes, which "will not just be transitionally," K.-H. Ladeur, "Can Methodology Change So as to Cope with the Multiplication of the Law," in *Epistemology and Methodology of Comparative Law*, ed. M. van Hoecke (Oxford: Hart, 2004), 103; and for human diversity as essential to necessary biodiversity, D. A. Posey (dir.), *Cultural and Spiritual Values of Biodiversity* (London: United Nations Environment Programme/Intermediate Technology Publications, 1999), notably at xi.

[31] L. Collins, *Dicey and Morris on the Conflict of Laws*, 11th ed. (London: Stevens, 1987), 32–33. The statement has been removed subsequently. The title has remained because of "the obvious inconvenience of changing a name which has been in use since the seventeenth century."

[32] See, e.g., A. Watson, *Joseph Story and the Comity of Errors* (Athens: University of Georgia Press, 1992), 78 ("There was really no conflicts law.").

the violence of European legal history, moreover, derived from attempts to impose uniformity (religious or other) in given territories. Thus, the case that a multiplicity of laws creates conflict cannot be taken as a given. Much will depend on the thinking underlying of the relations of laws. Poirier has thus written that the entire problem of development consists of "rendering complementary that which appears to be contradictory,"[33] and Haack has written of new and more "powerful" forms of logic, including multivalent or multivalued logic, with greater conciliatory potential than classic binary logic.[34] Multivalent "both/and" logic may well take us further than binary "either/or" logic, because multivalued laws require a multivalent logic. A logic of contradiction is required, as opposed to a law of noncontradiction (Glenn 2010, chap. 10). Woodman (2008, 35, and similarly in this volume) thus concludes that "since in many instances there is not a conflict so much as a search for accommodation, the term choice of law seems preferable," pointing out that even state law admits of "degrees of seriousness" of prohibited acts and that "two conflicting norms [may] coexist for very long periods, each being observed, and being disobeyed, to a certain extent."

Much of the argument for uniformity of laws is based on underlying ideas of human equality and "like cases" being decided in "like manner." The difficult questions, however, are equality for whom, and how do we decide which cases are like cases? Uniformity and equality within a state mean inequality and difference at its borders, and nationalistic justifications of inequality and discrimination at borders today appear less and less persuasive. They would be based on what Sen has described as the "unique categorization" of peoples, the idea that the people of the world can be uniquely categorized according to some singular and overarching system of partition, with human beings as members of exactly one group. The idea of a clash of civilizations, moreover, would be "conceptually parasitic" in such a unique categorization (Sen 2007, xii, xv, 10). Uniformity within a state, and like treatment of cases presumed to be like, therefore would represent not a solution to problems of conflict but one of its principal causes. There are reasons that justify the failure of rule of law efforts in much of the world.

Equality in the enjoyment of human rights has, however, achieved some transnational significance, even if means of enforcement are largely lacking. Can there be,

---

[33] J. Poirier, "Éléments de réflexion pour une théorie du droit Africain," in A la recherche du droit Africain du XXIe Siècle, ed. C. K. Kuyu (Paris: Connaissances et Savoirs, 2005), 41 ("Tout le problème du développement consiste sans doute à rendre complémentaire ce qui paraît être des contradictions"); and for the talent of Mongolian grasslanders in "making use of contradictions to strike a balance while achieving two goals with one action," as opposed to Han Chinese, who would "promote the east wind overpowering the west wind," Jiang Rong, Wolf Totem (New York: Penguin, 2008), 376.
[34] S. Haack, "On Logic in the Law: Something, but Not All," Ratio Juris 20 (2007): 2, 11 ("many-valued logic" as one of "more powerful logical techniques now available," part of "success of the new logic"); and for "trivalent" logic dealing with actions that are "good," "bad," and "indifferent," recalling the multiple gradations of Islamic law, M. Kalinowski, "Logique Formelle et Droit," Annales de la Faculté de Droit et des Sciences Économiques de Toulouse 15 (1967): 209–10.

and should there be, uniformity in the application of human rights norms? There is much to be said for negative answers to both of these questions. The negative response to the first question is based on both the unlikelihood of any form of global governance and enforcement and its undesirability in any event.[35] The negative response to the second question is consistent with the idea of sustainable diversity in law. The idea of human rights would be too Western, too abstract, and too underdetermined to admit of uniform application throughout the world and its different legal traditions.[36] In discussing the rights of women, Harrington and Chopra (2010, 19–21) argue for abandonment of a dichotomy between "customary" norms and formal legislative approaches, insisting on the need to "empower women to navigate whichever forum they find most available, convenient, effective and cost-efficient," while resisting efforts to "hijack" custom. The European Court of Human Rights has insisted on the need for a margin of appreciation of state conduct in compliance with European human rights norms (Arai-Takahashi 2002; Sweeney 2005). Uniformity is not necessary in advancing the cause of human rights.

Is the rule of law, however, in whatever form somehow necessary as a means of economic development? Much development literature has taken this to be the case, but there is a growing, more nuanced literature. There are obvious counterexamples, most notably China, to the link between Western-style rule of law and economic development, whereas specific studies have recently concluded that transplanted institutions create greater legal uncertainty than do domestically developed solutions;[37] that "local, informal institutions can support social substitutes for the enforcement of contracts";[38] and that, at least in the European context, "diversity is positively correlated to productivity."[39] Local institutions thus would not be

---

[35] For Kant's limited proposal of a loose world federation with a notion of "cosmopolitan law" limited to a right of temporary mobility between states, I. Kant, *Perpetual Peace*, trans. M. C. Smith (New York: Cosimo, 2005); and for contemporary hostility, D. Zolo, *Cosmopolis: Prospects for World Government* (Cambridge: Polity, 1997).

[36] M. Delmas-Marty, *Towards a Truly Common Law* (Cambridge: Cambridge University Press, 2002), 79, 80 (content of human rights weakly ["faiblement"] determined); and see M. Goodale, "Introduction: Locating Rights, Envisioning Law between the Global and the Local," in *The Practice of Human Rights*, ed. M. Goodale and S. E. Merry (Cambridge: Cambridge University Press, 2007), 3, 4 (international human rights as "decentered," existing "as part of preexisting legal and ethical configurations.").

[37] P. Grajzl and V. Dimitrova-Grajzl, "The Choice in the Lawmaking Process: Legal Transplants vs. Indigenous Law," *Review of Law & Economics* 5 (2009): 646 ("This paper contributes to a growing body of research, which argues that the appropriate path of institution-building critically depends on local conditions.").

[38] V. Gauri, "How Do Local-Level Legal Institutions Promote Development?," Justice and Development Working Paper Series 6/2009 (Washington, DC: World Bank, 2009), notably at 4 for 86 percent of respondents in Indonesia preferring informal to formal procedures; and see Tamanaha in this volume for high percentages of cases already resolved by non-state tribunals.

[39] E. Bellini et al., "Cultural Diversity and Economic Performance: Evidence from European Regions," Nota di Lavoro 632009 (Milan: Fondazione Eni Enrico Mattei, 2009), www.feem.it/userfiles/attach/Publication/NDL2009/NDL2009-063.pdf.

incompatible with economic development and would contribute to a type and level of economic development compatible with local norms.

CONCLUSION

The rule of law has become a contested concept and a liability in much of the world. This should not be surprising, though it continues to receive the support of state actors and governments in most parts of the world. This support cannot be taken, however, as indicative of the fundamental legitimacy of rule of law projects. It is not only the rule of law that is tenuous in much of the world, but also state organizations themselves. This does not imply the abandonment of either state or non-state institutions, but more active support of means of their conciliation. "Multiple normative strategies" appear to be the order of the day (Singer 2009, 847). Historically, the rule of law has been a useful concept in some parts of the world; it could well be replaced by the rule of laws.

REFERENCES

Adler, Daniel, Caroline Sage, and Michael Woolcock. 2009. "Interim Institutions and the Development Process: Opening Spaces for Reform in Cambodia and Indonesia." Working Paper 86, Brooks World Poverty Institute, University of Manchester.

Aoun, Marc, ed. 2009. *Les Statuts personnels en droit comparé*. Leuven: Peeters.

Arai-Takahashi, Yutaka. 2002. *The Margin of Appreciation Doctrine and the Principle of Proportionality in the Jurisprudence of the ECHR*. Antwerp: Intersentia.

Badie, Bertrand. 2000. *The Imported State: The Westernization of the Political Order*. Stanford, CA: Stanford University Press.

Barron, Patrick, Claire Q. Smith, and Michael Woolcock. 2004. "Understanding Local-Level Conflict in Developing Countries: Theory, Evidence and Implications from Indonesia." Social Development Papers, Conflict Prevention and Reconstruction Paper 19, World Bank, Washington, DC.

Castillo, Graciana del. 2008. *Rebuilding War-Torn States: The Challenge of Post-Conflict Economic Reconstruction*. New York: Oxford University Press.

Coleman, Jules. 2007. "Beyond the Separability Thesis: Moral Semantics and the Methodology of Jurisprudence." *Oxford Journal of Legal Studies* 27 (4): 581–608.

Dicey, Albert V. 1902. *Introduction to the Study of the Law of the Constitution*. London: Macmillan.

Gaillard, Emmanuel. 2008. *Aspects philosophiques du droit de l'arbitrage international*. Leiden: Martinus Nijhoff.

Glenn, H. Patrick. 1997. "The Capture, Reconstruction and Marginalization of 'Custom.'" *American Journal of Comparative Law* 45 (3): 613–20.

―――. 2005. "Doin' the Transsytemic: Legal Systems and Legal Traditions." *McGill Legal Journal* 50: 863–98.

―――. 2010. *Legal Traditions of the World*. Oxford: Oxford University Press.

Harrington, Andrew, and Tanja Chopra. 2010. "Arguing Traditions: Denying Kenya's Women Access to Land Rights." Justice for the Poor Research Report 2, World Bank, Washington, DC.

Huyse, Luc, and Mark Salter, eds. 2008. *Transitional Justice and Reconciliation after Violent Conflict – learning from African Experiences*. Stockholm: International Institute for Democracy and Electoral Assistance (IDEA).

Jong, Martin de, and Suzan Stoter. 2009. "Institutional Transplantation and the Rule of Law: How This Interdisciplinary Method Can Enhance the Legitimacy of International Organisations." *Erasmus Law Review* 2 (3): 311–30.

Kim, Sang-Ki. 1993–94. "Confucian Capitalism: Recycling Traditions." *Telos* 94: 18.

Koskenniemi, Martti. 2005. "Global Legal Pluralism: Multiple Regimes and Multiple Modes of Thought." Paper presented at Harvard Law School, Cambridge, MA, March 5. www.helsinki.fi/eci/Publications/MKPluralism–Harvard-05d%5B1%5D.pdf.

Mabiala, Ruffin V. 2009. *La Justice dans les pays en situation de post-conflit*. Paris: L'Harmattan.

Maru, Vivek. 2009. "Access to Justice and Legal Empowerment: A Review of World Bank Practice." Justice and Development Working Paper Series 9/2009, World Bank, Washington, DC.

Michaels, Ralf. 2009. "Global Legal Pluralism." *Annual Review of Law and Social Science* 5: 1–35.

Perrot, Roger. 2008. *Institutions Judiciaires*. 13th ed. Paris: Montchrestien.

Sarfaty, Galit A. 2009. "Why Culture Matters in International Institutions: The Marginality of Human Rights at the World Bank." *American Journal of International Law* 103: 647–83.

Sen, Amartya. 2007. *Identity and Violence: The Illusion of Destiny*. New York: W. W. Norton.

———. 2009. *The Idea of Justice*. Cambridge, MA: Harvard University Press.

Singer, Joseph. 2009. "Normative Methods for Lawyers." *UCLA Law Review* 56: 899–982.

Sweeney, James. 2005. "Margins of Appreciation: Cultural Relativity and the European Court of Human Rights in the Post-Cold War Era." *International and Comparative Law Quarterly* 54 (2): 459–74.

UNDP (United Nations Development Programme). 2004. *Human Development Report 2004: Cultural Liberty in Today's Diverse World*. New York: UN Development Programme.

United Nations. 2004. "The Rule of Law and Transitional Justice in Conflict and Post-Conflict Societies." Report of the Secretary General, United Nations Security Council, United Nations, New York.

Woodman, Gordon. 2008. "The Possibilities of Co-existence of Religious Laws with Other Laws." In *Law and Religion in Multicultural Societies*, ed. R. Mehdi, H. Petersen, E. Sand, and G. Woodman. Copenhagen: DJØF.

World Bank. 2009. "Concept Note: Legal Pluralism and Development Policy." Justice for the Poor, World Bank, Washington, DC. Unpublished. On file with the author.

7

Legal Pluralism 101

William Twining

I. INTRODUCTION

The purpose of this chapter is to try to demystify the mainstream literature on legal pluralism for foreign consultants or activists concerned with poverty reduction in the global South. The chapter proceeds on the working assumption that such interventions are legitimate, welcome, and well informed.

My standpoint is that of a British jurist interested in jurisprudence, legal anthropology, "Law and Development," and the implications of "globalization" for the discipline and practice of law.[1]

The mainstream literature on legal pluralism draws on several disciplines and does not belong to a single intellectual tradition. It is accordingly difficult to generalize about it. However, I suggest that a high proportion of the anthropological and sociolegal literature up to the mid-1990s approximates to a single ideal type, here characterized as *social fact legal pluralism* (sflp). In the past fifteen years, the idea of *global legal pluralism* (glp) has become fashionable, but I argue that this is in many respects based on a qualitatively different lot of concerns and that, if there is a single subject or field encompassed by this idea, it needs to be relabeled.

The mainstream literature contains a rich heritage of particular studies and some rather less satisfactory theorizing. One of the problems is that it has been bedeviled by an obsession with perennial jurisprudential problems surrounding the concept of law and legal positivism. It has rather neglected other theoretical issues about both pluralism and general normative theory. Part of the problem is that there is almost systematic ambiguity with regard to some of the central concepts. Thus, we need to start with some conceptual clarification.

---

[1] My main relevant experience has been in East Africa: Sudan, Tanzania, Uganda, Kenya, and to a lesser extent Rwanda and Ethiopia, mainly in the period from 1958 to 1965 and in the mid-1990s. My main relevant writings are Twining (2009a, 2009b, 2010). This chapter draws heavily on all of these. I am grateful to the participants in the World Bank workshop on legal pluralism in April 2010, and especially to Doug Porter and Brian Tamanaha for helpful comments.

II. SOME BASIC CONCEPTS

Pluralism

Plural, usually contrasted with singular, means more than one and is applied to persons or objects. It assumes that these units are discrete or individuated. The primary meaning of *pluralist* is "the state of being plural."[2] *Pluralistic* can mean diverse or varied. Pluralism is used as both a normative and a descriptive concept. For example, in ethics, pluralism, typically contrasted with monism, refers to "[a] theory or system of thought that recognizes more than one ultimate principle." Alternatively, *belief pluralism* refers to a situation in which different cosmologies or belief systems coexist, a social fact of considerable significance in the current context of "globalization," not least in relation to claims about the universality of human rights or natural law principles (Twining 2009a, 131 passim).

A related usage equates pluralism with multiculturalism. For example, Webster gives as a second meaning of *pluralist*: "the nature of a society within which diverse ethnic, social, and cultural interests exist and develop together" (Webster 1981). However, in some contexts the term *multiculturalism*, contrasted with assimilation, has been extended from referring to a social fact about a society to a normative concept referring to strategies and policies in such a society directed at respecting and maintaining cultural diversity in various ways.[3]

Here it is worth noting three points. First, to talk of objects in the plural presupposes that they can be individuated. Second, there is a general tendency in some contexts to move from an empirical to a normative usage, as illustrated by the two primary usages of *multiculturalism*. Third, it is always important to ask: plurality of what precisely?

Individuation

Plural means more than one. This presupposes that one can identify some discrete objects or units. In jurisprudence there has been much discussion of questions such as: What counts as one law or rule? What is a complete rule (Raz 1980)? There is widespread agreement among jurists that nearly all rules, norms, or laws belong to some larger agglomeration such as a system, order, or code. This is helpful, but it merely pushes the problem of individuation to a more abstract level. For

---

[2] There are certain special applications that we can set on one side: for example, "a pluralist" can refer to "one who holds two or more offices, especially ecclesiastical benefices, at the same time" (Webster 1981). The *Oxford English Dictionary* (*OED*) suggests that this was the original usage and that other meanings are extensions. The *OED* recognizes a special meaning of "pluralism" in ontology as "the theory that the knowable world is made up of a plurality of interacting things."

[3] More directly related to legal pluralism is the special meaning of "pluralism" in political science, rendered by the *OED* as "[a] theory which opposes monolithic state power and advocates instead increased devolution and autonomy for the main organizations that represent man's involvement in society."

example, legal pluralism is often taken to refer to the coexistence of two or more legal orders in the same time-space context. But what constitutes an order can be very vague; not all normative and legal orders have precise boundaries; and there are plenty of warnings in the literature about the dangers of "reifying" or "essentializing" such units or treating them as more homogeneous or monolithic than they really are.[4] The same applies to concepts such as culture and community. Talk of "pluralism" presupposes individuation. We need concepts such as order, system, code, community, and culture, and we talk about them as if they are discrete units (Twining 2009a, chap. 15). But we also need to be aware of the pitfalls.

Normative Pluralism[5]

We all encounter normative pluralism every day of our lives. When I ask my students to list all the sets of norms that they have encountered in the past week, very few do not get to a hundred. We accept this situation as a social fact; we navigate these complexities daily without undue difficulty, and we rarely puzzle about the phenomenon. Despite this, many lawyers are puzzled about "legal pluralism"; some even deny the concept, and there has been much theoretical debate about it. There has been much less theorizing about normative pluralism, which raises some profound philosophical problems in the general theory of norms (Twining 2010, 479–85).

Non-state law. How to conceptualize law is a central problem of jurisprudence. Although still contested, it is increasingly accepted that a conception of law confined to state law (or to municipal law and classical public international law) leaves out too many significant phenomena deserving sustained juristic attention, including religious law, customary law, and certain other kinds of transnational and supranational normative orders. Nearly all studies of legal pluralism assume or assert some conception of non-state law. This is presupposed by the very idea of legal pluralism and opposed by one version of state-centrism – namely, that state law is the only real law. Accepting the idea of non-state law leads almost inevitably to the view that legal pluralism is an important, pervasive, and complex phenomenon. How to distinguish between "legal" and other social phenomena has been an almost obsessive concern of lp studies. In my view, this concern has been largely unnecessary, because in most contexts not much turns on where, or even whether, the line is drawn.

Legal pluralism. I have for many years found it helpful to treat legal pluralism as a species of normative pluralism. If normative pluralism refers to a situation in which different sets of norms or two or more institutionalized normative orders coexist in the

---

4 An extreme example of the dangers is the creation of the categories of Hutu and Tutsi in Rwanda, which reportedly contributed significantly to the genocide of 1994 (e.g., Prunier 1995). Recent literature on religious minorities in Europe repeatedly warns against ignoring internal diversity within such "communities" or "groups" (e.g., Bano 2007).
5 In this context, *normative pluralism* refers to the existence of a plurality of norms (i.e., rules or prescriptions) or of normative orders as a social fact. This is narrower than the ordinary usage of *normative*, contrasted with empirical, meaning evaluative or prescriptive.

same time-space context, then legal pluralism is the species that includes those kinds of sets of norms or normative orders that merit the appellation *legal* in a given context (Twining 2009a, chap. 4).[6] This move does not solve the problem of the definitional stop – how to have a broad concept of law without including all social phenomena – but it domesticates the problem in a number of ways. First, it decenters the state (on which more is discussed in the next part). Second, it raises the issue of how to classify normative phenomena: normative theory tells us that depends on context and the purpose of the inquiry (Twining 2010). Third, it brings out the point that in many contexts, the scheme of classification and which borderline cases are subsumed or excluded from "the legal" are of little or no practical importance. I argue later that in the present context the main relevant point is that law reformers, policy makers, and importers of foreign laws and ideas need to be aware of the existence and nature of significant normative orders, whether or not they are recognized locally to be "legal" or to have some theoretical claim to that status. Of course, whether a particular order or set of norms is *recognized* by the state as "legal" or legally relevant occasionally may have practical consequences, but such issues are nearly always resolved in specific contexts.

Recently, several scholars of legal pluralism have moved toward treating legal pluralism as a species of normative pluralism or abandoning the term altogether. They have made this move for different reasons. Simon Roberts has written "against legal pluralism" mainly because he thinks that talk of legal pluralism obscures the distinctiveness of state law and governance as specific forms (Roberts 1998, 2005).[7] John Griffiths is prepared to drop the concept of law as part of constructing a general theory of social norms (Griffiths 2003, 2006). Brian Tamanaha (2008), alternatively, sees this move as a way of rescuing "legal pluralism" as a worthwhile field of inquiry or focus of attention. Like me, he thinks this will help shift attention away from the debilitating problems of conceptualizing law. The move does not solve the problem but contextualizes the concern and makes it less important.

State Centralism (or Centrism)

In 1986, John Griffiths launched a sharp attack on legal centralism, which he treated as an "ideology" (Griffiths 1986, 3). In this view, "law is and should be the law of the state, uniform for all persons, exclusive of all other law, and administered by a

---

[6] On the need in this context to work with two conceptions of law (law as ideas – as in legal traditions – and law as institutionalized normative orders or practices) and the conceptual framework this entails, see Twining (2009a, chaps. 1, 3, and 4). This chapter concentrates on social fact legal pluralism (sflp) that treats institutionalized normative orders (and to a lesser extent sets of norms) as the main units; another strand, following in the footsteps of Geertz, treats cultures (and related concepts) as the main units (see Sally Merry's chapter this volume).

[7] Discussed in Twining (2009a, 371–75). In my view, most of Roberts's concerns can be met by using terms such as *state law* or *municipal law* instead of *law* and not making law do too much work as an analytical concept.

single set of state institutions." This ideology is a mixture of assertions about how the world ought to be and a priori assumptions about how the world actually and even necessarily is. In Griffiths's view, legal centralism was "the major obstacle to the development of a descriptive theory of law" (1986, 3).

Attacks on "legal centralism" and "state centralism" have continued, but the grounds have been diverse. In light of subsequent discussions, the idea of state centralism needs to be disaggregated into a series of distinct but related propositions of different kinds:

(a) At the level of description, the state is the only institution that contributes to social order.
(b) The empirical claim that, at least in modern societies, state law is in practice the most important form of law: it is dominant, technically superior, and more powerful than other forms of institutionalized ordering (e.g., Galligan 2007, chap. 10).
(c) The normative claim that the state has sole and supreme authority in a given territory or space, and it has a monopoly of the legitimate use of force.
(d) The ideological claim that the state is the political form that offers the best or only hope for the realization of liberal democratic values, such as democracy, equality, human rights, and the rule of law.

Most people who have thought about it would contest (a) as an empirical statement about nearly all societies. Conversely, asserting that legal pluralism is a social fact involves no general claims about the de facto importance, technical sophistication, and power of modern bureaucratic states (b). Such claims are difficult to test empirically. The issue is central to discussions about the decline of the state, not least in the context of globalization, but inquiries about its relative power and importance are extraordinarily elusive. (c) and (d) are both generally contested in political theory.

The idea of legal pluralism, and the importance of the phenomenon, are widely recognized in recent scholarly literature. Legal pluralism mainly challenges (a). However, it would be wrong to assume that state-centrism is dead.[8] Most Western academic law and legal practice is focused almost entirely on domestic municipal law of sovereign states and is likely to remain so.[9] Even in circles in which the idea

---

[8] An interesting example of a moderate form of state-centrism is provided by the leading sociolegal scholar, Denis Galligan: he recognizes that there are forms of non-state law that coexist and intersect with state legal orders; he acknowledges that many claims made for the state's social role are extravagant, that it can be ineffective or worse, and that non-state normative orders, whether recognized as legal or not, often have social utility. However, he concludes that the modern democratic state provides the best hope for achieving some social goods, including human rights, the rule of law, and democracy (Galligan 2007, chap. 10). In respect of the subordination of non-state law, he recognizes that there can be semi-independence or semiautonomy but denies claims to complete autonomy (2007, 176–77).
[9] Underlying most regimes of legal education and training is a concern about the practical relevance of what is being studied. The maxim "lawyers don't practice non-state law" is sometimes true. It is also

of legal pluralism is accepted, a milder form of state centralism prevails. In much of the literature, the focus is still largely on the interactions between state and non-state law: how the state does and should respond, where it should hold the line, how minority communities should adjust, and how they can make their voices heard in policy formation. Typically, foreign development agencies and consultants have to work through governments with the result that, even if they are sensitive to the phenomenon of legal pluralism, it is difficult for them to avoid being state-centric in this weaker sense.

There are also fundamental ideological questions about the desirability of many forms of legal pluralism. This raises a range of both normative and empirical issues that extend far beyond the topic of "legal pluralism." Some of these issues concern broad questions of general political theory about the role of the state, its claims to a monopoly of legitimate force, and claims to independence or autonomy by or on behalf of non-state legal orders. Some believe that the bureaucratic state offers the best, perhaps the only, hope for maintaining democracy, human rights, and the rule of law. These are important and complex political issues with wide ramifications. Sociolegal research on legal pluralism can inform debates about them, as it has done recently with regard to ethnic and religious minorities in Europe,[10] but on its own it cannot purport to resolve such fundamental issues of political and democratic theory. In this context, it is important to remember Boaventura Santos's admonition against romanticizing legal pluralism, as some scholars have tended to do: "[T]here is nothing inherently good, progressive or emancipatory about legal pluralism" (Santos 1995, 114–15).

In development circles, especially at higher levels, state-centrism may be due to ignorance, deliberate policy, indifference, or downright hostility. A strong, but not untypical, example of hostility to customary law is a speech in 2006 by the secretary-general of the Commonwealth Secretariat:[11]

> The drawbacks of customary law are manifold. For a start, just take its perceived failure to adapt to the expectations created by modern statehood, education, new technology, and global development. It lacks a contemporary comprehensiveness. It fails to address the emerging issues and needs of children, women and the disadvantaged. (McKinnon 2006, 651)

---

self-confirming, but it is being eroded in multicultural societies and, for example, in international arbitration.

[10] For example, Shah and Menski (2006), Bano (2007).

[11] The Rt. Hon. Don McKinnon was addressing a legal conference on "Courting Justice: Rule of Law Reform in Africa" in London in April 2006. After listing a series of "deep-seated and harmful social values and practices" (including female genital mutilation, enforced female servitude, prolonged mourning rites, and so forth), he concluded: "From these examples, it is clear that the greatest single damage done by the persistence of customary law is to women, children and the poor. How far this has been a bar to our achievement of the Millennium Development Goals – particularly the 2nd to achieve universal primary education; the 3rd, to promote gender equality and empower women; and the 5th, to promote maternal health – remains a matter for concern" (McKinnon 2006, 651).

A significant example of indifference, bordering on hostility, is that of Jeffrey Sachs, the director of the Millennium Project. His powerful book *The End of Poverty* does not mention customary law or religion, but tellingly has a significant heading in the index for "cultural barriers" (Sachs 2005, index).[12] This is not atypical of writing about development by economists, though there are some exceptions. Not all discussions of customary law, culture, and tradition are so sweeping. Frontline development practitioners may be more sensitive to local complexities. There is, of course, a body of literature, much of it based on detailed empirical research, that presents a more complex and balanced view.[13] This kind of negativity, illustrated by McKinnon and Sachs, tends to be based on a number of dubious assumptions: that women are always at a disadvantage under customary law, that customary law is static rather than dynamic, that it is rigid rather than flexible, that it is incompatible with sustainable development, that it is always economically inefficient, that it is not concerned to conserve resources, and that values involved in economic development strategies (including the Millennium Development Goals) are intrinsically morally superior to customary values.[14]

"*Coexistence* in the same time-space context" refers to phenomena that in principle can be studied empirically, for example, human behavior, attitudes, institutions, processes, even beliefs. This fits law conceived in terms of social practices, institutions, and processes. But law is also conceived in terms of concepts, norms, traditions, and cultures independently of their institutionalization on the ground (and which may never have been so institutionalized, or about which we have no data).[15] The idea of "coexistence" in time and space in relation to these is problematic. Where is justice? Where are rights? are puzzling questions. As Franz von Benda-Beckmann (2002) suggests, whether we can make sense of the idea of coexistence depends on the context and purpose of the inquiry (cf. Walker 2009).

Interlegality. Santos's useful concept refers to relations and interactions between legal orders and sets of norms. Interlegality is best viewed as a dynamic process rather

---

[12] The longest passage reads: "Even when governments are trying to advance their countries, the cultural environment may be an obstacle to development. Cultural or religious norms in the society may block the role of women, for example, leaving half of the population without economic or political rights and without education, thereby undermining half of the population in its contribution to overall development. Denying women their rights and education results in cascading problems. Most important, perhaps, the demographic transition from high fertility to low fertility is delayed or blocked altogether" (Sachs 2005, 60–61; see also 36–37, 72).

[13] For example, Örebach et al. (2005). A central theme of the book is: "[E]ach customary law system needs to be evaluated on its merits" (Bosselman, id. at p. 441). See also Perreau-Saussine and Murphy (2007) and Rajagopal (2007, 276–82).

[14] Counterexamples to most of these overgeneralizations can be found in Örebach et al. (2005). On "chthonic law" and the environment, see Glenn (2007, 72–76). Because generalized hostility to customary law tends to be ignorantly ethnocentric, it does not follow that there are no problems (discussed in Twining 2009a, 11.6 ["Non-state law; the forgotten factor"]).

[15] For example, there is a rich, largely unempirical literature about Shari'a as ideas, but relatively few empirical studies of Muslim institutionalized social/legal practices.

than in terms of static structures. It is an empirical concept that draws attention to the dynamism and diversity of such relations, but it is generally acknowledged that interlegality does not necessarily involve conflict or competition. How normative and legal orders interact and interrelate is an empirical and interpretive question covering a range of possibilities, including symbiosis, subsumption, imitation, convergence, adaptation, partial integration, and avoidance as well as subordination, repression, or destruction.[16] Any attempt to classify these elusive relations in the abstract is likely to fail.

Recognition[17]

The idea of recognition (of states, foreign laws, and so forth) has a long history in public and private international law. In legal pluralism studies, the term mainly arises in connection with the relationship between the state and non-state legal orders. There are no consistent uses of the term. In this context, it is important to distinguish between a state *according* recognition and communities, groups, or even individuals *claiming, demanding, or asking* for recognition by the state. These are not coextensive and have different variants. For example, a state may *acknowledge* the existence of a non-state order without giving it any legal status, or it may or may not *take into account* the existence of norms or practices in the exercise of judicial or administrative discretion – for example, in sentencing or provocation, or in framing specific policies or legislation. It may undertake to *enforce* such norms; it may *incorporate* some as part of the official legal system, with or without modification, or subject to certain conditions or limitations. It may *integrate* to a greater or lesser degree certain institutions, practices, or tribunals into the state legal system.[18] It may *defer* to private ordering, as with certain kinds of arbitration or other forms of self-regulation, or it can *outlaw* certain practices, thereby acknowledging that they exist, and so forth.

In considering demands or claims for recognition, it is important to clarify what precisely is being asked for. It is also important to realize that (a) what the state accords or imposes may not be what a given group wants and that (b) such demands or claims may be contested within a given population. For example, in the debate in Britain following the archbishop of Canterbury's speech advocating recognition of some decisions of Islamic Councils with respect to family law, there was not only a (largely Islamophobic) outcry against this suggestion, but British Muslims were

---

[16] Tamanaha (2008) emphasizes conflict as being the most problematic aspect but recognizes that there are other kinds of relations between normative orders; I am inclined to use the concept of interlegality as an open-ended concept that refers to all kinds of relations – what these are in any given context is an empirical and interpretative question.
[17] This section is indebted to Ghai and Cottrell (2009).
[18] For example, on the Basoga in Uganda in the colonial period, see Fallers (1969).

split on the issues (Bano 2007, 2010). There is no agreed terminology with respect to recognition, but there is widespread agreement that it is a highly political matter.

This sample of problematic concepts could be extended to include several others that have been extensively discussed in other contexts, including religion (and religious law), custom (and customary law), tradition, culture, and authority.

II. SOCIAL FACT LEGAL PLURALISM

Social Fact Conceptions of Legal Pluralism: An Ideal Type

The mainstream legal pluralism literature has quite diverse intellectual roots. Generalization is dangerous, except that the very idea of legal pluralism typically presupposes a conception of non-state law. However, one can construct a fairly robust ideal type of social fact (legal) pluralism (sflp) to which most anthropological and sociolegal studies up to the mid-1990s approximated, based on the following points:

1. If one adopts a broad, positivist conception of law, legal pluralism is as much a social fact as normative pluralism.[19]
2. It is important to distinguish between state legal pluralism (sometimes called weak legal pluralism), legal polycentricity (the eclectic use of sources within different sectors of one state legal system) (Petersen and Zahle 1995), and legal pluralism conceived as the coexistence of two or more autonomous or semiautonomous legal orders or sets of norms in the same time-space context.[20]
3. Legal pluralism is pervasive in all multicultural societies, which in today's world means most societies.
4. Legal pluralism is not new. Indeed, from the perspective of world history, the near monopoly of coercive power by a centralized bureaucratic state is a modern exception, largely confined to the Northern Hemisphere for less than two hundred years.

---

[19] Accordingly, it is quite misleading to talk of "legal pluralists" as a marginal school or sect or a particular theoretical perspective (Benda-Beckmann 2002, 72–74). This is one of the best general articles on legal pluralism, and I am in general agreement with its thrust.
[20] Twining (2010) uses a series of case studies to illustrate some standard distinctions in sflp: ordinary statutory interpretation, not interpreted as "pluralism": *Sudan Govt. El Baleila Balla Baleila* (1958) *Sudan Law Journal and Reports* 12 (interpretation of the Sudan Penal Code invoking English concept of "the reasonable man" and Baggara values relating to cattle in relation to provocation in homicide); state ("weak") legal pluralism: the S. M. Otieno burial case (Kenya) (Egan 1987) (customary law as an integral part of state law); "genuine" legal pluralism: Santos's Pasagarda Residents' Association (Brazil) (Santos 1995, 2002), the Common Law Movement (United States) (Koniak 1996, 1997); Romani law (transnational) (Weyrauch and Bell, 1993; Weyrauch 1997); pluralism of discourse: Bowen's studies in Indonesia where argumentation in state, Islamic, and customary tribunals regularly involves weaving together state, Islamic, and traditional norms and concepts (Bowen 2003). Some of these distinctions are now challenged in the context of globalization (Michaels 2009).

5. Legal pluralism is here to stay. *Custom* and *tradition* may be more dynamic and flexible than these labels suggest, but insofar as institutionalized normative orders are grounded in settled ways and beliefs and a sense of identity, they are intransigent and resistant to change from the outside. For aspiring "social engineers" who perceive them as obstacles, they are more like mountains than molehills.
6. From the standpoint of subjects, users, and victims, situations of legal pluralism sometimes, but not always, provide opportunities for "shopping" for advice, norms, or fora.
7. Acknowledging legal pluralism as a social fact involves no necessary commitment to any of the following propositions:
    a. State law is unimportant.
    b. The state is withering away.
    c. Acceptance of legal pluralism as a fact involves a denial or weakening of such ideals as liberal democracy, human rights; and the rule of law.
8. It is a distortion to think of interlegality – relations and interactions between coexisting legal orders – as typically entailing conflict and competition.
9. Sflp studies were empirically oriented and focused mainly on institutionalized normative orders, as opposed to state centrism. It was generally not much concerned with normative questions about legitimacy, authority, justification, obligatoriness, and official policies toward non-state normative orders and laws.

Normativity

We have noted in relation to the concept of pluralism that there is a tendency in the literature to slide from the descriptive to the prescriptive. But sflp studies tell us almost nothing about the internal or external legitimacy, obligatoriness, or legality of non-state legal orders. Their existence as a social fact, their nature, and their internal and external relations have been their main concern. But questions arise at all levels of legal ordering about how coexisting orders should view each other.

In recent years, legal philosophers have devoted a great deal of attention to the topic of "the normativity of law." The central question is whether (state) law is by its nature obligatory, binding, and authoritative or whether obligations to obey, observe, and respect the law are based on contingencies external to the law itself.[21] Three aspects of this trend stand in sharp contrast to the mainstream literature on legal pluralism: first, the focus is on the domestic law of a given society; second, the idea of law is confined to state law; and, third, the standpoint is that of participants in or subjects

---

[21] For example, in a stimulating book, Sylvie Delacroix argues that laws are human creations that are obligatory for judges, lawmakers, and citizens "if law is deemed to promote a set of moral and prudential concerns essential to a 'good' way of living together" (Delacroix 2006, xiv, 206). In other words, the normative force of law is itself a creation of the moral aspirations and sense of responsibility of its subjects as members of a community. See also Simmonds (2009).

of that legal system. The question for them is: what is my responsibility toward *my/our* legal system? This differs from sflp, which (typically) (a) is not confined to nation-states, countries, or societies conceived of as units; (b) extends the concept of law to include at least some kinds of non-state law; and (c) adopts the standpoint of an observer of legal orders who is external to them but takes account of the internal point of view of citizens, lawmakers, judges, and other participants.

Such differences look like a rerun of juristic debates between positivists and non-positivists resurfacing in the context of discussions of legal pluralism. However, the situation is more complicated than that for two main reasons: First, some supporters of the idea of legal pluralism are non-positivists.[22] Second, many writers about legal pluralism have normative concerns, both at the level of ideology (opposing "state-centrism") and in relation to practical problems facing policy makers, judges, legislators, and other participants in legal processes. However, as just noted, most classical social fact accounts of legal pluralism, like legal positivism, provide little or no guidance on normative issues, other than suggesting that the phenomena are too empirically important to be ignored.

III. GLOBAL LEGAL PLURALISM – A NEW "PARADIGM"?

A radically ambiguous idea introduced largely in response to "globalization" – that is, since the mid-1990s – is that of global legal pluralism (glp). Each of its elements is problematic. We have already noted the ambiguities of "pluralism" and "legal." "Global" is almost as ambiguous and is currently overused and misused (Twining 2009a, chap. 1.4). It can mean (a) genuinely worldwide, (b) widespread geographically, (c) anything transnational or supranational, or (d) anything related to increased interdependence.[23] A crucial point is that most so-called global legal phenomena and patterns are sub-global, related to empires, diasporas, alliances, trading blocs, languages, and legal traditions. But "g-talk" is prone to exaggeration and hyperbole.[24] For example, there is a tendency in anglophone discussions

---

[22] An interesting example of the first group is Emmanuel Melissaris (2009), who constructs a sustained argument that ideas of legal pluralism and non-state law can be accommodated within nonpositivist legal theory on the basis of people's shared experiences and sense of law that are to some degree universal. Philip Selznick is perhaps the most substantial sociolegal theorist who seeks to transcend the is/ought divide. His concepts of incipient law and responsive law may be of particular relevance to development activists confronting non-state law (Kagan, Krygier, and Winston 2002; Krygier, forthcoming).

[23] For example, see the attitude of René David to custom as symptomatic of French attitudes (discussed in Twining 2010).

[24] The oversimplification of loose "g-talk" is illustrated by the claim that "English is the global language." That English is important and powerful in many countries and contexts is undeniably true. But how many people count as "English speakers," and how are they distributed? In about seventy countries, English is the official or dominant language, but in many of these only a small percentage of the population have it as their first or second language or have a working knowledge of it. For example, in "Anglophone" Uganda, the best, but purely speculative, estimate was that in 1994 perhaps 11 percent of

of legal pluralism and "law and development" to extrapolate from the practices and hangovers of the British Empire (itself a sub-global phenomenon) to generalize about the whole postcolonial situation. Anglo-American discourse in this area often understates the differences between the practices, attitudes, and postindependence legacies of different traditions of imperialism and colonialism – for example, in relation to conscious policies of indirect rule or attitudes to customary law.[25]

Despite the confused terminology, the concerns are real, but the answers to the question "plurality of what?" are different from those of sflp: for example, fragmentation of public international law, multiple geographical levels of ordering,[26] proliferation of supranational tribunals and of significant legal actors, proliferation of human rights, and so forth. Associating glp with "postmodernism" – itself an ambiguous concept – further muddies the waters. A major question is: is glp an extension of lp or sflp or a new "paradigm" (Michaels 2009, 243–44)? My view is skeptical. *Pluralism* may not be a good focus or label for these concerns, many of which are normative – relating to institutional design, state and supra-state policy, rights-based approaches to development, and so forth.[27]

"Globalization" is challenging some of the settled assumptions of Western traditions of academic law.[28] Legal pluralism studies, especially sflp, are perhaps less wedded to some of these assumptions: they oppose state centrism, they accept some idea of "non-state law," they take religion seriously, and they have more of an empirical orientation than doctrinal legal studies.[29]

However, several factors challenge any strong claims to continuity.

First, sflp grew out of a tradition that focused largely on small, face-to-face local communities at a subnational level; the range of subject matters and actors was a far cry from questions about international terrorism, the fragmentation of international

---

the population claimed English as their second language. That is to say that almost 90 percent of the population could not understand the language of the laws, courts (including magistrates' courts), or most official business (Crystal 1995). On the complexities of assessing such claims, see Crystal (2003).

[25] I have argued elsewhere that *law and development* is an American term, adopted in due course by some British scholars, but virtually unknown in the discourse of French, Dutch, and Portuguese colonial and postcolonial literature (Twining 2009a, 327, 330–31). Almost all of the papers in this volume are by anglophone scholars, and in some papers one can detect an American bias toward emphasis on pathological aspects of law – disputes, litigation, courts, and cases – in contrast to codes, principles, structures, and routines. Lauren Benton has plausibly suggested that different colonial strategies may mask more common patterns and problems than appear on the surface.

[26] See Appendix B.

[27] Of course, a multiplicity of normative and legal orders can be perceived at transnational, regional, and global levels; they interact with each other horizontally, vertically, and in more complex ways; they are as much a social fact worthy of attention as legal and normative pluralism at national and more local levels. But this is only one facet of the variety of phenomena that tend to get lumped together under "glp."

[28] See Appendix A.

[29] This is developed in Twining (2010).

law, regulation of transnational finance and commerce, regional integration, and trafficking of drugs or humans.

Second, sflp was mainly concerned with plurality of coexisting institutionalized normative orders. So-called global legal pluralism gives a much more varied answer to the question: plurality of what? Here, the term *pluralism* has been applied indiscriminately to almost any kind of complexity or diversity. Moving the central legacy of insights onto a world stage involves significant changes in scale, subject matters, and central concerns. The idea of glp applied to actors, courts, schools of thought, centers of power, sources of norms, levels of relations and ordering, authority, culture, or even the proliferation of human rights means little more than diversity. Postmodern enthusiasm for fragmentation, diversification, and indeterminacy further threatens to reduce the value of "pluralism" as an analytic concept. We are swamped with a not very illuminating plurality of pluralisms. It is not clear how helpful the heritage of sflp studies can be in interpreting these very varied topics.

Third, and equally significant, insofar as sflp studies have been largely descriptive rather than normative, one should not expect much practical normative guidance about such issues as institutional design, state policy, or rights-based approaches to development.

Fourth, as borders become more porous and state sovereignty is challenged, are sharp distinctions between the internal and external aspects of state legal systems still tenable? From a global perspective, state (weak) legal pluralism, conflicts of laws, and the politics of recognition transcend distinctions between state and non-state law (Michaels 2009).

Fifth, mainstream lp studies have bequeathed us a rich heritage of particular studies and a rather less impressive body of theorizing. Moving the central legacy of insights onto a world stage involves significant changes in scale, subject matters, and central concerns.

IV. CONCLUSION

From the point of view of development practitioners, the central lesson of sflp is that local knowledge is important. The phenomena of legal pluralism are so varied and complex that a general World Bank strategy toward non-state legal orders would almost certainly be unwise, even dangerous. Douglas Porter, in commenting on this chapter, suggested that many frontline development practitioners are well aware of the existence and intransigence of plural normative orders and bodies of rules. They realize that they are ubiquitous, elusive, likely to persist, and difficult to change. What they want is guidance on how to deal with such situations. From that point of view, this chapter is rather negative in that it suggests that the literature of sflp can be used to back up such perceptions, but it does not provide much general guidance beyond the following, rather anodyne conclusions.

Sflp literature, by emphasizing the fact of the coexistence of significant institutionalized bodies of social norms and practices, is helpful in at least five ways:

(a) in drawing attention to the existence of non-state orders, practices, and norms that are often ignored, overlooked, arcane, or even invisible;
(b) in the context of diffusion/transplantation, it provides a reminder that norms based on foreign models are rarely introduced into a vacuum (the blank slate fallacy) but will inevitably have to interact with preexisting local arrangements, which will often include significant institutionalized normative orders;
(c) it warns that many claims to convergence, harmonization, or unification may refer mainly or only to surface law (Twining 2009a, chap. 10);
(d) it focuses attention on interlegality – the many different and complex ways in which multiple legal and normative orders can relate to one another and interact; and
(e) it focuses attention on issues of state policy concerning relations between the state and different communities and belief systems in a multicultural society. But insofar as one adopts a social fact view of normative pluralism, this will on its own provide little direct guidance on normative questions about legitimacy, justification, toleration, and recognition of non-state legal orders.

APPENDIX

A. *Western Traditions of Academic Law: Some Simplistic Assumptions*[30]

(a) law consists of two principal kinds of ordering: municipal state law and public international law (classically conceived as ordering the relations between states) ("the Westphalian duo");
(b) nation-states, societies, and legal systems are very largely closed, self-contained entities that can be studied in isolation;
(c) modern law and modern jurisprudence are secular, now largely independent of their historical-cultural roots in the Judeo-Christian traditions;
(d) modern state law is primarily rational-bureaucratic and instrumental, performing certain functions and serving as a means for achieving particular social ends;
(e) law is best understood through "top-down" perspectives of rulers, officials, legislators, and elites, with the points of view of users, consumers, victims, and other subjects being at best marginal;
(f) the main subject matters of the discipline of law are ideas and norms rather than the empirical study of social facts;

---

[30] Adapted from Twining (2009a, 5–7).

(g) modern state law is almost exclusively a Northern (European/Anglo-American) creation, diffused through most of the world via colonialism, imperialism, trade, and latter-day postcolonial influences;
(h) the study of non-Western legal traditions is a marginal and unimportant part of Western academic law; and
(i) the fundamental values underlying modern law are universal, although the philosophical foundations are diverse.

B. *Levels of Law*[31]

Law is concerned with relations between subjects or persons (human, legal, unincorporated, and otherwise) at a variety of levels, not just with relations within a single nation-state or society. One way of characterizing such levels is essentially geographical:

- global (as with some environmental issues, a possible *ius humanitatis* and, by extension, intergalactic or space law) – for example, mineral rights on the moon;
- international (in the classic sense of relations between sovereign states and, more broadly, relations governed, for example, by human rights or refugee law);
- regional (for example, the European Union, the European Convention on Human Rights, and the African Union);
- transnational (for example, Islamic, Hindu, Jewish, and Romani ["gypsy"] law; transnational arbitration; a putative *lex mercatoria*; Internet law; and, more controversially, the internal governance of multinational corporations; the Catholic Church; or institutions of organized crime);
- intercommunal (as in relations between religious communities, Christian churches, or different ethnic groups);
- territorial state (including the legal systems of nation-states, and subnational jurisdictions, such as Florida, Greenland, Quebec, and Northern Ireland);
- sub-state (e.g., subordinate legislation, such as bylaws of the borough of Camden) or religious law officially recognized for limited purposes in a plural legal system; and
- non-state (including laws of subordinated peoples, such as native North Americans, Maoris, or gypsies or illegal legal orders, such as Santos's Pasagarda law, the Southern People's Liberation Army's legal regime in Southern Sudan,[32] and the "common law movement" of militias in the United States). Which of

---

[31] Adapted from Twining (2009a, 69–74).
[32] The Southern Peoples' Liberation Army operated a system of courts dealing with both civil and criminal cases in areas they occupied in the civil war in the southern Sudan (Kuol 1997).

these should be classified as "law" or "legal" is essentially contested within legal theory and also depends on the context and purposes of the discourse.

REFERENCES

Bano, Samia. 2007. "Muslim Family Justice and Human Rights: The Experience of British Muslim Women." *Journal of Comparative Law* 1 (4): 1–27.

———. 2010. "Beyond the Sacred and the Secular." In *Rights in Context: Law and Justice in Late Modern Society*, ed. Reza Banaker. Aldershot: Ashgate.

Benda-Beckman, Franz von. 2002. "Who's Afraid of Legal Pluralism?" *Journal of Legal Pluralism* 47: 37–82.

Bowen, John R. 2003. *Islam, Law and Equality in Indonesia: An Anthropology of Public Reasoning*. Cambridge: Cambridge University Press.

Crystal, David, ed. 1995. *The Cambridge Encyclopedia of the English Language*. Cambridge: Cambridge University Press.

———, 2003. *English as a World Language*. 2nd ed. Cambridge: Cambridge University Press.

Delacroix, Sylvie. 2006. *Legal Norms and Normativity: An Essay in Genealogy*. Oxford: Hart.

Egan, Sean, ed. 1987. *S. M. Otieno: Kenya's Unique Burial Saga*. Nairobi: Nation Newspapers.

Fallers, Lloyd. 1969. *Law without Precedent*. Chicago: University of Chicago Press.

Galligan, Denis. 2007. *Law in Modern Society*. Oxford: Oxford University Press.

Ghai, Yash, and Jill Cottrell, "The Rule of Law and Access to Justice," unpublished manuscript on file with author.

Glenn, H. Patrick. 2007. *Legal Traditions of the World: Sustainable Diversity in Law*. 3rd ed. Oxford: Oxford University Press.

Griffiths, John. 1986. "What Is Legal Pluralism?" *Journal of Legal Pluralism* 24: 1–55.

———. 2003. "The Social Working of Legal Rules." *Journal of Legal Pluralism* 48: 1–84.

———. 2006. "The Idea of Sociology of Law and its Relation to Law and to Sociology." In *Law and Sociology*. Vol. 8 of *Current Legal Issues*, ed. Michael Freeman. Oxford: Oxford University Press.

Kagan, Robert, Martin Krygier, and Kenneth Winston, eds. 2002. *Legality and Community: On the Intellectual Legacy of Philip Selznick*. Lanham, MD: Rowman and Littlefield.

Koniak, Susan. 1996. "When Law Risks Madness." *Cardozo Studies in Law and Literature* 8 (1): 65–138.

———. 1997. "The Chosen People in Our Wilderness." *Michigan Law Review* 95 (6): 1761–98.

Krygier, Martin. Forthcoming. *Ideals in the World: The Thought of Philip Selznick*. Stanford, CA: Stanford University Press.

Kuol, Monyluak Alor. 1997. "Administration of Justice in the (SPLA/M) Liberated Areas: Court Cases in War-Torn Southern Sudan." Refugee Studies Programme, University of Oxford.

McKinnon, Don. 2006. "The Rule of Law in Today's Africa." *Commonwealth Law Bulletin* 32 (4): 649–55.

Melissaris, Emmanuel. 2009. *Ubiquitous Law: Legal Theory and the Space for Legal Pluralism*. Aldershot: Ashgate.

Merriam-Webster. 1981. *Webster's Third New International Dictionary of the English Language*.

Merry, Sally. 2008. "International Law and Sociolegal Scholarship: Toward a Spatial Global Legal Pluralism." *Studies in Law, Politics and Society* 41: 149–68.

Michaels, Ralf. 2009. "Global Legal Pluralism." *Annual Review of Law and Social Science* 5: 1–35.

Örebach, Peter, Fred Bosselman, Jes Bjarup, David Callies, Martin Chanock, and Hanne Petersen. 2005. *The Role of Customary Law in Sustainable Development*. Cambridge: Cambridge University Press.

Perreau-Saussine, Amanda, and James Murphy, eds. 2007. *The Nature of Customary Law: Legal, Historical and Philosophical Perspectives*. Cambridge: Cambridge University Press.

Petersen, Hanne, and Henrik Zahle, eds. 1995. *Legal Polycentricity: Consequences of Pluralism in Law*. Aldershot and Brookfield, VT: Dartmouth Publishing.

Prunier, Gérard. 1995. *The Rwanda Crisis*. New York: Columbia University Press.

Rajagopal, Balakrishnan. 2003. *International Law from Below: Developing Social Movements and Third World Resistance*. Cambridge: Cambridge University Press.

Raz, Joseph. 1980. *The Concept of a Legal System*. Oxford: Oxford University Press.

Roberts, Simon. 1998. "Against Legal Pluralism: Some Reflections on the Contemporary Enlargement of the Legal Domain." *Journal of Legal Pluralism* 42: 95–106.

———. 2005. "After Government? On Representing Law without the State." *Modern Law Review* 68 (1): 1–24.

Sachs, Jeffrey. 2005. *The End of Poverty: How We Can Make It Happen in Our Lifetime*. London: Penguin.

Santos, Boaventura de Sousa. 1995. *Toward a New Common Sense*. London: Routledge.

———. 2002. *Toward a New Legal Common Sense: Law, Globalization and Emancipation*. 2nd ed. London: Butterworth.

Shah, Prakash, and Werner Menski, eds. 2006. *Migration, Diasporas and Legal Systems in Europe*. London: Routledge-Cavendish.

Simmonds, Nigel. 2009. *Law as a Moral Idea*. Oxford. Oxford University Press.

Tamanaha, Brian. 2008. "Understanding Legal Pluralism: Past to Present, Local to Global." *Sydney Law Review* 30: 375–411.

Twining, William. 2009a. *General Jurisprudence: Understanding Law from a Global Perspective*. Cambridge: Cambridge University Press.

———, ed. 2009b. *Human Rights: Southern Voices*. Cambridge: Cambridge University Press.

———. 2010. "Normative and Legal Pluralism: A Global Perspective." *Duke Journal of Comparative and International Law* 20: 473–517.

Walker, Neil. 2009. "Out of Place: Out of Time: Law's Fading Co-ordinates." *Edinburgh Law Review* 14: 13–46.

Weyrauch, Walter, and Maureen A. Bell. 1993. "Autonomous Lawmaking: The Case of the Gypsies." *Yale Law Journal* 103 (2): 323–99.

Weyrauch, Walter, ed. 1997. "Romaniya: An Introduction to Gypsy Law." *American Journal of Comparative Law* 45 (2, Symposium on Gypsy Law): 225–35.

8

The Development "Problem" of Legal Pluralism

An Analysis and Steps toward Solutions

Gordon R. Woodman

Legal pluralism may be defined for the present purpose as *the situation in which a population observes more than one law.*

Various questions of conceptual analysis arise from this and similar attempts to summarize the notion of legal pluralism, but these are not especially significant in considering its relevance to development policies. This is true of what are perhaps the most hotly debated of all of these questions, namely, whether the concept of "law" is limited to state law, and, if not, how "law" is to be distinguished from socially observed normative orders in general (Tamanaha 2001, chap. 7; 2008, 396). (See also F. Benda-Beckmann 2002 for a helpful study of issues in the conceptual analysis of legal pluralism.) The reason why these are not significant is that pluralism of normative orders poses questions for development policies regardless of whether all such orders are called "laws." It would be an unduly narrow approach to limit discussion to pluralism within state laws (although such discussion must not be excluded and can make a valuable contribution). The question of whether state law is or should be regarded as a special type of law, as clearly distinguishable from "non-state" alternatives or as more worthy of support in development projects, raises a series of issues that are noted below.

In one respect, however, this discussion may need to give primacy to the state. International development agencies deal mainly with state agents and, when aiming to bring about social change, act through them. Consequently, a realistic discussion of development policy and legal pluralism must for the present be concerned primarily with relations between state law and other laws and the possibilities of amendment to state laws. As Twining (in this volume) points out, foreign development agencies and consultants cannot easily avoid being "state-centric" in this weak sense. But this need not lead to the stronger form of state-centrism. To recognize that it is necessary to examine the relations between state and non-state law is not to concede the claims of the state to a monopoly of legal authority.

WHY IS LEGAL PLURALISM SEEN AS A PROBLEM?

I consider here a number of possible grounds for the view that legal pluralism is a problem for development policies. I first take two fundamental and extreme views and then consider three further, more qualified views.

First, it is sometimes claimed that development projects promoted through the use of state laws are liable to be frustrated by people's adherence to non-state normative orders and their consequential disregard of state law. Thus, when state laws are made to enable or encourage economic enterprise, non-state laws may effectively discourage the use of the opportunities offered by state laws. Non-state law may drive an entrepreneur to favor his or her lineage or ethnic group in giving employment to unqualified relatives or selling goods to them at a loss, frustrating the aim of maximization of economic returns. Projects intended through state law to promote gender equality may encounter a strong adherence from non-state family laws that discriminate against women. Good governance projects intended to eradicate official corruption, promote the rule of law, and assist economic development on a national scale may have to work through state law officials whose unofficial laws encourage or even require them to engage in corrupt practices or to exercise their discretions in biased ways to advantage members of the smaller circles to which they belong (Bierschenk 2008; Nuijten and Anders 2009). Non-state laws often encourage people to identify with and form loyalty to smaller populations than that of the state, with the result that their interest in the well-being of larger communities is restricted.

Second, development projects directed at strengthening the "rule of law" may be conceived of as being directed to strengthening the rule of *state* law.[1] Here legal pluralism is likely to be seen as an obstacle per se, because if subjects observe non-state laws in parts of their lives, the scope and effectiveness of state law are less than they otherwise would be.

Both of these views point to the conclusion that development policies must aim to eliminate non-state normative orders or to subordinate them totally to state law. This perception of legal pluralism as a problem arises from an obsession with state law to be found not only in state governments but also in international development agencies. These institutions are apt to take the view that state law is the only true law and ought to be fully effective in a modern state. Hence the view that the rule of law must mean the rule of state law.[2] In the field of development policy, this view leads to conclusions that "skip straight to Weber," with an unrealistic optimism as

---

[1] We may take the rule of law, as it features in development projects, to be formal legality, according to which both government officials and citizens act according to legal rules (Tamanaha 2004, 91–99; in this volume). Stephenson (2009) argues that development policy makers are unclear about what they mean by the rule of law but that this type of formal definition is sometimes adopted. Tamanaha (2004, 94) suggests that the World Bank adopts it.

[2] The view that the rule of law means the rule of state law was not only the basis for much work in the mainstream of law and development studies (e.g., Seidman and Seidman 1994), but also seems

to the effects to be achieved by a rationally acting state bureaucracy (Pritchett and Woolcock 2004). It is thought that social change can and should be produced by state law alone.

The principal objection to this view is that in fact state laws do not comprise the entire world of law, large parts of many people's lives being guided by non-state laws, and it will be impossible to change this in the foreseeable future. The requirements of the rule of law can be satisfied by the rule of non-state laws. It can also be argued that this condition should not to be regretted as a "problem" because it also means that there is a barrier to state law becoming unduly powerful. Because state law, just as non-state laws, can fall under the control of a faction that gives priority to objectives other than development and other goods, it is undesirable that state law should have a unique and overriding power.

The other three grounds for viewing legal pluralism as a problem for development policies characterize it not so much as a complete block to the realization of these policies as an impediment that sometimes may be overcome without the need to remove it.

The third problem is that legal pluralism complicates the planning of development projects. It compels the development practitioner to seek to operate on a number of fronts of action, taking account not only of state law but also of other effective, influential normative orders. So, for example, the planners of a project aimed at gender equality cannot stop at considering the best way of entrenching the equality principle in state law backed up by state bureaucratic and judicial institutions. They need also to consider how other, non-state laws may obstruct gender equality, for example, through marriage laws that permit polygyny or through land tenure laws that restrict women's access to land. The project needs to include plans to bring about change in those particular aspects of each of these non-state laws inimical to gender equality. Similar examples could be given of other development projects, such as those for the expansion of primary education. These may need not only a framework of state law for the setting up and ordering of new schools, but also changes in non-state laws that keep girls at home to help with household work. In all such instances, the development practitioner has to deal with a much larger database and a far more complex scene.

Fourth, legal pluralism potentially gives rise to conflicts between the different normative orders that are observed by one or more of the populations within a state. These conflicts produce inconsistency and uncertainty in the normative field. Uncertainty in the law and conflicts between laws are contrary to the ideal of the rule of law (Tamanaha, in this volume). Projects that aim at more efficient and just legal systems need to deal with the prospect that state laws requiring certain forms of conduct coexist with non-state laws that penalize that conduct, and that

---

to be implied in more recent work (e.g., Jayasuriya 1999; Faundez 2005). This view is contested by Tamanaha (2008).

state laws that attribute legal consequences to, for example, written wills coexist with non-state laws that recognize no such possibilities. However, these features are not unequivocally undesirable or problematic. Uncertainty as to which law governs an issue can provide opportunities for the forum- or law-shopper, as can conflicts between laws, so that injustices within one law may be moderated by recourse to another. The development of laws toward more satisfactory and just provisions can be assisted by such conflicts, through which previous laws are changed and different possibilities for the future are fought over and tested. Admittedly, they are, on the whole, more likely to benefit those who are already powerful and able to exploit the possibilities than the relatively powerless (Lund, in this volume). But it can be responded that development projects may select those existing laws that favor development and intervene to give them added effect, and that this is more likely to produce results than seeking to secure the observance of entirely new laws.

Fifth, the multiplicity of norms within situations of legal pluralism renders it very unlikely that any development agent, even if he or she has a high degree of expertise in one normative order, will have an adequate knowledge of other coexisting orders that also need to be taken into account in a development project. Judges and legislators may be able to adjudicate and legislate skillfully and effectively in cases governed by the state law in which they have been trained, and they and development practitioners may well be able to develop and adjust it to meet the requirements of a development project. But none of them may be readily able to discover or understand another law observed within the population of the state when they are required to defer to it or wish to use it to promote development.

Before these problems are considered further, it is necessary to develop somewhat the analysis of legal pluralism.

TOWARD AN ANALYSIS OF ELEMENTS OF LEGAL PLURALISM

Various suggestions have been made as to the categorization of instances of legal pluralism. Griffiths, in a seminal theoretical discussion, drew a distinction between legal pluralism "in the strong sense" (where state law coexists with other, non-state laws, all being observed from a social-scientific perspective) and "in the weak sense" (where pluralism is seen only as a characteristic of state law, and the ideology of state law is dominant) (Griffiths 1986). Merry (1988) distinguished between "classic legal pluralism" arising primarily in colonial societies and continuing in postcolonial societies, and "new legal pluralism" in noncolonized societies, especially the advanced industrial countries of Europe and the United States (but cf. F. Benda-Beckmann 1988). I have found it helpful to distinguish between deep legal pluralism (in which state law coexists with non-state laws) and state law pluralism (in which there is a real but limited pluralism within state law) (e.g., Woodman 1998). Tamanaha (2008,

397–400) gives a list of six groupings of "systems of normative ordering in social arenas." All of these analyses may assist in clarifying understandings of the historical global development and current conditions of legal pluralism. However, for the present purpose I suggest some other analyses and classifications that may be more directly helpful.

(a) *Categories of normative orders.* For the present purpose it seems especially instructive to categorize normative orders in terms of the types of populations that observe them. The following listing of types aims only to demonstrate the very wide incidence of state and non-state laws. It does not follow a single criterion for identifying groups, nor does it claim that there is no coincidence or overlapping of instances from different groups.

> (i) Many populations are defined by *ethnicity*. The members of an ethnic group often identify themselves in part by their observance of a customary law that has been developed within the group. Such a population may be a minority within a larger population that also observes some particular law. Thus, in many African states the population of the nation-state observes to a certain extent the particular law of the state but is divided into a number of populations consisting of ethnic groups, each a minority within the state and each observing to a certain extent its own law. The population may, alternatively, be a majority or the entirety of such a larger population, as in an ethnically uniform state. A population defined by ethnicity may be indigenous to the territory where it is resident, as in the case of the indigenous minorities of North and South America and Australia and the indigenous majorities of ancient states such as Nepal or some European states. It may be an immigrant population, such as the immigrant minorities of Europe and the immigrant majorities of some states that were formed by settlers in the period of European colonization.
>
> (ii) Some populations are defined by their members' common *economic activity*. This is the case where the followers of a particular profession, such as medicine or law, have developed a normative order that regulates the manner in which they practice that profession. Similar instances are the groups of workers within particular industries or workplaces who develop a sense of solidarity and observe norms of conduct in their work and relations inter se. Another outstanding instance is the global population of those engaged in transnational economic transactions (Teubner 1997).
>
> (iii) Other populations are defined by members' *voluntary activity*, where this is continuing and ordered. Instances are political parties and religious organizations such as the regular congregation of a particular place of worship or the membership of an organized religious group. They include a population consisting of the adherents of a particular religious creed insofar as they observe a body of norms of social behavior.

(iv) Some populations are defined by a common *imposed status*, such as the inmates of a prison or military conscripts. Often, in addition to the normative order imposed on them by the state that administers the penal institution, prisoners develop their own normative order.

(v) Finally, the population that observes a *state law* is in the standard case the population that is defined by that law as subjects of that state, largely by reference to presence within a defined territory. The subjects of a state, thus defined, normally observe the law of that state to a certain degree. The nonstandard cases are those where a significant part of the population claimed as subjects by a state law do not observe it at all. Instances are those where the state is seeking to extend its power over a population that has not yet been coerced or persuaded to accept it or if a section of the population that formerly observed that state law is in revolt against its continued subjection. Cases of limited observance by sections of the population are still included on the grounds that the analysis does not set a criterion for inclusion in terms of any particular degree of observance: laws have a social existence if they are observed to any degree.

The incidence of these various types of populations, all with their own extensive or not so extensive normative orders or laws, means that legal pluralism is and has long been ubiquitous. (Benton [2002] opened up new perspectives in this respect.) It would also seem that it is not realistic to predict the total cessation of observance of many of these laws, and one can envisage the emergence of newly identified populations observing their own laws. Any development project aiming to produce a wide range of social change is therefore likely to encounter, and to need to respond to, more laws than just state law. Being universal, legal pluralism should not be seen as a "problem" in the sense that, for example, violent crime is a problem that can be contained, reduced, and perhaps virtually eliminated.

Further, if some societies are more in need of development than others, the difference between them cannot be that the former are in the condition of legal pluralism, whereas the latter are not. Legal pluralism pervades the globe. It also seems unlikely that societies in more need of development have greater degrees of legal pluralism than others, assuming that it is possible to measure and compare spatiotemporal variations in degrees of legal pluralism (cf. Sezgin 2004).

(b) *Categories of relations between normative orders: content of norms.* The relations between normative orders in situations of legal pluralism vary widely. Not every case of legal pluralism involves opposition and contradiction. We may consider this in terms of the individual norms that are the constituent parts of every normative order.[3]

---

[3] On the relationship between different laws, Tamanaha (2008, 403–9) examines "relations and strategies between and among systems in situations of clash," and "common types of fundamental orientation clashes" (while accepting that the relationship is not always that of "clash"). It is suggested that the analysis presented here in terms of norms may also be instructive.

Admittedly, both state and non-state laws in practice depart from the strict, formal notion of rule orientation to a certain degree (Dworkin 1977 on state law; Tamanaha, in this volume, on "alternative legal forms," or non-state law), but norms in the form of rules remain important. A prominent theoretical analysis of law identifies two principal categories of norms, namely, imperative norms, such as the prohibitory rules of criminal law and norms of validation, or facilitative norms, such as the rules designating the manner in which people may transfer title to land (Hart 1961). By way of illustration, we may take for each category an example of a state law norm that may have some bearing on a development project and then note the possibilities of norms on the same subject in another, coexistent law.

(i) First, a state law may contain an imperative norm. For example, a norm enacted as part of a development project may require the parents and guardians of all children older than the age of five to send them to school. Another coexistent order, such as a customary law that is also observed by the population, may contain an imperative norm with effectively the same content, for example, requiring parents and guardians to do all in their power for the well-being of their children, which it interprets in the circumstances as requiring them to send their children to school. Alternatively, it may contain a norm with the opposite content, for example, by requiring parents and guardians to keep their children away from bad influences, interpreted as including the ideas of independent behavior believed to be instilled at school. But it may also contain no imperative norm referring to this conduct, adopting a policy that it is within the discretion of parents and guardians to decide how their children are to be brought up.

In the first of these cases, the two laws would be compatible and would not present any problem for the development project. In the second, they would be in conflict, and the non-state law would be a problem for the project. In the third case, they would be different, but compatible. This conclusion as to the third case is important, because it seems likely that there are large numbers of such cases, in which legal pluralism involves differences in content between the coexistent laws, but not conflict.[4]

(ii) Second, a state law may contain a norm of validation, providing, for example, that a valid sale of land is completed by the execution of a document and its registration with a state agency. Another coexistent order may then contain a norm to the same effect, having determined that the only way to validly sell land should be by complying with the state law. Alternatively, the other order may specify a different procedure, such as the performance of a ceremony on the land before witnesses,

---

[4] A complicating factor is that the other law may adopt a different classification of objects, so excluding a simple one-to-one comparison of the laws. For example, the other law may make different provisions for male and female children. In that case, the norm of the first, state law would need to be considered as if it also consisted of two norms: one requiring infant male children to be sent to school and the other requiring infant female children to be sent. Each of these would then be compared with the corresponding norm of the other, non-state law.

as sufficient to complete a sale of land. Or again, the other order may not contain any norms enabling valid sales of land. Any of these situations could confront a development project concerned either with encouraging the development of a land market or with restraining a rampant land market that is producing social problems.

Here the first instance would be a case of compatibility of the two laws, and no problem would be presented to the development project. The second instance also would not necessarily present a problem, in that each of the coexistent laws would provide means of carrying out the transaction. There would be complexity, but not conflict. A development project, concerned either with making the procedure more efficient or with restricting the use of the procedure, would need, to be successful, to take account of both laws. There would, however, be a problem if either of the laws held that its specified procedure was not only sufficient but also necessary for a valid sale. In this case, the two laws could over time produce different conclusions as to existing, valid land titles. This would entail conflict or contradictions between the laws, which a development project would need to confront. The third case does not entail incompatibility and, it may be remarked, appears common. In effect, one of the laws (the non-state law) withdraws from a field of activity and leaves it to be regulated by the other (the state law), although not expressly as in the first case.

These suggestions as to the relations between individual norms need to be seen in the context of pluralism of entire laws. In practice we confront not single norms in isolation but clusters of related norms, which are likely to include both imperative norms and norms of validation. So, for example, a non-state law containing a norm validating land sales by a procedure that is not the same as that of state law may also contain another, imperative norm forbidding attempts to sell land by recourse to the state procedure. But still the main contention is supported: a development project is likely to be more successful if the elements of the situation of legal pluralism are studied and taken into account rather than regarded as an obstacle to be removed. For example, to encourage a land market, it might be more effective to encourage the adoption in state law of a new procedure that accords with the principles of the non-state law rather than simply seek to overrule the non-state law that forbids recourse to the existing state procedure.

It is apparent that although legal pluralism entails legal complexity, it does not necessarily result in legal contradiction. Moreover, when contradictions do exist and pose problems for development practitioners, they may be of limited scope. There can indeed be multiple opportunities for persons to engage in "shopping," not only as forum shopping (K. Benda-Beckmann 1981), but also by shopping between alternative substantive laws. In these cases, it may be said that legal pluralism is an "opportunity," although not for development practitioners, but for subjects who may be able to take advantage of the plurality of choice. The development planner may find ways to enable subjects to choose alternative modes of producing development.

(c) *Categories of relations between normative orders: "recognition."* It has been suggested that a law may effect a policy toward another law not of opposition but of toleration or acceptance of the legitimacy of the other. This may conveniently be referred to here as "recognition." Instances of recognition fall into two categories.[5]

(i) *Normative recognition* is given when one law accepts that in certain matters the norms of the other law are valid and to be observed. Thus, a non-state law may incorporate a principle that the state criminal law ought to be observed. In the case of norms of validation, as we have seen, one law may accept a transaction carried out according to the requirements of another law as valid, whether or not it also provides its own procedure for the same purpose.

Normative recognition may involve no more than a passive acceptance that the norms of the other law are valid. But the recognizing law may go further, applying in its own institutions the norms of the other. The most obvious examples here are those where state institutions are required by a state law to give effect to non-state laws observed by parts of the state population. The general effect is that "state law pluralism" is added to the preexisting "deep legal pluralism" in that state. In the formulation of development policies, this means that, even with an exclusive concentration on state law, the existence of legal pluralism cannot be overlooked. However, it carries the danger that, if the recognized law is found to be an impediment to the program, it will be thought sufficient to change or repeal the provisions on recognition. This conclusion arises from the fallacious assumption that the recognized law exists as law through its recognition by the state. In practice, it is likely that, whatever changes may be made in state law, the observance of the non-state law outside the reach of state institutions will continue as before.

(ii) *Institutional recognition* is given when one law provides that it will accept as legally valid the decisions reached by institutions of the other. An instance occurs when state law accepts as valid the decisions of a non-state tribunal. Again, this may be a passive recognition, in which the recognizing law leaves to the institutions of the other law the task of enforcing their own determinations. Alternatively, institutional recognition may be active, as when the institutions of the recognizing law enforce the decisions of the other's institutions. For the development practitioner, there is, again, less possibility of overlooking the institutions of non-state origin once they have been recognized by the state.

A problem that can arise in both types of recognition flows from the need for those who administer the recognizing law to have a considerable knowledge and understanding of the recognized law, especially where the recognition is active. This understanding may be difficult to achieve because the culture of the population observing the recognized law, of which the law is a part, may differ considerably from that of the officials of the recognizing law. (On the differences between legal cultures, see Merry, in this volume, referring to Geertz [1983].) As a result, it has

---

[5] On the many senses that "recognition" may carry in reference to legal pluralism, see Twining, in this volume. The object here is simply to examine certain common situations, which are some among the various instances in which the term is used.

become an almost commonplace observation in African states that there is a divergence between "lawyers' customary law" or "official customary law," as expounded by the state courts in the processes of normative recognition, and the "living customary law" or "practiced customary law," which is observed by the population. Equally, it may happen that institutional recognition results in the enforcement of erroneous versions of decisions in the recognized law. This difficulty results not only from misunderstanding of the recognized law but also from the frequent impossibility of incorporating its norms or institutional decisions into the procedures of the recognizing law without radically changing them. So, for example, a norm or a decision stating that disputants must negotiate a compromise may be impossible to incorporate into state law in a form that can be given effect by state institutions (Woodman 1969, 1988, 2010).

(d) *The extent of the "problem."* If legal pluralism is a problem, it is not so often a problem on account of conflicts between coexistent laws but because of the complexity of laws. However, the problem of conflicts may tend to increase as the number of laws and their volumes increase. Conflicts between laws are more likely if both consist of large numbers of norms and apply to all fields of social relations than if both have modest volumes, each applying to limited fields of social activity. This problem may be exacerbated by a development policy. Development programs often require the making of more legal norms, typically by the state. Thus, a policy of development may result in an increase in conflicts between laws.

POSSIBLE "SOLUTIONS"

I now return to the list of problems set by legal pluralism to development projects. Several types of legal measures have been proposed to solve these problems. All can be included in development projects designed to make the law in a state more conducive to social and economic development or to advance the rule of law and promote human rights.

(a) *Unification of laws in a state.* It is sometimes suggested that all problems of legal pluralism might be solved by this process, whereby a uniform state law becomes the sole law observed by the population. This result, it is supposed, may be achieved by confirming norms of the previous state law, by replacing them with norms derived from a non-state law, by enacting entirely new norms, or by a combination of such measures. This is the elimination of legal pluralism, and it may be considered a solution if the very existence of legal pluralism is seen as a problem. It may also be seen as an effective way of removing the complexity, uncertainty, and conflicts that are endemic in situations of legal pluralism.

Whether unification is possible is a different question. In view of the many and varied populations that observe particular laws, it would seem that it is impossible to achieve unification in the foreseeable future. Moreover, the process of attempting it would entail a totalitarian policy that would almost certainly cause injustice. Where a population observes different laws in different situations and the state contains populations that observe different laws, it is likely that every one of these laws provides the most satisfactory solution for some issues.

(b) *Harmonization of laws.* This is a process that aims to eliminate conflicts between laws without removing legal pluralism. It thus attempts to address the problem that legal pluralism gives rise to inconsistency and uncertainty as to the applicable law.

Harmonization of laws may be attempted in some instances by changing portions of one law to remove conflicts with other laws. If this effects genuine change in the observed laws, it contributes to harmonization, although it is unlikely that such measures will be very extensive.

A more comprehensive harmonization process aims to establish meta-rules, or choice of law rules (Barron, Smith, and Woolcock 2004, 18–20). These stipulate precisely the circumstances in which each law is to be applied, so that instances in which two or more laws according to their own terms apply to the same situation with different results, and there is no clear way to determine which prevails and which will no longer arise. Choice of law rules are already well established in the private international laws of individual states.

Frequently, this allocation of jurisdictional space between two or more coexistent laws through choice of law rules is tacit. But where state law gives explicit normative recognition to non-state laws, it has been common for the provisions that prescribe recognition to also include express choice of law rules.

Such meta-rules are not likely to be effective if they are made in only one of the laws, even state law. Explicit choice of law rules in a state law may harmonize the laws in state law pluralism, but they cannot regulate the relationship between state law and living customary law. Indeed, an attempt to determine through norms of state law the fields of operation of non-state laws would be an attempt to establish state law hegemony and to eliminate deep legal pluralism. Alternatively, a development in which agents of both or all of the legal orders participate, aiming to remove conflicts between them, akin to the international process aimed at harmonizing the private international laws of different states, could remove the problem of conflict. A development project may aim to facilitate this, but it is a much more difficult exercise than securing the enactment of some rules in state law.

(c) *Ascertainment of laws.* Another problem mentioned previously is the lack of knowledge of one law by agents of another law, in particular when these agents are required to give effect to provisions for the recognition of that other law. To avoid the resultant failures in the rule of law, programs have been initiated for the ascertainment, clarification, and publicizing of non-state laws.

The strongest of these measures is codification of non-state law. The object is to state the substance of non-state law in a form that will be legally determinative as state legislation. In practice, populations that observe their own non-state laws usually continue to do so regardless of state law demands. If a code is complete and accurate at the time it is compiled, it may appear to be observed, because the population will continue to observe its own law. But insofar as the code differs from the observed law, conduct usually will not accord with the code.

A further problem confronts codification. After a code has been completed, the observed non-state law is likely, like all such laws, to change over time (Scott 1998, chap. 1). Unless the observed non-state law is constantly monitored and the code frequently revised, the conduct of the population will increasingly diverge from that which is enjoined by the code to an even greater extent than it did originally.

As a result of experience with codes, there has been in some parts of the world a practice of compiling written "restatements," or records of non-state laws as "ascertained" by investigators. Such documents are intended to provide guidance to officials and others who are required to effect recognition of those laws but have no direct experience of them. This carries the same risk of divergence from the observed law as codes and the same risk of increasing divergence over time.

Codes and restatements sometimes avowedly go further than stating the existing non-state law and purport to amend it, for example, to bring it into accord with international human rights laws. The problem here is the same as that with choice of law rules enacted in state law. Where the content of a non-state law is at issue, state law cannot determine the question, however worthy and enlightened the motives of the state lawmakers. There is a possibility that ascertainment of law projects are producing statements that are inaccurate and that state endorsement of these statements may be increasing the incidence of conflicts between state and non-state laws. These conflicts could eventually produce progressive changes, but development projects that overlook their existence are not realistic.

THE ISSUES OF BOUNDARIES BETWEEN LAWS AND INTERNAL VARIATIONS IN LAWS

Hitherto this discussion has proceeded, like most discussions of legal pluralism, as if the boundaries of the state and its laws were clear, as if the "population" (or "group," "people," *Volk*) that observes any particular law were a definable, relatively stable group of persons, and as if the extent of observance of a "law" were always stable and clear. Because it has been suggested that the distinction between state and non-state law is not significant as a matter of classification, it is not intended to debate specifically the boundaries of the state (for discussion with respect to Africa, see Lund 2007). On the identification of individual laws, as Twining (in this volume) points out, there are many difficulties in the individuation of laws or legal orders, although we need such concepts, and we talk about them as if they were discrete units. Two aspects of the issue, turning on the difference between the ideal types used in theoretical debate and the observed social reality, must be mentioned.

First, and especially in today's globalizing world, individuals and groups are socially mobile, and many people observe different laws to varying degrees at different times. So individuals who migrate from one district to another, whether in the same country or in a different country or continent, may in their new place of residence initially seek out people from their own place of origin. They may continue to observe the non-state law they previously observed. They may use communication technology to maintain daily contact with relatives and friends in their area of origin. But they may also begin to spend much of their daily life among people who observe a different non-state law. They may tend to observe the local state law, but it is also quite possible that they will begin to observe the non-state law of their new fellow workers and friends, becoming integrated to a certain extent in this population. The legal observances of migrants thus may change, while switching in the reverse direction when they go on holiday to their home area or return there in retirement. People who observe different laws increasingly engage in relations with each other, and the boundaries between populations may blur into areas of hybrid laws. (On the effects of population mobility on forms of legal pluralism, see especially F. Benda-Beckmann, K. Benda-Beckmann, and Griffiths 2005.)

A second, related feature of legal pluralism is that there are often internal variations in what may be claimed to be a single law. None of the categories of populations referred to above is necessarily homogeneous. Attempts to record customary laws of ethnic groups sometimes contain lengthy accounts of local variations (as, for example, in Obi 1977). I have developed more fully both of these points in my contribution to Bavinck and Woodman (2009) (cf. Twining 2009, chap. 3).

The effect of these features is a greater possibility of uncertainty about the applicable norms in each case. The operating choice of law rules are more complex even than the standard picture suggests: they need to take account of changes in the scope of operation of laws and to provide for choice between different variants of the "same" law. Also, there is likely to be uncertainty about the content of those non-state laws that contain internal variations.

CONCLUSION: ARE THERE SOLUTIONS?

The development practitioner needs to always take account of the existent social reality of observed laws. An analysis of legal pluralism shows that we are confronted with complex situations in which state law, far from being the entirety of the socially significant normative scene, wields limited authority. It is not realistic to suppose that legal pluralism will decline or can be eliminated in the foreseeable future. The development practitioner is faced with laws more numerous, complex, uncertain, contested, and variable in form and substance than is often assumed.

The problems for development policies are heightened by the fact, already noted, that development programs nearly always seek to act through the state and its law. This may not be avoidable, but change to "public discussion and exchange" (Sen 1999) and "deliberative development" (Evans 2004) need considerable effort and planning.

From the perspective of developmental action through the state, legal pluralism is not so much a problem as an inescapable fact that requires a sensitive appreciation of the normative entirety of each situation. Each new case, and each new proposed application of a principle, needs to be researched and reflected on. It will not be possible to develop a generally applicable "diagnostic decision tree" (Pritchett and Woolcock 2004, 204). The results of local research may show that we need to suspend attempts to put some of our preferred principles into operation in some instances. They will not always demonstrate that situations of legal pluralism must be accepted. Not only will situations need to be modified, but there will be occasions when the degree of legal pluralism prevailing in a field needs to be reduced. What is likely to emerge from greater knowledge of such situations is that to bring about significant social change through change in law will often be difficult, no matter how desirable it may be. It is likely to lead to the conclusion that some principles will have to be given priority over others, to an even greater degree than had been previously thought. In short, when we do develop an understanding, it is likely to produce a better appreciation of the limits to what may be achieved by a development policy.

REFERENCES

Barron, Patrick, Claire Q. Smith, and Michael Woolcock. 2004. "Understanding Local-Level Conflict in Developing Countries: Theory, Evidence and Implications from Indonesia." Social Development Papers, Conflict Prevention and Reconstruction Paper 19, World Bank, Washington, DC.

Bavinck, Maarten, and Gordon R. Woodman. 2009. "Can There Be Maps of Law?" In *Spatialising Law: An Anthropological Geography of Law in Society*, ed. Franz von Benda-Beckmann, Keebet von Benda-Beckmann, and Anne Griffiths, 195–218. Farnham and Burlington, VT: Ashgate.

Benda-Beckmann, Franz von. 1988. "Comment on Merry." *Law & Society Review* 22 (5): 897–901.

———. 2002. "Who's Afraid of Legal Pluralism?" *Journal of Legal Pluralism* 47: 37–82.

Benda-Beckmann, Franz von, Keebet von Benda-Beckmann, and Anne Griffiths, eds. 2005. *Mobile People, Mobile Law: Expanding Legal Relations in a Contracting World*. Aldershot: Ashgate.

Benda-Beckmann, Keebet von. 1981. "Forum Shopping and Shopping Forums: Dispute Settlement in a Minangkabau Village in West Sumatra." *Journal of Legal Pluralism* 19: 117–59.

Benton, Lauren. 2002. *Law and Colonial Cultures: Legal Regimes in World History, 1400–1900*. Cambridge: Cambridge University Press.

Bierschenk, Thomas. 2008. "The Everyday Functioning of an African Public Service: Informalization, Privatization and Corruption in Benin's Legal System." *Journal of Legal Pluralism* 57: 101–39.

Dworkin, Ronald. 1977. *Taking Rights Seriously*. Cambridge, MA: Harvard University Press.

Evans, Peter. 2004. "Development as Institutional Change: The Pitfalls of Monocropping and the Potentials of Deliberation." *Studies in Comparative International Development* 38 (4): 30–52.

Faundez, Julio. 2005. "The Rule of Law Enterprise: Promoting a Dialogue between Practitioners and Academics." *Democratization* 12 (4): 567–86.

Geertz, Clifford. 1983. *Local Knowledge: Further Essays in Interpretive Anthropology*. New York: Basic Books.

Griffiths, John. 1986. "What Is Legal Pluralism?" *Journal of Legal Pluralism* 24: 1–55.

Hart, H. L. A. 1961. *The Concept of Law*. Oxford: Clarendon Press.

Jayasuriya, Kanishka, ed. 1999. *Law, Capitalism and Power in Asia: The Rule of Law and Legal Institutions*. London: Routledge.

Lund, Christian, ed. 2007. *Twilight Institutions: Public Authority and Local Politics in Africa*. Malden, MA: Blackwell Publishing.

Merry, Sally Engle. 1988. "Legal Pluralism." *Law & Society Review* 22 (5): 869–96.

Nuijten, Monique, and Gerhard Anders, eds. 2009. *Corruption and the Secret of Law: A Legal Anthropological Perspective*. Farnham and Burlington, VT: Ashgate.

Obi, Samuel Nwankwo Chinwuba. 1977. *The Customary Law Manual: A Manual of Customary Laws Obtaining in the Anambra and Imo States of Nigeria*. Enugu, Nigeria: Government Printer.

Pritchett, Lant, and Michael Woolcock. 2004. "Solutions When the Solution Is the Problem: Arraying the Disarray in Development." *World Development* 32 (2): 191–212.

Scott, James C. 1998. *Seeing Like a State: How Certain Schemes to Improve the Human Condition Have Failed*. New Haven, CT: Yale University Press.

Seidman, Ann, and Robert B. Seidman. 1994. *State and Law in the Development Process: Problem-Solving and Institutional Change in the Third World*. Basingstoke: Macmillan Press.

Sen, Amartya. 1999. *Development as Freedom*. New York: Alfred A. Knopf.

Sezgin, Yüksel. 2004. "Theorizing Formal Pluralism: Quantification of Legal Pluralism for Spatio-temporal Analysis." *Journal of Legal Pluralism* 50: 101–18.

Stephenson, Matthew. 2009. "Rule of Law as a Goal of Development Policy." The World Bank. http://web.worldbank.org/WBSITE/EXTERNAL/TOPICS/EXTLAWJUSTINST/0,,contentMDK:20763583~menuPK:1989584~pagePK:210058~piPK:210062~theSitePK:1974062,00.html.

Tamanaha, Brian Z. 2001. *A General Jurisprudence of Law and Society*. Oxford: Oxford University Press.

———. 2004. *On the Rule of Law: History, Politics, Theory*. New York: Cambridge University Press.

———. 2008. "Understanding Legal Pluralism: Past to Present, Local to Global." *Sydney Law Review* 30 (3): 375–411.

Teubner, Gunther. 1997. "'Global Bukowina': Legal Pluralism in the World Society." In *Global Law without a State*, ed. Gunther Teubner. Aldershot: Ashgate.

Twining, William L. 2009. *General Jurisprudence: Understanding Law from a Global Perspective*. Cambridge: Cambridge University Press.

Woodman, Gordon R. 1969. "Some Realism about Customary Law – the West African Experience." *Wisconsin Law Review*: 128–52.

———. 1988. "How State Courts Create Customary Law in Ghana and Nigeria." In *Indigenous Law and the State*, ed. Bradford W. Morse and Gordon R. Woodman, 181–220. Dordrecht: Foris.

———. 1998. "Ideological Combat and Social Observation: Recent Debate about Legal Pluralism." *Journal of Legal Pluralism* 42: 21–59.

———. 2010. "A Survey of Customary Laws in Africa in Search of Lessons for the Future." In *The Future of African Customary Law*, ed. Jeanmarie Fenrich, Paolo Galizzi, and Tracy Higgins. Cambridge: Cambridge University Press.

9

Institutional Hybrids and the Rule of Law as a Regulatory Project

Kanishka Jayasuriya

LEGAL PLURALISM AS TECHNOLOGY OF LEGAL REGULATION

Legal pluralism – as practice and theory – is frequently viewed as a functional response to the diversity of legal culture and practices around the globe, or, as Michaels (2009) so succinctly observes, as a process driven by pressures from below for the recognition of local customs or norms. Such a bottom-up perspective elides the questions of "who" promotes these experiments and for "what" reason. In essence, we argue that legal pluralism should not be judged by its own terms, but rather understood as a technology of jurisprudence that provides templates for institutional entrepreneurs such as transnational agencies as they develop novel institutions of legal governance. This essay is a first cut at analyzing the emergence of legal pluralism as a regulatory project within the field of "law and development." The term *regulation* is extensively used here to describe the system of rules and standards governing the conduct of agents or organizations. Regulatory projects[1] grounded in the theory and practice of legal pluralism are attempts to steer "rule of law" programs via the incorporation of private or civic actors within institutional hybrids. These projects carve out spaces of legal governance that lead to the juridification of civic or customary legal regimes. Using customary regimes – often around reinvented customary practices – has resonance with regimes of legal governance in the late colonial state (Mamdani 1996).

A regulatory focus places the accent on those new institutional forms through which localized legal and social norms are given recognition and authority in seeking to implement the rule of law. Institutions, not the diversity of legal culture, need to be

---

[1] For an overview of this regulatory approach, see Jayasuriya (2001, 1999).

I wish to thank Veronica Taylor and editors for very useful comments on this chapter. The usual disclaimer applies.

at center stage in the study of legal pluralism.[2] Within a law and development context, we need to ask why legal pluralism has become such an important question for many transnational actors and organizations involved with legal and governance reform? Proceeding from this question – rather than from the usual question, "What is legal pluralism?" – allows us to problematize rule of law projects as forms of institutional bricolage,[3] that is, the conscious attempt of actors to weave new institutional forms by drawing on past social and cultural practices. More than that, the diverse institutional experiments subsumed under the label of legal pluralism are not a product of the purely "local" circumstances and norms, but rather stand at the intersection of the local and transnational legal order.

Within law and development practice there has been a marked shift toward the implementation of rule of law projects through the use of soft law mechanisms. The recent spate of interest in legal pluralism parallels the significant development of new forms of legal innovations that distinguish the second generation of law and development reforms (Rittich 2005). These soft law initiatives work with non-state actors and often use standards and codes of conduct to implement policy goals. However, what is distinctive about regulatory projects associated with legal pluralism, and possibly constituting a third wave of law and development, is the way in which rule of law itself has become a project that works indirectly through the regulation of institutional spaces furnished with reinvented local social and cultural forms located within scales of legal governance that are neither simply "national" nor "global." In fact, legal pluralism becomes a handy bit of technology – a set of templates and models – through which the non-state orders are regulated and authorized.

An implication of this perspective on legal pluralism is the capacity to understand institutional experimentation as a regulatory project that seeks to implement public law principles or objectives through civic or customary governance. Hence, a distinctive aspect about recent innovations in rule of law projects is that regulation is directed at incorporating elements of public law, or even constitutional principles, within systems of non-state ordering. The great diversity of this institutional experimentation can be seen in the rapid development of alternative dispute mechanisms, the rise of private governance mechanisms such as international arbitration and the development of systems of legal pluralism in areas as diverse property rights, and customary justice in peace building, whether in Iraq or Afghanistan. As such, these new hybrid regimes reflect a relocation and rescaling of public law rather than its retreat in favor of non-state law.

---

[2] For a survey of this interest in legal pluralism, see Santos (2002, 2006), Benda-Beckmann (2007), and Tamanaha (2008). In addition, there is substantial literature on European legal order and pluralism. See, for example, Zumbansen (2006).

[3] For an illuminating discussion of institutional bricolage, see Cerny (2010).

The reason for this appeal to non-state legal regimes is the general failure, so far, of legal reform and rule of law programs to achieve the ever-expanding objectives of transnational organization to build markets, create transparency, and expand access to the justice system (Taylor 2009). The crucial question for the new legal reform programs – in some respects paralleling the debate on the failed state – is the extent to which rule of law programs can engage with state-based legal systems. The problem this "prescription poses for rule of law assistance is that all legal systems are plural, and even legal formalists in the world of rule of law assistance are beginning to acknowledge that developing and transitional legal systems have both state and non-state components" (Taylor 2009, 47). As a result of these failures, there has been an interest in supporting initiatives to facilitate local or customary norms in order to generate support for and strengthen rule of law programs.

These initiatives help to constitute relations of authority between transnational as well as local actors not recognized in the usual dualisms of state and non-state legal ordering that pervade much of the legal pluralism literature (Faundez 2006). By posing the problem in terms of the efficacy of state against non-state law, we overlook the fact that these reform initiatives are part of the ensemble of relationships that are often multilevel, crisscrossing public and private boundaries. I suggest that the significance of legal pluralism as theory lies in its function as sociological jurisprudence that allows institutional entrepreneurs to recognize, authorize, and legitimize the use of these systems of private or non-state ordering. For this reason, a simple focus on such systems of non-state ordering obscures the role that legal pluralism plays in providing the "jurisprudential mask" for systems of regulation that bring together the diverse regimes located at transnational, state, and non-state levels.

Such a relocation of public law also involves a "localization" of legal governance in a way that rescales legal regulation by reducing complex social processes to an operation of informal rules or social mechanisms. One of the implications of the emergence of various institutional hybrids is that it represents a reconstitution of "social" in a way that valorizes traditional or customary practices. As with earlier colonial attempts to reinvent tradition, such institutional engineering has an authoritarian and conservative potential to constrain projects of social transformation even to the limited extent evident in the first generation of law and development theory and practice.

In the next section of this chapter, I examine the emergence of new forms of institutional hybrids and the institutional politics of the relationship between non-state and state law within these hybrids. In the following section, I go on to explore how the contemporary practices of legal pluralism reconstitute the "social" in a way that gives priority to local social norms and underlying cultural forms, resulting in a devaluation of the political conflict over the allocation of material resources. The final section of the chapter explores how the notions of the rule of law become contested within, and between, contending regulatory regimes. I discuss briefly the way in which the "rule of law" can be understood in this context of institutional conflict and accommodation.

INSTITUTIONAL HYBRIDS AND REGULATION

The argument so far is that the theory and practice of legal pluralism should be understood as an institutional description of the complex emergence of new forms of institutional hybrids that bring together public and private actors in innovative governance spaces, thereby enabling a mode of regulation through non-state (market or civic) regimes. Such an approach challenges the view of those who tend to regard customary law as an alternative to or substitute for state legal regimes that implicitly assume the autonomy of private and civic ordering. Instead of such assumed autonomy of private or civic systems of ordering, our approach suggests that we need to recognize that these are new "legal hybrids" – a term I borrow from Teubner (1986) – that produce novel configurations of the public and private. It is such novel institutional configurations, rather than the intermingling of state and non-state regimes, that distinguish the regulatory perspective on the rule of law.

Diverse legal reform experiments produced results that paradoxically lead to the juridification of non-state orders challenging some of the pluralist assumption of the autonomy of private or civic regimes. These developments, of course, do not go unrecognized within policy literature on justice reform. For example, Menzies's (2007) analysis of the Solomon Islands draws attention to the fact that civic ordering works in the shadow of legal hierarchy. These institutional hybrids then become the means through which transnational actors and agencies pursue "rule of law" objectives. What matters is not the shift from law to nonlegal forms of regulation, but the *relationship* between "hard law" and soft social norms of private or civil society actors and the resultant proliferation of institutional "hybrids." These innovative governance settings are obscured by those who emphasize the shift from formal and legal to informal and nonlegal forms of dispute resolution. It is not the relative emphasis on law or non-law that is important, but the relationship between these elements within the regulatory architecture.

It is certainly the case that non-state systems of ordering can function relatively autonomously, but only to the extent that they are now seen to further certain kinds of policy objectives, and indeed have "rule of law" reasoning and principles incorporated within these systems. As such, their evolutionary trajectory necessarily becomes entangled within systems of transnational regulation. On this point there is an intriguing similarity between justice and legal reforms that rely on private ordering and the increasing regulatory character of private law. In a provocative work, Collins (1999) has suggested that private law has a regulatory character – in contrast to libertarian assumptions about the autonomy of private law – that impinges on or collides with other forms of regulation and social and economic reasoning. His point is that the "result of the collision between discourses has been the reconfiguration of private law reasoning, so that instrumental or policy concerns within its normative orientation becomes the dominant force of its evolutionary trajectory" (Collins 1999, 53). This has important ramifications for the analysis of justice reform where customary law and arrangements become the institutional means that enable transnational agencies and organizations to pursue specific policy objectives, such as legal empowerment (Golub 2003) that might stand in tension with the reasoning of those within the customary institutions.

This tension between competing legal discourse and reasoning is not an aberration from some pure model of legal pluralism, but part and parcel of the fabric of these institutional hybrids. A significant advantage of this understanding of institutional hybrids is that it becomes possible to include a wide array of new forms of "rule of law" regulation, ranging from private law to customary arrangements, because we are concerned about the tensions between competing legal discourse and institutional structures. Competing legal discourses are often located at different scales of governance between, for example, transnational, national, and local actors. Legal hybrids are a mechanism through which these collisions and tensions of competing legal discourse can be managed and ordered. This is something along the lines of what Benton (2002) calls jurisdictional politics, where these institutional collisions are shaped by a "jurisdictional politics," which means "... conflicts over the preservation of, creation and nature of and extent of different legal forums and authorities" (Benton 2002, 10).[4]

Hence, this regulatory approach to rule of law projects enables us to go beyond the bright lines drawn between governmental and nongovernmental systems of ordering to analyze the relationships, accommodation, and collisions within and between these orders. We need to focus much of our theoretical and practical policy work on the dynamics of these institutional hybrids rather than on an obsessive concern with social norms or traditional authority of the law and economic literature or the legal pluralist literature. It is not the fact that actors are private or public per se that is important, but the relationship between private and public actors in new governance settings that challenge the "public" and "private," and "national" and "global" binaries of the Weberian and Westphalian notions of statehood. Simply put, it is these new formations of public and private that now are increasingly central to emerging forms of legal governance across a wide range of states (Jayasuriya 2008). Instead of being diverted by arguments about the intractability of customary law or non-state ordering, we should understand the emergence of institutional hybrids as producing and transforming categories of legal subjects, forums, and procedures of legal governance.

---

[4] Jurisdictional politics provides a useful heuristic framework for analyzing how transnational regulatory regimes create new jurisdictional practices that reach into, and beyond, national constitutional boundaries.

For example, in the Aceh, the United Nations Development Programme has supported the *Majelis Adat Aceh* (Aceh *Adat* Council) to implement guidelines for customary law (or *adat*) actors through a participatory process to inform them of public law standards in such areas as human rights and other relevant legislative conditions (Wojkowska and Cunningham 2009). The point of this institutional exercise is to "create greater clarity, among *adat* actors on the types of cases that *adat* is allowed to handle, to fortify the relationship between *adat* and the formal justice system" (Wojkowska and Cunningham 2009, 18). There is more than a hint here of the late colonial practice of indirect rule. But where it differs from such practices is that in contemporary times, institutional hybrids operate in governance settings that include both "public" and non-state actors and processes. Moreover, to analyze *adat* in this context as an indirect system of customary system is to lose sight of the explicit regulatory role that this council plays in pursuing specific policy objectives. Hybrid institutions incorporating *adat* are products of institutional engineering made possible by the jurisprudential technology of legal pluralism.

These emerging public/private hybrids are not confined to customary law. The strength of this approach is that it can include a range of institutional hybrids, particularly through transnational private law. For example, market governance is shaped by standard-setting programs such as the Organisation for Economic Co-operation and Development (OECD) Guidelines for Multinational Enterprises. The OECD guidelines are voluntary codes of conduct, but accompanied by what are called National Contact Points (NCPs) that police these guidelines.[5] The NCP system allows nongovernmental organizations to have a monitoring role in private economies, whereby it becomes an instrument through which regulatory principles are implemented. But the novelty of this innovation lies in the fact that the incorporation of various forms of public law is now located within new systems of institutional bricolage.

Similar examples can be found in the development of various forms of corporate conduct that have evolved in the aftermath of several scandals over health and safety conditions in complex multinational production chains (Locke, Qin, and Brause 2006, 3). Reinforcing these codes of conduct has been a move by transnational agencies such as the International Labour Organization away from a labor rights perspective for the protection of labor standards toward an emphasis on substance rather than process, with greater attention to decentralized systems of enforcement (Arthurs 2001; Alston 2004). It is a "trajectory that has involved a gradual hardening of initially soft standards, an incremental strengthening of supervisory processes, and the adoption with the acquiescence of governments and other actors of innovative

---

[5] Any interested party such as a nongovernmental organization that believes a violation of the guidelines has occurred can take up the issue with NCP of the country where the alleged violation took place or the NCP of the country where the company has its headquarters. For the guidelines, see www.oecd.org/document/28/0,2340,en_2649_34889_2397532_1111_00.html, accessed May 26, 2007.

promotional and other measures" (Alston 2004, 461). In a transnational context, these new private law hybrids illustrate Collins's (1999) argument that public law reasoning permeates the operation of private law. It creates a public domain within private economic regimes – a system of indirect rule – which at the same time diminishes the impact of formal rights mechanisms and instruments with respect to labor standards (Alston 2004).

Form this regulatory vantage, we can explore within these institutional hybrids the inherent tension between elements of "public law" and the logic of non-state ordering. The example of *adat* law examined previously raises a curious paradox: institutional innovation in non-state ordering that is premised on the facilitation of supportive social practices simultaneously leads to legalization or juridification of these non-state systems. Teubner's (1986) notion of a "regulatory trilemma" may be useful in understanding these issues. He has suggested that the impact of juridification on social rules and practices may produce the following outcomes: legal rules may not have an impact on social conduct or practice; they may end distorting social norms; or, alternatively, law itself may lose its own coherence by placing a high priority on nonlegal discourse. In other words, regulation may lead to "either 'incongruence' of law and society, or, the 'over legalisation' of society or the 'over socialization' of law" (Teubner 1986, 309). It seems clear that in the literature on justice reform and non-state arrangements, the avoidance of the first part of this trilemma – the "incongruence" of law and society of the trilemma – can come at the cost of overlegalization of non-state ordering and losing the internal coherence of formal law. This is an inevitable aspect of all such institutional hybrids, but the adoption of a regulatory perspective allows for a more reflexive understating of the policy dilemmas.

Leaving aside these difficulties, this chapter highlights the importance of understanding the growing importance of institutional experimentation within legal pluralism in the context of an emerging transnational legal order rather than as a representation of the diversity of global legal culture. This relational approach suggests that the practices and discourse of legal pluralism that underpin hybrid legal regimes are best conceived as a process or relationship between civic actors and public actors in new arenas of legal governance. As such, it also involves the "metagovernance" of relationships and conflicts between distinctive institutional domains, often at various scales of governance. Taking this view allows us to see emerging forms of legal pluralism in the global legal order as constituting a set of regulatory mechanisms working through the governance of market or civic actors.

Michaels has convincingly argued that legal pluralism is now inescapably a process shaped by the transformed context of legal globalization, whereby it is defined more "from the top down than from the bottom up: an internal differentiation of global law, not a multitude of varied local laws" (Michaels 2009, 247). He suggests a possible, though somewhat problematic, intellectual genealogy of legal pluralism that shifts from a first notion of classical "legal pluralism" – concerned with the colonial world – to a second conception of "new pluralism," applying these concepts to the "West," and to a third notion he calls "global legal pluralism." Leaving this typology aside, the benefit of this approach is to contextualize legal pluralism as the relationship of legal orders in a specific context of a transnational legal order, rather than to place an emphasis on diversity of social groups or practices (Teubner 1996; Michaels 2009). This constitutive view of legal pluralism and the global legal order has parallels with Benton's (2002) argument that legal pluralism of the early modern era was similarly constitutive of an emergent global order.

Approaching the contemporary discourse and practice of legal pluralism as a historically specific system of regulatory governance enables us to have a clear focus on the underlying conflicts and accommodation between legal orders at many different levels and spaces. It is this complex institutional ensemble that challenges the primacy of the national state as the author of binding legal norms. It is through these systems of governance that public law is relocated within new legal hybrids. This process is as much about creating new patterns of authority through a process of institutional bricolage as about the recognition of "socially embedded" legal systems.

REGULATING THROUGH SOCIAL NORMS

In legal experiments such as the *adat* example noted in the previous section, there is more than a faint echo of various forms of late colonial practices of indirect rule that relied on supportive institutions of customary law. There is an assumption that "customary social norms" are simply out there, and to the extent that formal law operates, it must be supportive of these elements rather than distort these practices (Menzies 2007; Michaels 2009). Here the assumption that informal institutions are intractable or merely a set of embedded norms is not only sociologically naïve, but it also obscures power relationships that may favor certain kinds of conflicts – such as those based on culture – while obscuring others. Despite these similarities, there are crucial differences, at least with respect to legal reform programs. These include the explicit focus on the rule of law, the existence of national systems, and the scope and range of innovative institutions to incorporate non-state systems in all states ranging far beyond customary law. Perhaps the most important difference between these regimes and forms of indirect rule is that these regimes have a transnational regulatory character that distinguishes them from those modes of governance that Mamdani identifies as "late colonial."

Yet the more important dimension of this shift toward social norms in the law and development literature is what Rittich (2005) has so persuasively argued: the reconstitution of the social in a way that depoliticizes social conflict. Legal pluralism as a jurisprudential technology shifts toward an emphasis on social norms or informal rules. In fact, these trends are part of a broader thrust of legal policy making and theory toward the use of informal institutions and soft law as a substitute for formal lawmaking. Here is the nub: in the fabrication of such social processes in the construction of institutional hybrids, there is a reduction of complex social processes to simple rules or norms that mimic formal law.

In much of the developed law, this move towards "soft law" and informal institutions lies in the critique of the welfare law and the perceived efficiency of private ordering in ensuring economic efficiency (Collins 1999). Here the argument is that social norms provide for the regulation of social behavior, and the role of the law is to either facilitate or obstruct the operation of these social norms. Indeed, the growing influence of the literature on social norms within the law and economic literature has led one scholar to dub it as the "new Chicago school" (Lessig 1998; see also Duxbury 2001). The cardinal assumption of this literature is that social norms and the informal institutions are order-creating arrangements with a rational basis in terms of the costs and benefits to individuals for adhering to those norms. Examining dispute resolution between cattle ranchers in California, Ellickson (1991) found evidence for the widespread use of informal institutions and norms – rather than formal legal mechanisms – for the resolution of conflicts. There is scant discussion in these examples of how and why social norms originated in the first instance, though some have argued that social norms are signaling devices that allow individuals to distinguish between "good" and "bad" types (Posner 2000).

In the law and economic literature that, as we have noted, has been influential in the design of some rule of law programs, there is an assumption that formal legal regulation can be cumbersome and inefficient and can interfere with the operation of private market ordering. Of course, this assumption has been at the core of much of the libertarian critiques of welfarism. The point is that the recent trends in law and economics literature toward the emphasis on social norms and the notion of "order without law" (Ellickson 1991; Posner 2000) have come to occupy critical positions within rule of law and legal reform programs in advanced industrial as well as developing societies. The more important point is that the jurisprudence of law and economics by naturalizing social norms and rules obscures the political and institutional contexts through which these social norms are given policy effect. Overlooking these facts obscures the understanding of private ordering as an instrument of regulatory control.

As these jurisprudential technologies have come to play an influential role in the engineering of innovative legal institutions, they have constituted a view of the social as apolitical and free of conflict. According to this view, then, legal order is about facilitating order through social norms rather than being a mechanism of social transformation.

An analogous slant on the role of social norms can be readily identified in some of the recent work on legal pluralism, particularly as it manifests in legal reform projects in developing countries. In this context, the turn toward culture exemplified in recent law and development literature, as Cohen (2009) so persuasively argues, is an "effort to enable ordinary citizens to instill within themselves normative desires for particular configurations of modern legal rule, processes and institutions"

(Cohen 2009, 517). She cites the "contemporary turn to culture as a tool of governance as an effort to implement the rule of law through the self ordering of individual people, and as the idea that through culture interveners can make law and development internal and can regulate individual from the inside" (Cohen 2009, 584).

The thread that runs through both the new Chicago school and the legal pluralism work on institutional reform is the notion that social norms and informal institutions provide an alternative regulatory model to state-centered law. Implicit in this sociological jurisprudence is the idea that social norms or non-state ordering are sticky, and often difficult to transform, and contain within them elements that resemble the ordering of law by formal mechanisms. As Cohen (2009) so superbly demonstrates with the example of the use of culture as regulatory tool, the pluralist emphasis on social norms in law and development comes at the cost of moving away from the politics of social conflict. Consequently, the institutional innovations often assume that to be effective, law needs to act within, rather than against, the grain of social norms or culture.

The influence of this sociological jurisprudence about social norms and culture as a regulatory component of the rule of law can be seen in institutional innovations as diverse as negotiated regulation or the use of the jirga (Wardak 2002) in Afghanistan. One way or another, these institutions depended on social norms as a regulatory tool in the implementation of rule of law projects. To be sure, the emphasis in these programs, as Taylor (2009) correctly notes, is on ordering through customary norms and alternative dispute resolution mechanisms. But the crucial role of these customary or informal institutions lies in the incorporation of sets of social norms – selective and localized – within new systems of non-state ordering (Faundez 2006). As we have argued, it is as much a *reconstitution* as it is the recognition of informal institutions. For example, we find a policy brief on building the rule of law in Afghanistan suggesting that "[w]ithout the rule of law and good governance it is difficult for societies to make the transition from war-related lawlessness to peace and social justice. Often overlooked during the reconstruction process are the traditional conflict resolution mechanisms that continue to serve portions of the population" (TLO 2008, 1). Such assumptions about sticky social norms – particularly in legal reform programs – provide a telling contrast to the first generation of the law and development movement, in which law was seen as a tool of social transformation.

Afghanistan is not an isolated case. These ideas about legal pluralism and the role of customary law have been especially influential in a recent review of justice reforms in failed states. For instance, in states such as East Timor and the Solomon Islands, initial disappointment with the outcomes of justice reform has witnessed a newfound practical interest and policy innovation in engaging with customary law. Menzies (2007) (see also Brown 2005) – has suggested that justice reform initiatives in the Solomon Islands, which have often had a strong state-centric bias, have failed to reflect the social and legal pluralism that underpins traditional modes of conflict resolution. Indeed, the Australian-led intervention in the Solomon Islands was initially designed to rebuild traditional statelike functions – including those in areas of legal reform – but, as in the case of Afghanistan, these interventions produced dismal results (Nixon 2006). The assumption is that there are "limits to the speed at which the full complement of state institutions can be introduced as legitimate instruments of governance" (Nixon 2006, 85).

It is these considerations that have prompted a call for the use of traditional and non–state-centric methods of conflict resolution.[6] These institutional innovations depend on the assumption that implicit social norms – whether market or traditional authority – make transformative legal projects difficult and problematic. Hence, the attraction of legal pluralism is that it provides a technology to guide institutional experiments that gives greater recognition to the role of custom and tradition in the design of justice reforms and legal reform projects. However well-meaning these experiments may be, we should not lose sight of the fact that it is not culture that is important but the way in which legal governance shifts the shape and form of conflict toward culture or customary issues.

Ironically, the way legal pluralism is used in these justice reform projects suggests that these approaches are stuck within the very same state-centric framework they critique. Legal pluralism as deployed in these rule of law projects is the mirror image of state-centered law. It is this fact that leads to the failure to recognize that these projects – legal reform or otherwise – build regulatory transnational spaces of governance. This may be an eminently feasible approach, but situating it within the straightjacket of state versus non-state law misses crucial features of this emergent regulatory regime. This point is reinforced in the recent innovative work of Hameiri (2010) on state-building programs, which demonstrates that projects associated with programs such as developing indigenous legal systems should be understood as political enterprises projects that enable new forms of political rule to be exercised in variously constituted spaces of governance.

The impact of the jurisprudence of social norms lies in the localization of legal governance not only through its territorial relocation in local communities but also through its rescaling of social complexity. It rescales social complexity by reconstituting the shape and form of legal and social conflict by embedding these governance institutions in local cultural practices. This dual-tracked regulatory rescaling of the rule of law is at the heart of the diverse institutional experimentation in the reform of the rule of law.

This regulatory approach to institutional hybrids situates the discourse and practice of legal pluralism in a process of rescaling and relocating the sites of legal governance. I suggest that this process of rescaling is fundamental to new regulatory innovations in "rule of law programs."

---

[6] See Charlesworth (2007), who, in a summary of the experience of Timor Leste, notes that the "UN did not seem to be aware of the local paradigms and made no serious attempts to accommodate them" (Charlesworth 2007, 5).

CONTESTING CONCEPTIONS OF LEGALITY

A pivotal aspect of regulation through non-state-centric regimes is the way in which public law principles are now relocated within hybrid legal regimes. It challenges our conception of the rule of law in three ways. First, these new forms of global regulation have multiple sources, are increasingly fragmented, and challenge the rule of law assumption about the notion of legal supremacy and a single source of sovereignty. Second, new types of global regulation often depend on new forms of representing a "public" – defined in functional or policy terms – and challenge the notion of rule of law as somehow linked to, or connected with, notions of political representation. For instance, consider who is represented in the example of regulation through *adat*. Third, transnational regulation works through increasingly flexible soft forms of standard setting and challenges the notion of rule of law as consisting of legal predictability and certainty.

More important, the conflict between institutional domains reflects a deeper contestation regarding the nature and form of legality. Contestation over legality in the operation of the non-state-centric regimes –for example, the imposition of labor standards against the libertarian notion of private law – reflects the tensions and contradictions as individuals and groups contest their inclusion and treatment within particular domains (see, for example, Collins 1999; Zumbansen 2006). Writing from a systems theory standpoint, Zumbansen (2006) argues that the law has a tendency to develop "rules and norms that are informed by yesterday's and today's definition and assignment of legal/illegal, and that will serve as a guiding post and reminder when applied to conflict situations tomorrow" (2006, 556). However, this seems of little help in sorting contested ideas of legality within and between regulatory domains. The point that needs emphasis is that political struggles have to be framed in terms of competing legal understandings of the nature and form of legality. But the very fact that contestation over the rule of law now takes place within these institutional settings is itself a reflection of the broader social and political forces at work in these regulatory regimes.

At one level, this contestation may mitigate the impact of legal instrumentalism in these new regulatory spaces. In a provocative analysis, Tamanaha has argued that legal instrumentalism leads to the advance of private good at the cost of its "manifestation as *public* power that is to be wielded in furtherance of the *public good*. The legitimacy of the law, its claim to obedience, is based upon this claim" (Tamanaha 2005, 65). Certainly legal instrumentalism is an important dimension of the emerging regulatory governance, but as we have seen, this legal instrumentalism can sometimes be used in furtherance of a concept of the "pubic good" in these regulatory regimes. Paradoxically, however, this public good is often defined in instrumental terms in relation to its functional purposes, such as regulating property rights. Tension and contestation within hybrid regimes is not simply about different forms of legal reasoning; it also involves contestation about the nature of the public good involved in hybrid regimes. One of the contributions of the regulatory approach to institutional hybrids outlined in this chapter is the suggestion that we need to foreground this contestation rather than simply resort to a depoliticized notion of culture that excludes some notion of legal and social conflict.

The approach to institutional hybrids as forms of institutional mediation between different forms of legal reasoning may well provide an insight into the management of conflict between legal orders within and beyond the national state. Institutional hybrids are not just localized forms of legal governance. They stand at the intersection of local and global legal regimes. They contain and mediate competing forms of legal reasoning; furthermore, they also operate within multiple and fragmented legal orders within and beyond the national state. The question, then, is: how can the communication between legal orders be achieved? Michaels's (2009) approach is helpful in arguing that it is the relationship between discourses of law that is crucial to legal pluralism within the specific context of globalization. Working within what could be called a "communicative" framework, he places a great deal of emphasis on pluralism as the developing aspect of interinstitutional legality. His argument suggests that recognition is vital here, but, crucially, this is a set of practices for the recognition of law rather than a "universal criterion of validity for the recognised law" (Michaels 2009, 256). This approach to legal pluralism will turn Hart on his head (Hart 1997).

Echoing this Hartian emphasis on recognition, Palombella (2009) has advocated a notion of communicative pluralism. He argues that the conflicts between contending legal regimes can over time be accommodated through practices of recognition that provide some guidance as to the general notions of legality that might mitigate or accommodate contending notions of legality. The existence of these practices of recognition permits communication between contending legal orders within an international legal order.

CONCLUSION

This is a first cut at a regulatory approach to legal pluralism, and our approach has the potential to illuminate the complex network of relationships that structure institutional hybrids and their broader relationship to the fragmented and multiple legal order. The point is that it is important to capture the *nature* of these relationships rather than one or another element of the networks.[7] The question is: how do we go about defining the nature of this political relationship, and more important, what is to represent the "public" in the relocation of the rule of law to new legal hybrids?

This contribution of this chapter is to situate recent rule of law projects within a system of regulatory governance. Our approach places the analytical emphasis on the institutional relationship between, and within, legal regimes. In particular, our emphasis on the constitution of institutional hybrids draws attention to the way

---

7 See Rubin (2005) for an elaboration of the idea of public law as a network of relationships.

legal pluralism serves to legitimize and give expression to new forms of regulatory innovation. One of the effects of legal pluralism conceived as a jurisprudential template is the reconstitution of the social in a way that highlights social conflict by naturalizing social norms. At the same time, it relocates various elements of the relocation of public law within new institutional configurations. In this respect, our understanding of regulatory innovations in rule of law programs has much to gain from the literature on legal geography. This literature has revealed the way in which law and legal processes create and operate within a particular spatial architecture (Blomley 1994).[8] One of the advantages of this approach is that it enables us to explore the process by which new scales of regulatory governance are created.

One of the virtues of this regulatory perspective is that it takes us beyond a notion of legal pluralism as the shadow of legal centralism. Indeed, much of the work on legal pluralism seems trapped within the ideological framework of state centralism as its mirror, or inverse, image. The approach adopted here is intended to move us beyond these questions of state centralism and allow us to explore how institutional hybrids shape distinctive patterns of legal and regulatory spaces. Legal pluralism is the "jurisprudential mask" of the proliferating multiple legal orders within a transnational order, similar to the manner in which legal monism masked state-centered law.

Ironically, these new modes of legal governance are echoed in earlier colonial forms of legal governance. Indeed, in the growing salience of social and customary norms and institutions in legal governance, there appears to be a problematic return to notions of tradition and custom that were influential within the colonial state. As Mamdani (1996), among others, has argued, the colonial state – especially the late colonial state – ruled through the use of traditional mechanisms and instruments of governance, relying on reified notions of culture and tradition. Systems of indirect rule incorporated individuals into customary modes of rule, with state-supported agencies and organizations defining the nature and scope of such customary rule. As he argues, this tends to invoke "authoritarian possibilities" within such systems of customary law. There is a danger that the recent embrace of legal pluralism in various rule of law regulatory projects carries with it a risk for authoritarian possibilities associated with systems of indirect rule.

This chapter seeks to advance a distinctive political conception of legal pluralism as an "assemblage of rules, principles, canons, maxims, customs, usage and manners that condition and sustain the activity of governing" (Loughlin 2003, 30). As with earlier systems of indirect rule, it creates new political subjects, but in a different context of legal globalization. In seeking more effective legal reform programs – an

---

[8] One of the few to consider the relationship between territoriality and legal transformation is Raustiala (2003), who, in his innovative essay, analyzes what he terms "legal spatiality." Legal spatiality, he argues, is transformed by broad shifts in the structure of international relations. Walker (2008) has expanded on these issues in the context of the relocation of the rule of law. For a more general argument about scaling of governance, see Brenner (2004).

imperative for access to justice programs – it is essential that we squarely address and recognize the nature of rule of law as a regulatory project and incorporate this into our understanding of institutional hybrids.

REFERENCES

Alston, Philip. 2004. "'Core Labour Standard' and the Transformation of the International Labour Rights Regime." *European Journal of International Law* 15 (3): 457–52.
Arthurs, H. W. 2001. "Private Ordering and Workers' Rights in the Global Economy: Corporate Conduct as a Regime of Labour Market Regulation." In *Labour Law in an Era of Globalization: Transformative Practices and Possibilities*, ed. J. Conaghan, K. Klare, and R. Fischl. Oxford: Oxford University Press.
Benda-Beckmann, Keebet von. 2007. "Transnationalisation of Law, Globalisation and Legal Pluralism: A Legal Anthropological Perspective in Globalisation and Resistance." In *Law Reform in Asia Since the Crisis*, ed. C. Antons and V. Gessner, 53–80. Oxford: Hart.
Benton, Lauren. 2002. *Law and Colonial Cultures*. New York: Cambridge University Press.
Blomley, Nicholas. 1994. *Law, Space, and the Geographies of Power*. London: Guildford Publications.
Brenner, Neil. 2004. *New State Spaces: Urban Governance and the Rescaling of Statehood*. Oxford: Oxford University Press.
Brown, Kenneth. 2005. *Reconciling Customary and Received Law in Melanesia: The Post-Independence Experience in Solomon Islands and Vanuatu*. Darwin, South Australia: Charles Darwin University Press.
Cerny, Philip. 2010. *Rethinking World Politics: A Theory of Transnational Neopluralism*. Oxford: Oxford University Press.
Charlesworth, Hilary. 2007. "Building Democracy and Justice after Conflict." Occasional Paper 2/2007, Cunningham Lecture 2006, Academy of Social Sciences, Canberra.
Cohen, Amy J. 2009. "Thinking with Culture in Law and Development." *Buffalo Law Review* 57 (2): 511–86.
Collins, Hugh. 1999. *Regulating Contracts*. Oxford: Oxford University Press.
Duxbury, Neil. 2001. "Signaling and Social Norms." *Oxford Journal of Legal Studies* 21 (4): 719–36.
Dyzenhaus, David. 2006. *The Constitution of Law: Legality in a Time of Emergency*. Cambridge: Cambridge University Press.
Ellickson, Robert. 1991. *Order without Law: How Neighbors Settle Disputes*. Cambridge, MA: Harvard University Press.
Faundez, Julio. 2006. "Should Justice Reform Projects Take Non-State Justice Systems Seriously? Perspectives from Latin America." In *The World Bank Legal Review: Law Equity and Development*, vol. 2, ed. C. Sage and M. Woolcock. Washington, DC: World Bank.
Golub, Stephen. 2003. "Beyond Rule of Law Orthodoxy: The Legal Empowerment Alternative." Rule of Law Series, Working Paper 41, Carnegie Endowment for International Peace, Washington, DC.
Hameiri, Shahar. 2010. *Regulating Statehood: State Building and the Transformation of the Global Order*. Basingstoke: Palgrave/Macmillan.
Hart, H. L. A. 1997. *The Concept of Law*. Oxford: Oxford University Press.
Jayasuriya, Kanishka. 1999. "Globalization, Law, and the Transformation of Sovereignty: The Emergence of Global Regulatory Governance." *Indiana Journal of Global Legal Studies* 6 (2): 425–55.

———. 2001. "Globalization and the Changing Architecture of the State: Regulatory State and the Politics of Negative Coordination." *Journal of European Public Policy* 8 (1): 101–23.
———. 2008. "Regionalising the State: Political Topography of Regulatory Regionalism." *Contemporary Politics* 14 (1): 21–35.
Lessig, Lawrence. 1998. "The New Chicago School." *Journal of Legal Studies* 27 (2): 661–91.
Locke, Richard, Fei Qin, and Alberto Brause. 2006. "Does Monitoring Improve Labour Standards? Lesson from Nike." *Sloan School of Management Working Paper 24*, Massachusetts Institute of Technology, Cambridge, MA.
Loughlin, Martin. 2003. *The Idea of Public Law*. Oxford: Oxford University Press.
Mamdani, Mahmood. 1996. *Citizen and Subject: Contemporary Africa and the Legacy of Late Colonialism*. Princeton, NJ: Princeton University Press.
Menzies, Nicholas. 2007. *Legal Pluralism and the Post-Conflict Transition in the Solomon Islands*. New York: Guilford.
Michaels, Ralf. 2009. "Global Legal Pluralism." *Annual Review of Law and Social Science* 5: 243–62.
Nixon, Rod. 2006. "The Crisis of Governance in Subsistence States." *Journal of Contemporary Asia* 36 (1): 75–101.
Palombella, Gianluigi. 2009. "The Rule of Law beyond the State: Failures, Promises, and Theory." *International Journal of Constitutional Law* 7 (3): 442–67.
Posner, Eric. 2000. "Law and Social Norms: Reflections on Henri Lefebvre, Urban Theory and the Politics of Scale." *International Journal of Urban and Regional Research* 24 (2): 361–78.
Raustiala, Kal. 2003. *"The Evolution of Territoriality: International Relations and American Law."* UCLA School of Law Research Paper 05-6, University of California, Los Angeles.
Rittich, Kerry. 2005. "The Future of Law and Development: Second Generation Reform and the Incorporation of the Social." *Michigan Journal of International Law* 26: 199–242.
Rubin, Edward. 2005. *Beyond Camelot: Rethinking Politics and Law for the Modern State*. Princeton, NJ: Princeton University Press.
Santos, Boaventura de Sousa. 2002. *Toward a New Legal Common Sense: Law, Globalization and Emancipation*. 2nd ed. Cambridge and New York: Cambridge University Press.
———. 2006. "The Heterogeneous State and Legal Pluralism in Mozambique." *Law and Society Review* 40 (1): 39–75.
Tamanaha, Brian. 2005. "The Perils of Pervasive Legal Instrumentalism." Montesquieu Lecture Series, Tilburg University, Tilburg.
———. 2008. "Understanding Legal Pluralism: Past to Present, Local to Global." *Sydney Law Review* 30 (3): 375–411.
Taylor, V. 2009. "Frequently Asked Questions about the Rule of Law (and Why Better Answers Matter)." *Hague Journal of the Rule of Law* 1 (1): 46–52.
Teubner, Gunther. 1986. "After Legal Instrumentalism? Strategic Models of Post Regulatory Law." In *Dilemmas of Law in the Welfare State*, ed. G. Teubner. Berlin: De Gruyte.
———. 1996. "Global Bukowina: Legal Pluralism in the World Society." In *Global Law without the State*, ed. G. Teubner. London: Dartsmouth Publishing.
TLO (The Liaison Office). 2008. "Between the Jirga and the Judge: Alternative Dispute Resolution in Southeastern Afghanistan." TLO Program Brief 1, The Liaison Office and U.S. Institute of Peace, Kabul.
Walker, Neil. 2008. "Beyond Boundary Disputes and Basic Grids: Mapping the Global Disorder of Normative Orders." *International Journal of Constitutional Law* 6 (3–4): 373–96.

Wardak, Ali. 2002. "*Jirga*: Power and Traditional Conflict Resolution in Afghanistan." In *Law after Ground Zero*, ed. J. Strawson. London: Cavendish.
Wojkowska, Ewa, and Johanna Cunningham. 2009. "Justice Reform's New Frontier: Engaging with Customary Systems to Legally Empower the Poor." Legal Empowerment Working Paper 7, International Development Law Organization, Rome.
Zumbansen, Peer. 2006. "Systems and Places: A Systems Theory Approach to Regulatory Competition in European Company Law." *European Law Journal* 12 (4): 534–56.

10

Some Implications of the Application of Legal Pluralism to Development Practice

Doug J. Porter

Development is an artifact of liberalism and the extension of empires. Thus, it has had from the outset to contend with the existence of multiple contending normative orders. Colonial officials were preoccupied with the impact of plural orders on durable answers to four core societal governance questions: what resources will be mobilized for productive purposes, how will production be organized, who will bear the benefits and costs, and who shall be empowered to make decisions with respect to these questions? These questions remain central to development work today. But in the decades following the establishment of the Bretton Woods institutions – when singular regimes of development were more deliberately and decidedly crafted to answer these questions – the existence of multiple legal and normative orders was typically regarded as one of the principle constraints to transforming societies and economies in ways that replicated the trajectory of Western capitalism and liberal democracy. As this volume implies, this is no longer the case: legal and normative pluralism is regarded as an established and enduring fact. And, in ways that echo the inventive forms of governing crafted by colonial authorities, development agencies today are just as likely to seek ways to instrumentalize normative plurality as they are to ignore or outlaw this reality when designing schemes to regulate social and economic activity.

This chapter is a speculative review of some of the implications of the resurgence of interest in legal pluralism in contemporary development policy and practice. Although it is true that "there is nothing inherently good, progressive or emancipatory about legal pluralism" (Santos 1995, 114–15), this chapter argues that legal pluralism – both as a de facto process and when actively promoted by development interventions – does have normative implications for societies' abilities to create durable institutional arrangements that enable peaceful and workable

I wish to acknowledge my ongoing work with David Craig, which informs this chapter, as well as the insightful comments made by Dan Adler and Tobias Haque on an earlier version of this chapter.

settlements around the core societal governance questions noted previously. Discussing this point involves broad generalizations around five key points, so some caveats are in order about concepts and context around which these remarks are made.

First, I am not concerned with doctrinal disputes about the intellectual traditions from which the concept of legal pluralism springs, nor do I dwell on otherwise important distinctions, such as those between social fact pluralism and global legal pluralism, discussed elsewhere in this volume. Rather, this chapter needs only to note that legal pluralism speaks to the pervasive situation of all development interventions, where different sets of norms, and correspondingly different sets of institutions and practices, coexist in the same time-space context. From this, several points scholars make about legal pluralism logically have immediate resonance with development practice: for instance, where it is also taken as a given that the monopoly of state law is a modern exception (as, incidentally, is the notion of "intentional development" [see Cowen and Shenton 1996]), and that mutable non-state institutions (e.g., custom and tradition), as manifestations of pluralism, are "here to stay." Thus, both concepts, legal pluralism and development, immediately draw attention to multiple orders, norms, and practices, but also to the fact that the transport of new norms, institutional arrangements, and precepts always interact with preexisting modes of governance, that is, that developmental spaces are "already governed." Both concepts also alert us to the fact that even where globally inspired modern/liberal norms appear to be harmonized with domestic arrangements, other highly illiberal ways of governing will coexist. Also, despite being opaque to development's liberal sensibilities, the layering of multiple forms of governing may seriously jeopardize the socially transformative aspirations that all but "development cynics" continue to hold dear (Craig and Porter, forthcoming).

Second, regarding context, it is obvious that development interventions occur in an extraordinarily diverse range of contexts and circumstances and that they seek to influence outcomes around an equally wide array of socially contested issues. Obviously, we are not talking about contexts where the institutional rules of the game are stable, regarded locally as legitimate, and functioning in ways that effectively contain and convey social contests, allowing decisions to be made, executed, and enforced in a relatively peaceful manner. Law has not been consolidated in the state. Here the issue is not simply that political order is commonly constituted by "hybrid" institutional arrangements (Boege et al. 2008). Rather, basic governing arrangements are actively contested, and there are typically high degrees of inequality in power and opportunity to influence the outcomes of these contests. Furthermore, in these contexts, although local disputes – around production, allocation, distribution, and authority – may overwhelmingly be contained in long-standing non-state institutions (Golub 2006; Piron 2006), the institutions more likely to be applicable at higher levels of scale and territory will be more recent imports that have not evolved through collective political contest. They will tend, in other words, to be the global artifacts of capitalism or schemes of liberal developmentalism that have traveled to these context through "executive short cuts" (Craig and Porter 2006).

This latter point highlights a key normative aspect of contemporary interest in legal pluralism in development. Namely, throughout this volume we are talking of country contexts where the task of creating local and national institutions that can peacefully resolve social contests and provide the stability and predictability needed for sustained economic growth will always be deeply affected by the commercial, diplomatic, and security decisions made by actors well beyond the country concerned. At the same time, the view that legal pluralism is entrenched – "here to stay" – necessarily implies that the trajectories of social change will be unlikely to mimic that of Western capitalism and liberal democracy. Thus, if it is not assumed that the state in these contexts will at any time possess a monopoly over law or political or economic orders, it may be prudent – as Tamahana (this volume) suggests – to assume that the predominance of social life will be dealt with through non-state orders. These facts, then, suggest the enormity of the challenge – how to best support local leaders in sorting out the kinds of institutions that make sense locally, will prove popular, and will promote consensus and social inclusion while also being robust enough to deal with social and economic changes at a level of territorial scale and over periods of time that are unfamiliar and for which long-standing non-state institutions are likely unsuited.

Finally, when considering how ideas about legal pluralism might be elaborated or the implications of their more general application, I have in view the kinds of situations that have become increasingly common in the past two decades, namely, those where states have recently emerged from conflict, are struggling to deal with the vastly superior power of transnational resource companies, or for these and other reasons have been framed by development agencies as "fragile." These are societies experiencing a long-term shrinkage in effective public authority (Moore, Schmidt, and Unsworth 2009). Fragile states in these countries are typically defined by gaps, lacks, or failure; they are unable to achieve a monopoly of violence within their territories, to equitably deliver services or regulate conduct in markets or social life, to achieve Western normative standards about the election and representative behavior of leaders, and to use international assistance in effective or accountable ways. Looked at differently, these tend to be countries where authoritative power has shifted from the state to unofficial, non-state actors and neo-patrons who manipulate a range of illicit, donor, and state resources to buy loyalty, trust, and security. In these contexts, patronage is the key principle in how they function. They are by definition normatively plural. But regardless of whether they are more or less stable and more or less on the border of being considered criminal or legitimate locally or internationally, they operate in familiar ways that should be considered when schemes are advanced to promote legal pluralism.

With these caveats in mind, this chapter suggest that efforts to foster legal pluralism can have unforeseen effects on the ability of societies to achieve stable, socially inclusive institutional arrangements that enable them to sustain ongoing contests around the four core questions of governance noted in the introductory paragraph of this chapter. In closing, I counter this provocation by relaxing these caveats and consider contexts and ways in which this might not be the case. Before this, some observations are needed about the common interests of development policy and scholarship around legal pluralism.

LEGAL PLURALISM AND DEVELOPMENT: REGULATING SOCIAL CONTEST THROUGH HYBRID INSTITUTIONS

Contemporary interest in legal pluralism is evidence of a wider recognition of the role development workers play in societal contests about these core governing questions. In these contests, elites – whether developmental, political or commercial, foreign or local – and everyday people actively contest efforts to make particular activities legible, assessable, and taxable and create workable monopolies for the purposes of advancing particular norms, constituencies of interest, and control over resources and territories. The present instrumental interest in legal pluralism is thus simultaneously recognition of elite contest and of the fact that concerted efforts of elites to absorb people in unified systems of economic or administrative governance will be resisted. Legal pluralism surfaces as a "problem" of development policy and operations for two reasons. One is that national elites selectively resist or partially incorporate the ostensibly progressive tenets of state law and liberal institutions promoted by development – a process scholars have referred to as "isomorphic mimicry" (Di Maggio and Powell 1991). Another reason is that people everywhere have resisted efforts by elites to demarcate, seize, tax, or otherwise administer on their behalf natural assets (e.g., land, forest, minerals, fish), their movements, their labor, and their identities to encourage their settlement and registration in taxable villages and their subordination of higher levels of governance (Scott 2009). People everywhere have created multiple and often durable systems for resisting these kinds of incorporation. This is especially the case where the dominant rule systems of the state are weakened by the kinds of conflict or economic turbulence associated with historical change or intentional development processes. Yet all too often, development workers assume that there exists a widespread "demand for good governance" or for unified "rule of law" systems. Just as often, the policy conceit follows that such demands are simply waiting to be facilitated through capacity building or incentivized by the distribution of rents from aid. But, as is repeatedly lamented by development agency evaluations of such projects, people often regard the fact that there is no single governing system – that there are multiple and fragmented local, national, and global aid systems for managing resources and ongoing contests about the authority of customary, political, and administrative agencies to decide what is to be done with proceeds – as much an "opportunity" as a "constraint" to be overcome.

From a different perspective, Jayasuriya's chapter (this volume) alerts us to the implication of this way of seeing normative/legal pluralism. He directs our attention to the process "through which these plural legal systems take form as components of a broader regulatory regime." In development work, the imperative to govern through an ordering of plural systems necessarily involved the purposive creation of institutions, in other words, of "intentional hybrids." Colonial governing was achieved through the juridification of non-state orders. This was part of deliberate strategic response to active resistance, where legal hybridity featured in particular ways. According to Frederick Lugard, architect of the colonial system of indirect rule (perhaps the first example of a deliberate "intentional hybrid"), the "[p]rinciples do not change, but their mode of application should vary with the customs, the traditions and the prejudices of each (administrative) unit" (Lugard 1922, 194). Thus, in Lugard's Nigeria and then Uganda, non-state legal orders were granted a semiautonomous status, but within a wider hybrid system that borrowed lessons from the Raj, drew on Mughal India, and was patched together with systems of imperial governance and reinventions of plural local "tradition." In practice, as Mamdani notes, the British worked with a single model of customary authority across Africa that mirrored images of traditional European monarchy and patriarchy (Mamdani 1996, 39). This individuation of plural systems entailed all the dangers of reification and essentializing non-state normative orders of which contemporary observers of legal pluralism warn (see, for instance, Twining, this volume). Early on, this model came to grief with the "hyrdra-headed" Yoruba and then dense forest acephalic Ibo territory, both non-state polities that had adapted to survive the plunder and pillage of slave trading (Craig and Porter 2006, 40).

As with institutional hybridity, the concept of "recognition" that lies at the heart of legal pluralism is widely present in historical and contemporary accounts of development work. Awareness of how this was instrumentalized by colonial authorities for the purpose of governing social contestation was perhaps first documented in irrigation schemes (e.g., Punjab, from the 1880s to early 1920s) (see Ali 2003). Here, colonial orders and officials would, at different times, for different purposes, acknowledge or deny the existence of contending non-state legal orders. They would actively and selectively take into account different norms and create bylaws to deliberately integrate them into state legal ordering arrangements and enforce such norms. Alternately, they would adroitly outlaw, defer to, or treat such systems at arm's length. In contemporary development work, state officials, development workers, and farmers alike routinely and in unpredictable ways in fact "forum shop"; they make political claims and appeals in multiple fora and thus selectively appeal to constitutional law to prosecute customary claims in order to resist imposition of statutory rights – around access to water, for instance – or have such decisions overturned by de facto norms articulated by religious, party patrimonies, or collective action (Craig and Porter, forthcoming).

LEGAL PLURALISM AND RESCALING GOVERNANCE

I will shortly illustrate five possible implications of renewed interest in legal pluralism in aspects of development practice. Before this, it is useful to underscore the point of Jayasuriya's chapter in this volume: namely, that contemporary interest – in development policy and legal pluralism scholarship – in non-state legal orders has reemerged in tandem with new modes of regulation that have been developed over the past twenty or so years. As a result, new and predominantly non-state hybrid forms of institutions are being used to regulate the interaction of local and global actors. This process, which has dramatically reframed the role of states in development, was clearly under way during the period of frank structural adjustment that followed the 1980s debt crisis. One aspect of this process involved what observers referred to as the hollowing out of the state. Another aspect, occurring in tandem, was that key functions of the state were rescaled, both to supranational institutions and to subnational, local institutions (Craig and Porter 2006). Renewed interest in legal pluralism, particularly as it focused on non-state, local institutions, was one element of this process of relocating legitimacy, authority, and power in governance to sites outside the state.

By the end of the 1980s, the definition of social rights and the command over decisions about how resources would be accumulated and used was shifting away from national cabinets and out onto the trading floors and into the boardrooms of financial institutions that were masquerading as the "free market" or into global institutions that were more actively defining and policing public rights and state obligations. As Jayasuriya (this volume) remarks, "It is through these systems of governance that public law is relocated within new legal spaces," a process corresponding with Michaels's (2009, 247) observations regarding legal globalization in which norms are defined "from the top down (rather) than from the bottom up." But it was more than this, which is where legal pluralism came again to the fore. At much the same time as the "vertical" reassignment of state regulatory functions was occurring, a "horizontal" reassignment was also under way. Here, state functions were hived off to non-state institutions, nongovernmental organizations (NGOs), private providers, and a host of newly decentralized local authorities, including reinvented "traditional" organizations. This horizontal reassignment of state functions occurred for both ideological and pragmatic reasons. Just as the market economy was believed to operate best unfettered by state regulation, so too would local social and political markets flourish if multiple sources of authority, identity, and obligations were fostered. Then, propelled by the social protests and instabilities of economic transformation during the 1990s, local political and social pluralism gained added momentum as efforts were made to put a "human face" on neoliberal economic reform. Various projects oriented to social welfare, basic service delivery, and local security all hoped, pragmatically, to peg governance functions to a range of new subnational scales, including quasi-government bodies, farmers' associations, clan or kinship groups, and water or health committees. These plural institutions had the added merit of drawing on the legitimate face of "community" rather than the oppressive "singularity" of the state.

SOME IMPLICATIONS OF REGULATORY PLURALISM

What this regulatory lens suggests is that there is nothing coincidental about contemporary interest in legal pluralism or, indeed, in this collection's thematic interest in the implications of legal pluralism for development work. Far from reflecting a curiosity about the multitude of local laws and norms in practice, this theme is part of a wider internal differentiation in global law, in which, as Jayasuriya suggests, "legal pluralism itself becomes a kind of jurisprudential technology – a set of templates and models – through which the non state legal orders are regulated and authorized." From this viewpoint, the remainder of this chapter charts and illustrates five possible implications of the elevation of non-state legal orders in contemporary development work.

First, as many others have remarked, this process of vertical and horizontal rescaling of governance meant that the core societal governance questions noted in the introductory paragraph could no longer be plausibly mapped and resolved at the scale of the nation-state. This has had a number of implications, each of which has had the effect of adding to legal pluralism. It has challenged the primacy of the nation-state as the sole source of binding norms, notions of citizenship, entitlements, and the public interest. Instead of societal governance questions being principally or even predominantly defined through societal contest within the constitutional containers of national states (in a sense, "bottom up" through plural representational politics), in contexts where states are defined as fragile and incompetent, new policy processes apply. Norms – about rights related to production, allocation, distribution, and authority – are defined externally, if not through truly "global" institutions, then through supranational processes. These are then exported globally through executive shortcuts and then ensconced in practice through non-state institutions at the "community" level (Craig and Porter, forthcoming).

This "pluralizing" of governance has several effects. One is that global norms are articulated in local territories and social groupings in ways that "reach over the heads" of national representational politics. Jayasuriya references the work of Alston (2004) to show this process at work with regard to labor rights. The Millenium Development Goals (MDGs) at face value are a more benign instance of this process; less benign is the host of collateral norms and global disciplinary systems around revenue, budget making, and expenditure management systems that more pervasively curtail national representational politics toward MDG outcomes. This process of creating direct relations between global and local scales of social ordering has important implications for how national institutions are capable of sustaining social contest – a point I return to. The practical implications of this process can be illustrated in health sector work. Here, the engagement of non-state actors – NGOs, private for-profit service providers – has been particularly pronounced. This has often brought undoubted benefits in terms of the efficiency of spending and quality of services. Here the pinning of globally sanctioned standards to individualized notions of health involves the contractualizing of public health services by supranational agencies to nongovernment agencies made vertically accountable "downward" to "community health committees" and "upward" to global norms and standards. This can have transformative effects on how governance is conceived and carried out. A more conventional, "unreformed" social compact between states and citizens would entail populations of "citizens" acting politically to negotiate workable and locally legitimate rights and entitlements for health through constitutionally mandated territorial authorities. Once reformed, people are repositioned to negotiate as individual clients for services delivered according to quite narrow, technically defined "service outputs." "Citizen entitlements" can be claimed through representative political processes; "client rights" are often a poor, marketized proxy.

Second, the interest in non-state forms of normative pluralism is often conceived of as a challenge to state centralism and hegemonic notions of development. Project documents for efforts as diverse as rural development or alternate dispute resolution will frequently persuade reviewers that "community participation" will do far more than simply improve the quality of services delivered by state agencies. Indeed, it is implicitly argued that empowerment – of elders, religious or traditional leaders, or community representatives appointed to quasi-territorial jurisdictions defined by projects – will result in the elevation of non-state regulatory norms. These arrangements, thus, will somehow "colonize" the state and transform it in the image of plural "community" values, norms, and regulatory arrangements. This is only one possibility. Just as often, what occurs is the appropriation, reshaping, and instrumentalizing of non-state institutions in the image of global regulatory systems, rights, and ordering principles.

This process is often evident in the host of "community-driven decentralizations" that have become popular in the past fifteen years (e.g., Mansuri and Rao 2004). On one level, these interventions have radically pluralized local politics and opened multiple sites where citizens can directly negotiate societal governance questions – about raising and allocating resources, resolving disputes about how authority is exercised, and making decisions about who benefits or bears the costs of decisions. In this setting, a host of different and ostensibly "local" political formations have been promoted around identities both new (women, youth, conflict mediators) and old (elders, jirgas, traditional authorities). Of course, what happens depends on context. But at the same time that "plurality" appears to be flourishing, it is striking how the honoring of community diversity and normative plurality is typically overlaid with globally standard systems for shaping up community groups, encouraging them to plan and allocate budgets in templated ways, read from a standard menu of legitimate investments, and adopt particular disciplinary systems for accounting, performing, and sanctioning their actions. In this process, the legitimacy of things "community" – values, normative orders, authority, and, most important, apparent plurality – is effectively appropriated at the same time they are being made globally legible and, it turns out, relatively easily incorporated into arrangements that suit governing elites (as in the case of Cambodia in Craig and Porter, forthcoming). This incorporation of non-state orders into neopatrimonial arrangements is often taken as an indicator of successful "community empowerment." Ironically, it can also represent a thorough "bounding" of local politics and the redirection of its energies into avenues most comfortable for those keen to sustain the status quo.

Third, the proliferation of intentional hybrids, that is, legal pluralism in practice, has been observed to have important implications for political accountability, the fragmentation of politics, and the increased strength of neopatrimonial systems of rule. What Jayasuriya describes with regard to law and justice sector reforms is also evident in other areas of development. Recognition of plural non-state norms, forms of legitimacy and authority, and their articulation under the banner of "community" has resulted in a splendid array of hybrid institutional arrangements – for delivering services and resolving disputes related to health, security, education, water, land, and forest management. This has been most marked in settings where the state's territorial reach is chronically weakening (Moore, Schmidt, and Unsworth 2009) or is actively contested, as occurs in the aftermath of civil conflict, or where it is overwhelmed by the special political economies of extractive industries (on the latter, see Human Rights Watch 2007; Watts 2004, for the case of Nigeria's "ungoverned spaces" in the oil-rich delta states). Irrespective of whether local communities are remote from state power or geographically close to its heart, it is not uncommon to find upward of one or two dozen governing authorities for the health project, the savings and credit group, the local justice group, the poultry committee, the parents and teachers association, two or three rural development planning committees, (with some shaped up to "demand good governance") – all mixing up electoral, kinship, and generational norms, identities, and authorities – reporting up, down, and sideways, and all predominantly to non-state authorities. This is legal pluralism at work in development practice. The consequence is typically a fragmentation of accountability – "more accountabilities do not add up to more accountability" (Craig and Porter 2006). The prospect of effective state territorial authority – administrative and justice systems accountable through representative political systems – can be disabled by the proliferation of globally attuned quasi-territorial authorities that are wrapped around narrow conceptions of rights and identity politics.

The fourth practical implication of legal plurality/hybridity can also be most pronounced in post-conflict settings. Here, the proliferation of hybrid regulatory institutions can have an enormous impact on the practical autonomy and legitimacy of states. The promotion of contending normative and legal orders can in some settings have the desirable effect of contesting the power, legitimacy, and authority of ugly regimes. But normative institutional pluralism at the local level needs to be seen in the context of a similar global proliferation of "rights" – extending from the post–World War II rights agendas through the vastly extended range of "poverty indicators" to the MDG framework of the past decade. These plural global norms proliferate at the same time the remits of multiple ethnically or locality-specific community, traditional, and other normative orders are being extended, often through populist engagements by development workers. They all make claims on the entitlements of national citizenship in different ways. In turn, these are projected into obligations on the state – in a sense, from above and from below. This has the effect of challenging the practical autonomy of the state – as it must "respond" or see its legitimacy eroded (both from above and below) – and at the same time, the range of obligations it must somehow administer is rapidly ramped up well beyond what is fiscally or administratively possible (see World Bank 2010). When states are perceived as not performing – not meeting this rhetorically expanded range of obligations – the result is what the fragile and conflicted states literature terms "the expectations gap" and "institutional overloading" (cf. Dinnen, Porter, and Sage 2010). This can translate into grievance, the steady withdrawal of popular legitimacy, and an undermining of state authority. This is noted as a common "driver" of the high probability of a relapse into conflict faced by post-conflict societies (World Bank 2011).

Finally, the purposive engagement of development with non-state regulatory orders can have important implications for the socially transformative aspirations on which development ultimately depends for credibility. Although there is nothing normatively good or bad about legal pluralism, it is arguable that many proponents of legal pluralism in development work inherently believe that the engagement of non-state normative orders related to land governance, service delivery, or dispute resolution around natural assets like forests or fish are normatively positive milestones on the route to social transformation. To be sure, as Jayasuriya points out, one of the drivers of the rescaling of regulatory functions to non-state actors is the disappointing record of legal and justice reform programs acting predominantly through the formal state sector. In practice, as Adler and So elaborate in this volume with regard to Cambodia's land reform process, non-state social norms are ensconced in "tradition" or party patrimonies and prove to be highly durable or "sticky." Most regulatory success, at least in this example, is to be found in those instances where "they formalize, rather than radically transform, existing social norms and power relations. Areas in which the transformative power of the law is called upon have been those where progress has been most challenging" (Adler, Porter, and Woolcock 2008, 4).

CONCLUSION

Contemporary interest in legal pluralism resonates strongly with trends in development practice over the past two decades. In one respect, it is a response to the apparent inability of state-centric rule of law projects to successfully extend and ensconce singular systems of law and institutions. The spread of such orders is not inexorable – and this is especially the case at the outer reaches of scattered archipelago nations or geographically remote border territories. Unless they hold aesthetic or natural resources attractive to global markets and local elites or exhibit forms of "unrest" that threaten the orders they wish to maintain, plural non-state legal orders are likely to endure in many territories as the principal means by which societies govern themselves. By implication, the five sets of observations made in this chapter about the active promotion of legal pluralism clearly will not apply here – despite the fact that the process of incorporation of such areas into global markets or governing systems may indeed be inexorable.

Elsewhere, to be sure, these provocative observations will apply according to context. Obviously, where states are simply dysfunctional rather than being oppressive or politically illegitimate, the promotion of service delivery, dispute resolution, or wider social ordering through non-state forms may indeed free the state from its own incapacities. There exist a wide slew of territories and peoples where either, or both, circumstances apply.

Nevertheless, most territories today are within the active reach of states and development agencies that contest decisions people make about what shall be produced, how the benefits and costs will be distributed, and who shall govern those decisions. Here, the resonance between interest in legal pluralism and development needs to be seen through a regulatory lens. Both are manifestly concerned with societal contests occurring at multiple scales in which efforts are being made to regulate and authorize non-state orders in ways that appear to be quite new. This reality requires more than an awareness that the harmonies sometimes achieved between recently arrived and preexisting formal governing arrangements are likely to rest on accommodations with semiautonomous non-state orders. The concepts of "intentional hybridity" and "recognition," drawn directly from the scholarship of legal pluralism, hark back to the sophisticated colonial technologies developed in the nineteenth century to govern fractured territories and resistant peoples. In this sense, we might be advised to suspect that there is a strong line of descent between this heritage – what Mamdani calls "decentralized despotism" – and contemporary forms of development that hope to promote flourishing plural non-state orders.

In this light, and in these places, normative pluralism becomes far more than an academic curiosity. It requires scholarship that empirically maps the counterfactuals to the generalizations carried in the five points made in this chapter about the potential consequences of activism around legal pluralism. Under what circumstances does the instrumentalizing of non-state orders have the implications suggested above for citizenship? Where and how might the appropriation of local forms of legitimacy and authority limit the practical autonomy of citizens and their states? Contrarily, how might it curtail or create incentives that redirect the actions of elite coalitions that otherwise would not act in the public's interests? In other words, under what circumstances and by what means could the socially transformative power of the law be called on?

REFERENCES

Adler, Daniel, Doug Porter, and Michael Woolcock. 2008. "Legal Pluralism and Equity: Some Reflections on Land Reform in Cambodia." Justice for the Poor Briefing Note 2, World Bank, Washington, DC.

Ali, Imran. 2003. *The Punjab under Imperialism: 1885–1947*. Oxford: Oxford University Press.

Alston, Philip. 2004. "'Core Labour Standard' and the Transformation of the International Labour Rights Regime." *European Journal of International Law* 15 (3): 457–52.

Boege, Volker, Anne Brown, Kevin Clements, and Anna Nolan. 2008. "Towards Effective and Legitimate Governance: States Emerging from Hybrid Political Orders." *Australian Centre for Peace and Conflict Studies*, University of Queensland, Brisbane.

Cowen, M. P., and Robert Shenton. 1996. *Doctrines of Development*. London: Routledge.

Craig, David, and Doug Porter. 2006. *Development beyond Neoliberalism: Governance, Poverty Reduction and Political Economy*. London: Routledge.

——— . Forthcoming. *Winning the Peace: New Institutions and Neo-patrimonialism in Post-Conflict Cambodia*. Ann Arbor: University of Michigan Press.

Di Maggio, Paul, and Walter Powell. 1991. "The Iron Cage Revisited: Institutional Isomorphism and Collective Rationality in Organizational Fields." *American Sociological Review* 48 (2): 147–60.

Dinnen, Sinclair, Doug Porter, and Caroline Sage. 2010. "Conflict in Melanesia: Themes and Lessons." Background Paper for World Development Report 2011, World Bank, Washington, DC.

Golub, Stephen. 2006. "A House without a Foundation." In *Promoting the Rule of Law Abroad: In Search of Knowledge*, ed. T. Carothers. Washington, DC: Carnegie Endowment for International Peace.

Human Rights Watch. 2007. "Chop Fine: The Human Rights Impact of Local Government Corruption and Mismanagement in Rivers State, Nigeria." Revenue Watch 19, no. 2(A), Human Rights Watch, New York.

Lugard, Frederick. 1922. *The Dual Mandate in British Tropical Africa*. Edinburgh: Frank Cass and Co.

Mamdani, Mahmood. 1996. *Citizen and Subject: Contemporary Africa and the Legacy of Late Colonialism*. Princeton, NJ: Princeton University Press.

Mansuri, Ghazala, and Vijayendra Rao. 2004. "Community-Based and -Driven Development: A Critical Review." *World Bank Observer* 19(1): 1–39.

Michaels, Ralf. 2009. "Global Legal Pluralism." *Annual Review of Law and Social Science* 5: 1–35.

Moore, Mick, Anna Schmidt, and Sue Unsworth. 2009. "Assuring Our Common Future in a Globalised World: The Global Context of Conflict and State Fragility." Background paper prepared for the Department for International Development, London. Unpublished.

Piron, Laure-Helene. 2006. "Time to Learn, Time to Act in Africa." In *Promoting the Rule of Law Abroad: In Search of Knowledge*, ed. T. Carothers. Washington, DC: Carnegie Endowment for International Peace.

Santos, Boaventura de Sousa. 1995. *Toward a New Common Sense*. London: Routledge.

Scott, James. 2009. *The Art of Not Being Governed: An Anarchist History of Upland Southeast Asia*. New Haven, CT: Yale University Press.
Watts, Michael. 2004. "The Sinister Political Life of Community: Economies of Violence and Governable Spaces in the Niger Delta, Nigeria." Economies of Violence Working Paper 3, Institute of International Studies, University of California, Berkeley.
World Bank. 2010. "Solomon Islands Growth Prospects: Constraints and Opportunities." Discussion Note, The World Bank, Washington, DC.
World Bank. 2011. *World Development Report 2011: Conflict, Security and Development*. Washington, DC: The World Bank.

PART III

From Theory to Practice

11

Legal Pluralism and International Development Agencies

State Building or Legal Reform

Julio Faundez

I. INTRODUCTION

In the early years of this century, most of the legal and judicial reform work of international development agencies (hereafter IDAs) focused mainly on state institutions. Their assumption was that once state institutions were reformed in accordance with prevailing market-friendly policy prescriptions, non-state mechanisms would promptly wither away. The almost exclusive focus on state institutions during this initial period of IDAs was, in all likelihood, also prompted by the fact that, at the time, most development practitioners regarded normative structures operating outside or against the framework of the state as disorderly, corrupt, unimportant, or even potentially subversive. Today, however, things have changed. After the disappointing outcomes of many years of legal and judicial reform, and in view of the enormous challenges posed by state building in numerous fragile and failed states, IDAs are beginning to accept that governance and justice mechanisms that operate either outside the framework of the state or in the fringes between state and society – non-state justice systems (hereafter NSJS) – are indispensable components of reform processes aimed at improving the overall performance of legal and judicial institutions.

The new awareness about the importance of NSJS is reflected both in the policy literature on legal reform and in the components of projects approved by a variety of IDAs, including the World Bank and regional development banks. Indeed, such is the enthusiasm with which IDAs have embraced NSJS that it is tempting to conclude that, if this wider and more comprehensive approach to reform had been applied two decades ago, the numerous legal and judicial reform projects implemented by IDAs would have been more successful in achieving better and more sustainable outcomes. The current awareness about the importance of NSJS is, undoubtedly, a welcomed development. Nevertheless, it also entails an important risk: namely, that in their incessant search for a magic wand, IDAs underestimate the difficulties and dangers involved in engaging with NSJS and, in the end, encounter the same disappointing results that have plagued most legal and judicial reform projects since their inception.

NSJS are so varied in their origin, nature, and functions that even the most refined attempts to develop guidelines on how to engage with them are pitched at such a high level of generality that it is unlikely that they can be of much use at the operational level (DFID 2004; UN Development Group 2008). Indeed, this is an area of development policy where the discredited "one-size-fits-all" cannot be made to work. Although I am certain that most IDAs are aware of the scale of the challenge, I doubt whether they have fully taken into account the political and operational problems involved in engaging with NSJS. Consider, for example, the following recommendations provided by a recently published policy brief on how to engage with traditional justice institutions in Afghanistan in areas cleared of insurgents (Dempsey and Coburn 2010):

- Identify local trusted actors who can help with the program design
- Encourage relationship building among program implementers
- Conduct thorough research to ensure proper understanding of local power
- Identify primary challenges to stabilizing cleared areas (local land disputes)
- Secure government buy-in to traditional justice programs, but allow communities to decide on the membership of their dispute resolution institutions (*jirgas* or *shuras*)
- Encourage respectful and regular dialogue on justice needs between state and traditional actors
- Bear in mind that individuals should not be required to participate in traditional dispute resolution against their will
- Be patient and keep expectations realistic

These recommendations, though sensible, are too general to provide a clear guide for action. They also raise important questions that are not always easy to answer. What, for example, are the aims and objectives of IDAs when they engage with NSJS? In the case of Afghanistan, the answer is simple: external agencies in Afghanistan are attempting to win the hearts and minds of local people in order to secure stable and sustainable peace. This clear objective does not, of course, make the task simple or even realistic. But what if we ask the same question about external programs in connection with justice institutions of indigenous communities in Bolivia, Guatemala, or South Africa? How, for example, should IDAs intervene in relation to NSJS in countries where the government and the elites are either in denial about the existence of these institutions or are openly, or covertly, fighting them in order to secure national economic, social, or political objectives? Indeed, if this is so, then any external intervention is not only an attempt to lift, empower, or modernize NSJS, but also involves a major attempt to change state policies in areas where governments are often reluctant to change. It would thus seem that any successful engagement with NSJS would require close coordination and cooperation with state authorities. If this is so, then the process of engagement instantly becomes both openly political and much more challenging than the more modest tasks of improving court management systems or updating the legal skills of lower court judges. The political nature of almost any form of external engagement with NSJS suggests – contrary to widely held assumptions – that states, in general, do not ignore these institutions. Indeed, as the work of historians, sociolegal experts, and legal anthropologists shows, most states are in constant interaction with NSJS, although, admittedly, this interaction generally does not yield improvements on the rule of law or produce results that further good governance.

The foregoing suggests that IDAs' engagement with NSJS is a hazardous venture that makes traditional legal and judicial reform work appear simple. As well as being politically complex, it is also resource intensive and requires long time frames, because change in this area is painfully slow and often difficult to sustain. I do not think, however, that this should deter IDAs from becoming involved. Yet they should be fully aware of the pitfalls and obstacles along the way. Accordingly, the objective of this chapter is to identify, albeit schematically, some persistent problems arising from attempts to engage, ignore, or regulate NSJS. The materials discussed in this paper, drawn from Latin America and Africa, suggest that any successful engagement with NSJS requires a deep understanding of both local state structures and political processes. It also requires an in-depth understanding of the state and community within which NSJS operate. Indeed, as this chapter shows, successful engagement should be seen as part of a continuing process of state building. Unless IDAs are willing to take a wider and more political approach to their involvement with NSJS, they will not achieve meaningful progress in rule of law and governance projects.

The following section (Section 2) examines some aspects of the debate over the failure of most African states to establish centralized systems of land tenure. This debate suggests that the ensuing legal pluralism is both a consequence of the capacity of traditional institutions to resist change and a solution to overcoming unrealistic land tenure policies. Section 3 shows that legal recognition of indigenous rights often yields positive outcomes, especially when it is combined with popular mobilization. Yet this section also argues that states are not helpless when they confront NSJS. Indeed, as illustrations from Latin America and Africa show, governments are well versed in the art of manipulating the rights of traditional communities and indigenous peoples in order to serve their own objectives. Section 4 examines and compares the difficulties that Bolivia and South Africa face as they attempt to reconcile NSJS within their respective constitutions, opting for a more comprehensive approach. Ultimately, however, as Section 5 shows, states often opt for less comprehensive regulatory approaches that combine limited regulation with an effective acknowledgment that NSJS perform critically important functions and thus cannot be fully regulated or ignored.

II. ENDURING SOCIAL PRACTICES: CUSTOMARY SYSTEMS OF LAND TENURE

One of the major problems that IDAs face is that NSJS and traditional institutions are seemingly resistant to change. Yet it is not only international donors that face the apparent immovable force of local practices and mechanisms of governance. In Africa, for example, the difficulties that most states have had in establishing a unified and centralized system of land tenure illustrate the problem. Indeed, as Patrick McAuslan argues, even though newly independent states in Africa tried to establish a centralized system of land tenure under the control of the state, most of them, in one way or another, have failed in this objective (McAuslan 2005, 2007). Customary systems of land tenure have proved more durable and resistant to change than expected by development experts, who advocate allocating individual land titles to facilitate the operation of the market for land, and African political leaders, who regard customary land rights as inconsistent with their aim of modernizing state structures. Several authors have also noted that the introduction of Western legal forms in colonial and postcolonial settings has not succeeded in displacing customary land rights (Chanock 1985; Benda-Beckmann 2001; Deininger 2003). Benda-Beckmann offers a succinct explanation: "Since local property rights are often intimately interwoven with other social relationships, they could not simply be 'taken out' of such a system of multi-stranded and multi-functional relationship. Consequently, there was usually no increase in legal security, both in the sense of clarity and stability of the rights. On the contrary, in many cases the introduction of new legal rights added to the already existing legal insecurity" (Benda-Beckmann 2001, 50).

According to McAuslan, in order to address the problem of the failure of centralized land tenure systems, policy makers must begin by acknowledging that this is not a legal problem, but a problem of power. Although he does not identify the main actors in this power struggle, it is clear that the issue of power can be equally characterized as the lack of capacity of the state to rule over its people and the whole of its territory. Thus, McAuslan calls for a full recognition that land law in Africa is governed by a legal system made up of two components, one of which is customary and the other statutory. He argues for the recognition of these two components based on clear principles, including the following (McAuslan 2005, 2–6):

- Collective ownership must be accepted and built on
- Both sets of norms should be equal, but must observe constitutional and international norms (gender equality, administrative justice, protection of private property)
- People should be able to opt from one system to another
- Customary approaches to dispute settlement must be respected

- Customary tenure and law are essentially local — accordingly, decisions about land taken at the local level will differ between each other
- Customary interests in land should be recorded

These principles are undoubtedly sensible. What is not clear, however, is whether, and if so how, these principles may contribute to resolving the issue of power, which, according to McAuslan, is the root cause of the problems associated with land law in Africa. On the contrary, it would seem that the principles listed previously could only be applied after the question of power is satisfactorily resolved. Consider, for example, the principle that people should be able to opt in and out of the formal and customary systems at will. How feasible is this choice of law principle? Wouldn't this principle have the effect of undermining either one or the other component of the single system envisaged by McAuslan? If so, would this otherwise sensible principle end up being resented by stakeholders who lose out in the choice of law competition? Likewise, the principle that calls for the mutual recognition of methods of conflict resolution raises familiar issues regarding the technical competence and impartiality of traditional procedures when compared with state court procedures. According to McAuslan, customary approaches to dispute settlement should be respected, even though they may yield results that are not uniform throughout the country. I am not sure, however, that international development economists, concerned as they are with the design and implementation of coherent national development strategies, would favor a system that can potentially generate innumerable conflicting regulatory outcomes. The notion that local methods of dispute resolution should be respected is also a matter of serious concern to most lawyers and state officials, whose concerns would be whether people without technical qualifications should be allowed to make final decisions on matters such as land tenure. Ironically, in the case of Tanzania, McAuslan, in his capacity as a government advisor, rejected the Presidential Commission's recommendation that village elders (*baraza la wazee*) should have original jurisdiction on all land matters, civil and criminal (McAuslan 1998, 533; Shivji 2000).

Nevertheless, in his recent writings McAuslan appears to have retracted from this view, adopting a position that is very close to that of Issa Shivji, chair of Tanzania's Presidential Commission. Customary tenure, argues McAuslan, is one of the foundational elements of land law in Africa. It is therefore, not an add-on to the received (Western) law, but the reverse. It is the received Western legal traditions that should adapt and adjust to Africa's indigenous law. Accordingly, he argues that those who should be most interested in advancing the case of legal pluralism are the proponents of received legal traditions (McAuslan 1998, 12). Shivji would not disagree with this statement, although he would articulate it in a slightly different way. Indeed, he proposes that the well-known repugnancy clause of colonial times should be turned on its head. Instead of requiring customary practices to be consistent with the core values of (received) Western legal systems, it is the received legal traditions that "should not be repugnant to Basic Principles of National Law Policy and principles of justice, fairness and equity held in common by Tanzanian communities" (Shijvi 2000, 51).

III. RECOGNITION AND MANIPULATION OF INDIGENOUS RIGHTS

In Latin America, indigenous peoples are among the poorest and most discriminated-against groups. Their exclusion dates back to colonial times and has been directly related to the plunder of their land and resources. Exploitation and exclusion continued after independence but were concealed under a false republicanism that called for their assimilation to the nation. In recent years, however, many countries in the region have responded to the political mobilization of indigenous communities by inserting in their constitutions clauses that recognize indigenous peoples as distinct groups with specific rights, including the right to govern themselves in accordance with their own traditional laws and the right to recover their ancestral lands. The Colombian Constitution, for example, recognizes the right of indigenous people to their ancestral lands (*resguardos*). Similar, though slightly more ambiguous, provisions are found in the constitutions of Argentina, Brazil, Paraguay, and Venezuela (Yashar 2005; Van Cott 2007).

Unsurprisingly, the implementation of these constitutional provisions has been painfully slow. It has faced three familiar problems. First, governments fail to enact the required legislation, so the constitutional provisions remain dead letter. Second, even when implementing legislation is adopted, other state institutions in the administration and the judiciary fail to provide timely responses to those seeking assistance in the enforcement of their rights. And third, because today most indigenous communities are not in possession of their land, their claims overlap with recently established property rights over the same land. These bureaucratic legal obstacles are familiar in the civil law culture of Latin America, but they are also a reflection of underlying social and economic conditions, which encompass long-drawn military conflicts (Perú and Colombia), drug trafficking (Bolivia, Colombia, and Guatemala), and the inability or unwillingness of the states either to resist the pressure of foreign investors (Ecuador, Nicaragua) or to discipline lawless speculators from home and abroad (Brazil) (Faundez 2010).

Contrary to expectations, however, some indigenous communities have made significant progress. Political mobilization by indigenous communities and the occasional but valuable support of IDAs and nongovernmental organizations (NGOs) have persuaded governments to make meaningful efforts to adopt policies that have empowered indigenous communities. In the case of Bolivia, for example, the World Bank and Danida (the Danish Development Agency) provided critical support that encouraged the government to adopt quite radical measures of decentralization, which, in turn, provided indigenous communities in rural areas with a platform to develop stronger and more coherent political demands in defense of their claims to land and self-governance (Andolina, Laurie, and Radcliffe 2009). Although it is difficult to establish whether the activities of IDAs in support of indigenous communities in Bolivia are causally linked to the electoral victory of President Evo Morales, there is little doubt that IDAs' activities there played an important role in raising the political and legal awareness of indigenous communities (Dunkerley 2007). Whether the current political situation in Bolivia will encourage IDAs to continue supporting indigenous communities elsewhere is an open question.

States are not helpless when they confront NSJS. They often make positive gesture toward recognizing indigenous and traditional communities but in effect are more interested in manipulating them to serve their political interests. In the case of Latin America, several academic activists (Hale 2005; Sierra 2005; Speed and Collier 2000), familiar with the plight of indigenous peoples in Latin America, offer us a sobering reminder that although many constitutions in Latin America recognize the rights of indigenous peoples, the political and legal processes continue to be seriously tipped against their interests. Thus, for example, Charles Hale, after presenting three case studies of multiculturalism in Central America, concludes that concessions to disadvantaged cultural groups are little more than a restructuring of the political arena and do very little to improve their subordinate position (Hale 2005, 24–25). In Mexico, recent studies confirm that although state authorities are happy to make concessions, such as the ratification of International Labour Organization (ILO) Convention No. 169 and the adoption of constitutional amendments acknowledging some rights of indigenous communities, they consistently refuse to translate these broad concessions into national legislation or state policy (de la Peña 2006, 279–302). The Mexican government's failure to implement the 1996 San Andrés Agreement, which brought to an end one phase of its long-standing conflict with the Zapatista movement, is one of the best-known recent illustrations of their approach. This agreement recognized indigenous peoples' right to self-determination, their own normative systems, mechanisms of political representation, and their ancestral lands. The government of the day did not comply with this agreement. Six years later, a new administration secured the approval of a constitutional amendment that purported to give effect to the demands of indigenous peoples but was a much watered-down version of the original San Andrés Agreement (de la Peña 2006, 289–91). In some respects, the Mexican government's failure to implement its agreement with the Zapatistas could be seen as politics as usual, because it confirms the traditional disdain displayed by most Latin American governments toward members of indigenous communities. Yet, despite showing no respect for them, either as individuals or as members of distinct communities, governments have not hesitated to use them to further their political agenda. In Mexico, for example, although the government is tough and unforgiving in its policies toward indigenous communities that sympathize with the Zapatistas, it is generous and manipulative toward indigenous groups willing to offer unconditional support to its political party (Speed and Collier 2000, 886).

Political manipulation of indigenous and ethnic groups as a technique of governance also has a long history in Africa. It was used by colonial powers in the form of indirect rule, giving way to the colonial creation of the notion of "customary law," which has been described as the tiny portion of self-governance allowed to indigenous groups, provided they did not engage in "repugnant" practices, as characterized by the colonial authorities (Allott 1970, 145–81; Young 1994, 116; Mamdani 1996, 109–37; Chanock 2006, 339–43). This ambivalence toward indigenous and traditional authorities continued after independence. Authoritarian one-party states made use of traditional authorities as an adjunct of governance (Malawi, South Africa), and when elections were required they were also handy because chiefs also delivered votes. The preservation of traditional authorities was also a useful stabilizing factor because it involved a form of social and political segmentation that kept widespread political mobilization at bay (Moore 1986, 316). Unsurprisingly, the colonial and apartheid regimes in South Africa also developed detailed regulatory structures that combined recognition of traditional authorities within an overall framework of racial subjugation (Republic of South Africa 2003a, 15–24). This relentless political manipulation explains why the African National Congress government in South Africa had great difficulties formulating a policy toward traditional authorities, because many of the "official rights" they had acquired were granted by colonial authorities to further racist policies (Mamdani 1996; Murray 2004). The political manipulation of traditional authorities also explains why socialist movements such as *Frelimo* in Mozambique were hostile to traditional authorities, regarding them as reactionary elements that had no role in the construction of a modern, developed socialist order (Santos 2006, 64). Yet, despite their widespread rejection, traditional authorities in Africa have proved more resilient than expected by both new and old "state builders." Not unlike the situation in many Latin American countries, where the institutions of indigenous communities continue to play important roles – despite the attempt by the state to ignore their existence – traditional authorities in Africa also continue to play an important role in governance. The continuing relevance of traditional authorities and indigenous communities in Africa and many Latin American countries is a direct consequence of the weakness of state institutions.

IV. IMPLEMENTING CONSTITUTIONAL PROVISIONS – BOLIVIA AND SOUTH AFRICA

Even though states may be reluctant to acknowledge the existence of NSJS in their constitutions, they often do so, either because they need to reconcile it with the principle of constitutional supremacy or because, under pressure from internal or external interest groups, they are keen to comply with international human rights obligations. In many Latin American countries, for example, the constitutional recognition of indigenous peoples' institutions – a fairly recent phenomenon – was prompted by the combined effect of the process of democratization that took place in the final decades of the twentieth century and the impact of ILO Convention No. 169, ratified by a large number of countries in the region (Van Cott 2007). As noted constitutional recognition of indigenous peoples' rights has not resolved the critical question of how an indigenous justice system fits within the prevailing state justice system. Constitutions generally either gloss over this question or provide that the legislature will offer detailed regulation.

Bolivia

An interesting departure from this tradition is the case of Bolivia. Its new constitution, adopted in 2009, recognizes the right of original indigenous peasant communities (*naciones y pueblos indígenas originario campesinos*) to administer justice in any civil or criminal dispute arising within their territory, applying their own principles, cultural values, norms, and procedures (Articles 190 and 394) (Bolivia 2009). Thus, the constitution places community justice administered by peasant communities at the same level as justice dispensed by state courts. It is not justice of a lower or less important nature. The constitution does provide, however, that in the exercise of their judicial functions, peasant communities must respect the right to life, the right to legal defense, and other constitutional rights and guarantees.

The law that regulates the delimitation of jurisdictions between indigenous community justice and state justice institutions reiterates the commitment to respect the principles of legal pluralism, cultural diversity, and gender equity (Bolivia 2010). It reaffirms the constitutional prohibition of the death penalty and bans any form of violent punishment against children, adolescents, and women. It acknowledges that indigenous peasant communities have broad powers to resolve civil and criminal disputes that, historically and traditionally, have been within their jurisdictions. Nevertheless, the law excludes from their jurisdictions a wide range of criminal offenses, including murder, rape, crimes involving violence against children and adolescents, crimes against state security, war crimes, crimes against humanity, offenses involving drugs, corruption, and infringement of customs regulations. It also excludes from their jurisdiction any civil matter in which the state is a party and any issue relating to labor law, social security law, mining and hydrocarbon law, forestry law, agrarian law, and international law. The law does not establish any mechanism for the resolution of conflicts of jurisdiction between indigenous and state judicial institutions. Perhaps the legislature in Bolivia did not think this mechanism was necessary because it had so drastically restricted the judicial jurisdiction of indigenous communities. Indeed, the law merely calls on state and indigenous peasant institutions to exchange information about their respective activities and to conduct a dialogue on issues relating to the implementation of human rights. This vague call for coordination contrasts sharply with the approach taken during the parliamentary discussion of this law. Indeed, an earlier draft provided that conflicts of jurisdiction between state and indigenous courts would be resolved by the Constitutional Court. It also provided for the establishment of joint indigenous and state tribunals to hear petitions of habeas corpus against indigenous courts (Bolivia 2009).

It is too early to make a definitive assessment of Bolivia's experiment with indigenous justice. It is important, however, to highlight three points. First, the absence of a mechanism to resolve conflicts of jurisdiction between state courts and indigenous justice institutions is clearly not an oversight. On the contrary, it can be explained by the fact that, given the constitutional provision that places indigenous justice institutions and state courts at the same level, the establishment of an external mechanism to resolve conflicts of jurisdiction would have been regarded as inconsistent with the constitution. Second, because the Bolivian legislature drastically reduced the jurisdiction of indigenous courts, it is likely that it did not foresee that there would be many major conflicts of jurisdiction. The greatly reduced jurisdiction of indigenous courts may also explain why the law focuses exclusively on coordination and cooperation between state and indigenous institutions. And third, the law also contains a clause calling upon all courts in the country to apply an intercultural method of interpretation. It defines this method of interpretation as the obligation that all courts have to take into account all the different cultural identities existing within the Bolivian state. At one level, this provision could be regarded as a fairly innocuous attempt to ensure that courts respect legal pluralism. Yet the notion of intercultural interpretation could also be used by indigenous communities to condone practices that are inconsistent with fundamental rights protected by the constitution. Indeed, during the parliamentary debates leading to the approval of this law, the government had proposed that "intercultural interpretation" could be invoked by indigenous communities to override constitutional rights (Bolivia n.d.).

Regardless of whether Bolivia's attempt to regulate indigenous justice is successful, it will not benefit the majority of its indigenous people. Indeed, the constitutional provisions on indigenous justice will only benefit indigenous people living in rural areas. Those who live in cities – according to some reports, 50 percent of Bolivian citizens – will continue to be under the jurisdiction of state justice institutions (UNDP 2007, 101). Thus, Bolivia still has a major task ahead. It has to ensure that the judicial institutions of the state fully respect legal pluralism so that the majority of its population can enjoy meaningful access to justice.

South Africa

South Africa's long-drawn attempt to enact a law regulating traditional courts illustrates the difficulties involved in reconciling NSJS with the principles of a democratic constitution. In South Africa, delays in the adoption of legislation on traditional courts have, to a large extent, been due to concerns for democracy and human rights.

Indeed, although this issue has been thoroughly and carefully discussed in the country for many years, the government is still unable to get its proposals adopted by the National Assembly. In 2003, after a lengthy process of consultation and deliberation, the South African Law Commission published an important report on the judicial functions of traditional leaders. This report contained detailed recommendations as well as a draft bill (South African Law Commission 2003). Aware of the importance of this issue, the government did not rush into action, but on the contrary proceeded cautiously. It launched another process of consultation with relevant stakeholders, and five years later – in March 2008 – it introduced in the National Assembly the Traditional Courts Bill (Republic of South Africa 2008). The National Assembly deferred the discussion of the bill for a further two years to allow time for yet another period of consultation.

The delay in the approval of the Traditional Courts Bill stems from serious concerns among various groups within South Africa over issues such as discrimination, gender balance, poor procedural safeguards, lack of technical expertise, inconsistent decisions, and lack of legal representation. The South African constitution, like most modern progressive constitutions (sections 39 and 211[3]), accepts that customary law may be applied but requires that its application be consistent with the constitution (Republic of South Africa 1996). The constitution recognizes the right to culture, but it provides that this right cannot override other rights protected by the Bill of Rights (sections 30 and 31). It also recognizes traditional authorities and acknowledges that they apply customary law in accordance with the constitution (sections 211 and 212). In order to align traditional courts with these broad constitutional principles, the new legislative framework will, inevitably, have to introduce important changes to the way traditional courts currently operate. The difficulty, of course, lies in whether these changes can be imposed by the stroke of the legislature's pen or whether it will take time for these courts to evolve into institutions consistent with constitutional principles.

In South Africa, poverty and underdevelopment in rural areas, combined with the legacy of apartheid, further complicate efforts to regulate traditional courts. Indeed, despite its modern constitutional framework and relatively developed industrial and financial sectors, close to 20 million people in rural communities in South Africa live under the authority of traditional rulers (Republic of South Africa 2003a). This is a reality that liberal ideas, however progressive, cannot erase or ignore. Likewise, it is not easy to ignore the historical relationship between the state and traditional authorities established before the advent of democracy. Indeed, in 1927 the Black Administration Act recognized traditional chiefs' courts as part of the state judicial system and gave the government the power to grant criminal and civil jurisdiction to traditional authorities. Although the state closely controlled the power of the chiefs (through commissioner's courts presided over by white officials), chiefs, did, nonetheless, exercise limited judicial power within their respective jurisdictions (Bennett 2009). Although in 1994 the Black Administration Act was repealed, the sections that give judicial power to chiefs remain in force until the Traditional Courts Bill is approved by the National Assembly.

The bill, introduced by the government in the National Assembly in March 2008, seeks to achieve three main complementary objectives: 1) to bring traditional courts into line with the principles of the constitution through the establishment of a uniform legislative framework; 2) to affirm traditional courts' values of restorative justice and reconciliation; and 3) to promote access to justice for all. It specifically notes that the objective of aligning traditional justice systems with the constitution requires traditional courts, as well as all other courts, to promote human dignity, freedom, and equality, taking especially into account the need to eradicate direct and indirect discrimination with respect to gender, age, and race.

The type of disputes that traditional courts currently hear include domestic violence, witchcraft, marriage matters, disputes over *lobola* payments, damage to crops by stray animals, theft, common assault, and malicious damage to property. The bill significantly reduces their jurisdictions. In the area of civil disputes (section 5), it prohibits traditional courts from hearing or deciding cases involving 1) constitutional matters; 2) questions of nullity, divorce, or separation arising out of customary or civil unions; 3) matters relating to the custody or guardianship of minors; 4) matters relating to the validity or interpretation of a will; 5) any matter arising out of customary law and custom where the claim or the value of property in dispute exceeds the amount determined by the minister; and 6) matters arising out of customary law and custom relating to any category of property determined by the minister. The bill also restricts the criminal jurisdiction of traditional courts to the following offenses: 1) theft, whether under the common law or a statutory provision, including the theft of stock where the amount involved does not exceed an amount determined by the minister by notice in the *Gazette*; 2) malicious damage to property, where the amount involved does not exceed an amount determined by the minister by notice in the *Gazette*; 3) assault, where grievous bodily harm has not been inflicted; and 4) *crimen injuria*, where the amount involved does not exceed an amount determined by the minister. In criminal disputes, traditional courts are not allowed to impose any of the following (section 10): a) inhumane, cruel, or degrading punishment, or punishment that involves any form of detention, including imprisonment; b) banishment from the community; or c) fines in excess of the amount determined by the minister. The bill provides that magistrates' courts have jurisdiction to consider appeals and review decisions by traditional courts.

The bill follows the recommendations of the South African Litigation Centre (SALC) on all but a few critically important points. On the question of the appointment and constitution of traditional courts, the SALC initially recommended that the government should consider three options: a) at least half of the members of the courts should be women; b) the insertion of a clause affirming the need for reasonable representation of men and women; and c) the insertion of a clause stating that in order to comply with constitutional requirements, traditional courts should include both men and women. The bill, however, is silent on the issue of gender balance and instead (section 4) gives the minister broad powers – in consultation with provincial authorities – to appoint senior officers to traditional courts. The only reference that the bill makes to the issue of gender is in section 9, which provides that women should be given equal and full participation in proceedings before traditional courts. The bill does, however, provide that the manner in which traditional leaders are designated will be further elaborated through regulations.

The other important area where the bill does not follow the SALC's recommendation is the transfer of cases from traditional courts to other traditional courts or to state courts. The SALC had proposed that parties to cases before traditional courts should have the right to request such a transfer to the registrar for customary courts in the event that traditional courts either unreasonably delay the adjudication of the dispute or unreasonably refuse to hear and adjudicate on such dispute. The bill does not give parties the right to request the transfer. Instead (section 19), it gives the presiding officer of the traditional court the power to decide on the transfer of cases if he or she is of the view that the traditional court does not have jurisdiction over the dispute or if the matter involves complex questions of law or fact that should be dealt with by a magistrate's or a small claims court. Likewise, the bill allows prosecutors, in criminal cases, and magistrates or commissioners of small claims courts to transfer cases to traditional courts if either traditional courts have jurisdiction over the dispute or the dispute is a matter that can be more appropriately handled by a traditional court.

One of the important features of the bill is that it clearly defines the place of traditional courts within the constitutional order. It provides (section 7) that traditional courts are distinct from official state courts and that their objective is to prevent conflict, maintain harmony, and resolve conflicts in ways that promote restorative justice and reconciliation. Because this statement about the role and nature of traditional courts significantly reduces their jurisdictions, it is not surprising that traditional leaders have reservations about the bill. They also resent the widely held view that traditional courts discriminate against women and other vulnerable groups (Parliamentary Monitoring Group 2008). There is little doubt that the so-called living customary law applied by traditional courts today is inconsistent with constitutional and international principles of gender equality. The problem is whether a further period of consultation on the bill could yield an agreement acceptable to major stakeholders and consistent with constitutional principles. The government is obviously aware of the important political role played by traditional leaders (Republic of South Africa 2003b), but it also knows that it has to ensure that traditional courts operate within the framework of the constitution. Thus, other critics of the bill rightly point out that the government seems unconcerned with the undemocratic nature of traditional courts, and through the powers delegated to the minister, it seems determined to treat the appointment of traditional leaders as a purely administrative procedure. These are valid points, but they should not overshadow the enormous dilemma that the South African government is attempting to resolve (Sibanda 2010, 34).

V. ALTERNATIVES TO REGULATION

It is likely that in some instances a state may be unwilling fully to commit itself to the regulation of NSJS because it is uncertain as to the relative advantages of regulation or because it does not have adequate resources to enforce it. The case of Mozambique offers an interesting illustration of this problem. Upon independence, the new government vowed to rid the country of the reactionary legacy of traditional authorities in order to build a modern revolutionary state. It established popular courts that were meant to act as conduits for political mobilization and for the development of peoples' power (Gundersen 1992). In 1992, these politically inspired institutions were dismantled and replaced by community courts. These courts, which are not very different from their predecessors, are not formal courts, as they have been removed from the judicial system. Their objective, according to the law that established them, is to enable citizens to resolve minor differences and contribute toward harmonizing diverse practices of justice. Community courts have been described as inhabiting a legal limbo, because they are not part of the official legal system (though notionally under the jurisdiction of the Ministry of Justice) and there is no appeal from their decisions (Santos 2006, 56). Traditional leaders continued to perform their functions, including dispensing justice, alongside community courts. The government, however, continued to regard them with suspicion, as they had sided with the opposition during the civil war.

In June 2000, prompted partly by the availability of IDA funding, the government enacted a Decree (15/2000) establishing principles for the participation of community authorities in public administration. The notion of community authorities was defined broadly to include traditional leaders, village secretaries, and other community authorities. Community leaders were given the power to collaborate with the authorities on a variety of issues, including education, health, tax collection, and maintaining social order and harmony. The Decree does not, however, specify in any detail the role of traditional leaders and village secretaries in conflict resolution. Nevertheless, in line with colonial tradition, the Decree grants community leaders the right to a uniform, to use state symbols, and to keep a proportion of the tax they may collect (Institutions for Natural Resource Management n.d.).

In the absence of regulation on how community institutions are to discharge their dispute resolution responsibilities, local communities and local state officials developed their own guidelines and practices. In the rural district of Sussundenga, the main interest of the local police was to reduce crime rates and reassert its authority by reaffirming its exclusive jurisdiction over serious criminal offenses. Accordingly, it developed detailed guidelines setting out the scope of the jurisdiction of community and traditional authorities (Kyed 2009, 46–48). The guidelines provided that state courts had jurisdiction over serious crimes, including offenses that violate land rights or involve violent attacks on persons, such as homicides, bloody fights, rapes, serious theft, arson, and armed robbery. Local chiefs were expected to notify these crimes to the police and were warned that they would be severely punished if they exercised jurisdiction over these offenses. The police guidelines gave community institutions jurisdiction to settle so-called social cases, which included adultery, beating without bleeding, minor threats and insults, divorce, marriage payments, and land disputes.

Helen Maria Kyed, in her study of 243 cases in the district of Sussundenga, found that local people did not appear to understand the classifications contained in the guidelines. The difficulty was that seemingly simple disputes, such as divorce, often led to more serious offenses such as arson, serious bodily harm, or even homicide. Kyed also points out that the legal characterization of the offenses also presented serious difficulties. A case the police had initially classified as statutory rape (involving sexual intercourse with a fourteen-year-old female) turned out to be a family dispute over marriage payment (*lobola*) that had already been resolved by a local chief, who had ordered the payment of a fine. Because in any event the couple intended to get married, the case could be characterized as a "social case" (Kyed 2009, 51). Kyed does not tell us the outcome, but several questions arise from this case. Had the police enforced the fine ordered by the traditional authority, would this have amounted to a violation of the young woman's rights? If a state court had found the young man guilty of rape, would this finding have enhanced the status of state courts among the local community? Had the police demanded a bribe from the young man in return for dropping the investigation against him, would this have contributed to furthering good relations between the police and the local community? Kyed rightly points out that the difficulties in classifying these offenses also stem from the conflicting interests between the police and community authorities. Although the police are interested in upholding their authority, they are also keen to ensure that their policing methods do not alienate members of the local communities. Local chiefs, for their part, though under pressure from the police, are also keen to ensure that they keep their people happy, because most of them prefer to claim compensation rather than demand the imprisonment of the person who has committed an offense (Kyed 2009, 56–59). Thus, unsurprisingly, neither the police nor local community leaders in the district of Sussundenga follow police guidelines on the allocation of jurisdiction. What prevails instead is an uneasy, or rather a creative, mix of state and non-state law based, as ever, on the relative power of the two sides. Whether this type of situation provides IDAs with a realistic entry point to promote the rule of law and support vulnerable people remains an open question.

The difficulty of identifying an entry point for IDAs in cases such as the allocation of jurisdiction is further compounded when, in the absence of proper policing and adequate judicial services, local communities take direct action to protect their property and personal security. The case of the *Rondas Campesinas*, in the state of Cajamarca in northern Perú, is a case in point. The *Rondas* can be classified either as vigilante or grassroots groups that seek to compensate for the governance deficit in the region. They emerged as a response to cattle rustling carried out by organized gangs from another region. The victims denounced the crime to the authorities, but neither the police nor the local judge provided any support, either because they feared reprisals from the criminals or because they were in collusion with them. The victims thus decided to form vigilante groups to protect their cattle and to punish those caught committing crime. Those apprehended by the *Rondas* were judged and convicted by an assembly of local neighbors. The punishment involved various forms of community service and often also involved flogging. The *Rondas* were a resounding success, reducing criminal activity, and soon similar community institutions sprung up in other rural areas of Perú (Gitlitz and Rojas 1983).

The *Rondas*'s success in maintaining law and order at the local level brought about an expansion of their jurisdiction. They soon became organs of community governance. Local state authorities, however, were not impressed by their success and sought to prosecute *Ronda* members, accusing them of usurping state authority. The central government (in Lima), however, sought to capitalize on the success of the *Rondas* in two ways: first, to further its electoral strength, and later to enlist the *Rondas* in their fight against the terrorist group the Shining Path. Simultaneously, *Ronda* members and their local NGO supporters lobbied Congress to secure the adoption of legislation that would legitimize their activities and confirm that they were authorized to administer justice (Faundez 2005). Several questions arise from the experience of the *Rondas*. Would IDAs advise the state to ignore or engage with the *Rondas*? Would they advocate formal regulation of the *Rondas*? Or would they be more inclined to favor informal approaches? In any event, it is perhaps misleading to assume that there are alternatives to the regulation of NSJS. Indeed, as the cases of Mozambique and Perú show, one way or another, members of local communities who rely on NSJS for survival cannot easily escape the reach of the state, and neither can the state afford to ignore them.

CONCLUSION

This chapter welcomes the interest that IDAs have recently shown in legal pluralism and, more specifically, on NSJS. Its objective is to remind practitioners that NSJS are complex institutions that should be approached with great caution. Although NSJS are not formally part of the official state apparatus, they are not entirely outside the prevailing framework of governance. As a consequence, attempts to engage NSJS inevitably risk disturbing finely tuned governance arrangements that are not always easy to uncover or conceptualize using orthodox notions drawn from modern legal, political, or economic theory. As noted above, the persistent failure to impose a centralized system of land tenure in Africa is as much a consequence of the well-known resistance to change that characterizes most traditional institutions as it is a consequence of policy makers' failure to properly understand the multistranded nature of customary forms of land tenure. Lack of, or very poor, local knowledge, combined with ideologically inspired economic or legal policies, further aggravates this problem. Although states often fail to transform traditional institutions, they are not oblivious of their existence. Indeed, states are permanently formulating policies or responding to events that have a direct or indirect impact on NSJS. As a consequence, attempts by external agents to engage with NSJS may often disrupt an already fragile and unstable political equilibrium, which, though not consistent with textbook models of good governance and the rule of law, provide local populations with a measure of stability and security. The task of gauging whether, how, and when to launch an externally funded project in this area requires a considerable amount of knowledge of the complex political arrangements underlying NSJS and adjunct structures. In any event, it is often delusional to expect IDA engagement with NSJS to be instrumental in bringing about change from below, thus circumventing state policies.

IDAs are, of course, not totally unprepared to deal with the challenges posed by NSJS. Indeed, the shift from a technically based approach toward a broader approach focused on governance and institutional reform has given IDAs a taste of the complexity of reform processes involving multiple state institutions. The participatory grassroots approaches to project development and implementation should also provide IDAs with useful lessons in their engagement with NSJS. In any event, as the materials in this chapter demonstrate, any engagement with NSJS requires a profound knowledge about the nature of the state and the communities where these institutions operate. As the cases of Bolivia and South Africa illustrate, the process of defining the most appropriate relationship between NSJS and state institutions is fraught with difficulties. In both cases, national policy makers are determined to bring NSJS within the framework of their constitution. The differences in approach reflect divergent views not only about law and legal institutions, but also about democracy and constitutionalism. Yet, despite these differences, both Bolivia and South Africa share the belief that law can bring about social change. Perhaps their faith in the power of law as an instrument of social change will prove to be correct. Or perhaps it is misplaced and will end up disrupting other aspects of their constitutional and legal orders. In any event, the difficulties that both countries are facing in designing policies to bring NSJS into the fold of state regulation provide helpful reminders to IDAs about the nature and scale of the problems. They also confirm that legal reform cannot be successfully implemented if it is detached from wider political and institutional processes. Indeed, it is to be hoped that IDAs' interest in NSJS will persuade both practitioners and academics that comprehensive approaches to legal reform are part of the wider and continuing process of state building. If this is so, I am hopeful that the renewed interest in legal pluralism will reenergize the academic study of law and development.

REFERENCES

Allott, Antony. 1970. *New Essays in African Law*. London: Butterworths.
Andolina, Robert, Nina Laurie, and Sarah A. Radcliffe. 2009. *Indigenous Development in the Andes*. Durham, NC: Duke University Press.
Benda-Beckmann, Franz von. 2001. "Legal Pluralism and Social Justice in Economic and Political Development." *IDS Bulletin* 32 (1): 46–56.
Bennett, Tom W. 2009. "Re-introducing African Customary Law to the South African Legal System." *American Journal of Comparative Law* 57 (1): 1–31.
Bolivia, Government of. 2009. *Constitución de 2009*. http://pdba.georgetown.edu/Constitutions/Bolivia/bolivia09.html.
———. 2010. *Ley de Deslinde Jurisdiccional*. Ley N³ 073, December 29, 2010, *Gaceta Oficial de Bolivia* (on file with the author).
———. n.d. *Anteproyecto de Ley de Deslinde Jurisdiccional* (on file with the author).
Chanock, Martin. 1985. *Law, Custom and Social Order: The Colonial Experience in Malawi and Zambia*. Cambridge: Cambridge University Press.
———. 2006. "Customary Law, Sustainable Development and the Failing State." In *The Role of Customary Law in Sustainable Development*, ed. Peter Orebeck et al. Cambridge: Cambridge University Press.
Deininger, Klaus. 2003. *Land Policies for Growth and Poverty Reduction*. World Bank Policy Research Report. Washington, DC: World Bank; and Oxford: Oxford University Press.
Dempsey, John, and Noah Coburn. 2010. "Traditional Dispute Resolution and Stability in Afghanistan." Peace Brief 10, U.S. Institute of Peace, Washington, DC.
DFID (Department for International Development). 2004. "Non-state Justice and Security Systems." DFID Briefing (May), Department for International Development, London.
Dunkerley, James. 2007. "Evo Morales, the 'Two Bolivias' and the Third Bolivian Revolution." *Journal of Latin American Studies* 39 (1): 133–66.
Faundez, Julio. 2005. "Community Justice Institutions and Judicialization: Lessons from Rural Perú." In *The Judicialization of Politics in Latin America*, ed. Alan Angell and Rachel Sieder, 187–209. New York: Palgrave Macmillan.
———. 2010. "Access to Justice and Indigenous Communities in Latin America." In *Marginalized Communities and Access to Justice*, ed. Yash Ghai and Jill Cotrell, 83–109. London: Routledge.
Gitlitz, John S., and Telmo Rojas. 1983. "Peasant Vigilante Committees in Northern Perú." *Journal of Latin American Studies* 15 (1): 163–97.
Gundersen, Aase. 1992. "Popular Justice in Mozambique: Between State Law and Folk Law." *Social and Legal Studies* 1: 257–82.
Hale, Charles. 2005. "Neoliberal Multiculturalism: The Remaking of Cultural Rights and Racial Dominance in Central America." *Political and Legal Anthropology Review* 28 (1): 10–26.
Institutions for Natural Resource Management. n.d. "Implementing CBNRM in M'punga." Briefing, University of Sussex, Brighton.
Kyed, Helen Maria. 2009. "Traditional Authority and the Localization of State Law." In *State Violence and Human Rights*, ed. Andrew M. Jefferson and Steffen Jensen, 40–59. London: Routledge.
Mamdani, Mahmood. 1996. *Citizen and Subject: Contemporary Africa and the Legacy of Late Colonialism*. Princeton, NJ: Princeton University Press.

McAuslan, Patrick. 1998. "Making Law Work: Restructuring Land Relations in Africa." *Development and Change* 29 (3): 525–52.

———. 2005. "Legal Pluralism as a Policy Option: Is It Desirable, Is It Doable?" Paper presented at the UNDP – International Land Coalition Workshop, "Land Rights for African Development: From Knowledge to Action," Nairobi, October–November 2005.

———. 2007. "Improving Tenure Security for the Poor in Africa. Synthesis Paper: Deliberations of the Legal Empowerment Workshop – Sub-Saharan Africa." Food and Agricultural Organization (FAO), Rome.

Moore, Sally Falk. 1986. *Social Facts and Fabrications: "Customary" Law on Kilimanjaro, 1880–1980*. Cambridge: Cambridge University Press.

Murray, Christina. 2004. *South Africa's Troubled Royalty – Traditional Leaders after Democracy*. Centre for International and Public Law, Law and Policy Paper 23. Canberra: Australian National University.

Parliamentary Monitoring Group. 2008. "The Traditional Courts Bill: Parliamentary Research Units Briefing [B 15–2008]." Parliamentary Monitoring Group, Cape Town. http://www.pmg.org.za/report/20080620-traditional-courts-bill-parliamentary-research-unit-briefing.

Peña, Guilllermo de la. 2006. "A New Mexican Nationalism? Indigenous Rights, Constitutional Reform and the Conflicting Meanings of Multiculturalism." *Nations and Nationalism* 12 (2): 279–302.

Republic of South Africa, Government of. 1996. *Constitution of the Republic of South Africa*. http://www.info.gov.za/documents/constitution/index.htm.

———. 2003a. "The White Paper on Traditional Leadership and Governance." Department of Provincial and Local Government, Cape Town.

———. 2003b. Traditional Leadership and Governance Framework Amendment Act, 2003. *Government Gazette*, No. 25855, December 19, 2003.

———. 2008. Traditional Courts Bill. *Government Gazette*, No. 30902, March 27, 2008. www.justice.gov.za/legislation/tradcourts/B15-2008.pdf.

Santos, Boaventura de Sousa. 2006. "The Heterogeneous State and Legal Pluralism in Mozambique." *Law and Society Review* 40 (1): 39–75.

Shivji, Issa G. 2000. "Contradictory Perspectives on Rights and Justice in the Context of Land Tenure Reforms in Tanzania." In *Beyond Rights Talk and Culture Talk*, ed. Mahmood Mamdani, 37–60. New York: St. Martin's Press.

Sibanda, Sanale. 2010. "When Is the Past Not the Past? Reflections on Customary Law under South Africa's Constitutional Dispensation." *Human Rights Brief*. American University Washington College of Law, Washington, DC.

Sierra, María Teresa. 2005. "The Revival of Indigenous Justice in Mexico: Challenges for Human Rights and the State." *Political and Legal Anthropology Review* 28 (1): 52–67.

South African Law Commission. 2003. "Report on Traditional Courts and the Judicial Function of Traditional Leaders (Project 90)." South African Law Commission, Pretoria.

Speed, Shannon, and Jane E. Collier. 2000. "Limiting Indigenous Autonomy in Chiapas, Mexico: The State Government's Use of Human Rights." *Human Rights Quarterly* 22 (4): 877–905.

UNDP (United Nations Development Programme). 2007. *Informe Sobre el Desarrollo Humano en Bolivia – El Estado del Estado (Human Development Report Bolivia)*. La Paz: UNDP. http://hdr.undp.org/es/informes/nacional/americalatinacaribe/bolivia/name,3394,es.html.

United Nations Development Group. 2008. "Guidelines on Indigenous People's Issues." Office of the High Commissioner for Human Rights, Geneva.

Van Cott, Donna Lee. 2007. "Building Inclusive Democracies: Indigenous Peoples and Ethnic Minorities in Latin America." In *On the State of Democracy*, ed. Julio Faundez, 196–214. London: Routledge.

Yashar, Deborah. 2005. *Contesting Citizenship in Latin America – the Rise of Indigenous Movements and the Postliberal Challenge*. Cambridge: Cambridge University Press.

Young, Crawford. 1994. *The African Colonial State in Comparative Perspective*. New Haven, CT: Yale University Press.

12

Access to Property and Citizenship

Marginalization in a Context of Legal Pluralism

Christian Lund

> What Jesus blatantly fails to appreciate is that it's the meek who are the problem.
> *Monty Python*, Life of Brian

I. LAW IS A QUESTION LARGER THAN LAW

Introduction

Few things are more fundamental in social life or politics than what we have and who we are – *avoir* and *être*. Property and citizenship, in the broadest sense, are perhaps the most overt and familiar manifestations of these core dimensions of community life. In poor countries, few entities connect the two facets more intimately than land, where claims to land are partly defined by social identity, and social identity is partly defined through property.

Property and citizenship have obvious legal dimensions but are hardly reserved for the legal domain alone. Ultimately, no single institution either fully determines or fully controls all of the issues that surround these two important societal assets. Thus, with regard to property and citizenship, it is important to bear in mind that legal pluralism is embedded in a broader institutional pluralism.

In the following, I briefly develop three conceptual considerations and discuss some of their implications in relation to recent research on marginalized groups' access to property and political influence in Niger. In that country, there are examples of both chronic marginalization as well as more successful developments. The conceptual issues can be summarized in the following way: 1) No institution is state

---

I am grateful to Marie Monimart, Marthe Diarra, and Eric Hahonou for commenting on this chapter. Their research provides important primary material to its argument. I also draw in part on work done in collaboration with Thomas Sikor (Sikor and Lund 2010). Although he has generously allowed me use a few phrases of our common work, all shortcomings are mine alone.

as such; rather, "state" is the *quality* of an institution being able to define and enforce collectively binding decisions on members of society, a quality that is not solely the preserve of government institutions; 2) institutional and normative plurality means not only that people struggle and compete over access to land, but that the legitimate authority to settle conflicts is equally contested. Struggles over property are therefore as much about the scope and constitution of authority as about access to resources; and 3) although legal and institutional pluralism may prevail, access to such institutions in the pursuit of justice is highly unequal. In fact, whereas some have many options, others, particularly women and those at the lowest economic levels, have few or no institutional fallback options.

Institutional Pluralism

One of the defining distinctions between more- and less-developed societies appears to be the existence of so-called meta-rules that ensure communication and order between the multitude of subsystems. As Rose and Miller (1992, 174–76) point out regarding what they call the modern state, "[t]o the extent that the modern state 'rules,' it does so on the basis of an elaborate network of relations formed amongst the complex of institutions, organisations and apparatuses that make it up, and between state and non-state institutions.... Political power is exercised today through a profusion of shifting alliances between diverse authorities in projects to govern a multitude of facets of economic activity, social life and individual conduct." This suggests that a critical difference between more- and less-developed societies lies not in more or fewer institutions as such, or in whether or not relations between them are contentious; instead, it lies in the degree to which interaction between them is institutionalized and regulated. In other words, the disparity stems from the extent to which there is a clear division of jurisdiction between institutions, as well as structured hierarchies and procedures for dealing with discord and conflict.[1]

In Africa, as in most developing societies, there is no shortage of institutions that attempt to exercise public authority and define property. Not only are multiple layers and branches of government institutions (the judiciary, the central administration, local governments, the police, the agricultural and forestry services, and so on) present and active to various degrees, but so-called traditional institutions bolstered by government recognition also vie for public authority. Much of the literature on African politics and history details how government institutions and chieftaincy institutions negotiate, forge alliances, and compete to constitute and assert public authority and political control (Bayart 1989; Berry 1993; Boone 2003). In addition, associations and organizations that do not appear at first to be political may also exercise political power and wield public authority, for example, development

---

[1] See the chapter by Glenn in this book for a discussion on "meta-rules" and "sustainable diversity in law."

organizations, political parties, private companies, religious organizations, and so forth. Similarly, ostensibly nonpolitical occasions may reveal themselves to be active sites of political negotiation over what is legitimate ownership (see Lund 2006).

A conventional way to look at pluralism is to distinguish between government institutions and statutory law, on the one hand, and customary institutions and law, on the other. However, property rights do not fall neatly into these categories. Government as well as customary institutions are plentiful, and some institutions are hard to categorize, including, for example, development agencies, political parties, hometown associations, and so on. They all operate to define and enforce collectively binding rules – with varying degrees of success. Moreover, the sources of law – the normative repertoire – do not always match the institutions. Although a particular set of norms is more likely to be invoked by some institutions than others, an institution may well refer to "religion," "tradition," "*the* law," "human rights," or "progress" to justify its decisions regardless of its institutional character. Which source of authority is accepted and enforced often depends on the respective powers and interests of the antagonists and the institutions themselves (for more elaborate discussions, see Moore 1978, 1986; Geisler 2000; Mattei and Nader 2008).

In such cases, it is difficult to ascribe exercised authority to the "state" as a coherent institution. Rather, public authority becomes the amalgamated result of a variety of local institutions' exercise of power and external institutions' imposition of it, joined together with the *idea* of a state. Hence, the practice of governance varies from place to place and even from field to field, such as "security," "citizenship," "property," and so on. Indeed, in some areas, institutions may exercise near-hegemonic command in one sphere, while at the same time, their authority in other domains may be ferociously contested. Whatever the label, it seems that a variety of institutions may constitute themselves as de facto public authorities, albeit with greater or lesser ambit and success, even though they have no firmly institutionalized hierarchy.

Although we may entertain the notion of "state" as shorthand for organized political power, it is difficult to imagine any society where several institutions do not compete for political authority. Institutions form centers of power and develop procedures, norms, hierarchies, and codes proper to themselves. This means that no institution is state as such; "state" is, rather, the *quality* of an institution being able to define and enforce collectively binding decisions on members of society. Such decisions may have a longer or shorter shelf life as the institution maintains or loses its state quality. This is the key point: state quality can wax and wane. It can also dwindle and be lost. Hence, institutions with state quality are never definitively formed but are in a constant process of formation. Such institutions operate in a kind of "twilight" between state and society, between public and private (Lund 2006; see also Das and Poole 2004; Neubert 2009). State quality is not lodged in a single institution through time.

Tilly reminds us that what turned out to be the states of present-day Europe were the successful survivors from among an amorphous array of institutional coalitions competing for the power to define and enforce rules over a particular territory (1985). We often tend to reserve state qualities for government institutions, but this is more a reflection of our idea of an "ideal" end result than of the messy process of state formation itself. Government institutions may indeed have state quality, but it is more appropriate to treat this as an empirical question than as a preestablished fact. Likewise, it behooves us to be open to the possibility that state quality can reside in institutions other than government.

Competing Institutional Interests

A central dynamic connects the competing claims to the right to exercise authority. The institutional and normative plurality prevailing in many poor societies means that people struggle and compete over access to land. At the same time, the legitimate authority to settle conflicts is also contested. It usually is a question not only of land but also of property more broadly – and social and political relationships in a wider sense. Struggles over property are therefore as much about the scope and structure of authority as about access to resources (Berry 2002; Lund 2002). The process of recognizing claims to property simultaneously works to imbue the institution that provides such recognition with the acknowledgment of its authority to do so. This is the "contract" that links property and authority. Property is only property if socially legitimate institutions sanction it, and politico-legal institutions are only effectively legitimized if their interpretation of social norms (in this case, property rights) is heeded and enforced (MacPherson 1978; Rose 1994; Lund 2002). In other words, the process of seeking authorization for property claims also works to authorize the authorizers, as it were, and institutions underpinning various claims of access – and hence catering to particular constituencies – simultaneously undermine rival claims to the same resources.

Simply put, claimants seek out sociopolitical institutions to authorize their claims, and sociopolitical institutions look for claims to authorize in order to assert their authority. The relationship is a dynamic one. Although parties in a dispute may go "forum shopping," taking their claim or dispute to the institution that they deem the most likely to produce a satisfactory outcome, institutions also use disputes for their own, mainly local, political ends. According to Keebet von Benda-Beckmann, "besides forum-shopping disputants, there are also 'shopping forums' engaged in trying to acquire and manipulate disputes from which they expect to gain political advantage, or to fend off disputes which they fear will threaten their interests. They shop for disputes as disputants shop for forums" (Benda-Beckmann 1981, 117).

Thus, institutions are simultaneously actors, arenas, and manifestations of power relations. All three aspects are important for an understanding of the political processes involving institutions. First, as an actor, a politico-legal institution is personified by its governor – for example, the mayor, the district chief executive, the district commissioner, the magistrate, the chief, the party boss, the "strongman" – defining and enforcing collectively binding decisions and rules, or rather *attempting* to define and enforce them, because this capacity is rarely fully accomplished and is often challenged. At the same time, an institution is also an arena where competing social actors struggle to influence the way rules and rulings are made. And finally, as arenas, these politico-legal institutions are also manifestations of structures and power relations, which, in the course of time, have established a structure of entitlement and prerogatives as well as exclusion.

The fact that some rights and social relations appear to endure and remain stable is not a sign that nothing is happening. On the contrary, various actors, individuals, and organizations actively and continuously reproduce these social relations and confirm property rights (among many other matters). Social conventions such as property regimes are not concrete *things* that are present or not; they are what people *do*. Moreover, institutions are only as robust, solid, and enduring as the ongoing reproduction, or institutionalization, that enables them to persist. One might lose sight of this when talking about "old" institutions as if they were perpetuated from the past by some mysterious force. They are no more solid than people make them. However, because they generally reflect prevailing power relations, they are not random constructs.

As a consequence, the individual and/or institutional contestants' pursuit of control over land involves them inadvertently in the competition over public authority, including its consolidation, reconfiguration, and erosion. This competition is not necessarily done with the intention of state formation and law creation at the local level, but to check and overcome competitors and benefit from the advantages of power. Nonetheless, the result is, in part, institutional.

Pluralism: In the Eye of the Beholder

If legal pluralism is embedded in a pervasive institutional pluralism – an institutional tug-of-war – and the institutions that make up this landscape are neither neutral nor inert, what are the implications? In particular, what does it mean in concrete terms for poorer people?

Scholarship on legal pluralism, including by this author, sometimes sees this kind of pluralism as an opportunity for individual resistance to inequality in the context of unequal power relations. Although this is not untrue, it is not the full picture. In a comprehensive article, Pauline Peters takes issue with the recent increasing attention to the negotiability of rules and socioeconomic position in Africa.[2] Although the notion of negotiability was once a welcome challenge to simple economic premises about the insecurity of all property that is not privately owned, Peters argues that it has gained so much currency that processes of inequality and social differentiation drift out of focus. We should, she argues, pay as much attention to processes that

---

[2] For a debate between these positions, see Berry (2002) and Peters (2002, 2004).

limit negotiation and exclude certain groups (Peters 2004, 305). There is much to be said for this argument. Certain groups are marginalized economically and politically, and people in poorer countries are very unequally positioned in their ability to negotiate how land rights and property are to be defined. As Amanor states, "[t]he majority of people are merely forced to abide by interpretations of what is determined to be customary by the powerful, or to operate outside legality" (Amanor 1999, 44).

However, if efforts to contest prevailing patterns are ignored or classified as insignificant merely because they may have been unsuccessful, actual outcomes become endowed with a quality of *inevitability*. Although the excluded or the poor are unsuccessful in radically changing their situation, their actions – however mundane or foolhardy – are hardly inconsequential to the reproduction of the forms of exclusion. The key, it would seem, is to look for structural and political constraints and opportunities for negotiation.

Agarwal employs a bargaining approach to her analysis of household property relations that is useful in a wider perspective. A person's "bargaining power would be defined by a range of factors, in particular the strength of the person's fallback position (the outside options which determine how well off he or she would be if cooperation ceased), and the degree to which his/her claim is seen as socially and legally legitimate" (Agarwal 1994, 54). We can usefully extend this to talk about institutional fallback positions – that is, *where* can a person seek recourse if cooperation ceases? Some obviously have more leverage and more options than others. This often is not a narrow legal issue, but has to do with broader enabling conditions for staking a claim and backing it up (see Gloppen 2009).

In the context of institutional pluralism, there is a large number of what we could call legal avenues, referring to institutions to which a person can turn with problems concerning his or her rights. However, there is a significant difference between existing legal avenues (on paper) and actually available avenues (in practice). What may seem to be a bewilderingly wide array of institutions to an external observer with little at stake may be a good deal narrower to someone whose political and economic endowments are scarce and who faces structural constraints to even voicing a claim. The choices may look more like narrow alleyways than nicely paved legal avenues.

Research on citizenship and belonging has demonstrated how access to vindication of claims is conditioned on citizenship – or, alternatively, social identity (Berry 2009; Geschiere 2009; Jacob and Le Meur 2010). It is not that social identity automatically entails rights, but that this identity can make it legitimate to claim them. Conversely, not belonging – not being a local citizen – may outright deny the person a legitimate opportunity to stake a claim. The category of "citizen" – meaning those entitled to seek entitlements – is not carved in stone; persons or groups can slide out of this category while others enter into it and entrench themselves.

II. SOME EVIDENCE FROM NIGER

Some examples from Niger can illustrate this phenomenon. Niger is one of the poorest countries in the world, and its rural poor are among the poorest on the planet. Rural society in Niger is stratified along gender and social lines, and women (especially from farming communities) and descendants of slaves generally occupy the least powerful positions in society. These groups face such overwhelming obstacles that it is extremely difficult for them to access existing political arenas and legal avenues – let alone prevail in conflicts over property.

Research on land conflicts and land reform in Niger in the past two decades demonstrates extensive legal and institutional pluralism (Lund 1998, 2001, 2009). Land conflicts, often prompted by imminent government reform measures, were dealt with by a host of institutions. Village chiefs, canton chiefs, and even the sultans were active mediators or provided forums for adjudication, as did the imams, prefects, *sous-prefets*, police, magistrates, and, indeed, political parties. Niger adopted a land tenure reform – a Rural Code – in the 1990s, making it possible to register customary land rights and land transactions. The reform also established district and local tenure commissions in charge of registering rights and transactions and resolving disputes, adding to the range of available institutions without definitively eliminating any already existing ones.

Although these institutions were formally organized in a procedural hierarchy, my research has shown how the same dispute would move from institution to institution, irrespective of such hierarchy, and that any settlement would often be temporary (Lund 1998). For example, research from the Zinder region in southern Niger shows that a very large proportion of households had been engaged in land disputes and that most had been dealt with by two or more institutions (Lund 1998; see also Kelley 2007, 2008). A range of norms were usually invoked as legitimate references for decision making, but this often meant that unclear and sometimes outright contradictory statutory rules could be cited alongside equally flexible religious, customary, and "historical" norms.

Conspicuously absent was women's participation in disputes, for two apparent reasons. First, for most women who had conflicts over land, the dispute was an intrahousehold affair that was generally dealt with within the household. This was so not least because the structural inequity within the household made it very difficult for women to take the affair elsewhere. Second, when engaged in land conflicts outside the household, brothers, fathers, or husbands generally represented the women. Although not universally the case, this was the dominant picture.

Other structural inequities stemmed from persistent social and economic divisions within society based on economic wealth or privilege (see below). For example, Kelley's research shows that nobles (that is, the wealthy landowners) have successfully reclaimed land that was traditionally farmed by their slaves and their descendants

(Kelley 2008). My research also demonstrates how politico-legal institutions historically have been dominated by nobles, and decisions therefore have weighed in favor of descendants of the group that was believed to have settled first and thus gained political seniority (Lund 1998).

Women's Land Rights in Niger

Marthe Diarra[3] and Marie Monimart (2006; Doka and Monimart 2004; Monimart and Diarra 2009) have researched women's access to and ownership of land in southern Niger in the Maradi region. They document a number of discouraging trends involving the exclusion of women, with consequences for ownership and control over land, as well as opportunities for redressing these trends.

Hausa women are active farmers. Traditionally, they have participated in most or all farming tasks on the household land and have cultivated small fields of their own to cover personal needs (Doka and Monimart 2004, 2). A Hausa woman's individual plot is supposed to feed her and her children during the dry season. However, different processes have worked against women's interests over the past decades.

Diarra and Monimart show how increasing land scarcity has engendered a renegotiation of social norms to the detriment of women. First, this land scarcity has led to a fragmentation of family farms, and gradually the households have less and less land to farm. This has meant not only that women's fields have become smaller, but also that they are expected to cover a greater part of the needs of their children from this smaller area than was traditionally the case. In the past, as long as it was possible to have a reasonably sized field of their own in their husbands' households, few women claimed their inheritance from their parents according to Islamic law. It was seen as more appropriate to leave this land to – or at least in trust with – their brothers. In any case, as a woman moved to her husband's village upon marriage, it was often inconvenient, and sometimes impossible, to actually cultivate the land she had inherited in her native village.

Now, however, because women are increasingly squeezed on their husbands' holdings, some have begun to claim their inheritances. (According to Islamic law as practiced in Niger, women inherit half the share of their brothers.) Yet, even if successful in this endeavor, with land commoditization, women who claim land often decide (with or without pressure) to sell their inherited plot (located in their family village) to their brothers in order either to acquire some land in their husbands' village or to buy animals. More and more often, the inherited plots are so small (after being shared between the multiple heirs) that they are no longer appropriate for use as fields.

Certain social practices affecting women have developed in conjunction with land scarcity. Although it is difficult for husbands to outright deny their wives access

---

[3] Marthe Diarra wrote as Marthe Doka before 2006.

to their own fields, increasingly early marriages to girls as young as twelve years of age create tremendous difficulties for women. Because girls generally learn to farm from their mothers, if they are married off at the young age of twelve, they have little knowledge – and still less experience – with farming and will have a very tough time acquiring it. Moreover, the practice of seclusion, presented as ostentatious religious piety, is on the rise in land-scarce communities. Traditionally a sign of wealth whereby a husband could demonstrate that he could care for his household without putting his wife or wives to work, seclusion has now become a means for men in land-poor households to deny women access to and control over parts of the household's land. This happens not entirely without resistance, however, as rare instances can be found where women quit seclusion because their husbands are unable to take care of their wives and children. Finally, the demographic pressure on land has become matched by a social pressure on women to transfer their individual fields to their sons and not their daughters, even though the latter are also in need of land.

Diarra (then Doka) and Monimart demonstrate how the increasing land scarcity – moving from the north toward the south in the Maradi region – corresponds to the increasing exclusion of women.

> The process of excluding women corresponds to the need to readjust or find a social balance between a resource and its potential beneficiaries. a) Where land is plentiful, women have access to it and enjoy their land heritage. [...] b) When this resource starts to become scarce (no free land) and societal control begins at farm level, there is a perceptible change in the portion of land granted to women, who progressively lose access to land. Inheritances are still shared out according to Muslim law, but the woman's share is given to her brothers and returned to her if she divorces. [...] c) After the 1984 drought women progressively lost access to land as the [household fields] were dispersed to spread the risk of production, and with the application of customary regulations (or Islamised customs). This [...] marked the beginning of women's exclusion from land ownership. [...] d) This [...] is followed by another phase that sees women lose access to all land apart from the ever-diminishing [individual field]. The custom of preventing women from inheriting land is a crucial factor in perpetuating land insecurity for Hausa women, while society's refusal to allow them access to land ownership also represents an element of control over their mobility. [...] e) The final level of societal control observed is the loss of the [individual field]. Does this signal the beginning of a de-feminisation of agriculture? And does the fact that women, even when they do claim their share of land, give it to their sons or husbands, mean that they now see farming as a masculine activity? (Doka and Monimart 2004, 11)

As a result of this process, there are now villages in southern Niger where women have not cultivated land for two generations – something quite difficult to reverse.

It is striking how social norms, customs, and traditions change according to circumstance. New religious customs are invoked as traditional, and traditions supporting women's property rights are being expunged. This malleability is troubling – and holds promise at the same time.

In the 1990s, as mentioned previously, Niger adopted a land tenure reform program – a Rural Code – to register customary land rights and land transactions and to establish district and local tenure commissions in charge of registering rights and transactions and resolving disputes. However, Monimart and Diarra (2009) find that these commissions have proved unable to secure women's rights or even to view their claims as legitimate. The mandatory appointment of women to the commissions has had no discernable effect. In fact, the registration of land process tends to favor men across the board, as men register household lands as theirs while women generally register their fields in the names of their husbands or brothers. It is well known from land registration programs that registration entails simplification, because only the rights of primary right holders are registered, and often the only the name of the so-called head of the household – the oldest man – is listed. Such simplification often leads to the disenfranchisement of secondary right holders (Lund 2008, 15 and 182; Toulmin 2009).

The institutional landscape in southern Niger in theory offers a range of institutional or legal avenues. Practice, however, shows that many of these avenues are not relevant or accessible to women. It could even be said that questions of land access and ownership for women are almost "pre-legal," in that structural impediments to even voicing interests as claims need to be addressed before women could possibly anchor those claims as rights (see Vincent 1994; Biddulph 2010; Harrington and Chopra 2010). Currently, the predominant problem facing women is not the multitude of institutions and norms but rather their ability (or lack thereof) to access even one legal avenue in pursuit of rights to property.

Politics of the Descendants of Slaves in Niger

The descendants of slaves are another group of socially marginalized people in Niger. Eric Hahonou (2006, 2008, 2009, 2010, 2011) has researched the social and political transformation in Niger ushered in by political decentralization. Society in most parts of the country is highly stratified. "Aristocrats" or "nobles" are pitted against "commoners" and descendants of slaves. Historically, nobles have controlled the labor of their slaves as well as the ownership of land in various ways. Although slavery is now banned, various forms of servile labor have persisted. Certain kinds of menial work continue to be reserved for commoners, whereas other functions have been the privilege of nobles or aristocrats. Moreover, social stigma is still alive in the political culture. Despite their small numbers, positions of power within the customary polity have been appropriated by nobles as a matter of course, which suggests a general societal internalization of this fixed social order. Appointments of locals to different positions have systematically favored the nobles, and "the status as servile is *a priori* incompatible with exercise of the function of political representation" (Hahonou 2008, 171 [author's translation]). Until 2004, elections to local assemblies had never taken place. Since independence from France in 1960, there have been universal elections only to the National Assembly and the presidency – and these elections were frequently interrupted by coups and long periods of military rule. Few parliamentarians in the National Assembly were ever of poor or slave origin.

Decentralization reforms in 2002 heralded change. The creation of municipalities with a new range of tasks and powers created a new political arena, as local politics could be played out in the municipality as well as in existing institutions. Moreover, because the scope of its authority included public investment and land tenure commissions (among other matters), the new municipality was coveted by the elite and excluded alike. City people – businessmen and active and retired civil servants – originating from different villages sought election to local councils, testifying to the perceived importance of the added arena.

Hahonou describes the differing results in these local elections. In some municipalities, the elite managed to monopolize seats. Among the Songhay in Gorouol, for example, the aristocracy succeeded in controlling the election list of the most powerful party, and despite being in the minority, they prevailed to win all the seats in the council. In some neighboring municipalities, however, the outcome was different. Among the Kel Tamasheq in Bankilaré, the aristocracy had been equally entrenched in their positions, but a local association was able to mobilize and organize people of slave origin who were the majority of the electorate. The association – called *Timidria* – not only managed to mobilize voters, but also successfully made connections with political parties in the capital to get access to the party lists for their candidates. *Timidria* effectively proved to be a campaign vehicle for candidates who were descendants of slaves, several of whom had been civil servants and experienced in public administration. The association also secured financial support from a businessman from the village who, despite his low social status, had become wealthy. In the end, descendants of slaves won a majority of seats, and the mayor was chosen from among them.

Hahonou points out that although the political change in this case is significant, the emergence of local councils dominated by the descendants of slaves did not result in the disappearance of all the other elite-dominated institutions. Thus, the distinct powers of the new municipalities likely will not go uncontested amid the usual wrangling of local politics.

Another interesting finding from Hahonou's research is the significant change that decentralization did bring – despite the continued domination of elites in some areas. The political culture changed such that today, slave descendants are seen as legitimate leaders, just as free men or aristocrats. However, although the change offered a possibility for a group hitherto excluded from political influence to access a new political arena and, in some cases, dominate it, there has been little impact on the political culture with regard to the style of rule and the management of public goods. Despite their origins, the new political players did not play politics differently from those they had partially replaced – and partially joined. Patronage, corruption, embezzlement, nepotism, and extraction of political rent by no means disappeared merely because of the change in leadership. Hahonou cites a local source who said, "Those that used to make do with mutton neck now can pick the morsel of their choice" (Hahonou 2008, 181 [author's translation]). It is too early to say whether the change in access to *political* office will have a long-term impact on society's entrenched *economic* inequalities. The "new people" in powerful positions seem likely simply to reconfigure coalitions of privilege rather than eliminate privilege altogether. The changes may thus turn out to be more of an "elite phenomenon" than a wider structural social transformation.

This research from Niger echoes the findings by Prag in his research on women in local politics in Senegal (2010). Women's participation in a range of overtly non-political associations (especially the business women's associations) enables them to draw on organizational and financial resources, campaign, and mobilize voters, and they have been very successful in accessing the local councils in that country. However, as Prag observes, the way of doing politics in Senegal changed very little, if at all. Instead, ambitious female politicians draw on their networks, repay favors, mobilize supporters, and exclude adversaries in ways virtually identical to those of their male colleagues and predecessors.

Clearly, the presence of people of humble origin on a municipal council does not necessarily guarantee justice for others of the same social and economic status. On the contrary, they most likely will still have to pay to be heard, just like anybody else. But the main point is that in Niger, despite the continued limitations, they now have, in some areas at least, access to vent grievances, and as institutions compete, venues other than the municipal council are likely to open up as conduits for those grievances. This does not ensure that hitherto disenfranchised people will succeed, but it does make it possible for them to articulate interests and stake a claim. In contrast to women, people of low economic status in Bankilaré and similar places have managed to establish themselves as citizens – admittedly poor citizens in a corrupt society, but citizens nevertheless. A certain relationship of accountability has been established in which politicians are compelled (at least to some degree) to acknowledge this particular group and its grievances. This may prove to be the prerequisite for being able to act politically and pursue interests legally.

By contrast, women's institutional "fallback position" in relation to property rights in Diarra and Monimart's research remains dismal. If women do not manage to negotiate a satisfactory arrangement of ownership and property within the household, there is virtually nowhere else for them to turn. Immediate alternative options seem nonexistent, although there are some initiatives on the part of nongovernmental organizations in assisting women to buy land collectively. Without an institutional alternative, poor women in southern Niger fall into an institutional void. In light of increasingly poorer conditions for negotiating satisfactory arrangements, this is ominous.

Descendants of slaves, however, have managed to improve their situation and gain access to other institutional fallback options. If they have a disagreement over property, they enjoy a certain degree of effective citizenship that enables them to seek entitlement. Success in such a venture obviously hinges on a range of other resources and contacts as well as a measure of chance, but their institutional opportunities have been broadened.

Access and Property

In a piece about the connections between resource access and property, Thomas Sikor and I argue that there is a partial overlap between the two (Sikor and Lund 2010). On the one hand, property is not the only means by which social actors are able to benefit from resources. Law or other social norms do not sanction and encompass all forms of possession. People gain and maintain access to resources in many ways that do not amount to owning property (Leach, Mearns, and Scoones 1999; Ribot and Peluso 2003). The difference between access and property implies that people may derive benefits from resources without holding property rights to them. They may derive benefits from an agricultural field – for example, by way of occupation or market exchange – even though they do not hold any rights to the land. Actual possession can be worked into property rights in situations where people try to secure their possession with recognition from a politico-legal institution. For this to be successful, however, there needs to be an accessible institution through which to convert, as it were, simple access to recognized, legitimate, and durable ownership.

On the other hand, people may hold formal property rights to some resources without having the capacity to derive any material benefit from them. One can argue that people lack effective rights if such rights are promised in law or by custom but denied in practice. This is where property and access overlap partially; property rights may or may not translate into "ability to benefit," and access may or may not come about as a consequence of property rights. But "ineffective" ownership or property rights are still distinct from no rights at all, even if those paper-only rights do not translate into ability to benefit here and now. Although rights may have no value at a certain point in time (such as women's customary rights to a field of their own), the fact that they are somehow enshrined in legislation or recognized by some politico-legal institution may be important if the political or other structural circumstances change. Formal (legal or customary) but currently "empty" rights *can* be worked into actual possession where people enjoy effective command over their property. Opportunities for successful claims may materialize in the future, so it is not unimportant that laws and customs recognize women's property rights, even if they are currently unrealized (see Moore 1992; Lund 2008).

Presently, the women in Diarra and Monimart's (2006) research do not have access to institutions that can protect their possessions, and the authors see a resulting erosion of women's access to land. With time, the customary right to land may indeed be diluted to the point of faint memory because it is persistently rebuffed and therefore ineffective. Thus, women's possessions are not turned into property, and even their ineffective formal rights are at risk for disappearing (see also Doka and Monimart 2004; Monimart and Diarra 2009).

The descendants of slaves in Hahonou's research, by contrast, have pried open an institutional avenue through which one may both attempt to consolidate current access and turn it into property as well as make sure that formal rights are not rendered entirely hollow.

Organization: Acquiring the Capacity to Claim Rights

As noted above, in societies marked by dramatic inequality, the ability to *access* politico-legal institutions is as much a problem as the existence of countless institutions (see, for example, O'Brien and Li 2006; Assiens 2009). In response, as much attention should be paid to the capacity of the disenfranchised to organize in order to access institutions, as to the institutions themselves.

The examples above suggest that a tremendous amount of footwork and political effort are required to establish credible and accessible institutional alternatives from where legal – or at least broad property – claims can be launched. One cannot overemphasize the importance of improvisation in such situations, which involve considerable uncertainty and risk, improvisation, including such actions as connecting to other groups, creating temporary or enduring alliances with resourceful actors, and prudently choosing the right forums for the resolution of claims and the coordination of interest in petitions, meetings, demonstrations, newspapers, and radio, and perhaps the odd press conference. Obviously, not everybody is equally capable of organizing at the moment of opportunity, as some may be citizens in name only. For this group, policies addressing basic *civic* needs, the very basic elements enabling people – in the present case, especially poor rural women – to exercise even minimal civic actions, suggest themselves. Literacy, reproductive health, farming and gardening skills, and so forth would seem to be prerequisites, or at least accompanying elements, to any modestly successful form of rights-awareness activity. However, these programs alone hardly ensure women's ability to access effective public decision making with regard to property.

Let us remind ourselves that there is no single land issue or a single issue of exclusion. Consequently, there is no single remedy or instrument to deal with poverty or land issues. Had there been a magic bullet, it almost certainly would have been fired by now. Frustration with the complexity of land-related problems may render decision makers susceptible to "clear-cut," "once-and-for-all," and/or seemingly "obvious solutions" (Mosse 2004; Fitzpatrick 2005; Lund 2010). Yet simplistic policies have a truly poor record in the developing world in general and in Africa in particular. If we rush we may not allow ourselves to ask the questions that should come first, namely, who has a problem, what does it consist of, to what extent and to what degree of precision is it desirable to regulate it, and who stands to benefit?

Experience with development clearly reveals a multitude of endogenous dynamic processes unfolding all the time. People do not necessarily wait for a cue from policy makers before they act. Moreover, people's actions and countless everyday struggles and negotiations form a variety of patterns with winners and losers. Strengthening, or outright crafting, institutions from "above" or "outside" may respond to some problems and may not always be ineffective. But very often, the groups that control existing institutions or currently have privileged access to them will find ways of capturing new ones as well, with little guarantee that groups struggling to gain access will be able to benefit. In the end, decentralization reform in Niger turned out to benefit some hitherto excluded groups, but far from all of them.

Therefore, when searching for constructive and feasible policy choices, policy makers and operators could do worse than to ask: What processes involved in peoples' efforts to change their lives can be identified, identified *with*, and furthered by policy? The challenge for social science research relative to policy lies in identifying dynamics, changes, movements, and the organization of societal interests that policy makers can support, strengthen, and promote. Obviously, this means that policy should relate to existing and expressed interests in society; it also probably means that at least as much attention should be paid to the group of people whose plight is the political concern as to any institutional structure.

Institutions are only as strong and resilient as the ongoing reproduction that enables them to persist. In this context, it is difficult to predict which institutions of "justice" will endure, and even more difficult to determine which institutions women would be likely turn to were they more conscious of their interests, capable of organization, and determined to act. Alternatively, enabling the disenfranchised to organize and engage as citizens with the politico-legal institutions of *their choice* to stake their claims may not hold the "charm" of institutional engineering, but it reflects people's experience and grasp of opportunities. That is not the worst place to start.

REFERENCES

Agarwal, Bina. 1994. *A Field of One's Own: Gender and Land Rights in South Asia.* Cambridge: Cambridge University Press.
Amanor, Kojo. 1999. *Global Restructuring and Land Rights in Ghana: Forest Food Chains, Timber and Rural Livelihoods.* Uppsala: Nordic Africa Institute.
Assiens, Willem. 2009. "Legal Empowerment of the Poor: With a Little Help from Their Friends?" *Journal of Peasant Studies* 36 (4): 909–24.

Bayart, Jean-François. 1989. *L'État en Afrique: La Politique du Ventre*. Paris: Fayard.
Benda-Beckmann, Keebet von. 1981. "Forum Shopping and Shopping Forums: Dispute Processing in a Minangkabau Village in West Sumatra." *Journal of Legal Pluralism* 19: 117–62.
Berry, Sara. 1993. *No Condition Is Permanent: The Social Dynamics of Agrarian Change in Sub-Saharan Africa*. Madison: University of Wisconsin Press.
———. 2002. "Debating the Land Question in Africa." *Comparative Studies in Society and History* 44 (4): 638–68.
———. 2009. "Property, Authority and Citizenship: Land Claims, Politics and the Dynamics of Social Division in West Africa." In *Politics of Possession: Property, Authority and Access to Natural Resources*, ed. T. Sikor and C. Lund, 23–45. London: Blackwell.
Biddulph, Robin. 2010. "The End of the Controversy? Divorced Women's Land Rights under Systematic Land Titling in Cambodia." Paper presented at EuroSEAS Conference, Gothenburg, August 25–28.
Boone, Catherine. 2003. *Political Topographies of the African State: Territorial Authority and Institutional Choice*. New York: Cambridge University Press.
Das, Veena, and Deborah Poole. 2004. "State and Its Margins. Comparative Ethnographies." In *Anthropology in the Margins of the State: Comparative Ethnographies*, ed. V. Das and D. Poole, 3–33. Santa Fe, NM: School of American Research Press.
Diarra, Marthe, and Marie Monimart. 2006. "Landless Women, Hopeless Women? Gender, Land and Decentralisation in Niger." IIED Issue Paper 143, International Institute for Environment and Development, London.
Doka, Marthe, and Marie Monimart. 2004. "Women's Access to Land: The De-feminisation of Agriculture in Rural Niger?" IIED Issue Paper 128, International Institute for Environment and Development, London.
Fitzpatrick, Daniel. 2005, "'Best Practice' Options for the Legal Recognition of Customary Tenure." *Development and Change* 36 (3): 449–75.
Geisler, Charles. 2000. "Property Pluralism." In *Property and Values: Alternatives to Public and Private Ownership*, ed. C. Geisler and G. Daneker, 65–86. Washington, DC: Island Press.
Geschiere, Peter. 2009. *The Perils of Belonging: Autochthony, Citizenship, and Exclusion in Africa and Europe*. Chicago: University of Chicago Press.
Gloppen, Siri. 2009. "Legal Enforcement of Social Rights: Enabling Conditions and Impact Assessment." *Erasmus Law Review* 2 (4): 465–80.
Hahonou, Eric. 2006. "En attendant la décentralisation au Niger: Dynamiques locales, clientélisme et culture politique." PhD diss., L'École des Hautes Études en Sciences Sociales, Marseille.
———. 2008. "Culture politique, ésclavage et décentralisation: La Revanche politique des descendants d'ésclaves au Bénin et au Niger." *Politique Africaine* 111: 169–86.
———. 2009. "Slavery and Politics: Stigma, Decentralisation, and Political Representation in Niger and Benin." In *Reconfiguring Slavery: West African Trajectories*, ed. B. Rossi, 152–81. Liverpool: Liverpool University Press.
———. 2010. *Démocratie et culture Politique en Afrique: En attendant la décentralisation au Niger*. Sarrebruck: Éditions Universitaires Européennes.
———. 2011. "Past and Present Citizenships of Slave Descent: Lessons from Benin." *Citizenship Studies* 15 (1): 75–92.
Harrington, Andrew, and Tanja Chopra. 2010. "Arguing Traditions. Denying Kenya's Women Access to Land Rights." Justice for the Poor Research Report 2, World Bank, Washington, DC.

Jacob, Jean-Pierre, and Pierre-Yves Le Meur. 2010. "Citoyenneté locale, foncier, appartenance et reconnaissance dans les Sociétés du Sud." In *Politique de la terre et de l'appartenance: Droits fonciers et citoyenneté locale dans les Sociétés du Sud*, ed. J.-P. Jacob and P.-Y. Le Meur, 5–57. Paris: Karthala.

Kelley, Thomas. 2007. "Exporting Western Law to the Developing World: The Troubling Case of Niger." *George Washington International Law Review* 39 (2): 321–66.

———. 2008. "Unintended Consequences of Legal Westernization in Niger: Harming Contemporary Slaves by Reconceptualizing Property." *American Journal of Comparative Law* 56: 999–1034.

Leach, Melissa, Robin Mearns, and Ian Scoones. 1999. "Environmental Entitlements: Dynamics and Institutions in Community-Based Natural Resource Management." *World Development* 27 (2): 225–47.

Lund, Christian. 1998. *Law, Power and Politics in Niger: Land Struggles and the Rural Code*. Hamburg: LIT Verlag.

———. 2001. "Precarious Democratisation and Local Dynamics in Niger – Micro Politics in Zinder." *Development and Change* 32 (5): 845–69.

———. 2002. "Negotiating Property Institutions: On the Symbiosis of Property and Authority in Africa." In *Negotiating Property in Africa*, ed. K. Juul and C. Lund, 11–43. Portsmouth, NH: Heinemann.

———. 2006. "Twilight Institutions. Public Authority and Local Politics in Africa." *Development and Change* 37 (4): 685–705.

———, ed. 2007. *Twilight Institutions: Public Authority and Local Politics in Africa*. London: Blackwell.

———. 2008. *Local Politics and the Dynamics of Property in Africa*. Cambridge and New York: Cambridge University Press.

———. 2009. "Les dynamiques politiques locales Face à une démocratisation fragile (Zinder)." In *Pouvoirs locaux au Niger*, ed. Maman Tidjani Alou and Jean-Pierre Olivier de Sardan, 89–112. Paris: Karthala.

Lund, Christian. 2010. "Approaching Development – an Opinionated Review." *Progress in Development Studies* 10 (1): 9–34.

MacPherson, Crawford B. 1978. *Property, Mainstream and Critical Positions*. Oxford: Basil Blackwell.

Mattei, Ugo, and Laura Nader. 2008. *Plunder: When the Rule of Law Is Illegal*. London: Blackwell.

Monimart, Marie, and Marthe Diarra. 2009. *Enjeux de genre: Foncier et regeneration naturelle assistée. Elements de reflexion collectés dans six communautés de la region de Maradi*. Copenhagen: Care.

Moore, Sally Falk. 1978. *Law as Process*. London: Routledge & Kegan Paul.

———. 1986. *Social Facts and Fabrications. "Customary" Law on Kilimanjaro 1880–1980*. Cambridge: Cambridge University Press.

———. 1992. "Treating Law as Knowledge: Telling Colonial Officers What to Say to Africans about Running 'Their Own' Native Courts." *Law & Society Review* 26 (1): 11–46.

Mosse, David. 2004. "Is Good Policy Unimplementable? Reflections on the Ethnography of Aid Policy and Practice." *Development and Change* 35 (4): 639–71.

Neubert, Dieter. 2009. "Local and Regional Non-State Actors at the Margins of Public Policy in Africa." In *Non-State Actors as Standard Setters*, ed. A. Peters, L. Koechlin, T. Förster, and G. F. Zinkernagel, 35–60. Cambridge: Cambridge University Press.

O'Brien, Kevin, and Lianjiang Li. 2006. *Rightful Resistance in Rural China*. Cambridge: Cambridge University Press.

Olivier de Sardan, Jean-Pierre. 2005. *Anthropology and Development: Understanding Contemporary Social Change.* London: Zed Books.

Peters, Pauline. 2002. "The Limits of Negotiability: Security, Equity and Class Formation in Africa's Land Systems." In *Negotiating Property in Africa*, ed. K. Juul and C. Lund, 46–66. Portsmouth, NH: Heinemann.

———. 2004. "Inequality and Social Conflict over Land in Africa." *Journal of Agrarian Change* 4 (3): 269–314.

Prag, Ebbe. 2010. *Women Making Politics in Rural Senegal: Women's Associations, Female Politicians and Development Brokers.* Saarbrücken: Lambert Academic Publishing.

Ribot, Jesse, and Nancy Peluso. 2003. "A Theory of Access." *Rural Sociology* 68 (1): 153–81.

Rose, Carol. 1994. *Property and Persuasion: Essays on the History, Theory and Rhetoric of Ownership.* Boulder, CO: Westview Press.

Rose, Nikolas, and Peter Miller. 1992. "Political Power beyond the State: Problematics of Government." *British Journal of Sociology* 43 (2): 173–205.

Sikor, Thomas, and Christian Lund. 2010. "Access and Property. A Question of Power and Authority." In *Politics of Possession: Property, Authority, and Access to Natural Resources*, ed. T. Sikor and C. Lund, 1–22. London: Blackwell.

Tamanaha, Brian Z. 2008. "Understanding Legal Pluralism: Past to Present, Local to Global." Legal Studies Research Paper Series 07-0080, St. John's University School of Law, Jamaica, NY.

Tilly, Charles. 1985. "War Making and State Making as Organized Crime." In *Bringing the State Back In*, ed. P. Evans, D. Rueschemeyer, and T. Skocpol, 169–91. Cambridge: Cambridge University Press.

Toulmin, Camilla. 2009. "Securing Land and Property Rights in Sub-Saharan Africa: The Role of Local Institutions." *Land Use Policy* 26 (1): 10–19.

Vincent, Joan. 1994. "On Law and Hegemonic Moments. Looking behind the Law in Early Modern Uganda." In *Contested States: Law, Hegemony and Resistance*, ed. M. Lazarus-Black and S. Hirsch, 118–37. New York: Routledge.

13

The Publicity "Defect" of Customary Law

Varun Gauri

This chapter examines the extent to which dispute resolvers in customary law systems provide widely understandable justifications for their decisions. The chapter first examines the liberal democratic reasons for the importance of publicity, understood to be wide accessibility of legal justification, by reviewing the uses of publicity in Habermas's and Rawls's accounts of the rule of law. Taking examples from Sierra Leone, the chapter then argues that customary law systems would benefit from making local dispute resolution practices, such as "begging" from elders, witchcraft, and customary law judgments, more widely accessible. The chapter concludes that although legal pluralism is usually taken to be an analytical concept, it may have a normative thrust as well, and that publicity standards would also apply to formal courts in developing countries, which are also typically "defective" along this dimension.

From the standpoint of theories of the liberal democratic state, contemporary customary law systems in developing countries can be considered defective along several dimensions. The first "defect" involves the substance of the laws. Although the norms and rules across customary law systems vary enormously, the following characteristics are not uncommon. Usually, customary laws do not allow women to inherit assets, manage jointly held property, or seek divorce. Customary laws permit parents to predetermine the occupations and life destinies of their children. Customary laws not only tolerate inequalities in status and power but often understand them to be essential for social order and grant unique prerogatives to elder males and other locally powerful individuals. Kin and co-ethnics of the dispute resolvers receive preferential access to and treatment under the law. Weak individual, or collective,

---

I would like to thank Junaid Ahmad, Jorn Sonderholm, and Michael Woolcock, the participants in a workshop on Legal Pluralism and Development Policy (Washington, DC, 2010), and two anonymous reviewers for their helpful comments. The arguments and opinions expressed in this chapter are those of the author alone and do not necessarily represent the views of the World Bank or its executive directors.

land titles dampen investment incentives. Assault, rape, and murder are sometimes conceived as property crimes. To redress a crime or even an insult, collective punishment of the family or village of the perpetrator can be appropriate. Ostracism from the social community is acceptable under some conditions. Processes of adjudication and punishment employ thin standards of procedural fairness. Overall, customary laws do not valorize the classic liberal rights – personal dignity, bodily integrity and privacy, free choice of a life plan – or many of the key liberal democratic political rights, such as the right to political membership and equality under the law.

The second "defect" concerns the enforcement power available in customary law systems. Unlike state law, customary law systems generally do not possess the coercive authority needed to enforce contracts, incarcerate criminals, or confront the executive. Indeed, it is for this reason that many have argued that customary law is not really law at all (Hart 1961, 229). Weber distinguished convention, which uses widespread disapproval expressed toward deviating behavior to create social conformity, from law, which entails a "staff engaged in enforcement" (Weber 1978, 34). More recently, Tamanaha (2008) has argued that the motivating idea behind the anthropological understanding of legal pluralism – that all "semi-autonomous social fields" are bodies of law – is fundamentally incompatible with the positive law conceptions exemplified in the work of Weber and Hart. The enforcement of law by a juridical-bureaucratic staff, moreover, requires a rational-bureaucratic process – a "rule of recognition" in Hart's terminology – on the basis of which "a suggested rule is taken as a conclusive affirmative indication that it is the rule of the group to be supported by the social pressure it exerts" (Hart 1961, 94). Arguably, these sorts of secondary rules are not available in customary law systems, or at least not in a systematic manner.

This chapter does not directly address these two "defects," which have received substantial attention in the literature. Rather, the focus is on a third problem. From the perspective of liberal democratic accounts of law, the purpose of adjudication is not only to resolve dispute but also to state publicly and to elaborate broadly acceptable reasons for the concrete application of the general laws as exemplified in the proposed resolution of the current dispute. Dispute resolvers need to justify their decisions. Public and explicit justification serves not only to persuade the parties to the case to accept the proposed resolution but also to alert other members of society that coercive power is being exercised according to principles that they can accept, and that it is safe for them to make life plans on the expectation that the same or similar principles will inform adjudication should disputes involving them arise.

But the justifications for dispute resolution decisions in customary law systems may not, generally speaking, be sufficiently public to stabilize expectations and promote rationally motivated cooperation among members of the society. When dispute resolvers in customary law systems – local chiefs, religious leaders, village elders, respected community members, and the like – make decisions, the basis for their decisions typically do not reference the many other decisions that have been made in related cases; use terms, concepts, and reasons that would be persuasive for community outsiders as well as insiders; or gain wide publicity and access. The problem is exacerbated by the fact that customary law systems are almost always partial systems, typically covering only certain legal domains, and operating alongside a variety of state-based and other legal systems. Thus, the justifications that they can offer must contend with rival explanations (whether real or hypothetical), and the range of the applicability of justifications under customary law systems – where "range" is understood as their potential extension into the future as well as to other potentially similar disputes in the present (in other words, the precedential value of customary law justification) – is in doubt from the beginning.

This chapter addresses this third "defect" of customary law systems. The following section expands on the importance of publicity from the liberal democratic point of view by drawing on the work of two prominent liberal theorists – Habermas and Rawls. The account of their work in that section is necessarily abbreviated, selective, and partial, but hopefully it uses their arguments in a way that at least illustrates what is at stake in the publicity "defect." The succeeding section draws out, from the account of liberal theory described in the previous section, a few normative implications for the processes of justification under customary law. That section attempts to assess, in a preliminary way, the extent to which the publicity "defect" really is a defect. The concluding section raises some issues not only for customary law but also for formal, state-based law in developing societies.

THE LIBERAL DEMOCRATIC CASE FOR PUBLICITY

On the face of it, it may seem odd to use the work of Habermas and Rawls, both committed liberals, to benchmark the processes of justification under customary law, which are usually not liberal in their core assumptions regarding the value of individuality, the sources of political authority, and equality. It may seem like an ethnocentric limitation, perhaps reminiscent of the way Christian missionaries judged indigenous religious practices outside Europe by the light of their Biblical interpretations.

But this approach may not be totally unfounded. Liberalism arose as an approach to overcome a cycle of fierce and deadly religious wars. Although in retrospect it seems difficult to relate to the animus that existed between Catholics and the sixteenth- and seventeenth-century "heretics," at the time the differences between them constituted an instance of extreme normative pluralism that was understood to be as irreconcilable as liberalism and "non-Western" views are believed to be today. The origins of liberalism lay in a simple cease-fire, or mere tolerance among various Christian faiths – a modus vivendi. One could say that in many developing societies, the state-based, more or less, nominally liberal legal system exists in a somewhat similar state of truce with customary law systems – there is tolerance, but not necessarily a lot of mutual understanding. More recently, and as described by theorists such as Habermas and Rawls, liberal theory, and perhaps also political practice in some societies, has moved beyond mere tolerance to something closer to a consensus on the procedures and styles of discourse necessary for accommodating extreme normative pluralism. Importantly, this near consensus (to the extent that it exists) is primarily about the procedures of government and the conditions that make the procedures legitimate rather than about philosophical or metaphysical values. As Olivier Roy (2006) describes it in another context:

> The perception of the opposition between the West and Islam in terms of a debate on "values" (are they Western or universal?) is biased because Western values are seen in the West as being consensual, which is nonsense. Dialogue between pro-lifers and pro-choicers, patriots and human-rightists, statists and free-marketeers, Christian rightists (from Saint Louis to the Vatican) and liberation theologians, conservatives and liberals, and so on, shows that in the West there is a debate on values, which could cross-cut the same debate in Muslim countries....
> The dominant and final consensus in the West is about institutions, not values. (Roy 2006, 15)

Roy's way of stating it may overstate the case because it may be impossible to establish a consensus on institutions and procedures without at least some minimal agreement on values. The agendas of Habermas and Rawls, however, show that only a relatively thin agreement on moral beliefs is necessary to establish a political consensus on the kind of government that can accommodate pluralism in values. One need not hold a romanticized conception of individuality, privilege the individual over community, or ascribe an identical schedule of rights to all individuals to support a liberal democracy in this sense. As Rawls puts it, this understanding of freedom is "political, not ethical" (Rawls 1993, 77). For both Habermas and Rawls, however, it seems that one of the political values that is important in this kind of government is publicity. If this version of liberal democratic arrangements is applicable to the kind of value pluralism that exists in developing countries with customary law systems, and if it is desirable for countries like Sierra Leone and Timor-Leste to move from mere tolerance of various normative systems to an endorsement of the possibility of diversity, then publicity might be important for dispute resolvers in those systems.

It is useful to begin with the significance of publicity in Habermas's account. The beginning point for Habermas is the modern situation, which is characterized by its normative pluralism – the fact that people disagree about ultimate values. There is, moreover, no authoritative external standpoint, such as divinity, a conception of nature, or transcendental reason, on which people can draw to resolve deep disagreements: the world is, in Weber's terms, "disenchanted." And economic and social processes, especially the division of labor and technical specialization, that multiply the various roles, tasks, and interest positions in societies have made societal coordination more important while at the same time demanding a stance of self-interested calculation that jeopardizes society-wide projects. As a result, the shared background assumptions that facilitate meaningful social communication have faded, and forms of social, political, and legal power need to be justified more explicitly.

In Habermas's account, any justification of political and legal power is problematic because of the tension between power ("facticity") and legitimacy ("normativity") that pervades all social practices and institutions. The roots of this tension are linguistic: when communicating and convincing, human speakers use reasons that are necessarily addressed to an idealized community of competent listeners, but their present audience can only grasp those reasons in a "good enough" and provisional way that is sufficient (or not) to motivate the joint effort necessary to tackle the problem at hand. The actions taken, then, never seem to live up to the norms used to justify them. Traditional societies, Habermas believes, merged the social power of chieftains, obligatory behavioral norms, and mythical sources in a manner that established enough of a background consensus to overcome this basic tension. Those societies could draw on that background consensus to build institutions of conflict resolution and political authority. No such background consensus exists in modern societies, which instead must rely on law.

It is worth emphasizing that for Habermas, the other potential basis for the legitimacy of law and political authority, bargaining based on the cold calculations of *homo economicus*, is obviously insufficient. There are strategic accounts of democracy that can explain *the idea* of political compromise – for instance, ruling elites might entrench liberal democratic rights and liberties because they know that one day they could lose an election and fall under the power of a vengeful rival party. But that does not explain why elites and their constituents should support a *particular* set of rules for sharing power, with its attendant implications for the distribution of political and economic resources in their society. Bargaining that results in legitimacy requires not only compromise but fair compromise, and the establishment of the latter requires communicative, not strategic, interaction. Legitimacy requires the perspective of a participant, not the perspective of an observer, which is what one becomes when calculating.

Without access to the shared background available in traditional societies, and given the limited legitimacy that can arise from bargaining, modern political communities, then, must establish their normative appeal using their own resources, as it were. Positive state-based law, which is the characteristic mode of establishing social coordination and collective action in modern societies, requires a foundation that has validity for modern participants. How Habermas develops his principle of validity is difficult to summarize in a short space. The end product, however, is the discourse principle: "Just those action norms are valid to which all possibly affected persons could agree as participants in rational discourses" (Habermas 1996, 117). This principle applies to all of the various modes of action norms, including moral principles, the criteria of fairness in bargaining, and positive state-based law. When applied to law, this means that "it must remain possible for everyone to obey legal norms on the basis of insight" (Habermas 1996, 121), although the law must not compel its addressees to conform to law on that basis and must leave open the option of external compliance on the basis of utility calculation. To state it another way, only those statutes are legitimate that, in principle, all participants could assent to in a communicatively open process of legislation that has been legally constituted. Habermas believes that this discourse principle establishes a sufficient and "post-metaphysical" foundation for the basic civil, political, and social rights.

For present purposes, it is important to emphasize that, for Habermas, putting the discourse principle into practice in the real world requires not only the system of rights, which protects classical private autonomy; popular sovereignty, which supports public autonomy and a collective capacity for mutual recognition; and the legal form, which stabilizes expectations in a complex society on the basis of principles such as consistency, precision, and non-retroactivity. It also requires "communicative power." The latter involves processes of "violence-free" mutual understanding, if we follow Habermas's reading of Arendt, and "undamaged intersubjectivity" (Habermas 1996, 151). These terms are hard to pin down, but they have to do with the absence of repression and inequality in the processes and procedures that authorize, undertake, and interpret collective action. The various identities, values, and interests in a society need to be given due consideration as the "general will" is developed. "Thus, along with the system of rights, one must also create the *language* in which a community can understand itself as a voluntary association of free and equal consociates *under law* [emphasis in original]" (Habermas 1996, 111).

The development of this language takes place in all of the various institutions of modern societies. Principles such as the autonomy of the public sphere from social interests and party competition promote this kind of discourse and its publicity. These are elements of the "publicity requirements that keep institutionalized opinion- and will-formation open to the informal circulation of general political communication" (Habermas 1996, 183). The ultimate goal is a form of public opinion in which issues, contributions, information, and arguments are not attached to particular people (public opinion is "subjectless") and in which they move unblocked from civil society to the public sphere and back.

The focus here, however, is on the narrow legal culture. In that domain, Habermas argues that judges are engaged in a fundamentally dialogic process. Legal "argumentation is characterized by the intention of winning the assent of a universal audience to a problematic proposition in a non-coercive but regulated contest for the better arguments based on the best information and reasons" (Habermas 1996, 228). To generate communicative power, judges should have the intention of speaking to a wide audience, and should do so when formulating the basis for their decisions. This process facilitates the action by which "the perspectives of participants and the perspectives of uninvolved members of the community (represented by an impartial judge) come to be transformed into one another" (Habermas 1996, 229). This is an argument for judges to render broadly accessible arguments. It is also an argument for the establishment of judicial procedures that support this kind of argumentation in court hearings:

> Procedural law does not regulate normative-legal discourse as such but secures, in the temporal, social, and substantive dimensions, the institutional framework that *clears the way* for processes of communication governed by the logic of application discourses. [emphasis in original] (Habermas 1996, 234)

Although more welcoming of public expressions of religious and nonliberal perspectives on ultimate values than Habermas appears to be, Rawls develops a broadly similar endorsement of publicity in the judicial sphere. Rawls's account starts with the idea that a society is to be understood as "a fair system of cooperation over time, from one generation to the next" (Rawls 1996, 16). In that kind of society, citizens would ask themselves: How should they, all free and equal citizens, establish the rules of fair cooperation in the society in which they are going to spend the rest of their lives together? Given that they are citizens sincerely committed to mutually advantageous rules, and that these fictional citizens have a developed sense of justice and capacity to formulate their life goals and rationally choose the best means to achieve them, Rawls believes that bargains struck among them would, under certain specified conditions, lead to the basic structure of a just society. To abstract from the advantages that accompany private information and unequal bargaining power, Rawls assumes that the representatives who meet to strike that bargain regarding society's basic structure would know nothing about the age, gender, race, ethnic group, social position, and religious outlook of the citizens they represent. Rawls argues that this imaginary procedure would produce two basic principles of justice: each person is to have an equal right to the most extensive scheme of equal basic liberties compatible with a similar scheme of liberties for others, and social and economic inequalities are to be arranged so that a) they are to be of the greatest benefit to the least-advantaged members of society (the difference principle), and b) offices and positions must be open to everyone under conditions of fair equality of opportunity. (Rawls modified his phrasing of these principles over the years, but that is not of concern for the argument here).

The representatives in the original position cannot appeal to metaphysical views ("comprehensive doctrines") to ground the bargain that leads to the principles of justice. What is most interesting for the present chapter is that irreducible pluralism means that real flesh-and-blood members of a liberal pluralist society ("you and I," says Rawls) also cannot appeal to metaphysical views when justifying their chosen principles of justice, whether those turn out to be identical to Rawls's principles or some other conception of liberal political justice that also accommodates value pluralism. In implementing and interpreting the principles they have agreed on, real citizens must use public justifications and public arguments that all citizens could agree to, whatever their private metaphysical commitments. That notion leads to a certain understanding of the criteria for reasonable public arguments ("public reason") and to the dispositions and opinions needed in real-life citizens. Without such dispositions and the commitment to public reason that those dispositions support, the just liberal society would not be stable. This means that real citizens (we) should be, in Rawls's terms, "reasonable" – that is, willing to propose fair terms of cooperation and abide by them, as long as others are willing to do so, and to refuse to impugn the reasonableness of people we disagree with when the disagreements are rooted in normal sources of argumentative uncertainty, such as different kinds of evidence, conceptual ambiguities, varying life experiences and normative considerations, and different priorities among the shared liberal values. Through reasonable behavior, the full justification of the just liberal society comes to be publicly known and supported. Rawls notes that:

> [o]nce [the publicity] condition is imposed, a political conception assumes a wide role as part of public culture. Not only are its first principles embodied in political and social institutions and in public traditions of their interpretation, but the derivation of citizens' rights, liberties, and opportunities also contains a conception of citizens as free and equal. In this way citizens are made aware of and educated to this conception. They are presented with a way of regarding themselves that otherwise they would most likely never be able to entertain. To realize the full publicity condition is to realize a social world within which the ideal of citizenship can be learned and may elicit an effective desire to be that kind of person. (Rawls 1996, 71)

Judicial activities are among the most crucial sites for the "derivation of citizens' rights, liberties, and opportunities." Indeed, for Rawls a supreme court is the branch of government that serves as the exemplar of public reason. He believes that the court gives "public reason vividness and vitality in the public forum" and that the court's role "is part of the publicity of reason and is an aspect of the wide, or educative, role of public reason" (Rawls 1996, 236–37). Although Rawls is particularly interested in apex courts in constitutional regimes with judicial review, his account of the educative power of judicial reasoning is relevant for other kinds of dispute resolvers as well:

> Citizens and legislators may properly vote their more comprehensive views when constitutional essentials and basic justice are not at stake; they need not justify by public reason why they vote as they do or make their grounds consistent and fit them into a coherent constitutional view over the whole range of their decisions. The role of justices is to do precisely that and in doing it they have no other reason and no other values than the political. (Rawls 1996, 238)

THE NEED FOR JUSTIFICATION IN CUSTOMARY LAW

States such as Sierra Leone draw on sources of legitimacy apart from their liberal democratic practices. This may be because liberal democratic values are not widely shared, or it may be that disenchantment, pluralism, and role diversification have not (yet) eroded the shared "lifeworld" of their inhabitants. Still, states in many developing societies are now broadly liberal democratic in form, and one can ask whether it makes sense to apply publicity standards to social, political, and legal practices there, both for the purpose of strengthening the normative basis for the formal liberal democratic state and for managing the value pluralism of those societies. It is possible, moreover, although this chapter does not make the case, to make normative arguments for publicity on the basis of political concepts drawn from the political traditions of those developing societies themselves, and without relying on Western normative imports, such as Habermas and Rawls. Amartya Sen (2005), for instance, describes autochthonous debates about how to manage value pluralism in India.

If, say, a section chief in Sierra Leone endorses a community's decision to ostracize a woman accused of witchcraft, should he (usually he is a male) be encouraged to do so publicly, with reference to related court rulings, with words and reasons that he believes can persuade nonresidents? Although those kinds of public statements – public derivations of individual and community rights and responsibilities – by village section chiefs and other dispute resolvers are not the norm in Sierra Leone, one can imagine interventions to encourage them: judicial training, nongovernmental organization advocacy that teaches people to ask dispute resolvers to give them justifications for their decisions, changes in the formal rules governing customary courts, and inducements for dispute resolvers to meet and publicly hash out tough cases. These interventions might or might not produce better legal justifications; indeed, given that the goal of customary law is often to restore the relationship among disputing parties rather than to develop general rules of conduct, the emergent legal justifications might at first look more like oral casuistry than precedential case law (Bennett 2004, 52). But the question here is: Would this be desirable even if it were clearly feasible, or would it be a mistaken application of a "best practice" that serves a purpose in the global North but would not work, or even be counterproductive, in poor and/or nonliberal societies?

Another way to think about this is to consider how law and development theorists, as well as practitioners, have reconciled themselves to the human rights "defect" mentioned previously. When, for example, a married man in rural Sierra Leone has sex with another man's wife, and the village chief requires the offender to pay a fine to the offended husband, outsiders for the most part view this as a tolerable outcome, even if the village chief later endorses more severe punishment for a married woman who has had sex with a married man. The reason that this may be tolerable, even though it diverges from an international standard of gender equality, is that it is difficult (though not impossible) to act as if someone's dignity has been violated if the woman punished does not make that claim. Outsiders view a case like this as a long-term challenge to increase the sense of agency and entitlement among women in Sierra Leone. In that way, human rights, even civil and political ones, are viewed under the lens of "progressive realization," which is usually applied only to social and economic rights. The goal becomes one of raising rights consciousness, rather than redressing all human rights violations immediately, and doing so in a manner cognizant of local practices and the alternative forms that dignity might take in different societies. In a similar manner, standards of publicity could be applied in a gradualist way over time.

When undertaking such a project, it is important to note that justification is distinct from both codification and documentation. Some have argued that codifying customary laws might rigidify current power relations and weaken the flexibility and responsiveness of customary law systems, which for those living under them is one of their most attractive features. Codification might also, perversely, make decisions and the justifications for them less, not more, public in circumstances where most people do not read and write well, if legal justification were to take a written form or even reference written texts. De Soto (2008) notes that actors in the informal economy in places such as Peru frequently document land titles and other economic transactions. Demonstrating the fact of contractual entitlement is a different endeavor, however, from justifying the legal basis for one's claim. One would not say that the publicity standard has been fulfilled if a dispute resolver merely compares the documents of two parties to a land dispute without explaining the source of the legal validity of the documents or the reasons one might be more salient than another.

Maru (2006) describes the case of "Kadiatu T.," a woman living in a neighborhood of east Freetown, Sierra Leone, whom a police officer beat and kicked into unconsciousness, and on whose behalf a paralegal filed a complaint and threatened private prosecution and a civil suit. The accused police officer responded to the allegations by apologizing and asking a senior police official to "beg for him" to the victim, Kadiatu T. "Begging" in Sierra Leone is a specific action in which someone apologizes and asks for forgiveness, often via a respected intermediary. Kadiatu T. accepted the officer's apology, as well as his compensation payment, and the legal case was dropped. In this instance, a paralegal mediated the conflict, so there may have been a less obvious opportunity for legal publicity than had a dispute resolver issued an opinion. Still, it may have been possible to talk to the police officer, his colleagues, and his superior concerning the reasons that this restitution was considered acceptable. (The case study does not indicate whether or not this in fact happened; I am assuming, for the sake of argument, that it did not.) Specifically, there may be a set of behaviors and indications of sincerity constitutive of "begging" in contemporary Sierra Leonean practice. There may be a common understanding of a kind of proportionality between the offense and the form the begging and compensation should take. There may be certain acts for which, or certain settings in which, victims should not accept someone's "begging." There may be criteria of competence, such as a person's age, before a victim is qualified to accept "begging." Developing and elaborating such descriptions of the practice, or at least taking opportunities to talk about them, may fortify the normative consensus on which they are based. This in turn could motivate members of the society who are otherwise truculent to accede to mediations and adjudications, could stabilize expectations regarding the likely legal responses to behavioral deviations, and could articulate the standards of the local customary justice system to outsiders to the community.

The absence of a normative consensus on the criteria for "begging" is evident in a case involving the distribution of rice (Manning 2009a). When the government gave bags of rice to the leaders of a poor rural community in southern Sierra Leone in 2004, a section chief held back, of the five bags allocated to his community, two for himself and a secret society ceremony. When a young man named "Mohammed" learned of this, he and a few others loudly protested. Then the paramount chief and other leaders sent a delegation of elders to investigate, and they decided to ask the protesters to apologize and pay a small fine. At first, all but Mohammed apologized. After repeated humiliations and threats, Mohammed finally relented and reluctantly begged for forgiveness. Begging in Sierra Leone contains at least two normative elements: deference to respected authorities and the recognition of a principle of righteousness. As this case indicates, sometimes these elements are in tension. The development of "case law," or perhaps a body of oral casuistry, concerning begging could help to clarify and strengthen the normative basis of the practice.

Then there is witchcraft. Maru (2006) also recounts the case of "Macie B.," a twenty-six-year-old woman from southern Sierra Leone whose three children died and from whom a diviner elicited a confession to have agreed to sacrifice her children to a coven of witches she had seen in a dream. Macie B.'s family and community rejected her. A paralegal convinced her family to take her back, for a time, by appealing to their love for her. Then a court required her husband's family to pay for prenatal care after she became pregnant a fourth time. (That child also died.) Here, the substance of a public legal argument would have involved the tension between witchcraft, a belief that is widespread in Sierra Leone and that may be a category for making sense of vulnerabilities, threats, and mental illnesses; and familial love, which not only is a naturally occurring sentiment but also is the basis for many familial and extrafamilial moral obligations. ("Ma," "Pa," and "brother," for instance, are frequently used terms to indicate affection and respect.) Dispute resolvers could promote a public discussion regarding the moral basis of obligations of societal support and the ways in which witchcraft and familial bonds affect moral commitments. In response, some might well say that witchcraft is better left unmentioned and unspoken, that courts and customary dispute resolvers could involve themselves in dangerous matters were they to undertake such public discussions, and that this is precisely the sort of "best practice" from the West that would be counterproductive in an African setting. I am not sure. The secrecy surrounding witchcraft may already be exacerbating suspicions and threats and stoking discord. And it may be reasonable to hypothesize that the lack of publicity, on balance, most serves those with things to hide.

Publicity in the narrow sense of open court hearings (in customary and formal courts), rather than in the broader sense of explicit and public justification for the basis of legal decisions, can expose wrongdoing. Manning (2009b) describes a case in which "Mr. K" raised money for rebuilding homes destroyed during the civil war but then absconded without finishing the promised construction. He was charged in magistrate court, but before the police had completed their investigation, and the court apparently disposed of the case without the presence of the police officer or community members, who were never repaid. Similarly, when some youths did not show up for the start of a road-building project, a local councilor sued them. A seventy-year-old male village chief refused to withdraw the case once it was filed – even though many villagers thought his action was extreme – probably because he wanted to impose fines on the youths and keep a share of the receipts for himself, which may indeed be what happened (Manning 2009a). Under a norm of publicity, a public account of the procedures for filing a suit, and the basis on which it could be withdrawn, is something that the community members would have expected, perhaps before, and certainly after, these events occurred.

CONCLUSIONS

In the anthropological and law and development literatures, legal pluralism is, for the most part, understood as an analytical concept. This chapter has argued that legal pluralism might also be understood to have a normative thrust, at least from the perspective of liberal democratic theory. Elaborating the legal and moral basis for decisions taken in customary law might help developing societies such as Sierra Leone to not only manage divergent values and moral concepts but also to create the conditions for the endurance of a society in which that diversity is seen as desirable and is understood to be an institutionally supported fact of social life. Of course, the lack of justification for legal decisions is a "defect" not only for customary law systems but for many formal state-based legal systems in developing countries. Formal courts often suffer from the absence of written records, insufficient public access to written records where they do exist, and poorly reasoned and even fiat-like legal decision making. Law and development practitioners have, in various places, lobbied for state courts to accord some degree of recognition and legitimation to customary law systems, which many people find more accessible and responsive than the formal system. That kind of recognition is, to an extent, a way in which customary law systems can gain public legitimation. But a deeper form of legal publicity would occur if judges in formal courts themselves presented better reasons for their decisions and did so more often, and if they themselves grappled with the content of customary law in a deeper and more systematic way. The normative thrust of legal pluralism pushes in both directions.

REFERENCES

Bennett, T. W. 2004. *Customary Law in South Africa*. Cape Town: Juta.
De Soto, Hernando. 2008. "Are Africans Culturally Unsuited to Property Rights and the Rule of Law? Some Reflections Based on the Tanzanian Case." In *Rights and Legal Empowerment in Eradicating Poverty*, ed. Dan Banik. London: Ashgate.
Habermas, Jurgen. 1996. *Between Facts and Norms: Contributions to a Discourse Theory of Law and Democracy*. Cambridge, MA: MIT Press.
Hart, H. L. A. 1961. *The Concept of Law*. Oxford: Clarendon Press.
Manning, Ryann Elizabeth. 2009a. "Challenging Generations: Youths and Elders in Rural and Peri-Urban Sierra Leone." Justice and Development Working Paper Series, vol. 1, no. 2, The World Bank, Washington, DC.
―――. 2009b. "Exploitation of Poor Communities in Sierra Leone: False Promises in Reconstruction and Development." Justice and Development Working Paper Series, vol. 1, no. 3, World Bank, Washington, DC.
Maru, Vivek. 2006. "Between Law and Society: Paralegals and the Provision of Justice Services in Sierra Leone and Worldwide." *Yale Journal of International Law* 31: 427–76.
Rawls, John. 1995. *Political Liberalism*. New York: Columbia University Press.
Roy, Olivier. 2006. *Globalized Islam: The Search for a New Ummah*. New York: Columbia University Press.
Sen, Amartya. 2005. "Human Rights and Capabilities." *Journal of Human Development* 6(2): 151–66.
Tamanaha, Brian Z. 2008. "Law." In *Oxford International Encyclopedia of Legal History*, ed. Stanley N. Katz. Oxford: Oxford University Press.
Weber, Max. 1978. *Economy and Society: An Outline of Interpretive Sociology*. Berkeley: University of California Press.

14

Unearthing Pluralism

Mining, Multilaterals, and the State

Meg Taylor and Nicholas Menzies

INTRODUCTION

The impact of mining on communities in developing countries is the subject of much documentation, debate, and global advocacy. Mining brings together those with diverse concerns, from environmental and social harm to corruption and the tracking of benefit flows. Discussion of the benefits and pitfalls of mining regularly includes a range of stakeholders, including both communities and policy makers in host countries, global nongovernmental organizations (NGOs), multilateral development agencies, and international mining conglomerates. The discourse is therefore complicated by the concurrence of different voices, visions, and understandings of the world. What can an awareness of legal pluralism bring to all this?

An attention to the diverse legal (and normative) systems that come to bear on mining can help provide insight into how mine-affected communities understand development in their localities, why they react the ways they do, and where and how they seek to mitigate the impacts of mining. Such insight can hopefully encourage development practitioners – and others – to contribute to policies and projects for more equitable and less conflict-prone mining. An attention to legal pluralism often focuses on the ways that multiple legal and normative systems weaken the position of communities to respond to development challenges. Legal pluralism can also offer opportunities for empowerment and redress that may not otherwise exist. In this chapter, we seek to highlight some of these opportunities through a discussion of work of the World Bank Group in Peru and Papua New Guinea. Through this we touch on the role of mining operations in highlighting the often diffuse nature of "stateness" in developing countries.

How Law and Legal Pluralism are Relevant to Mining

An understanding of legal pluralism is useful in thinking about mining and development, as it urges us to look at the functions of law as opposed to merely its institutional forms. Law – whether informal or formal – plays an important role in mining projects because it defines, among other things, who has rights to the resources (including ownership as well as the authority to access), who can participate in the management of the wealth (who benefits and by how much), and how grievances are dealt with (who decides and on what grounds). These issues are all central to determining whether a positive development outcome eventuates and for whom. The existence of multiple legal systems allows development practitioners to be expansive when looking at the levers of power and control that can be used so that citizens benefit from development. As Tamanaha points out earlier in this volume, state law is often not the primary source of social order, and its role varies by, inter alia, subject matter and location. Mining often occurs in remote sites where the reach of the state is particularly weak. Regulatory and service delivery functions are regularly fulfilled above, below, and around state institutions, with mining companies themselves playing a central role in governance.

Complexity arises not only because of the sheer number of stakeholders (be they local landholding communities, multilateral mining companies, government agencies, local communities, or NGOs), but also because the stakeholders are grounded in different regulatory traditions, with a divergence of views on rights, responsibilities, and processes. It is in this divergence of views that especially heated and intractable conflicts can arise.

Mining projects can become enmeshed in three main strands of pluralism. First, on the international level, multinational corporations (backed by global capital) play an important role in large-scale resource extraction. For particular projects, international financial institutions (IFIs) provide support, opening up avenues for dispute resolution, including within the IFIs themselves. Second, state law is often the main source regulating the entry and actions of mining ventures, and conversely, resource companies themselves influence the ways in which this regulation is formulated and applied. Third, the interaction of international and state regulation with the rules of specific "host" mining communities impacts ultimately on the way people within those communities experience development. Aspects of all three strands will be taken up below.

HOW MINING CAN THICKEN LEGAL PLURALISM

Mining projects can add layers of pluralism to the local context, as international norms and state law come to play an increasing role in community affairs. As development practitioners, we often approach legal pluralism from the perspective of the challenges it poses for development, but, as Woodman points out in this volume, "while legal pluralism may sometimes be a problem for development, development may perhaps be a problem for legal pluralism." Pluralism becomes more problematic as more strands of regulation are laid down. The impact of the "thicker" pluralism that results from mining can fall more heavily on some community members than others. In Papua New Guinea, the small island of Lihir in New Ireland Province provides an example of the impact of pluralism on women's rights within mine-affected communities.

In Papua New Guinea, most land is owned and held customarily, and under national law, landowners are entitled to a significant share of resources, including equity in mining projects and a share of the royalties flowing from them. The gold mine located on Lihir is situated in a society that has been historically structured along matrilineal lines. Owned by one of the world's largest gold miners, Newcrest, the mine has been operating since the mid-1990s. In this time, the new wealth that has been generated for local communities and the regulations flowing from national law and company policies to govern this wealth has changed the societal role of women on the island.

Papua New Guinean national law provides for the creation of landowner associations to negotiate for, receive, and manage benefit flows from mining. The corporatist principles and structures that these associations embody are adopted from Western practice, which invariably differs from local modes of organizing. Furthermore, when these corporate forms are introduced into particular affected communities, their local manifestations invariably do not include women – on their boards or otherwise in decision-making roles. Under state law, landowner associations' boards and management are not required to include women and are therefore legally entitled to make decisions without women's participation or reference to women's interests – even though this may not accord with the rules of the societies into which they have been introduced. A more recent push in a small subset of resource agreements (for example, under the Community Mine Continuation Agreements for the Ok Tedi Mine in Western Province) to set aside 10 percent of benefits for women and children is also not without flaws. Although empirical work on the impact of this type of "ringfencing" is limited – in Papua New Guinea or elsewhere – it is arguably only a limited step forward for equality if only 10 percent of the benefits is set aside for more than four-fifths of the population (more than 30 percent of the population in Papua New Guinea is younger than fifteen). It could also undermine the ability of women to influence the ways in which the remaining 90 percent is spent.

On Lihir, women's inheritance and decision-making rights are being undermined, as the corporate structures of the introduced landowner associations do not reflect matrilineal practices of inheritance, under which women are not only consulted but also can censor decisions. Some women have more recently reported changing inheritance patterns, with instances of landownership bequeathed through fathers, and have expressed concerns that with their role diminishing, a patrilineal system may be emerging. Furthermore, the presence of the mine has introduced a new economy that has displaced traditional distribution patterns, with obligations taking on new meanings. Commoditization is replacing traditional forms of social organization and acknowledgment of relationships. The concern of many women is that their role as feast makers – ensuring that food and wealth is distributed to clans across the island – is now being disrupted as new cash distribution patterns emerge.

Resource inflows and changing economic patterns combine on Lihir to shake gender roles and weaken traditional practices. As Lund discusses in this volume, women's rights can be "edited out" in the face of scarce resources, yet the example of Lihir illustrates how women's rights can also be diminished in contexts of abundance – when resource projects result in significant benefit flows.

HOW THICKER PLURALISM CAN RESULT IN MORE OPTIONS FOR DISPUTE RESOLUTION

In addition to the disruption that introduced regulatory arrangements can cause within local communities, international strands of pluralism can also offer opportunities. The Yanacocha gold mine in Cajamarca, Peru, provides an illustration of pluralism being both a problem for communities and a source of opportunity. The mining development in Cajamarca unearthed historical animosities, but international engagement with the venture provided an avenue through which to manage the conflict.

The geological formations that produce minerals are shaped by layers of sediment deposited over time. In unearthing these layers, historical understandings of development can also be tapped. In this volume, Merry entreats us to conduct an "archaeology of law," that is, to unpack historical complexity as a means of understanding contemporary forms of law and reactions to it. Merry recommends going at least as far as the colonialist expansion, because "... [t]o a large extent the roots of contemporary pluralities of global law are buried in the colonial era."

When applied to Yanacocha, the largest gold mine in Latin America, an archaeology of the law readily unearths the contemporary impact of colonial experiences on development. Begun in the mid-1990s, discontent was initially focused in rural areas closest to the mine, spreading to the city of Cajamarca in 2000 and intensifying following a spill of mercury. Protest against the mine has been grounded in "collective memory of events surrounding the Spanish conquistador Francisco Pizarro's... confrontation with the Inca King Atahualpa... in the plaza of Cajamarca..." in 1532 (CAO 2009, 3). In a scheme of deception against the Incas, Pizarro stole gold from the Cajamarca treasury, killed King Atahualpa, and seized control of the region. These events of almost five hundred years ago remain "present day" to many citizens of the area and have infused communities' understandings of their grievances against the contemporary actions of the mine. The conquistadores stole gold and people's inheritances, and it is popularly conceived that the mine is doing the same today.

Local communities have acted on their historically infused complaints by accessing international grievance mechanisms. The Federation of Female *Rondas Campesinas* of Northern Peru (FEROCAFENOP), a civil society organization, drew on national and international networks to protest against the mine, joining a global campaign run by Project Underground, a U.S.-based NGO, against Newmont, the mine's majority shareholder. Project Underground provided advice to

FEROCAFENOP, drafting a complaint to the International Finance Corporation's Office of the Compliance Advisor/Ombudsman (CAO). The CAO is an office established to review complaints from people affected by development projects undertaken by the International Finance Corporation and the Multilateral Investment Guarantee Agency, the two private-sector financing arms of the World Bank Group. The CAO conducts mediated settlements and compliance audits and provides advice on improving the social and environmental outcomes of projects. Critical to the availability of this dispute resolution mechanism for local communities around Yanacocha is the International Finance Corporation's equity and debt involvement with the mine operator. Access to an international strand of legal pluralism allowed local communities to find an alternative option for redress, namely, the grievance and dispute resolution mechanisms of international finance institutions.

In response to the complaints from Yanacocha communities, the CAO established a *mesa* (dialogue table) process in an attempt to address the grievances. Although the CAO could have conducted an audit in response to the community complaints and issued recommendations to the project operators and the communities, CAO staff judged that the lack of a forum within which the parties could engage with one another meant that an audit alone would be unlikely to lead to concrete outcomes. Instead, the CAO chose to focus on creating a mediated process. Economic and cultural pluralism within the affected communities as well as the historical archaeology contributed to a lack of trust between citizens, adding to the complexities of bringing people together to resolve the conflict. However, most affected groups believed outside intervention could catalyze needed improvements in the communities' relationships with the mine, and the CAO capitalized on this by using independent experts – with no connections to Yanacocha or the mining industry – to gain trust. Because the key issue of concern was contaminated water, rigorous technical studies and independent verification of water sampling by *vedorees* from the Rondas communities were required. This participatory approach, and later independent water monitoring by communities, gave technical credibility to the work of CAO scientific experts. That said, many groups did not participate in the *mesa* for fear of being castigated as *Felipillo* after the sixteenth-century Incan translator who allied with Pizarro to betray Atahualpa (CAO 2009, 16). Convening a critical mass of participants was a constant challenge. Over time, the *mesa* morphed into a locally run institution, and despite shortcomings can be seen as a practical example of a "measure of conciliation" (Glenn, this volume) to address conflicts that arise in part as a result of legal pluralism.

HOW MULTILATERALS CAN FOSTER ENDOWMENTS TO ENGAGE WITH PLURALISM

In addition to contributing to internationally sourced strands of dispute resolution, international development agencies can positively influence the outcome of resource extraction in plural contexts by focusing on citizens' "basic civic needs" (Lund, this volume). Lund highlights that a significant amount of effort is required for communities, and citizens within them, to be able to launch legal claims to protect and enforce their rights (that is, to avail themselves of even one strand of legal pluralism that may course through their lives). This effort is only likely to be mustered if people have the enabling elements to allow them to take civic actions. Lund's argument is that without such things as literacy, access to basic health services, or the ability to satisfy food production needs, citizens are very unlikely to even try to claim their rights. Although these elements are by no means sufficient, without them claims are almost unthinkable.

The World Bank supported attempts by the Women in Mining Initiative in Papua New Guinea to address some of these basic enabling elements so that women can more fully exercise their citizenship and participate in a more engaged manner in development processes. The initiative, run by the Papua New Guinea Chamber of Mines and Petroleum, works with women in mining-affected communities across the country. Women in Mining developed in response to the recognition that men invariably capture most mining-related benefits, such as royalty and other benefit flows, employment, and business opportunities that accrue to mine communities in Papua New Guinea. By contrast, women often bear the brunt of negative social and environmental impacts. The initiative has sought to address a lack of voice through the development of basic skills such as literacy, numeracy, and project management so that women can participate in the development process. It has also fostered entrepreneurial skills so that women can use benefit flows to establish businesses and tap into economic opportunities catalyzed by having mines in their localities. Women in Mining has also brought together women from mining affected communities across Papua New Guinea to share experiences, influence national policy makers, and develop priorities for government support. These priorities have been reflected in a Women in Mining National Action Plan endorsed by the Cabinet. The success of the initiative in increasing women's empowerment takes place in a broader context of inequity for women in Papua New Guinea.

ACTING LIKE A STATE: DIFFUSE STATENESS AND MINING AS A SOURCE OF LEGAL PLURALISM

Lund's formulation of "state" (in this volume) is particularly instructive with regard to mining, because in many contexts it is the extractors themselves who take on (whether willingly or otherwise) elements of "stateness." Lund argues that no institution or set of institutions should be assumed to be the state as such or have a monopoly on "stateness." Adopting a function over form characterization, "state" is best understood as the ability of an institution "to define and enforce collectively binding decisions on members of society." In exhorting practitioners to focus on circumstances as they exist, not what we wish them to be, Lund notes, "We often tend to reserve state qualities for government institutions, but this is more a reflection of our idea of an ideal end result of the messy process of state formation itself...." In many contexts, government and other institutions that normally make up the state – the judiciary, parliament, military – don't have much power or influence, or it is extremely variable – some have a lot and some very little.

In Papua New Guinea, Lund's formulation helps us see both the varied "stateness" of governmental institutions as well as the statelike quality and functions of extractives companies. Although the Papua New Guinean state has been referred to as "weak" and "fragile" (Allen and Hasnain 2010) and subject to "limited reach," a closer examination of institutions commonly associated with the state reveals clear variation. Some, like the Central Bank, formal courts, and the Ombudsman, have more authority, legitimacy, and efficacy (at least in certain spheres) than others, such as the police, many central government departments, and local government entities. On one key indicator of democratic states, electoral participation, Papua New Guinea appears healthy. Knowledge of parliamentary members is high, and electoral campaigning manages to touch even the remotest communities – bringing into starker question why basic services seem not to have similar reach.

State authority varies geographically and can change quickly over time, especially with changes in key personnel such as politicians, especially government ministers. In this regard, it is not uncommon for qualities of "stateness" to be bound up not just in a range of institutions, as Lund would have it, but also in individuals, with development outcomes reliant on personal qualities rather than structures and processes. The picture of who holds statelike power is further complicated by the role of mining companies, which regularly provide infrastructure and services, influence legal processes, and muddle any monopoly on the use of force. The delivery of services alone gives resource companies tremendous legitimacy and authority in communities. The statelike provision of infrastructure, such as roads and bridges, is actually encouraged by the state through a tax credit scheme. Under this scheme, money that would ordinarily flow to the national treasury as tax revenue (for the state to then provide infrastructure, among other things) is retained by the companies that build the infrastructure themselves. Companies also regularly provide other fundamental infrastructure normally provided by the state, such as schools and health clinics, either as part of agreements that permit the right to extract or as a means of cultivating a social license to operate. In this, companies are not alone. The provision of education and health services by churches rivals that of the state in Papua New Guinea, and in many areas the state explicitly outsources the provision of such services to churches, as they are unable to fulfill the task.

The impact that resource companies often have on the economy, both locally and nationally through infrastructure, employment, and revenue, provides companies with a level of control that is often used to impact the regulatory environment in which they operate. In Papua New Guinea, amendments to the environmental regime have been brought before Parliament to alter the power of the courts to review administrative decisions. In this case, the administrative decisions that the amendments are intended to quarantine from judicial review stem from the government's power to issue permits for the disposal of mine waste. The amendments were reportedly brought in response to requests from a mine operator whose permit to dispose of mine tailings at sea was being challenged in court. Another regularly espoused tenet of "stateness," a monopoly on the use of force, is also blurred with the use of private security firms by resource companies and the lack of regular police in remote locations.

CONCLUSION

In unearthing riches, mining developments often also unearth layers of pluralism as well as add fresh ones of their own. The rules of the extractives companies, and the resources they unleash, can quickly swamp preexisting norms. Divergences between the rights as understood by communities and those as granted to resource companies can lead to conflict. Compounding this are different conceptions about legitimate processes for resolving disputes: who should be involved, what remedies are available, and who ultimately decides. Because of significant imbalances in power and the capacity of parties to understand and bring legal claims, negotiation and resolution are fraught with difficulties. Furthermore, certain groups, such as women, do not benefit from the emergence of the newer forms of pluralism as they are captured by others more able to navigate them. But as the cases in this chapter show, pluralism offers opportunity, especially the ability of affected groups (including women) to access national and international protest networks, international financial institutions' grievance mechanisms, or development bank capacity-building projects.

We are generally cautious about the ability of international development practice to positively affect outcomes in contexts of legal pluralism. Multilateral development organizations such as the World Bank have organizational proclivities that make engaging with legal pluralism challenging. Undertaking an archaeology of the law or looking beyond government institutions to other entities that encompass "stateness" are not things most development organizations are naturally set up to do. International development's ahistorical bent (Woolcock, Szreter, and Rao 2009) makes archaeology difficult. This is in part driven by the way in which most international development practitioners operate: invariably not being from the places in/on which they work, working on many countries at once and conducting fleeting visits to each or living in a country for only a few years. It also flows from the nature of the development business itself, which is inherently forward looking with a focus on "solutions," an emphasis in the possibility of social change, and a privileging of interventions that are scalable across contexts, rather than a deep contextual knowledge of one place and what has come before. But the past is deeply embedded in the present through institutions that development practitioners seek to alter and is firmly present in the minds of citizens, with a strong influence on what is understood not only to be right (just) but also what is possible.

Looking beyond government institutions is familiar for development practitioners who work with NGOs and other state institutions. Lund's call to focus on the *nature* of "state" as opposed to its manifestation(s) crystallizes this in a conceptually useful way. However, practitioners working in multilateral development banks face particular challenges. The underlying structure of the organizations (with states as shareholders) and the prevailing modalities of engagement (through loans, preferably at scale) make the government the first – and sometimes only – likely point of call. These facets also make management in multilateral institutions particularly responsive to feedback from governments, even when project staff may be willing to more broadly engage. This does not, by any means, exclude more positive engagements, but it does serve to frame what is and is not likely and what drives donor attention.

REFERENCES

Allen, Matthew, and Zahid Hasnain. 2010. "Power, Pork and Patronage: Decentralisation and the Politicisation of the Development Budget in Papua New Guinea." *Commonwealth Journal of Local Governance* 6: 7–31.

CAO (Office of the Compliance Advisor/Ombudsman). 2009. "Building Consensus: History and Lessons from the Mesa de Dialogo y Consenso CAO-Cajamarca, Peru. Monograph 1: The Formation and the First Steps of the Mesa, 2000–2003." CAO, World Bank Group, Washington, DC.

Papua New Guinea, Government of, Department of Mining. 2007. "Women in Mining National Action Plan 2007–2012." Department of Mining, Port Moresby.

Woolcock, Michael, Simon Szreter, and Vijayendra Rao. 2009. "How and Why Does History Matter for Development Policy?" Working Paper 68, Brooks World Poverty Institute, University of Manchester.

15

The Problem with Problematizing Legal Pluralism

Lessons from the Field

Deborah H. Isser

For the past several years, a small but growing group of justice practitioners has been pushing against the state-centric rule of law orthodoxy, calling for recognition of and attention to alternative legal orders among those working to stabilize and promote the rule of law in war-torn societies. Their motivation is taken for granted in this volume – formal justice systems in such countries are, have always been, and will be into the foreseeable future incapacitated, inaccessible, and incapable of serving the justice demands of much of the population; moreover, customary and alternative legal orders are the primary locus of dispute resolution for the vast majority. Resistance is still strong in some pockets – the monopolistic legal establishment, the most strident defenders of international human rights, and ideologues of various sociopolitical agendas. But among a growing number of justice reform actors, engagement with non-state and customary justice systems has become a critical addition to their repertoire. Programs, policies, and draft laws addressing legal pluralism have taken center stage in donor activities in countries such as Afghanistan, Bolivia, Burundi, Timor Leste, Liberia, Sudan, and Somalia. This trend, however, does not seem to be leading to much of an improvement in the more narrow orthodoxy. But what is more alarming is that the extension of international intervention beyond the limits of formal institutions and into the everyday realities of the population can have a far-reaching detrimental impact on how people pursue justice.

This chapter explores what has gone wrong, taking as its point of departure a variant on one of the key questions posed to the contributors to this volume: Is legal pluralism a problem, an opportunity, or both for those seeking to promote peace, justice, and equitable development? Drawing on recent research and policy engagement by the United States Institute of Peace in Liberia and Southern Sudan, the chapter focuses on countries where violent conflict is ongoing or a serious threat, and that are subject to significant international interventions focused on state building. Although the analysis would be similar for more stable developing contexts, the issues are amplified in these countries given the heightened degree of state dysfunctionality and social fragility combined with the intensity of international engagement, the multitude of such actors, and their more overtly political objectives.

In these contexts, the concept of legal pluralism offers important and necessary correctives to the standard approaches to justice reform by demonstrating that law is not a uniform, state-provided good. But whereas it may have succeeded in making this an accepted empirical reality, it has failed to challenge the dominant paradigm of state building and rule of law, which presupposes a clear linear progression toward a particular end state. Thus, development actors problematize the fact of legal pluralism in reference to that end state. As legal pluralism is incorporated into this paradigm, interventions fall prey to the same criticisms levied against orthodox justice programs: they focus on forms over functions, they result in socially detached models of justice often based on transplanted best practices, and they fail to address the justice concerns of most of the population (Desai, Isser, and Woolcock 2011). Seen through this lens, legal pluralism is just part of the justice system as an isolated field that can be fixed through technical assistance. In reality, legal pluralism is a hotly contested arena in which all sorts of political, ideological, and social agendas play out. Development actors who fail to understand this are at risk of not only failing to instill meaningful change, but also unwittingly supporting a particular political agenda and/or shifting power balances and social accountability mechanisms, potentially worsening people's ability to pursue justice.

As it currently plays out, the focus on legal pluralism as a problem – or an opportunity – is a potentially dangerous distraction from the more crucial questions with which development actors should be grappling: What is the real problem we are trying to solve? Who gets to make that determination? What are the most effective means of trying to do so?

PROBLEMATIZING LEGAL PLURALISM

The rise of rule of law as a critical pillar of peace building over the past fifteen years, accompanied by a proliferation of definitions, guidelines, and best practices, has reinforced the notion that there are ideal and predetermined end states. These are largely the product of two dominant paradigms: the concept of the Weberian state (and its notions of sovereignty) and the universality of human rights. For many development actors, mandates flow accordingly: the objective is to build the capacity of the state to exercise a monopoly on force, which complies with international standards of human rights.[1]

---

[1] This rather simplified description of international development actors is worthy of further analysis in terms of the internal incentives, organizational cultures, and political nature of the various organizations. As "rule of law" has become a virtual industry, with a range of actors, including multilateral and bilateral agencies, nongovernmental organizations and for-profit companies, a detailed analysis of how these structures and ways of doing business impact the nature of rule of law programming would

Considered through this lens, the problems of legal pluralism are obvious. From a state-building perspective, legal pluralism is a threat to the supremacy, even sovereignty, of the state and its duty and right to define, regulate, and enforce the legal system and standards of justice. There is growing recognition among scholars and practitioners that state-building endeavors can and, in some cases, must accommodate the reality of legal pluralism. But in practice, such accommodation does not break the mold: the state is still assumed to be rightfully dominant as the ultimate regulator of other legal orders (Isser 2011). Twining (this volume) similarly notes the tenacity of a "milder form of state-centrism" in the legal pluralism literature that focuses on how the state should respond to non-state legal orders.

From a human rights perspective, legal pluralism poses three key challenges. The first relates to the normative content of alternative orders and the extent to which that deviates from international standards. This top-down value judgment often reveals considerable discrepancies, particularly regarding the rights of women and minorities, due process, and fair trial standards. The second concerns the possibility that legal pluralism yields different results for different people in like cases, challenging the principles of uniformity, certainty, predictability, and equal application of the law. The third focuses on the state as the legal guarantor of human rights under the international treaty regime, placing responsibility on state institutions to enforce these standards on alternative legal orders.

What then, under this paradigm, are the solutions to these problems? Ignoring legal pluralism becomes impossible; the goal, then, is to harness the good, mitigate the bad, and use this paradigm to serve the same goals of state building and compliance with international standards. For both state builders and human rights advocates, all but the most strident also see the opportunity in legal pluralism. The massive endeavor of getting the formal system up to par will take decades; alternative legal orders thus serve as necessary gap fillers. The restorative nature of many customary justice systems also holds appeal as a culturally appropriate – and less resource intensive – alternative to an adversarial, penal order for petty offenses.[2] But this does not represent a shift in paradigm. It is rather a simple dose of realism that is hard to avoid when one sees the justice system up close. Thus, legal pluralism is neither an opportunity nor a problem; they are two sides of the same coin.

Activities focus on two main areas. At the macro level, the focus is on legal frameworks that establish a coherent system of jurisdictional limitations, hierarchy, interaction, and regulation between the various legal orders. As one justice practitioner stated, the aim is to "build the big house." At the level of the constituent

---

be quite revealing. Aside from noting these complexities, such an analysis is beyond the scope of this chapter.

[2] Legal pluralism is also seen not only as an opportunity but also as a right in the case of indigenous peoples according to International Labour Organization Convention 169 and the United Nations Declaration on the Rights of Indigenous Peoples, adopted by the General Assembly in September 2007.

parts, programs aim to "fix" the individual legal orders such that they comply with the model of international human rights. This involves a standard menu of training, "sensitization," and capacity building, with some top-down regulation to ensure that the most critical human rights issues (usually serious crime, including sexually based violence, corporal punishment, and discriminatory practices) are kept out of their bounds. More ambitious efforts seek to introduce new mechanisms into non-state systems to shoehorn them into familiar forms of principles of certainty and predictability, such as some form of codification and recordation of customary laws and decisions.

The perceived problems are of flawed legal frameworks and substantive standards; the chosen remedies thus set out to fix them. The internal logic is sound, but the approach fails for its narrow approach to legal pluralism, ignoring the broader political and societal dynamics in which it exists.

LEGAL PLURALISM AS POLITICS

The case that legal systems are not simply pieces of technology that can be molded to an external ideal through technical inputs has been compellingly argued elsewhere. (Sage, Menzies, and Woolcock 2009; Isser 2011). They must be understood as an integral part of complex social systems; therefore, effective reform efforts must be embedded in the "prevailing social, economic, and political relations" (Adler, this volume). This is usually sensibly put forward as an argument for engaging with local rule systems on their terms, rather than pursuing idealized models. I focus on a different implication of this reality: that legal pluralism itself needs to be understood as a reflection of complex and dynamic social and political relations.

This is by no means a new revelation. The term "legal pluralism" emerged as colonial powers discovered local forms of justice and tried to order their interaction with imported colonial systems – a process laden with obvious political motives and consequences (Mamdani 1996). As Faundez (this volume) argues, legal pluralism continues to be an arena in which political agendas, manipulation, and competing claims to authority are played out. The Bolivia example he describes is perhaps a case of overt politics: the constitutional recognition of indigenous justice as equal to state justice is clearly motivated by the populist power base of the government. Other examples abound. During the civil war, Mozambique's FRELIMO party adopted the opposite approach, seeking to eradicate customary justice in favor of its modernist Marxist ideology (Lubkemann, Kyed, and Garvey 2011). The Guatemalan state's oppression of Mayan law throughout its civil war was in part ideologically based, but more significantly strategic in that traditional communities were seen as supporting the insurgents. The postwar movement in favor of legal pluralism had its own political agenda, namely, that of promoting indigenous self-determination (Hessbruegge and Garcia 2011). Saddam Hussein's policies on tribal law in Iraq shifted according to political need, moving from not recognizing it under the Baathist modernist rhetoric, to granting it official status when he needed the support of tribal leaders (Asfura-Heim 2011). Of course, the standard international approach to legal pluralism is also a manifestation of the political and ideological agenda of its agents – a mixture of universal norms, Weberian notions of statehood, and the particular bilateral motives of the various actors.

Whatever the motive, efforts to restructure the relations between legal orders have deep political implications in terms of the allocation of power, mechanisms of social accountability, governance structures, and the ethnic and ideological identity of the state. The way that legal pluralism is generally problematized – and "solved" – by both international and national actors is ultimately a function of their own political lens yet can have far more consequential effects than may be intended. The following cautionary tales demonstrate how seemingly technical approaches to addressing legal pluralism are manipulated and instrumentalized by the multilayering of political agendas, while the ultimate aim of improving people's ability to pursue justice is sidelined or even ignored.

CAUTIONARY TALE 1: SOUTHERN SUDAN

Since the 2005 Comprehensive Peace Agreement, which marked the beginning of the interim period that led to Southern Sudan's independence in 2011, the Government of Southern Sudan (GoSS) has sought to establish a common law legal system while grappling with the fact of legal pluralism: a robust proliferation of customary law and chiefs courts. Francis Mading Deng describes the paradoxical way that customary law is viewed by Southern Sudanese elites. It is simultaneously seen to be an integral part of Southern Sudanese identity – especially as southerners define themselves against the Islamic North – and as a backward system incapable of meeting the demands of a modern state (Deng 2010).

The GoSS and its international partners have coalesced around a policy of *ascertainment*, whereby the customary laws of the more than sixty ethnic groups would be identified and recorded in written form. Some advocates of ascertainment, including the current chief justice, see it as a means of taking customary law out of its local environment and making it the source of legislation and common law for the whole of Southern Sudan. Legalistic-minded advocates call for ascertainment as the first step in codification, which they believe is necessary to ensure predictability and certainty in its application. Some believe ascertainment should serve to preserve culture and customary law from the evils of modern society; others call for writing down customary law so that it can be modified to eliminate "negative practices." Many chiefs have jumped on the ascertainment bandwagon, believing that having a written code will enhance their status, especially vis-à-vis more dominant ethnic groups such as the Dinka, although they admit that a written code will not change the way they resolve disputes. The United Nations Development Programme, the leading international agency on justice reform in Southern Sudan, has entered the fray, promoting ascertainment as a means of creating a clear, unified, modern, and human rights–compliant legal system (and frankly because ascertainment is relatively easy to program).

What is fascinating about this debate is how the very same policy is put forth as a means of achieving very different political agendas. These tensions are clear in discussions about what the process of ascertainment should actually look like. Is it about writing down principles, local fixed rules, and sanctions and modifying them to create "harmony," or compliance with national law? According to whom, given that rules and principles within the community itself may well be contested? Is it meant to be applied as a legal code or a general cultural reference? Is the written product owned by the community or the state? Which way this will go is yet to be determined. But certainly this debate over legal pluralism is a proxy for complex and fundamental tensions regarding the role of the state in relation to local communities, the allocation of court fees, the power and status of chiefs, ethnic divisions, and the pace of social and economic change. All of this plays out in what is portrayed as a technical legal issue, but the actual impact it would have on the delivery of justice is rarely part of the discussion.

In fact, recent research demonstrates just how far removed the debate is from the justice needs of the population. Whereas policy makers see the multitude of systems as a problem to be fixed, in reality the legal pluralism on the ground is a much more nuanced system that has evolved locally in ways that are able to accommodate the complex and fluid nature of justice demands. In this period of fragility, social flux, and economic change, along with severely limited state capacity, it is the very contingent and dynamic nature of the interaction between customary and state law that makes it possible to find a reasonable balance between community restorative processes and government enforcement and adversarial processes, as well as to keep the power of the justice providers in check (Leonardi, Moro, Santschi, and Isser 2010). Policies of ascertainment and other ways of regulating customary law threaten this balance by privileging the voice of certain informants and elites in the determination of what the law is and by cutting off the ways in which more marginalized litigants can contest and thereby shape the norms and processes of the justice system (Leonardi et al. 2010). Driven by political and ideological agendas, GoSS and international policies on legal pluralism may result in less, rather than more, justice for Southern Sudanese while failing to address the real justice concerns of the population: the more general dysfunctionality of the governance and justice system and the abusive exercise of power by the military, the police, and other elites.

CAUTIONARY TALE 2: LIBERIA

Liberia's dual justice system is the legacy of the colonial-style indirect rule the Americo-Liberians exercised over the "hinterland" and its native population. A judiciary modeled on the United States was applied in Monrovia, while a hierarchy of chiefs' courts, regulated by the Ministry of Internal Affairs, presided over the rest under the Hinterland Regulations. Decades of predatory politics, including massive manipulation of the formal judiciary and ethnic discrimination, fueled a brutal civil war that began in 1989 and lasted fourteen years.

To the extent that today's international peace-building community, dominated by the United Nations, recognizes the existence of chiefs' courts, they are largely seen as an impediment to the goals of state building and human rights. The Hinterland Regulations have been scrutinized for violations of international standards, and customary law has become synonymous with the practice of trial by ordeal.[3] Under the mantra "One Liberia," legal pluralism is seen as a remnant of the discriminatory past that needs to be remedied by establishing a single justice system for all. This view is supported by much of the Monrovian legal elite, who, despite the severe dysfunctionality and corruption of the formal judiciary, advocate that under the principle of separation of powers, there can be no alternative adjudicative bodies. The dominant reform agenda is therefore to limit the jurisdiction of chiefs' courts, requiring serious crime (and, in particular, rape) to be referred to formal courts, to eliminate "odious practices," such as trial by ordeal, and to bring the chiefs' courts under the supervision and hierarchy of the formal judiciary. The key means of doing so include legislative reform, training and "sensitization" of chiefs, and top-down bans on certain practices. Although this agenda is driven largely by abstract ideals of justice, it is also a manifestation of internal politics and power struggles, including the respective roles of the judiciary, Ministry of Justice, and Ministry of Internal Affairs, as well as the ambitions of the National Council of Chiefs.

What does not seem to be driving the agenda is an understanding of how Liberians perceive and pursue justice in reality. Thus, the policy of limiting the role of the customary system, without a corresponding increase in the state's capacity, has served to widen what is effectively a justice vacuum, leading to violence and mob justice (Isser, Lubkemann, and N'Tow 2009). Efforts to ban trial by ordeal have been met with accusations that the solicitor-general must be a member of a particularly dangerous witchcraft association – the logic being that he is trying to increase his power by banning community mechanisms for combating witchcraft. A common reaction among rural Liberians to the "One Liberia" policy is that it is but another unwanted imposition on them from the Monrovian and foreign elite, who are responsible for impunity and injustice. Although the problematization of legal pluralism is undermining the power of chiefs and their ability to maintain social order, it is also lending them a new source of power. In recent consultations between chiefs and the legal establishment, the former were all too happy to discuss the formalization of their status as part of the judiciary, which may serve to protect

---

[3] Trial by ordeal is the practice of determining guilt based on an oath or a physically harmful test such as administering poison or touching a hot cutlass to the accused.

them from local contestation of their authority. None of this bodes well either for the state-building agenda or for practical solutions to justice gaps.

As in Southern Sudan, the fact of multiple orders is not the justice problem for Liberians. It is rather a sense that, in the words of one Liberian informant, "there is no justice for the poor" (Isser et al. 2009). Power imbalances, predatory behavior, and corruption pervade all systems, leaving Liberians to shop for the forum they think can best serve them based on their personal relations, social associations, and means of leverage.

MOVING BEYOND PROBLEMATIZING LEGAL PLURALISM

In this volume, William Twining extols the virtues of social fact legal pluralism while acknowledging that it does not provide much guidance to practitioners "on normative questions about legitimacy, justification, toleration, and recognition of non-state legal orders" (Twining, this volume). That is precisely why it is such a useful concept. It helps us move beyond the obsession with what justice systems *should* look like to an empirical inquiry as to what they *do* look like, with all of their complex forms of hybridity, interlegality, and local specificity. It allows us to understand how, in practice, disputes, rights, grievances, and wrongs are resolved – or aren't – and to see this as a function of broader social and political dynamics. This is particularly helpful in fragile and conflict-affected environments characterized by accelerated transitions involving uneven and messy changes in power relations, social values, demographics, and justice needs (Duffield 2001). In such cases, simplified dichotomies of state/non-state, formal/customary, and modern/traditional are distortions of the much more complex realities of both how justice institutions function and what people want. Normative prescriptions may look good on paper, but – as in the case of Southern Sudan and Liberia – they may well have significant adverse consequences on the ground. Instead, practitioners need to adopt justice reform efforts that are flexible, transitional, and context specific rather than determinative of particular end states.

This presents a new paradigm for mainstream justice reform practitioners in which one does not have to be "for" or "against" legal pluralism or customary law, and in which the problem is not how to "fix" the justice system to meet an ideal, but rather how to work with the realities of institutional capacity, legitimacy, and effectiveness to improve justice and development outcomes for the users. This has important implications for the methods, approaches, and goals of justice reform:

1. Invest in empirical analysis of the justice landscape in practice.

Standard justice assessments tend to be template questionnaires geared toward the particular mandate of the agency to enable a rapid plan for programming, usually carried out by a few expatriates over just a few weeks. They also tend to measure the extent to which the justice system deviates from the ideal. Accepting legal pluralism as a social fact implies a commitment to understanding it on an empirical rather than a normative basis and requires a much greater investment to develop a solid evidence base. A few points deserve mention:

- Research should focus on the actual experience of those seeking justice. Mapping actual dispute trajectories and focusing on user perspectives moves beyond particular justice systems – customary, formal, hybrid – to an analysis of justice as embedded in local social and power dynamics. As such, it can help identify practical obstacles, points of resilience, and opportunities to improve justice outcomes, including predicting the consequences of various policy directions.
- Research should not be seen as a one-time event, but as an integral part of the reform process. In addition to informing programming and policy, research can give voice to local communities and marginalized populations and can empower stakeholders to engage in constructive contestation processes. Building local research capacity and fostering a policy environment that is receptive to empirical studies is itself an important contribution.

2. Take a practical problem-solving approach: function over form

Both the Southern Sudan and Liberia examples show how seeing legal pluralism as a problem leads to an emphasis on legal forms – written codes and jurisdictional limitations – that threaten to worsen access to justice. Remaining neutral about legal pluralism as such can shift the focus to empirical determinations of the qualitative functions of justice. Instead of seeking to harmonize Liberia's dual justice system into a uniform, human rights–compliant legal framework, the question becomes, "How, given the realities on the ground, can the justice demands of the population be met?" This alternative formulation invites very different responses and policies that call for context-specific experimentation, for example, working with communities to find socially responsive alternatives to harmful forms of trial by ordeal or developing more nuanced criteria for jurisdiction over crime rather than blunt national policies. It may also reveal that the problem is not about law or the justice system at all but about broader questions of education, economic opportunity, security, and power imbalances.

This is not to say that the normative questions vanish. Taking a problem-solving approach means that someone gets to determine how the problem should be defined. Amartya Sen would suggest that we be guided by what the population perceives to be just (Sen 2009). In fragile and conflict-affected societies in particular, there will be multiple ways of defining this, which may also be at the core of societal fracture. This leads us to the third point.

3. Justice reform strategies should focus on promoting a constructive process of change, rather than on imposing an end state.

If legal pluralism is a social fact, meaningful efforts at justice reform need to change the social facts. In other words, justice systems emerge from and respond to the social, political, and economic processes in which they are embedded. End states imposed without engaging these processes effectively are likely to be either ignored or coerced, particularly in fragile and conflict-affected environments characterized by a severe disconnect and legitimacy gap between citizens and the state (World Bank 2011). Recognition of this implies a change in the role of development practitioners from providing technical solutions to fostering constructive processes of societal change.

As noted previously, research can be used to give voice to the marginalized, to structure dialogue, and to encourage innovation. Development practitioners can help create space for incremental steps, experimentation, evaluation, and adjustment. Empowerment strategies, including awareness, education, and legal assistance, can promote the ability of the less powerful to shape the system through contestation.

On a larger scale, where legal pluralism is imbued with political agendas, interventions aimed at breaking down hostility, misconceptions, and polarization and facilitating a cooperative and participatory approach to envisioning an end goal can be as valuable in promoting a more cohesive and sustainable peace as in producing better justice policies, particularly where questions of identity and inclusiveness were at the heart of the conflict. Here are some questions to be asked:

- What kind of balance – between (a) restorative and punitive justice, (b) social reconciliation and adversarialism, and (c) the individual and the community as the basic social unit – would best reflect the values of society and the interests of the state?
- In what sort of disputes should the state have the exclusive or overriding jurisdiction?
- How should the collective rights of certain ethnic, indigenous, and religious groups be balanced against individual rights guaranteed by the state?
- To what extent should justice be uniform and centralized versus pluralistic and decentralized?

These are not abstract questions pitting tradition against modernity, but questions that must be considered in the context of empirical realities and development trajectories. Development practitioners should seek to promote an inclusive and equitable process of working through these issues to forge new manifestations of legal pluralism that better reflect the needs of society.

This approach is not easy for practitioners. As an industry, the development world emphasizes action, spending, and measurable results within short time horizons. "Best practice" approaches from other contexts are highly rewarded as easy to program and "sell" to donors and clients. Practitioners are also constrained by the mandates and political agendas of their organizations, which may require the approval of governments unwilling to tackle what may be, from their perspective, sensitive or undesirable issues.

REFERENCES

Asfura-Heim, Patricio. 2011. "Tribal Customary Law and Legal Pluralism in al Anbar, Iraq." In *Customary Justice and the Rule of Law in War-Torn Societies*, ed. Deborah Isser. Washington, DC: United States Institute of Peace Press.

Deng, Francis Mading. 2010. *Customary Law in the Modern World: The Crossfire of Sudan's War of Identities*. New York: Routledge.

Desai, Deval, Deborah Isser, and Michael Woolcock. 2011. "Rethinking Justice Reform in Fragile and Conflict-Affected States: The Capacity of Development Agencies and Lessons from Liberia and Afghanistan." *World Bank Law Review* 3: 241–62.

Duffield, Mark. 2001. *Global Governance and the New Wars: The Merging of Development and Security*. London: Zed Books.

Hessbruegge, Jan, and Carlos Fredy Garcia. 2011. "Mayan Law in Post-Conflict Guatemala." In *Customary Justice and the Rule of Law in War-Torn Societies*, ed. Deborah Isser. Washington, DC: United States Institute of Peace Press.

Isser, Deborah, ed. 2011. *Customary Justice and the Rule of Law in War-Torn Societies*. Washington, DC: United States Institute of Peace Press.

Isser, Deborah H., Stephen C. Lubkemann, and Saah N'Tow. 2009. *Looking for Justice: Liberian Experiences with and Perceptions of Local Justice Options*. USIP Peaceworks No. 63.

Leonardi, Cherry, Leben Nelson Moro, Martina Santschi, and Deborah H. Isser. 2010. *Local Justice in Southern Sudan*. USIP Peaceworks No. 66.

Lubkemann, Stephen C., Helene Maria Kyed, and Jennifer Garvey. 2011. "Dilemmas of Articulation in Mozambique: Customary Justice in Transition." In *Customary Justice and the Rule of Law in War-Torn Societies*, ed. Deborah Isser. Washington, DC: United States Institute of Peace Press.

Mamdani, Mahmood. 1996. *Citizen and Subject: Contemporary Africa and the Legacy of Late Colonialism*. Princeton, NJ: Princeton University Press.

Sage, Caroline, Nicholas Menzies, and Michael Woolcock. 2009. "Taking the Rules of the Game Seriously: Mainstreaming Justice in Development. The World Bank's Justice for the Poor Program." In *Legal Empowerment: Practitioner's Perspectives*, ed. Stephen Golub. Rome: International Development Law Organization.

Sen, Amartya. 2009. *The Idea of Justice*. Cambridge, MA: Harvard University Press.

World Bank. 2011. *World Development Report 2011: Conflict, Security and Development*. Washington, DC: IBRD/World Bank.

Index

alternative dispute mechanisms, 27, 69, 146, 154

colonial authorities, 23, 162, 166, 184
colonization, 38, 41, 45
customary law, 14, 40, 44, 45, 56, 57, 68, 96, 98, 100, 114, 117, 118, 120, 123, 133, 135, 138, 139, 148, 149, 150, 152, 154, 158, 184, 187, 188, 189, 215, 216, 217, 218, 223, 224, 226, 241, 242, 243, 244
    inconsistency with liberal values, 215–216

development, meaning of, 96–97

empowerment, 58, 73, 76, 79, 90, 104, 149, 169, 170, 228, 233
enforcement, 3, 22, 24, 25, 31, 42, 54, 57, 59, 61, 62, 83, 85, 88, 107, 108, 109, 138, 150, 182, 216, 242
European Court of Human Rights, 53, 54, 60, 109

forum shop, 11, 87, 90, 136, 166
fragile states, 164

global capitalism, 21, 41, 43, 44, 45
global legal system as plural legal order, 26–28
global system as plural legal order, 28, 122–124, 151–152
Griffiths, John, 84, 85, 101, 102, 115, 116, 132, 141

harmonization, 125, 139
human rights and custom, 56–58
human rights and development overlap, 50

indigenous communities, 182–184
indigenous rights, 69, 179
    constitutional recognition of, 185–190
instrumental resort to law
    colonized or indigenous population, by, 24–25
intentional hybrids, 166, 170

judicial reform, 35–36
juridification, 145, 148, 151, 166
jurisdictional competition, 200–201
jurisdictional politics, 22, 30, 149
justification in customary law, 222–226

land rights, traditional, 180–182
law and development failures, 8, 35–36
law, levels of, 126–127
legal consciousness, 71
legal culture, 70–71
legal mobilization, 72–73
legal pluralism
    colonial origins of, 23–25, 39, 67–68
    conceptual critiques of, 101–103
    definition of, 34–35, 67, 115, 129
    development agencies and, 4–9, 237–238
    land rights and, 42–43, 86–87
    meta-rules and, 4, 9, 105, 106, 139, 198
    mining and, 228–231
    politics as, 240–241
    problems for development of, 9–12, 130–132, 165, 239–240
    social fact, conception of, 120–121, 244
legal uncertainty, 3, 47, 48, 109
liberal democratic theory, 217–222

normative orders, categories of, 133–134

pirates, 26
pluralism, meaning of, 113
postmodern view of law, 70

rule of law
  definition of, 34, 36–37
  economic development, and, 42
  failure in West of, 99–100
  Western institutional forms, 98–99

semiautonomous social field, 67
Sen, Amartya, 4, 54, 85, 100, 108, 142, 223, 245
social norms, regulation through, 152–155
soft law, 146, 152, 153

state centralism, 115–118, 158
state centric, 154, 155, 156, 171
subsidiarity principle, 52

traditional or customary institutions
  resort to, 36
transnational law, 69

unification, 45, 46, 69, 125, 138
Universal Declaration on Human Rights, 52
universality, 59, 113, 238

women and mining, 232–233
women's rights, 39, 41, 43, 44, 48, 69, 77, 206, 230, 231

For EU product safety concerns, contact us at Calle de José Abascal, 56–1°, 28003 Madrid, Spain or eugpsr@cambridge.org.

www.ingramcontent.com/pod-product-compliance
Ingram Content Group UK Ltd.
Pitfield, Milton Keynes, MK11 3LW, UK
UKHW020404060825
461487UK00009B/803